Union of American Hebrew Congregations

Judaism at the World's Parliament of Religions

Comprising the Papers on Judaism Read at the Parliament...

Union of American Hebrew Congregations

Judaism at the World's Parliament of Religions
Comprising the Papers on Judaism Read at the Parliament...

ISBN/EAN: 9783744730259

Printed in Europe, USA, Canada, Australia, Japan

Cover: Foto ©Suzi / pixelio.de

More available books at **www.hansebooks.com**

JUDAISM

WORLD'S PARLIAMENT OF RELIGIONS

COMPRISING THE PAPERS ON JUDAISM READ AT THE
PARLIAMENT, AT THE JEWISH DENOMINATIONAL
CONGRESS, AND AT THE JEWISH PRESENTATION

Published by the Union of American Hebrew Congregations

CINCINNATI
ROBERT CLARKE & CO
1894

INTRODUCTION.

When the idea of holding a Parliament of all Religions in connection with the World's Fair of Chicago was broached there was no denomination that hailed it with greater enthusiasm than the Jewish. The first advocates of a universal religion had been Israel's prophets, and this movement was the first pronounced step to be taken in our Western World toward giving active expression to the glorious hope of the uniting of all men in the name of the one God. Individual voices in the various Jewish pulpits throughout the land were raised in joy and gratitude. The first official action, however, in the matter was taken at the meeting of the Central Conference of American Rabbis held in New York City, July 6-10, 1892, when the committee to whom had been referred the suggestions in the annual message of the President of the Conference included in their report the following paragraph:

"We recommend, in reference to the Religious Congress of the Columbian Exposition, that after the matter has been given mature deliberation at the present session of the Conference, the Executive Committee of this Central Conference be given full power to act in conjunction with the committee already appointed by the Columbian Commissioners."

A number of suggestions were made as to what participation Judaism should take in the Congress, and the matter was disposed of by a resolution to the effect "that all matters concerning the World's Fair be referred to the Executive Committee, that all recommendations that the Executive Committee will have to make and all the reports of their transactions regarding the World's Fair be brought to the notice of a special session of the Conference to be held in Washington next December, in order to act in conjunction with the Council of the Union of American Hebrew Congregations."

At the special session of the Conference held in Washington on the fifth of the following December, it was resolved to address a communication to the Council of the Union of American Hebrew Congregations which was to convene on the next day asking the co-operation and support of the Union in the execution of the idea of the representation of Judaism at the Parliament.

Upon the receipt of this communication by the Council it was referred to a Committee of Five consisting of Messrs. B. Bettman,

Julius Freiberg, Simon Wolf, and Revs. Dr. Joseph Silverman and Louis Grossman. This committee submitted the following report which was unanimously adopted :

"*To the Council of the Union of American Hebrew Congregations:*

GENTLEMEN :—Your Committee, to whom was referred the communication from the Central Conference of American Rabbis, petitioning this Council to co-operate with it in a proper presentation of Judaism at the Congress of Religions which will be held in Chicago, August, 1893, beg leave to submit the following :

Inasmuch as all the religions of the world will be represented at the said Congress of Religions, and the Central Conference of American Rabbis has taken the initiative for a proposed representation of Judaism in it,

The subjects to be treated as follows :

I. HISTORICAL—

(a) Subdivided into Biblical, Mediæval, and Modern.

(b) The history of Jewish beliefs and the customs in the various lands and times.

(c) The history of the domestic and inner social life of the Jews in the various periods.

(d) A history of the education of the Jewish people, public and private.

II. ETHICAL—

(a) Biblical ethics from the historical standpoint.

(b) Talmudical ethics based upon and to begin with the Hellenistic literature.

(c) Ethics of the mediæval Rabbis down to our own time.

III. POLEMICS AND APOLOGETICS—

That is, the relation of the Jews to Heathenism, Christianity, and Islam.

IV. STATISTICAL—

(a) An estimate of the present statistics.

(b) European statistics.

(c) American Jewish statistics.

(d) Eastern Jewish statistics.

V. ARCHÆOLOGICAL—

Religious and national both as to results and desiderata.

These various topics will be assigned to well-known scholars who have made these branches their special study and they shall be requested to participate in person, or if that be impossible, by literary contributions. Furthermore, we recommend that the Conference should tender a special invitation to representative men and women to take part. Furthermore:

WHEREAS, The anti-Semitic agitation, undeterred by the verdict of the enlightened, still continues its unjust hostility in many lands, be it

Resolved, That besides the discussion of the topics recommended, we solicit the co-operation of all American Jews in sympathy with the cause, both individuals as well as societies, orders, and congregations to render the participation of the Jews in the Religious Congress of the Columbian World's Exposition a matter of international importance, to help to state clearly and emphatically the great aim and the objects of Judaism before the entire world and to substantially refute all the slanderous charges made against it through the successive ages by its declared foes; be it also

Resolved, That men of renowned, world-wide scholarship and impartiality of the Christian denomination and Jewish scholars of note be requested and authorized, at the expense of the American Jews, to write and publish exhaustive treatises on the anti-Semitic charges, in particular in regard to the blood accusations, which fill so dark a chapter in Jewish and Christian history, stating the facts and giving the result of their examination in decisive and clear terms. Furthermore, be it

Resolved, That these men be invited to come and to review publicly these charges before the enlightened representatives of the great religions of the world, in order to elicit the approval and assent of the world and silence slander in the name of humanity forever, at least within the pale of civilization.

In all of which the Council fully concurs and heartily indorses the proposed plan.

We recommend that this Council appoint a committee of eleven to co-operate with the Executive Committee of the Conference, and that the joint Commission be intrusted with full power to carry out this suggestion, with such modification as they may see fit for the proper representation of Judaism in the Congress, and that it shall convene as speedily as practicable, and furthermore, that the Executive Board be herewith authorized to provide such financial support to the Commission as may be necessary for the execution of the plan."

The suggestions in this report as to the subjects which should be treated in the papers to be read were adopted by the committee from the communication of the Conference. At the New York meeting above referred to, this plan had been presented.

In accordance with this resolution, the President of the Council, Mr. Emmanuel Werthheimer, appointed the committee of eleven, consisting of the following gentlemen:

B. Bettman, Cincinnati, O.

Isidore Bush, St. Louis, Mo.

Josiah Cohen, Pittsburg, Pa.

Solomon Hirsch, Portland, Oregon.

Adolph Moses, Chicago, Ill.

Simon W. Rosendale, Albany, N. Y.

Jacob H. Schiff, New York.

Lewis Seasongood, Cincinnati, O.

Oscar S. Strauss, New York.

Mayer Sulzberger, Philadelphia, Pa.

Simon Wolf, Washington, D. C.

Julius Freiberg, Cincinnati, O., *President of the Union of A. H. C., ex-officio.*

On March 26, 1893, a joint meeting of the Commission, consisting of this Committee of the Union, the Executive Committee of the Central Conference, the local committee of Chicago, and representatives of the Congress of Jewish women, was held in the parlors of the Auditorium Hotel, and on the succeeding days in the vestry-rooms of the Anshe Maariv Congregation. An organization of all these bodies was effected. Mr. B. Bettman was chosen chairman of the meeting and Rabbi Joseph Stolz, secretary.

The joint committee resolved to spread broadcast the following preliminary address, which states briefly and clearly the reasons why Judaism should be represented at the Parliament:

" In accordance with the authority vested in us by the World's Congress Auxiliary of the World's Columbian Exposition, we, the undersigned, representing the Union of American Hebrew Congregations, the Central Conference of American Rabbis, and the Local Committee on a Jewish Church Congress, send fraternal greetings to the Jews and friends of the Jews of all countries.

The World's Congress Auxiliary of the World's Columbian Exposition has formally and officially invited the professors of Judaism to be represented in the Parliament of Religions to be held in the Memorial Art Palace from September 11th to September 28th, and it behooves us to participate in this Congress of all living historical religions, that no link in the chain be missing, and the evidence be as complete as possible, that however manifold our titles may be, the beliefs, the hopes, the aims we all cherish in common are much more important and essential than a long-standing and deep-rooted intolerance has led mankind to believe.

Another reason of not less importance urges the Jews to be properly represented at this Congress. Although the history of Judaism covers a period of more than three thousand years, no religion has been more thoroughly misunderstood and misinterpreted. Misconceptions of it are so deeply rooted that ours is still the humiliation to see the most enlightened nations of the world not only giving credence to beliefs concerning us that have been invented by fanaticism, and have not the slightest historical foundation, but even persecuting our brethren upon the strength of them.

Since the existence of our religion, no such opportunity as this has ever been extended to the Jew to set himself right before the whole world. It would, therefore, be criminal negligence did we not embrace this chance to proclaim broadcast, through such men as by their learning, their ripeness of judgment, their character, and their works, will command general recognition and attention, what our fundamental doctrines, hopes, and aims have ever been, what are the chief spiritual contributions for which humanity is indebted to us, what is our attitude toward other religions, and in what respect Judaism is still indispensable to the highest civilization.

For these reasons, we beg leave to invite your moral support and hearty co-operation in this representation of Judaism for which the evenings of September 13th, 15th, and 16th have been assigned to us by the General Committee.

It is designed by the Auxiliary that also a Denominational Congress or Conference shall be held in Chicago for a more complete and extended presentation and discussion of such theoretical and practical questions as concern each denomination; and we herewith extend to you a hearty invitation to attend and participate in the sessions of our Denominational Congress, which will be held under the auspices of the Central Conference of American Rabbis during the week beginning August 28th, and which will form an officially recognized part of the World's Fair Religious Congresses.

All communications may be addressed to RABBI JOSEPH STOLZ, Secretary of the Joint Committee, 412 Warren Avenue, Chicago, Illinois.

Signed by—

    B. BETTMANN, Cincinnati, *President.*

    HON. JACOB H. SCHIFF, New York, *Vice-President*

    ADOLPH MOSES, Chicago, *Vice-President.*

    JULIUS FREIBERG, Cincinnati, *Vice-President.*

ISIDOR BASH, St. Louis, *Vice-President.*
HON. SOLOMON HIRSCH, Portland, Ore., *Vice-President.*
JUDGE SIMON W. ROSENDALE, Albany, N. Y.
HON. OSCAR S. STRAUSS, New York.
HON. SIMON WOLF, Washington, D. C.
JOSIAH COHEN, Pittsburg, Pa.
MAYER SULZBERGER, Philadelphia.
GEN. LEWIS SEASONGOOD, Cincinnati.
RABBI ISAAC M. WISE, Cincinnati.
RABBI DAVID PHILIPSON, Cincinnati.
RABBI CHARLES LEVI, Cincinnati.
RABBI JOSEPH SILVERMAN, New York.
RABBI TOBIAS SHANFARBER, Baltimore.
RABBI EMIL G. HIRSCH, Chicago.
RABBI ISAAC S. MOSES, Chicago.
RABBI JOSEPH STOLZ, Chicago, *Secretary.*
Joint Committee of the World's Congress Auxiliary on the
Jewish Denominational Congress."

The committee appointed by the chairman to prepare the program for the Denominational Congress and the Jewish Presentation at the Parliament submitted a report which was substantially carried out.

The Denominational Congress convened Sunday afternoon, August 28, in the Hall of Columbus, and continued its sessions until Wednesday morning, August 30th. The Jewish Church presentation took place on the evenings of the 13th and 15th during the sessions of the Parliament.

Mr. B. Bettman, the chairman of the joint committee, in his official report, presented to the executive committee of the Union, at its meeting held in Cincinnati, December 10, 1893, writes of the program and the manner in which it was carried out:

"This plan provided for a presentation of the cause of Judaism before the World's Congress of Religions and for papers to be read before the Jewish Denominational Congress, prepared by men selected from among the best and ripest Jewish scholars in the United States, and the results have exceeded the highest expectations of the warmest friends of the movement. Not only did Judaism for the first time in its history meet the other Religions of the World as an acknowledged equal entitled to and accorded a respectful hearing, but the brilliant presentation of its cause has made warm friends for it in hitherto hostile or at least coldly indifferent circles, and seed has been sown that will undoubtedly bring forth a harvest of esteem and good fellowship.

In addition its own champions and adherents have gained in confidence and encouragement, and another great cause for congratulation is in the eminent success achieved also for the first time by the American Jewish women in their exceedingly able public participation in the work of the Congress, which has resulted in conferring great honor upon themselves and the sacred common cause."

At this same meeting, the following communication addressed by the Rev. Dr. Isaac M. Wise to Mr. B. Bettman, on November 7, 1893, was presented :

"Herewith I have the honor to report to the Commission of the U. A. H. C., over which you preside, that the members of the Central Conference of American Rabbis and others associated with them have done their duty in the Congress and Parliament of all Religions, and have done it well. Judaism has been represented on this occasion fairly, fully, and frankly by able and eloquent champions, although none of the foreign brethren appeared. Also that cruel "blood accusation" was emphatically and effectually refuted—I dare say by our influence—by the great Catholic Archbishop of Zante in Greece, who declared it a base falsehood in Parliament. In the same manner anti-Semitism was denounced by Archbishop Ireland and others in both cases much better than we could have done it. We discussed fully all departments of Judaism, theoretical and practical, exactly according to plan and specification indorsed by your Commission at the meeting in Chicago.

None of our men hitherto asked any recompense, traveling expenses, any thing at all, and no foreigner gave us the honor, consequently no draft on the $1,000 was made to the best of my knowledge.

Therefore, I ask of the Commission (1) to order the inclosed bills of the Secretary paid, to which I have to add $50 for printing done on my order in preparation for the Congress and the Parliament. (2) The balance to be applied in the publication of the book which shall contain (a) all transactions in connection with this affair ; and (b) all papers and addresses by our people, men and women in that Congress and Parliament, together with those of the two archbishops mentioned.

This volume—I judge to be about 300 pages octavo—to be distributed thus: One volume to the archives of the Union, the College and every congregation of the Union A. H. C. One volume to each of the officers connected with the Congress and Parliament, to our writers whose presentation is in the volume, and to every member of the Central Conference of American Rabbis together about 300 volumes. 100 to be distributed in the various libraries of the country; 100 among the leading newspapers, and 100 in Europe, together 600 volumes. No less than 1,500 to be printed, and the balance to be sold for the benefit of the Union.

This publication will be the historical monument of the occasion, and for the future generations of American Israelites, to tell so we were, so we did, and so we stood in 1893."

A committee, consisting of Messrs. B. Bettman, A. A. Kramer and Alfred Seasongood, was appointed to take these suggestions into consideration, with power to act.

It is due to the generosity of the Union of American Hebrew Congregations, through its Executive Committee, that the publication of this volume has been made possible. It is sent forth as a memorial of Judaism's participation in the greatest religious gathering that the world has ever seen. The thanks of the Jews of this land are due to the public spirit of the officers of the Union, who have placed the funds for the publication of the work at the disposal of the committee.

There have been gathered, as far as possible, all the papers that were read at the Parliament proper, the Congress, and the Presentation. With but few exceptions, all the papers read are given. Where this is not the case, the committee, although making every effort to obtain the paper, did not succeed.

It had also been intended to include the papers read at the Jewish Women's Congress in this volume, but the committee, much to its regret, learns that it has been anticipated in this matter by the Jewish Publication Society of America, which has made all arrangements to issue the proceedings of the Women's Congress.

A number of the papers read before the Parliament, although not appointed by the joint commission, have nevertheless been included, in order that as complete an account as possible of what was spoken by the Jews on Judaism might be given.

The paper of Professor D. G. Lyon, of Harvard University, on "Jewish Contributions to Civilization," has been included, because of its bearing on the subject.

The strong words of the Archbishop of Zante on the blood-accusation, doubly important when the speaker who uttered them is considered, are reproduced.

The remarks of Archbishop John Ireland on Anti-Semitism, made at a meeting of the Jewish Women's Congress, and kindly furnished by their author for publication in this volume, will be welcomed as the expression of a broad and liberal-minded man upon a movement which calls for the condemnation of all friends of humanity.

This volume is sent forth with the prayer that it may serve toward spreading a knowledge of the past achievements, the present beliefs, and the future hopes of Judaism. These hopes center in the realization of the ideal of the Parliament of Religions, the acknowledgment of the Fatherhood of God, and the Brotherhood of Man. It was a rabbi who suggested the verse of the prophet that was adopted as the motto of the Parliament: "Have we not all one Father? has not one God created us?" May God speed the coming of the time when the thought implied in these words will be realized, and, the world over, the high hopes aroused by the Parliament be fulfilled.

CONTENTS.

VI. GENERAL.

JEWISH DENOMINATIONAL CONGRESS.

On the twenty-seventh day of August, in the Hall of Columbus in the Art Palace, in the presence of a highly interested audience, the Jewish Denominational Congress opened its sessions. It was the first of the many denominational congresses held in connection with the Parliament, and the general feeling seemed to be that it was particularly appropriate that the key-note of the Parliament should be struck by the mother of monotheistic religions.

The exercises opened with prayer by Rabbi I. L. Leucht, of New Orleans, La., as follows:

Almighty and most merciful God, Sovereign of the Universe! Deeply impressed with the solemnity of this moment, we approach Thee and crave for Thy blessing. Thou art the source of all wisdom, the light of our soul is but a spark borrowed from Thy glory, leading us to heights, where Thou alone reignest supreme.

O Father, we stand in need of that divine light shedding a ray of hope into the darkness of our mundane existence, that we may not be engulfed by the waves of selfishness and earthly glory, that we may find fortitude and faith in times of danger and pain, in hours of doubt and infidelity, enabling us, O Lord, to proclaim at all times that Thou art our God—and without Thee there is no salvation.

O God, of all nations, the children of all peoples have come hither to prove the wonders of human achievements, to show forth the treasures of the earth, and now they do assemble to acknowledge that they have not forgotten the Giver of all, proclaiming each, in his own tongue, that Thou art the King of all Kings, the Ruler of the world, the Preserver of all things. The first called to emphasize and to acknowledge, before the world, eternal fidelity and allegiance to Thee, great God, comes Israel.

O Father, from the beginning of our pilgrimage Thou hast en-

(xix)

trusted us with this mission, to walk before the peoples of the earth proclaiming Thy truth and Thy unity. From Abraham, the father of all nations, to Moses, Thy trusted servant, even to this day, we have never ceased to cry aloud, "Thou, Jehovah, art our strength." Every age has heard this cry, its echo vibrates throughout all lands, and from every mountain top thrilled the message, " Hear, O Israel, the Lord is our God ; the Lord is One."

Heavenly Father, we thank Thee for this great day, when fulfillment draws near—when all lands join in that great hymn of praise and thanksgiving, whose every verse is but a chord of that grand anthem, lifting all mankind to the same inspiration, the same father, the same ideal, the same God, who knows but one justice, but one love.

O God, let this gathering—only the beginning of a grand divine service, such as the world never witnessed, be sweet incense in Thy sight. Help us, O Lord, in our endeavor of binding man closer to man, linking heart nearer to heart. O, let it be a mountain of the Lord, where all nations gather to praise Thee. Let it be a Sinai, from whose crest once more will resound the trumpets of Revelation— announcing to those near and far—Thy Unity and Thy Love for evermore! Amen!

Mr. Charles C. Bonney, President of the World's Congress Auxiliary, and General President of the World's Congresses of 1893, thereupon delivered the address of welcome.

Masters and Teachers of Israel, Officers and Members of the Jewish Denominational Congress of 1893: The providence of the God of Abraham, Isaac and Jacob, who created man in his own image, and gave him from Sinai's glory-crowned summit the law of a righteous life, has so ordered the arrangements for the Religious Congresses, to be held under the auspices of the World's Congress Auxiliary of the World's Columbian Exposition, that, without any plan to that end, this Congress of the Jewish Church is the first of the series. The month of August having been assigned for the Congresses on Engineering, Art, Government, Science, and kindred subjects, the month of September was set apart for the Congresses of that greatest department of the World's Congress work, the Department of Religion. For this reason many efforts were made to fix a later date for this Congress, but it was found impracticable to do so ; and when the present date was finally settled, it was not then expected that place could be found for the sessions of the Congress in the Memorial Art Palace, but that one of the Chicago synagogues must be selected for them. But when the assignments of the August Congresses, which had the prior right to this week, were finally made, it was happily found that the Jewish Congress could be accommodated here where the other religious congresses will be held, and the arrangements were, with much pleasure, accordingly changed.

Thus the Mother Church, from which all the Christian denominations trace their lineage, and which stands in the history of mankind as the especial exponent of august and triumphant theism, has been called upon to open the Religious Congresses of 1893.

But far more important and significant is the fact that this arrangement has been made, and this Congress has been formally opened and welcomed by as ultra and ardent a Christian as the world contains. It is because I am a Christian, and the Chairman of the General Committee of Organization of the Religious Congresses is a Christian, and a large majority of that committee are Christians, that this day deserves to stand gold-bordered in human history, as one of the signs that a new age of brotherhood and peace has truly come.

We know that you are Jews, while we are Christians, and would have all men so, but of all the precious liberties which freemen enjoy, the highest is the freedom to worship God according to the dictates of conscience; and this great liberty is the right, not of some men, but of all; not of Christians only, but of Jews, and Gentiles as well. I desire from all men respect for my religious convictions, and claim for myself and mine the right to enjoy them without molestation; and my Master has commanded me that whatsoever I would have another do to me, I must also do to him. What, therefore, I ask for myself, a Christian, I must give to you as Jews. Our differences of opinion and belief are between ourselves and God, the Judge and Father of us all.

Through all the Sacred Scriptures of the Old Testament, we walk side by side, revering the creation; journeying through the wilderness; chanting the psalms and inspired by the prophecies; and if we part at the threshhold of the gospels, it shall be, not with anger, but with love, and a grateful remembrance of our long and pleasant journey from Genesis to Malachi.

The supreme significance of this Congress and the others is, that they herald the death of Persecution throughout the world, and proclaim the coming reign of civil and religious liberty.

O Religion! Religion! how many crimes have been committed in thy name! The crimes committed in the name of Liberty are but few in comparison.

Against Religious Persecution, all the religions of the world should be united and support each other with unfailing zeal. This is not saying that all religions are of equal worth. This is not saying that any one should yield one jot or tittle of his own peculiar faith. It is quite the contrary. For only when one is protected in his proper liberties, and can "act in freedom according to reason," can he properly examine his own faith or that of his fellow-man.

With perfect religious liberty, with comprehensive and adequate education, with a life according to the great commandments, mankind will come into closer and closer relations; into a better and better understanding of their social, political, and religious differences, and the living power of the truth, guided by the sovereign providence of God, will more and more make the whole world one in human brotherhood and service, and finally in religious faith.

Henceforth the leaders of mankind will seek, not for points of difference, but for grounds of union, striving earnestly to know the truth, that the truth may make them free from the bondage of prejudice and error, and more and more efficient in advancing the enlightenment and welfare of the world.

With these sentiments I welcome the Jewish Denominational Congress of 1893."

This address, received with marks of the highest approval, was followed by remarks introductory to the work of the Congress by the Rabbis Isaac M. Wise, of Cincinnati, Gustave Gottheil, of New York, and Emil G. Hirsch, of Chicago.

The work of the Congress proper was thereupon begun by Dr. K. Kohler, who read his paper on "The Synagogue and the Church and their Mutual Relations with Reference to their Ethical Teachings," which will be found elsewhere in this volume.

THEOLOGY.

AN INTRODUCTION TO THE THEOLOGY OF JUDAISM.

By REV. DR. ISAAC M. WISE.

I. A PROLEGOMENON.

The Theology of Judaism, in the opinion of many, is a new academic discipline. They maintain Judaism is identical with legalism, it is a religion of deeds without dogmas. Theology is a systematic treatise on the dogmas of any religion. There could be no theology of Judaism. The modern latitudinarians and syncretists on their part maintain we need more religion and less theology, or no theology at all, deeds and no creeds. For religion is undefinable and purely subjective; theology defines and casts free sentiments into dictatorial words. Religion unites, and theology divides, the human family not seldom into hostile factions.

Psychology and history antagonize these objections. They lead to the conviction that truth unites and appeases, while error begets antagonism and fanaticism—error, whether in the spontaneous beliefs or in the scientific formulas of theology, is the cause of the distracting factionalism in this transcendental realm. Truth well defined is the most successful arbitrator among mental combatants. It seems, therefore, that the best method of uniting the human family is to construct a well defined, rational, and humane system of theology, as free from error as possible, which will appeal directly to the reason and conscience of all normal men.

Research and reflection in the field of Israel's literature and history produce the conviction that a code of laws is not yet a religion. Legalism is but one side of Judaism. The underlying principles and doctrines are the essential Judaism; these are the material to the theology of Judaism, and these are essentially dogmatic. You take Judaism as a philosopheme, it is certainly dogmatic. It is neither empirical, skeptical, nor critical, hence it must be dogmatic. If you take it as a body of principle, doctrine, and precept embodied in Holy Writ, it certainly has its fundamental truths which, if formulated in *decreta* or *placita*, are always dogmas.

Let us consider a few particular points. The scriptures begin with an account of CREATION. Expound this as you may, it always centers in the proposition of the priority and superiority of a substantial being—call it spirit, causative power, God, or by any other name—prior and superior to all material being and its modalities; and this, however formulated, is a dogma.

The scriptures from the first to the last page advance the doctrine of DIVINE INSPIRATION AND REVELATION. Reason about it as you may, it always centers in the proposition: There exists a faculty of intercommunication between that universal, prior, and superior being and the individualized being called man; and this also is a dogma.

The scriptures teach that the Supreme Being is also Sovereign Providence. He provides sustenance for all that stand in need of it. He foresees and forcordains all, shapes the destinies and disposes the affairs of man and mankind, and takes constant cognizance of their doings. He is the law-giver, the judge, and the executor of his laws. Press all this to the ultimate abstraction and formulate it as you may, it always centers in the proposition of *Die sittliche Weltordnung*, the universal, moral theocracy, which is the base of all canons of ethics; and this again is a dogma.

The scriptures teach that virtue is rewarded and vice punished, inasmuch as they are voluntary actions of man; furthermore that the free and benevolent Deity under certain conditions pardons sin, iniquity, and transgression. Here is an apparent contradiction between justice and grace in the Supreme Being. Press this to its ultimate abstraction, formulate it as you may, and you will always arrive at some proposition concerning atonement; and this also is a dogma.

Furthermore, scriptures teach with special emphasis THE YHVH MONOTHEISM. This is not the indefinite theo-monism of the primitive element worshipers, nor the illative monotheism of the Shemitic or Aryan paganism, supposed to underlie the polytheism of elemental astrolatry or anthropomorphous theology. It has nothing in common with any god or gods made by human hand or fancy; nothing in common with the abstract deities or god-ideas of philosophy, ancient or modern, which are metaphysical postulates without substantial existence; nor with the artificial god or gods of inductive speculation, like Hegel's perpetually self-developing " Geist," which is the original of the Darwinistic and Auguste Comte's metaphysics; nor with the " Will " of Schopenhauer, the " Unconscious " (*Das Unbewusste*) of Ed. von Hartmann, the subsequent " Panlogism," or " Panpsychism," and the last phase of the whole, the " Unknowable " of British speculation. It is a unique YHVH monotheism without precedent or parallel in history which scriptures teach, a belief in an eternal living God, the author, preserver, and governor of the entire cosmos, who possesses, enlivens, and permeates the All without being submerged in, changed, or limited by this All, the self-conscious wisdom and benevolence in the All, without any dependency on the All. "God is he that is, and all the rest but seems to be." This Yuvh monotheism is no philosopheme; reason neither could nor did invent it, reason can not deny it, it can only construe it; it is a dogma. And according to all ancient and modern expounders of scripture, it is a dogma on which depends the salvation of man. Therefore it is correct to maintain that Judaism has its dogmas; hence there may be built up a theology of Judaism.

Whether it is necessary to formulate and establish these, other, or in fact *any* dogmas, in order to construct a system of theology, can be decided only after we have ascertained what theology is, what the theology of Judaism is.*

2. WHAT THEOLOGY IS.

Theology is the science of man's religious knowledge. Science is ratiocinated and systematized knowledge. Knowledge is any conception of fact, phenomenon or sentiment made permanent in consciousness. Man's religious knowledge is the complex of conceptions of facts, phenomena or sentiments concerning the Supreme Being of his own cognition, that Being's nature and commandments, man's duties, hopes or fears accordingly, and his relations to that Supreme Being. Since all religious knowledges center in man's cognition of the Supreme Being, the science of these knowledges is properly called theology, "a treatise or discourse on or of God."

The ratiocination of conceptions and knowledge entering into any system of science is the work of the faculty of reason. This is the point where theology and philosophy meet, but only to separate again from each other at the next step in advance. Theology is no metaphysics, no ontology, no psychology and no philosophy of religion, consequently its operations and methods differ from all of them.

We know that the attempt to formulate these dogmas by Moses Maimonides and other authorities, before and after him, proved a failure. No two of them agreed in the numbers, essence or wording of the dogmas. Maimonides himself in his philosophical book, *Moreh Nebuchim*—although his formulas were placed in the common prayer book of the synagogue—drops the last two, and in his Rabbinical code, *Mishnah Thorah*, emphasizes but two, viz: God and Revelation. See Yesode Hathorah i, and vii, 1: Joseph Albo's *Ikkarim*, section 1; Isaac Abarbanel's *Rosh Amanah* and Chasdai Kreskas' *Or Adonai*, and compare first Mishnah of section *Chelek* in *Sanhedrin*.

Ratiocination signifies the generation of a judgment from others actually in our understanding. I compare the conception or knowledge to be ratiocinated with those I possess; if there exists nothing contrary or contradictory to it in my consciousness, I hold it to be true, true for me; it is subjectively true. The next higher step is, I compare this new conception or knowledge with the knowledge of mankind, with that which all men know, and if there exists nothing contrary to it in the consciousness of mankind, I hold it to be objectively true; it is true with all rational beings.

In theology, as in every other transcendental science, none can nor need go beyond this for ratiocination. Whatever all men ever knew to be true is true to all; it is self-evident because it is evident to all. Theology can safely build its structure upon the universal knowledge of men. Philosophy in fact does the same. It can not produce facts or phenomena, or the conceptions of either. It can only reason on them, hypothetically determine the degree of possibility, or probability, analyze, construct and define that which it has adopted from the universal knowledge of mankind. Mankind knows much more than reasoners elaborated. Philosophy in these three thousand years elaborated but a few problems which mankind's reason begets. In all this, however, it relied on mankind's knowledge more than on the syllogism. None can reason on naught. Knowledge precedes the process of reason and claims justly the priority in time and superiority of evidence over all products of reason. Mankind's universal knowledge in each particular case is the conclusion of a syllogism, the antecedents of which the philosopher may or may not discover.

3. THE POSTULATES OF THEOLOGY.

As far back into the twilight of myths, the early dawn of human reason, as the origin of religious knowledge was traced, mankind was in possession of four dogmas. They were always present in men's consciousness, although philosophy has not discovered the antecedents of the syllogism, of which these are the conclusions. The exceptions are only such tribes, clans or individuals as had not yet become conscious of their own sentiments, those latter not yet having been crystallized into conceptions, in consequence whereof they had no words to express them ; but those are very rare exceptions. These four dogmas are :

1. There exists—in one or more forms—a Superior Being, living, mightier and higher than any other being known or imagined. (Existence of God.)

2. There is in the nature of this Superior Being, and in the nature

of man, the capacity and desire for mutual sympathy, inter-relation and inter-communication. (Revelation and worship.)

3. The good and the right, the true and the beautiful, are desirable, the opposites thereof are repugnant to the Superior Being and to man. (Conscience, ethics, and æsthetics.)

4. There exists for man a state of felicity or suffering beyond this state of mundane life. (Immortality, reward, or punishment.)

These four dogmas of the human family are the postulates of all theology and theologies; and they are axiomatic. They require no proof, for what all men always knew is self-evident; and no proof can be adduced to them, for they are transcendent (*trans conscientiam communem*). Philosophy, with its apparatuses and methods of cogitation, can not arrive at them, it can only expound them; it can not negate them, and no reasoner ever proved such negation satisfactorily even to himself.

All systems of theology are built on these four postulates. They differ only in the definitions of the quiddity, the extension and expansion of these dogmas in accordance with the progression or retrogression of different ages and countries. They differ in their derivation of doctrine and dogma from the main postulates; their reduction to practice in ethics and worship, forms and formulas; their methods of application to human affairs, and their notions of obligation, accountability, hope or fear.

These accumulated differences in the various systems of theology, inasmuch as they are not logically contained in the postulates, are subject to criticism; an appeal to reason is always legitimate, a rational justification is requisite. The arguments advanced in all these cases are not always appeals to the standard of reason—therefore the disagreements—they are mostly historical. "Whatever we have not from the knowledge of all mankind, we have from the knowledge of a very respectable portion of it in our holy books and sacred traditions"—is the main argument. So each system of theology, in as far as it differs from others, relies for proof of its particular conceptions on its traditions written or unwritten, as the knowledge of a portion of mankind; so each particular theology depends on its sources.

So also does Judaism. It is based upon the four postulates of all theology, and in justification of its extensions and expansions, its derivation of doctrine and dogma from the main postulates, its entire development, it points to its sources and traditions, and at various times also to the standard of reason, not, however, till the philosophers pressed it to reason in self-defense; because it claimed the divine authority for its sources, higher than which there is none. And so we have arrived at our subject:

4. WHAT THE THEOLOGY OF JUDAISM IS.

We know what theology is, so we must define here only what Judaism is.[*]

JUDAISM IS THE COMPLEX OF ISRAEL'S RELIGIOUS SENTIMENTS RATIOCINATED INTO CONCEPTIONS IN HARMONY WITH ITS JEHOVISTIC GOD-COGNITION.

These conceptions made permanent in the consciousness of this people form the substratum to the Theology of Judaism. They are recorded in the national literature of the Hebrews, and actualized in their history, which records also the temporary aberrations, the combat of the logical and illogical in the historical process.

This definition of Judaism is justified by the Hebrew records. It is presupposed in the opening chapters of Genesis, that the progressive development of the monotheistic religious knowledge in the human family was preserved by certain patriarchs—this is also the opinion of the Talmudical sages—and reached Abraham in the fullness of its opulence. Abraham was in his time the heir and exponent of mankind's monotheistic traditions, or perhaps the most prominent of that favored class, who represented an esoteric faith, which Abraham began to proclaim publicly in Canaan. It was a nameless faith. With Abraham begins the definite God of revelation. When this patriarch was ninety-nine years old, it is recorded, Genesis xvii. the first time in these records, God spoke to him of Himself, expounding what He is: "I am AIL SHADDAI, walk before me and be (become) thou perfect, and I will make my covenant between me and thee." Here is the first record of monotheistic religion, with its object, "to be (become) perfect," and its method, to walk before God, in the light of God, to think and act God-like, to shape the moral conduct according to the God-idea, which is its ideal and pattern, and identical with the religious knowledges ratiocinated in harmony with the God-cognition.

Four centuries of progressive development elapsed between the

---

[*] Judaism is a misnomer for the religion of Israel. It applies only to that status of religion which was developed and established in Judea, i. e., to one phase of that religion, and especially the one which was developed from and after the revolution under the Asmoneans (167 B. C.) Still the word is so old, venerable and popular, that it can not well be replaced by its original designation, which is יִרְאַת יְהֹוָה "The fear, veneration, and worship of Jehovah (Psalm xix, 10), which endureth forever."

God-revelation to Abraham and to Moses, characterized by the ethical height of Joseph, the faith and trust in God by the Elders of Israel in Egypt (Exodus iv, 27–31), and the prophetical powers of Moses. A new era of religion begins, it is the Mosaic dispensation. It begins not with a legislation; it begins with the revelation of God Himself to Moses (Exodus iv, 14–16). The God-cognition always precedes the embodiment of the religious idea into commandment and institution; for the God-cognition is the principle, first cause, and touchstone for all religious knowledges, ordinances, and institutions, all religious dogmas and practices, all of which must be effects of that first cause, legitimate conclusions from that principle, sequences of that antecedent. The law of laws is, " Whatever is in my cognition of God, is imperative in my religion; whatever is contrary to my cognition of God, is irreligious and forbidden to me." Israel did not make its God, God made Himself known to Israel, and its entire religion grew out of this knowledge; whatever is not in harmony with this principal knowledge is aberration, error. In Judaism, therefore, all religious sentiments must be ratiocinated into conceptions in harmony with its Jehovistic God-cognition. Therefore Israel's religion is called יִרְאַת יהוה " Veneration and Worship of Jehovah;" its laws and institutions are divine inasmuch as they are the sequence of this antecedent; and its expounders maintain that this monotheism is the only dogma of Judaism. Its formula is ה' אֱלֹהֵינוּ ה' אֶחָד and its categoric Imperative, its law of laws, is אַחֲרֵי ה' אֱלֹהֵיכֶם תֵּלֵכוּ.

The Theology of Judaism is the science of Israel's religious conceptions, these being the doctrinal, ethical, and practical sequences following legitimately from the one principle antecedent to them, which is Israel's God-cognition.

Its evidence is in the four postulates of all theology, the universal knowledge of mankind; in the revelations recorded in the Thorah, the universal knowledge of a large portion of mankind; in the standard of reason and the demonstration of history, to which it refers all doctrine not contained in the four postulates and in the Thorah.*

---

* Thorah signifies "*The* teaching," emphatically, even as the term *biblia* or Bible was adopted for "THE book," emphatically; also the Canon, the Law, to direct authoritatively man's reason, volition, and action. The five books of Moses are the Thorah, the primary sources of the "teaching and canon" of Israel's religion. The other books of Holy Writ are secondary sources, relating to the Thorah as commentaries by inspired men, as far as the "teaching and canon" are concerned; and all post-biblical writings on the "teaching and canon" as laid down in the Thorah and expounded in Prophets and Hagiographa, stand in relation to the Thorah as sub-com-

It consists of two main divisions:
1. God and His attributes as revealed in the Thorah.
2. The doctrinal, ethical, and practical sequences, following legitimately from this God-cognition.

We shall begin by considering the first.

5. GOD AND HIS NAMES ACCORDING TO THE THORAH.

We approach this most important, most solemn and sublime problem with deep veneration and profound reflection. It is the grandest and most inscrutable of all thoughts and ideals of men; it is God and his attributes we are to discuss. I only venture out upon this fathomless and boundless deep because I am to discuss this theme of the infinite under the limitation "according to the Thorah;" and the Thorah is a book, and a book may be understood correctly by an ordinary mortal, if his canon of exegesis harmonizes with the standard of reason.

I have to lay down, in this connection, the following rules of exegesis:

1. The Thorah maintains that its "teaching and canon" are divine. Man's knowledge of the True and the Good comes to his reason and conscience (which is unconscious reason) either *directly* from the supreme and universal Reason, the absolutely True and Good; or it comes to him *indirectly* from the same source by the manifestations of nature, the facts of history and his power of induction. This principle is in conformity with the second postulate of theology, and its extension in harmony with the standard of reason.

2. All knowledge of God and His attributes, the True and the Good, came to man by successive revelations, of the indirect kind first, which we may call natural revelation, and the direct kind afterward, which we may call transcendental revelation; both these reve-

mentaries to the original text and its inspired expounders. This is the historical position of Judaism. Those Bible critics who maintain that the five books of Moses in the form before us were written after Prophets, must admit that the main "teaching and canon" existed traditionally or in any other form prior to the prophets and psalmists; or they must postulate that inspired men of a later date abstracted from existent literature all "teaching and canon" and compiled it in this Thorah form; or they must place themselves upon the non-Israelitish and non-historical standpoint: for this is unexceptionally and incontrovertibly the historical Israelitish standpoint that the "teaching and canon" is in the Thorah, and it is therefore called Thorah or more explicitly. תורת יהוה (Deuter. iv, 8; xvii, 11. 19; xxxi. 24. 25; xxxiii, 4; Psalm xix, 18. See the author's "Pronaos to Holy Writ").

lations concerning God and His substantial attributes, together with their historical genesis, are recorded in the Thorah in the SEVEN HOLY NAMES OF GOD,* to which neither prophet nor philosopher in Israel added even one, and all of which constantly recur in all Hebrew literature.

3. The term *the God of Revelation* is intended to designate God as made known in the transcendental revelations, including the successive God-ideas of natural revelation. His attributes of relation are made known only in those passages of the Thorah, in which He Himself is reported to have spoken to man of Himself, His name and His attributes, and not by any induction or inference from any law, story, or doing ascribed to Him anywhere. The prophets only expand or define those conceptions of Deity which these passages of direct transcendental revelation in the Thorah contain. There exists no other source from which to derive the cognition of the God of revelation.

These passages are: Genesis xvii, 1, 2; Exodus iii, 6, 14. 15; xx, 1–5; xxxiii, 17–23; xxxiv, 5–10; Leviticus xix, 1. 2; Deuter. v, 6–10. Whatever is not predicated of God in these passages, none can predicate of Him.

4. God called in the Thorah by any of the seven holy names, or the God of Abraham, Isaac and Jacob, the God of the Fathers, the God of Israel, or by the prophets the God enthroned in Zion or Jerusalem, can not be understood to signify a tribal God, a national God, a local God, or any special God; it could signify only the one God revealed to the fathers, or known and worshiped by them; God revealed to Israel, known, worshiped, and proclaimed by Israel only, as all those revelations in the Thorah plainly and convincingly teach, the creator of heaven and earth, the judge of all the earth, the possessor of heaven and earth, exalted above all, prior and superior to all matter, time, and space. He can not be supposed to be also a tribal, national, special, or localized God.† The prophets and hagiographers never understood God otherwise than as the Eternal, Infinite, Absolute, hence Universal and Omnipresent God, the very highest, broadest, and deepest conception of Deity which human reason is capable of: and the prophets only knew of God and His attributes, what they had learned from the Thorah. They anthropomorphized the Deity in poetical tropes, metaphoric language, to interpret those sublime conceptions to the gross understanding of the common man, or to move

* שֶׁבַע שֵׁמוֹת שֶׁאֵין נִמְחָקִין, see Talmud in *Shebuoth,* p. 35, also in *Sopherim* iv, and Moses Maimonides in sixth book of his Code.

† The whole can never be thought of as a part of itself.

the heart to love and affection, to admiration, veneration, and worship.
Still they added no new name and no new predicate to the God of
Revelation, simply because human reason could not do it, could con-
ceive nothing higher than the highest.

We shall examine now the details as laid down in the sacred
texts. We begin with the SEVEN HOLY NAMES OF GOD.

1. אֵל AIL.

When primitive man became conscious of the law of causality
in him, he recognized elemental power about and above him which
governed him, and he had no control over it. He recognized a superhuman power, and this was to him the first revelation of a Superior
Being in the form of an empiric observation from the periphery of
nature.

Holy Writ maintains, that the first man, called Adam, recognized
his own superiority over his fellow beings, and the existence and superiority of a superhuman power, which the Shemites called אֵל (AIL)
an existent, superhuman, and superior power.

AIL is the positive term to the negative אֵל AL or לֹא Lo of the
same consonantal letters. The latter signify the relative or absolute
not-being, and AIL signifies being absolute, causative and constant.
Primitive man could call his primitive God-idea AIL only.

In Holy Writ, AIL retained its indefinite and appellative character.
It appears with the article הָאֵל and the possessive suffix אֵלִי; in patriarchal times with an explanatory term, as AIL ELYON. AIL ROI,
AIL OLAM, AIL SHADDAI, the conception of AIL had evidently been
enlarged; in Mosaic time AIL is used where anthropomorphous or elemental qualities are predicated of God, as AIL rachum wechannun, AIL
qanna, HA-AIL haggadol, haggibbor wechannora, evidently representing
God as immanent in nature, retaining its primary signification. In
post-Mosaic scriptures AIL is used for 'ELOHIM, mostly poetical, and
both frequently in the sense of immanence.

AIL is in Holy Writ the first name of God connected with the
names of persons and places. It appears in the Cain (Genesis iv, 18)
and the Sheth family (ibid. v. 15), and then in the family of the patriarchs, like Ishma-ail and Isra-ail; among the Syrians (ibid. xv. 3 and
xxii, 21), in Mesopotamia (ibid. xxvi, 15), and among the Edomites
(ibid. xxxvi. 4, 39. 43). The names of places with AIL, like Beth-ail
and Peni-ail are quite frequent in the old Canaanitish cities named in
Joshua xv, xviii and xix. Modern orientalists prove that the term
AIL, changed with some into אֵיל Eel or ILU, was there in all lands

and languages, from India to the desert of Sahara, wherever a Shemitic dialect was spoken, as the name of a god, or as an appellative
denoting divinity, power, or dominion, or as a title of distinction added
or prefaced to the names of persons or places. In the Koran also
the names of the angels have the Ail as last syllable.*

2. אלוה or אלה ELOVAHH.

The differentiation of the theo-monistic idea to a plurality and
variety of superior beings in prehistoric times is no doubt contemporary with the origin of the different languages. The primitive tribes
separated from one another, in course of time produced distinct dialects, gave different names to their AIL, and also different attributes,
according to the environs and fate of each tribe. One happily situated saw in AIL the good and benevolent god; the other, exposed to
the terrors of the elements, perceived in its AIL an angry and destructive deity, and a third may have experienced both sides of nature and
looked upon its AIL as a variable sovereign. When after centuries of
separation some of those tribes met and coalesced again, they brought
together a polytheism in a polyglot community, from which new languages, gods and cults developed in course of time. All this, however, was beneficial in the historical process; it prompted man to
behold Deity from different aspects; these were revelations from various standpoints, all of which became factors of progressive development. The historic material to establish those differentiations are
meager; we rely chiefly on retrospective inferences. The other and
apparently older differentiation of the God-idea in masculine and feminine deities in all ancient mythologies, from the north-west of Europe
to the south-east of Asia, all over the ancient world, is marked out in
the holy name *Elovahh*, after the form of זרוע.

Two different forces and elements of nature, the generative and
the proliferous, marked so distinctly in the organic kingdom, were observed by the primitive thinkers, and there was added to the AIL the
AILAH, the feminine manifestation of the AIL, the maternal aspect of
nature. This AILAH became the ALLATH of the Phœnicians and Assyrians, which Herodotus identified with Urania; the Allat of the pre-
Mohammedan Arabs, the Eloha of the Syrians, became Astarte among
the Chaldeans, Tethys, the wife and sister of Oceanus, according to

---

* Beiträge zur semitischen Religionsgeschichte, by Friedrich Baethgen,
Berlin, 1888, p. 270 sqq. and Excursus. See also אל in dictionary by
Menahem ben Seruk, Nachmanides to Genesis i, 1 and Lekach Tob,
ibid.

Homer the progenitors of all gods and men; Osiris and Isis in Egypt, the masculine and feminine gods the world over except among the Hebrews, who changed the АILAH into ELOVAHH, to change its gender, and used this term poetically only.

The term never occurs in scriptures prior to Moses, who has it twice in his last song, and there it is defined by the verb עָשֵׂיהוּ " its maker," its maternal power, while *Ail* is defined by מְחוֹלְלֶךָ " who has begotten thee," the paternal power.* The term was old in the time of Moses. It had become a poetical expression of the Deity, the maternal, soft, affectionate, and mild power of God, immanent in nature, revealed to man from its periphery. It marks an epoch in natural revelation, which remained permanently in all heathenism.

3. אֱלֹהִים ELOHIM.

With this third name of God, pronounced ELOHIM, we step upon purely Hebraic ground. Like the tetragrammaton, this *Elohim* or *Ha-Elohim,* is Hebrew exclusively. It occurs most frequently in Holy Writ and in connection with, or often in place of, the tetragrammaton. Neither of these two names of God occur in any language besides Hebrew.

The term *Elohim* contains the consonantal letters and the vowels (*except one*) of both *Ail* and *Elovahh* and the additional ם' *eem*, the plural masculine ending, which shows distinctly that the word was made of the two prior names of God. The feminine ה hai from *Elovahh* is retained and deposed by the masculine *eem*, to express the monotheistic idea of Almightiness, the abstract of almighty, the being that is the center and fountain of all might, force, power, causation, and is therefore the creator of the All (Genesis i, 1); who contains all existent power, the masculine and the feminine, and every other power thinkable or imaginable, producing the good here, evil there, and both simultaneously elsewhere. And yet he is not identical with this force, power, might, which we observe empirically from the periphery of nature; he is the abstract idea of all might, power, force, causation, he is *Elohim,* and that *im* or *eem* as in חַיִּים זְקֻנִים נִעוּרִים רַחֲמִים, or לֵאלֹהִים אֲדֹנִים לֹא. as also דְּבַר אֲדֹנֵי הָאָרֶץ אִתָּנוּ, and many similar passages, is the sign of abstraction. It signifies "Almightiness," or also the Almighty Being with the prefixed article ה. Here is the primitive Hebrew idea of God, a long distance beyond the elemental theo-monism, a step from

---

* See also Daniel xi, 37. Elovahh in apposition with חֶמְדַּת נָשִׁים.

the periphery to the interior of nature, from elements and forces to
the generating and moving soul of them. And yet it is primitive
monotheism only. It has in common with AIL the impersonal and indefinite signification. It is an appellative and no *nomen proprium*,
takes the definite article and the personal suffixes, and is homonymous
with false gods, angels, also judges and rulers. Like AIL it occurs
frequently in Holy Writ to express the idea of God immanent in nature. Elohim expresses a higher degree of natural revelation, as conceived primitively by the Hebrew mind, or by those bearers and exponents of mankind's traditions, of whom Abraham only became
known to posterity. It is the first step above materialistic conceptions
of primitive humanity.

4. אֲדֹנָי ADONAI.

With Abraham, according to the sacred records, in his old age,
natural revelation reaches its climax and transcendental revelation
opens its cycle. Abraham is the first man on record who proclaimed
the name of God, and proclaimed him as the God of heaven and earth
(Genesis xxiv, 3);* the first who prayed to God, and he prayed for
abject sinners; the first of whom it is said that God appeared to him;
the first whom Holy Writ calls a prophet, and his contemporaries
acknowledged a prince of God. Either he was himself the sublime
genius that lifted up his generation to a cognition of God, man and
the world, as recurred so often in the world's history, or his generation
advanced rapidly to higher thoughts and cognitions, and Abraham
was the favorite of Providence that rescued his name and fame from
oblivion for posterity. It is evident that a decided progress of the
religious idea and the God-cognition was achieved in his days. The
century marks the transition from the elemental to the moral God;
from the God immanent in nature to the God immanent also in man;
from the sovereignty of power, wisdom, dominion and fate to the
sittliche Weltanshauung, the ethical supremacy of freedom, justice and
love.

Abraham was the first man to call Gad ADONAI, and this is the
symbol, the ideograph, of that transition (Genesis xv. 2, xviii. 27 sqq.).
Adonai contains in Hebrew the same vowels as *Elohim*, with the plural
ending *ai*, to distinguish it from *Adonee*—my human master, ruler,
governor. It is a Shemitic term Hebraized on the pattern of *Elohim*,
and like it, it denotes the abstract lordship, mastership, majesty. It

---

* Siphri, Haasinu 313 and Lekach Tob ad locum. "Before he was made
known to people he was the God of heaven only; after that, he was the
God of heaven and earth."

follows in the texts pointed out, after or with historical data, something done or being done by God for man, and is defined in Abraham's prayer for the people of Sodom as " the Judge of all the earth," who punishes the wicked, but also spares the evil-doers on account of the righteous among them. *Adonai* is the name of God revealed in the history of man, the just and merciful ruler. It is the moral Lord, the principle of *Die Sittliche Weltordnung.* It is a great distance in the God-cognition from the elemental God or gods, one step higher than the *Elohim*-idea, a new revelation of the God immanent also in human nature.

This *Adonai*-period marks the highest stage of God-cognition in the pagan world. For *Adonai* is synonymous with Adonis, Baal, Bel, and Moloch, anthropomorphous and moral gods, lords, kings, rulers of men, no mere elemental powers. Although the original element of mythology was retained in the masculine and feminine gods and goddesses, and in the forms of worship, still these humanized gods mark the progress of the idea and the highest ever reached by paganism, reached primarily by Shemitic paganism only. The difference between the Abrahamitic *Adonai* and the heathen Adonis, Moloch, Baal, is that the *Adonai* is a successive development from the Hebraic *Elohim,* and the heathen Moloch and Baal are a successive development from *Ail* and *Elovahh.* The Shemites had reached the highest from their standpoint of dualism, so had Abraham reached the highest from his standpoint of pure monotheism. So far natural revelation went, so far human reason succeeded in the cognition of Deity. It never went beyond it, as history testifies. Therefore Abraham was prepared to receive the revelation of God directly, the first transcendental lesson in monotheistic theology.

5. אל שׁדי AIL SHADDAI.

When Abraham was ninety-nine years old, after a long life of contemplation and righteousness, God appeared to him. The Thorah notices this fact particularly. God appeared to none before. And God himself, it is stated, said to him: "I am *Ail Shaddai.*" He had said to none before Abraham, who or what he was. This is the first direct revelation. Here begins the God of revelation.

The substance of this revelation is in the word SHADDAI. The *Ail* was known, and is set before *Shaddai* to announce that the one revealed now is no other than the one revealed originally to man. Therefore *Shaddai* without *Ail,* especially in the book of Job, is a proper name of God.

Ail signifies the mighty one. In the development of the God-

idea from *Ail* to *Elohim* it had become the Almighty and Almightiness.
If *Shaddai* signified the same as AIL, as those suppose who derive it
from SHADAD, it would be a mere tautology and no revelation; yet
Shaddai evidently qualifies *Ail*.

In the Talmud it is suggested (Chagigah 12*a*) that 'ד *dai* is the
root of *Shaddai*, which was adopted by Septuagint, Saadia, Rashi and
others. But they do not account for the *shad*.

There is no reason discernible why *Shaddai* should not be the
nomen proprium of the Deity, after the form of שׂרי "Sarai" and many
others, contracted of שׂר and 'ד which accounts for the *dagesh* in *daleth*.
Shad, like *shadad*, as in *Shadayim*, signifies nourishing, supporting,
preserving. The term *Shaid*, for evil demon, is of late origin, when
the names of the supposed good demons were changed into evil
ones. 'ד signifies sufficient, superabundant, more than sufficient,

as ויהריק לכם ברכה עד בלי די. The *Ail Shaddai* signifies the Almighty, self-sufficient and self-existent supporter and preserver of the
All. This was an important revelation to Abraham. It imbued his
consciousness with the knowledge that the God of his cognition is
eternal, while all heathen gods were begotten and must therefore have
an end. The world depends on him for preservation and support, and
he depends on none. He is in this material world as its life-principle,
although he is also above and beyond it. He alone is self-sufficient
and self-existent. He is *Ail Shaddai*. *Adonai* is God's name in his relation to man; *El Shaddai* is his name in relation to all nature, man
included, and as such he is the God of transcendental revelation, not
reached by natural revelation.

It is evident from two facts that Abraham was the recipient of the
Ail Shaddai revelation, as maintained also by Moses (Exodus vi. 3).

(*a*). The *Ail Shaddai* occurs only in the history of the patriarchs
from and after Abraham, and then no more except the *Shaddai* absolute
in Hagiographa.

(*b*). Names of persons with the *shaddai* appended, like Zurishaddai
and Amishaddai (Numbers ii, 10, 12. 25), occur only after the time of
the patriarchs up to Moses, and nowhere else.

6. יה YAH.

There exists no reason whatever to suppose that *Yah*, the sixth
holy name of God, is an abbreviation of Jehovah. No passage in
Scriptures suggests it. No similar abbreviation can be cited. It is
evident that this name of God originated among the Israelites in
Egypt. It appears affixed to the names of persons for the first time

among those who were born in Egypt, as is evident from 1 Chronicles
iv, 19; v, 4. 24; vii, 2. 3; and then one hundred and fifteen times in
Scriptures. Its origin must be in Egypt after the death of the patriarchs. Right after the exodus we find *Yah* in Exodus xv, 2 יָהּ כֹּם עַל,
and before that (ibid. xv, 2) עָזִּי וְזִמְרָת יָהּ. The latter shows that
Yah is no abbreviation, for the identical phrase is quoted in Isaiah
and Psalms, always with *Yah*. In this passage *Yah* saved Israel at the
Red Sea, and is placed in parallel with *Ail*, *Elohim* and *Jehovah*, hence
it is no abbreviation of either. Still more striking is the fact, that in
Psalms, wherever the poet sings of the Exodus, or the passage through
the Red Sea, as Psalms lxxvii, 12; lxxxix, 9; cxviii; cii, 19; cxxii,
4; cxxxiv, 4, or only takes his metaphors from those events, he has
the *Yah* evidently as the name of God best known among the people
coming from Egypt.

The ancient Midrash also presumes that God was called *Yah* by
the Israelites in Egypt. Bityah, the daughter of Pharaoh, who married the Israelite Mered (1 Chronicles iv, 48), supposed to be identical
with the daughter of Pharaoh that saved Moses (Exodus ii), embraced
the religion of the Israelites, and was therefore called בַּת יָהּ, "Daughter of *Yah*." *Pirkai Rabbi Eliezer*, chap. 48, and *Rabbah* to Leviticus i.

The etymology of this divine name is given nowhere. In Arabic
"Ya" is the name of a god in names like Ya-gut and Ya-uk. "Io"
or Yo was a Greek name for Isis, always without definition. We can
define *Yah* only by inference from the contexts of Scriptural passages
in which it occurs. According to these passages—

YAH IS THE LIFE, מְקוֹר חַיִּים וֵאלֹהִים חַיִּים *manifested in this
sublunar world, the source, bestower and protector of the life of the individual beings and of nations living in constant co-operation and mutual support, like the members of every individual organism.* It is the *Ail Shaddai*,
also, of the nation's life.

Yah is not only the substance conception of *Adonai* and *El Shaddai*,
but also the nation's life as a nation, and as such a higher step in the
God-cognition of the Hebrews, from the abstract to the substance,
with the sanctification of national life. If life is the essence of
Deity, then His is the power, the will, the freedom, the intellectus,
and the goodness, for these are the accidents of life in all its manifestations,* and national existence is no less divine than that of the individual.

---

* See "The Cosmic God," p. 127 sqq. In Goshen the children of Israel
became a nation; there the revelation of God in the life of nation rose in

We need, it seems, no better proof of this definition of Yah than the closing verse of Psalms: "Every thing that hath breath (every living being) praise *Yah, Halleluyah.*" The reverse of this occurs in Psalm cxv, to which we refer later on.

Yah manifested in the life of the individual is clearly expressed in the prayer of King Hezekiah (Isaiah xxxviii, 11). He was sick, recovered, and prayed : "I said in the cutting off of my days, I shall go to the gates of my grave. I am deprived of the residue of my life." Then he continues thus:

> "I said I shall not see (again) *Yah,*
> *Yah* in the land of the living;
> I shall behold man no more
> With the inhabitants of the world."

To see *Yah* he must behold man and the other inhabitants of the world ; *Yah* is manifested in their life only ; he could see *Yah* nowhere else, for *Yah* is the source of life.

The same idea is expressed in Psalm cxviii, 17–19: "I shall not die, but live and declare the works of YAH. YAH hath chastised me sore, but he hath not given me over unto death. Open to me the gates of righteousness, I will go into them and I shall praise YAH."

As the life of the nation, *Yah* is praised in Psalm cxv, which, from verse 12, is a blessing to the entire nation. It proceeds (verse 12) thus: "The heaven is Jehovah's heaven, and he gave the earth to the children of man. The dead will not praise YAH, not all those that go down to silence (defunct nations). But we will bless YAH from now to evermore, Halleluyah."

The same view of the term *Yah* is expressed in the Talmud, *Menachoth* 29 on Isaiah xxvi, 4: "For in Yah Jehovah is the rock of eternity" (or of the two worlds); also *Bereshith Rabba* 9, and Yalkut in Tehillim 794 on Psalm lxviii, 5.

Few notices only reached us from the centuries of Israel's life in Egypt. Still we know from succeeding history, that many of the children of Abraham preserved the sacred traditions, and the Talmud adds that there arose prophets among them prior to Aaron and Miriam, among whom were also Kehath and Amram. There was a successive revelation between Abraham and Moses, for which this sixth holy name of God is no mean evidence. It leads to the YHVH revelation. It relates to Jehovah like *Ail* to *Elohim.*

their consciousness, and this consciousness was the primary cause of their salvation. See Exodus xv, 2. —יָהּ וַיְהִי לִי לִישׁוּעָה.

7. יהוה YEHOVAH.

YHVH, the tetragrammaton, the ineffable and perfect *nomen proprium* of the Absolute and Only God שם המכורש, engraved upon the golden diadem of the high priest, is given in Scriptures to God only. It is the last and highest of the seven holy names, and contains, besides the new revelations, all the revelations of Deity in the six prior names of God. Concerning this name of God, it is reported in Exodus (iii, 15) that the Almighty himself said : "This is my name forever, and this is my memorial throughout all generations." The prophet Zachariah expressed this revelation thus : "And Yehovah will be king over all the earth, that day Yehovah will be one, and his name will be one." The Absolute is immutable and eternal, so must be his name, if it represents him.

The etymology of the tetragrammaton is this : "It is purely Hebrew. It is a contraction of the consonantal letters of the three tenses of the verb *hawah*, " to be," viz :

היה הוה יהיה

" He was, he is, he will be." These are ten letters, viz., six letters ה *hai* represented in the tetragrammaton by two ה *hai* ; three י *yud* represented in the name by one, and the one ו *vav* forming the יהוה.

The verb הוה signifies to be, to become, and to have. This is also the threefold signification of the tetragrammaton.

1. YHVH is the Absolute Being, eternal, infinite, unconditioned, and immutable, all being besides him is relative, finite in time and space, conditioned, and mutable. He alone is self-existent and self-sufficient ; all other beings depend for existence on something outside of themselves, and are subject to genesis and katatesis. He is the necessary existence (מחויב המציאות), and all things are as long as they exist, because He is.

2. YHVH is the Eternal Becoming, as nothing could become from any source outside of the Absolute Being. His becoming power was manifested in the creation of the world. All possibilities potential in the world that have or will become realities, were ideally-actual in him in all eternity and remain so forever, as there can be no increase or decrease in the Absolute. Being and Becoming are but two aspects of the absolute and necessary being.

3. YHVH is the absolute Having. He alone possesses himself ; no relative being has or possesses itself ; all are possessed by something outside of themselves. He possesses the All and all, they were in Him before they were in reality and remain in Him forever. He is

קֹנֵה שָׁמַיִם וָאָרֶץ "the possessor of heaven and earth" (Genesis xiv, 19), and no finite being possesses, not even itself.

These three significations of the verb correspond to the three tenses represented in the tetragrammaton, as revealed to Moses (Exodus iii, 13–16). This is God and none besides him. None can think or imagine a being higher than the Absolute, two or more absolute beings in existence, or a world of beings without the Absolute as its cause or sustaining power. So far and no farther can reason penetrate into the mysteries of existence.

The vocalization of the tetragammaton, it is maintained by Moses Maimonides (Moreh Nebuchim, part II, chapters lxi and lxii), was forgotten after the destruction of the temple in Jerusalem. Leo di Modena, in his Minhaghai Haqqaraim, p. 169, quoted by Basnage, Part II, Book 3, § 16, maintains that the Pharisees only forgot this vocalization, because they would not pronounce the tetragrammaton; the Sadducees did pronounce the holy name, and did not forget it. The vowel signs in the Bible, it is further maintained, were originally established by the Karaites, and they preserved the Sadducean traditions. We must add to this, that the older names of God in Scriptures, Elohim, Eloah, Adonai, are vocalized like Jehovah, beginning with a Sheva and a Cholem, there is no good reason to consider this incorrect in ·the tetragrammaton. Least justifiable is the form Jahve which would make it a Hiphil, the verb hawah in the causative form, which would make of it "he who caused being," and not "he who is himself the being absolute and eternal," as the prophets understood it (Isaiah, xliv, 6; xlviii, 12).

8. THE ATTRIBUTES OF GOD.

Attribute (תּוֹאַר) is any thing that can be predicated of another, and which is inherent in its nature or its substance. The Infinite necessarily presents an infinite number of attributes, and every one in itself must be infinite. It is evident, therefore, the attributes of the Absolute can not be enumerated, or any of them defined in any language. It is no less evident that we know the existence, substance, and nature of any thing by its attributes. It follows, therefore, that we have no knowledge of the Absolute, except by revelation, as is also the case with the Absolute or Infinite itself. We canpredicate no more of YHVH than what He directly or indirectly revealed to Himself.

To illustrate : The forces of nature, like the mental qualities of man, are unknown as to their substance. We obtain·our knowledge of them by their manifestations. Change the term of manifestation to revelation—and they are synonymous—and you will feel convinced that all we know of the Absolute and His attributes we know by revelation.

Theology relies for its knowledge upon the universal knowledge of man—the four postulates—and its written or unwritten traditions, the knowledge of a large portion of humanity. The Theology of Judaism acknowledges the Thorah as the repository of its divine traditions; therefore it can predicate of YHVH only that which is either in the universal knowledge of man or in the Thorah, reported there as God's direct manifestations of Himself.

All attributes of God are expressed in the Thorah in the substantive form,* because in Him every thing is absolute, involved in the substance and unity of the necessary being. So also every attribute of relation in the Thorah is a verbal noun (שֵׁם נִגְזָר מִן הַכִּיעוּלָה). God and His attributes are one. They are expressed in the seven holy names of God, and then defined as attributes of relation in his dealings with humanity.

In the seven names God is revealed as:

   (a) The absolute and necessary existence (מְצִיאוּת).

   (b) The absolute oneness (אַחְדוּת).

   (c) The Eternal (קַדְמוּת וְנִצְחִיוּת).

   (d) The Omnipotence (יְכוֹלֶת).

   (e) The Life (חַיִּים).

   (f) The Intellectus (חָכְמָה).

   (g) The Goodness (חֲנִינָה).

All other substantial attributes of the Deity, such as infiniteness, immutability, omnipresence, providence and freedom, are logically contained in these seven.

9. HOLINESS.

Between the two kinds of attributes there is one which characterizes especially the God of revelation; it appertains both to the substance and to the relation, and this is Holiness. God reveals Himself as קָדוֹשׁ. "And the Lord said unto Moses, saying: Speak unto all the congregation, the children of Israel, and say unto them: Ye shall be (become) holy, for holy (kadosh) am I, Jehovah, your Elohim." (Leviticus xix.) The prophet (Isaiah vi, 3) hears the Seraphim on high praise the Lord as threefold holy, which is to express the idea of most holy, holiness inexpressible in human language. This attribute

---

*Compare also I Chronicles xxiv, 10-12, the grand benediction of King David.

of holiness recurs continually in Holy Writ, and always in the substantive form of KADOSH, and not in the adjective form of KODESH, after this special revelation to Moses. By this attribute of holiness the God of revelation is distinguished from all gods and God-ideas in the theology of the world. It represents Jehovah as the highest ideal of moral perfection, and it is made incumbent upon the congregation of the children of Israel to become holy, morally perfect. Here is the foundation of YHVH ethics, which was known to Israel only. The term *kadosh* is the predicate of a being, in which all moral excellencies in the highest degree are united, and this is moral perfection.

Holiness signifies not only to abhor the vicious, wicked, and false, but also to love the True and the Good, because they are true and good; it is the generic term of utmost goodness, including justice, mercy, benevolence, the delight in the practice *per se* of all which is good, true, and pure, and the abhorrence of the opposite thereof.

10. YHVH'S ATTRIBUTES OF RELATION.

These are revealed in the Decalogue and specified in the direct revelation to Moses recorded in Exodus xxxiv, 5–10.

After the establishment of the covenant of God with Israel as a people and a revelation of the conditions contained in the Decalogue to be fulfilled by the covenant people, they rebelled, violated the main condition of the covenant by making and worshiping a god besides YHVH, and forfeited their national existence, their "ornament from Mount Horeb" (ibid. xxxiii, 6) in the opinion and belief of Moses. Therefore he broke the two tables of stone, as the contract was broken, and moved his tent from the camp, as they were a covenant nation no longer. God, however, it is recorded there, pardoned also this rebellious transgression, and renewed his covenant with Israel under the same conditions. Moses could not understand how the great God of justice, of righteousness, the sovereign *Adonai*, "the judge of all the earth," should thus deal with a nation, and he prayed, "Let me know thy glory, let me know thy ways, I beseech thee, that I may know thee, and that I may find grace in thine eyes;" or in other words, "that I may know how thou, God, governest nations, and by doing as thou doest, find favor before thee." God answered his supplication thus, "I will cause all my goodness to pass before thee, and I will proclaim (fully expound) the name of YHVH before thee, how I am beneficent to whom I am beneficent and merciful to whom I am merciful." (ibid. xxxiii, 19.) Therefore he received the direct revelation, what YHVH as the eternal AIL, immanent in

nature and man, is to all human beings especially (ibid. **xxxiv, 5, sqq.**).
He is:

1. The True and Incomparable Love—love without any motive
aside of his own nature, which is the superlative of grace and truth.

Language has no adequate term to express the love of God, which
is so entirely different from what man calls love; therefore Scriptures
employed five different terms to express it approximately.

Love is first a sentiment, a feeling of kindly sympathy for any
being whose nearness pleases and delights us. This is expressed in
Rachum* (רחום). Mercy is but one side of *Rachum* and signifies that
kindly sympathy for the object of our love in a state of suffering;
Rachum signifies the constancy of that sympathy under all conditions.

Love is secondly a desire to sustain, support, and to make happy
the object of our sympathy in exact ratio to this sympathy. This is
expressed in *Chanun* (חנון), the benevolent, beneficent bestower of
all which gives sustenance, support, and happiness to the beings of
His sympathy.

Love, in the third place, is that unshaken and never-failing fidelity which adheres steadfastly to the object of its sympathy and never
withdraws from it its benevolent beneficence, however it fails, falls, degenerates, until it becomes necessary to heal the fallen man by the
infliction of punishment, and then it is done with sincere sorrow and
regret. This is God's "long suffering" (ארך אפים). He abandons
not the fallen sinner, individual, or nation; permits not the consequence
of sin—which is punishment—to overwhelm the sinner instantly, but
affords him time for self-correction.†

All this kindly sympathy, benevolent beneficence, and never-failing fidelity, which are the three elements of love, can only then be
called divine if the motive is pure goodness, unselfish, "free of every
expectation and possibility of recompense." Such is the motive of
Ynvu's love. He is the Supreme Goodness, the רב חסד "Supreme
Grace;" love is the attribute of his nature.

In the term "long suffering" there is involved the idea of punishment, which would seem contradictory to the supreme love; this,
however, is not the case if the punishment is intended for correction.
Therefore this revelation continues, Ynvu is רב אמת "Supreme

Rachum in other Shemitic languages signifies "love," and appears in
Holy Writ always in this signification as mercy, sympathy, or the like.

† So this divine attribute is defined in Proverbs xiv, 17. 29; Psalms xxv.
xxxii. li. lxxxvi. ciii. cxlv; Isaiah lv, 6–10; Jeremiah iv, 1. 2; Ezekiel xviii;
Hosea xvi; Jonah iii, iv; Micah vii, 18–20; Talmud in *Sanhedrin*, p. 111,
and elsewhere.

Truth," truthfulness and justice, which is also an attribute of his nature. Sins must be punished, wrongs must be righted, God's law must be enforced and sustained for the preservation of mankind and the benefit of the individual. But all punishment inflicted on the transgressor is at the same time from the motive of Supreme Grace as it is from Supreme Truth. So this fifth term complements the definition of the divine love, for which language has no word.

2. Ynvii's Supreme Love and Truth revealed in the life of nations, in the process of history, is the object of the second part of this revelation.

A nation is a complex or association of human beings. It must exist, develop, and prosper under the laws of a God as physical nature does, and stand the evil consequences of a deviation from these laws. These evil consequences are affliction, decline, and death. Nations die of their own sins. Man is a free agent, hence he may sin, deviate from the straight path of God's law, and this possibility must be included in God's law. Nations are composed of many such free individuals; hence nations may sin, deviate from the straight line of God's law, and run themselves to misery and self-destruction, if no remedy were provided in God's law, as was then the case with Israel making and worshiping the golden calf. Therefore this revelation of God's attributes announces that Ynvii " pardons (or rather bears with) iniquity, transgression, and sin," as outlined already in his attribute of " long suffering," although " he makes no sinner guiltless; " the sinner himself must eradicate cause and effect of his sins, urged to this by punishment or by his own voluntary action. So God's love deals also with the nations. He bears or forbears their iniquities, transgressions, and sins, and cleanses none of his sins who does not cleanse himself. How does God's love bear or forbear the sins of nations? In reply thereto this revelation announces a law of history, a law from the code of Providence, which affords an insight into the mystery of man's existence and progress in this world, notwithstanding the numerous mistakes, sins, and transgressions committed, and notwithstanding the holiness and justice of God. This law is :

The Good and the True existing in man, or evolved by man in the course of his history under the love of God, remains forever imperishable, indestructible, and unforgotten, and increases in quantity and quality as the historical process goes on, as this revelation announces " He preserveth grace (the Good and the True) to the thousandth generation," i. e., forever. On the other hand, the opposite of the True and the Good—evil, wickedness, and all that is nugatory to mankind, produced by " the iniquity of the fathers" by deviation from the straight line of God's law, with its evil effects upon humanity—will perish and not reach beyond the third or fourth generation of those who hate God. He, by a peculiar arrangement of transpiring facts, neutralizes the effects produced by the evil doers, so that they can not reach beyond the third or fourth generation. So God's love is manifested and actualized in the life of nations as well as individuals.

This involves the doctrine of man's perfectibility, and the visions of Israel's prophets who saw the golden age with all its glory in the distant future, when the True and the Good will have grown to be the sovereign power of humanity.

The same law governs also the individual man. God's love neutralizes for the penitent sinner the effects of his sins and transgressions by a peculiar arrangement of transpiring facts, as Joseph verily said to his penitent brothers (Genesis I, 19. 20). A very large number of men inherit the iniquities of their fathers, their diseases of body and mind, their oppressive institutions and laws, their errors and ignorance. Still all those evils remain unremedied with those only who hate God (Exodus xx, 5), who stubbornly refuse to see and embrace the True and the Good before them, and even then the evil effect reaches not beyond the fourth generation. This is the most intelligible revelation of God as Supreme Goodness.

This is Israel's God-cognition with its genesis in natural and transcendental revelation. It is the highest known to man, the utmost reason could comprehend. It is the immovable groundwork of all theology, hence also the Theology of Judaism. Whatever doctrine, precept, dogma, or canon rises logically from this principle, is a legitimate part of the system. Again, whatever theory or practice is contrary or contradictory to Israel's God-cognition can have no place in the Theology of Judaism. It comprises necessarily :

1. The doctrine concerning Providence, its relations to the individual, the nation, and mankind. This includes the doctrine of covenant between God and man, God and the fathers of the nation, God and the people of Israel, or the election of Israel.

2. The doctrine concerning Atonement. Are sins expiated, forgiven, or pardoned, and which are the conditions or means for such expiation of sins?

3. This leads us to the doctrine of Divine Worship generally, its obligatory nature, its proper means and forms, its subjective or objective import, which includes also the precepts concerning holy seasons, holy places, holy convocations, and consecrated or specially appointed persons to conduct such divine worship, and the standard to distin-

guish conscientiously in the Thorah the laws, statutes, and ordinances which were originally intended to be always obligatory, from those which were originally intended for a certain time and place, and under special circumstances.

4. The doctrine concerning the Human Will; is it free, conditioned or controlled by reason, faith, or any other agency? This includes the postulate of ethics.

5. The Duty and Accountability of Man in all his relations to God, man, and himself, to his nation and its government, and to the whole of the human family. This includes the duty we owe to the past, to that which the process of history developed and established.

6. This leads to the doctrine concerning the future of Mankind, the ultimate of the historical process, to culminate in a higher or lower status of humanity. This includes the question of perfectibility of human nature and the possibilities it contains, which establishes a standard of duty we owe to the future.

7. The doctrine concerning personal immortality, future reward and punishment, the means by which such immortality is attained, the condition on which it depends, what insures reward or punishment.

The Theology of Judaism as a systematic structure must solve these problems on the basis of Israel's God-cognition. This being the highest in man's cognition, the solution of all problems upon this basis, ecclesiastical, ethical, or eschatological, must be final in theology, provided the judgment which leads to this solution is not erroneous. An erroneous judgment from true antecedents is possible. In such cases the first safeguard is an appeal to reason, and the second, though not secondary, is an appeal to Holy Writ and its best commentaries. Wherever these two authorities, reason and Holy Writ, agree, that the solution of any problem on the basis of Israel's God-cognition is correct, certitude is established, the ultimate solution is found.

This is the structure of a systematic theology. Israel's God-cognition is the substratum, the substance; Holy Writ and the standard of reason are the desiderata, and the faculty of reason is the apparatus to solve the problems which in their unity are the Theology of Judaism, higher than which none can be.

SYLLABUS OF A TREATISE ON THE DEVELOPMENT OF RELIGIOUS IDEAS IN JUDAISM SINCE MOSES MENDELSOHN.

By G. GOTTHEIL, D.D.

A development of the ideas of Judaism took place, and could take place only, where the principle of reform was recognized. Elsewhere stability reigns. True men's views do change in course of time *malgré eux*, and by degrees imperceptible to themselves; just as their daily habits and modes of life change without their being aware of it. Notably in a century like ours, that witnessed so many and so wide departures from received ideas, it is not within nature that men's minds should remain unaffected. Freedom of thought and of speech, now conceded by all civilized governments, engenders a critical spirit. Old beliefs and institutions are challenged as to their right of continuance; their defense compels investigations by persons who, but for this exigency, would never have thought of them; and researches of that kind rarely leave men exactly where they found them. Even that bulwark of stability, the Roman Church, now recognizes the spirit of the time, and her present ruler earns general praise for the skill with which he steers his ship before the winds, and makes them swell his sails and bear him forward.

In theory, the orthodox Jew, or, at least, his spokesman, repudiates all ideas of change; but in reality, he is no more in all things like his forefather of a century ago than Maimonides was like Hillel, or, for the matter of that, as Mendelsohn was like that great light of the twelfth century.

Still, these moldings by the silent but potent hand of time can not be called developments. They lead to no conceptions recognized as new, result in no fresh statements of old truths, and are allowed no practical influence on the religious life of the community. There is no definite goal before the mind's eye toward which its energies are bent; on the contrary, all desire to change is stoutly denied, whilst in the case of a development the alteration is the very thing aimed at. The old, admitted as no longer adequate to the needs of the present, shall make room for the new. No breach with the past is intended; only an adjustment of both doctrine and life to the undeniable and not unwelcome facts before us, lest these facts ride over us and crush us out of existence.

Reformed Judaism originated in Germany, and is still found in those countries only to which German Israelites have carried it. Practically, all Western Jews are alike in regard to the observance of the rituals, but by none except Germans has the attempt been made to legalize their derelictions. The reform of Synagogue-worship in England has been feeble from the start, and has gained no strength during the fifty years that have elapsed since. In other countries, not even these weak beginnings were made.

In saying Germans, we disregard political limits and include in their number Germans living in Austria, Hungary, and other countries.

But it was not given to the Germans in Europe to carry to their full fruition the principles they had formulated, and to gather the prizes of their hard-won victories. A political reaction set in, too well known for needing description, that chilled their ardor—nay, made all further progress impossible. Governments frowned upon all things liberal, reformed congregations had to use the greatest circumspection to save their synagogues from being closed by the police ; anti-Semitism began to rage and to re-enact scenes of ages commonly called dark. Fanatics in our own orthodox ranks cried: " Behold now the fruit of your vaunted progress, the idol to whom you sacrificed our laws and time-honored usages! You might indeed liberalize your faith and your services, but you can not liberalize the people around you, nor prevent statecraft on the one hand and demagogism on the other from using you for their own political ends, by making once more your name a hissing and a by-word." No wonder the German Reformer lost heart ; no wonder his heart sank. The disenchantment was all too cruel. Amidst the general discouragement, all they could do was to try and save what had so far been gained for better days to come.

Ideas need for their development free air, a buoyant, hopeful spirit, and a sense of security. These elements America offered, and hither came men that stood high in the counsels of the German Reformers, men, moreover, whose learning and fervent spirit fitted them well for the pioneer's peculiar task. Most of their number have now gone to their reward ; but their work lives after them. It has prospered and spread to almost every state of the Union, and is steadily putting forth new strength. It shall not be denied that a good pruning of some wild shoots is necessary. The zeal of the younger generation of lead-

ers is not always according to knowledge; it is apt to run to extremes
and to do things which will have to be undone again. But, taking all
in all, the Reform Congregations of the United States may claim to
have continued the work begun some seventy years ago in Germany,
but interrupted by adverse circumstances, and to have carried that
work forward to permanent results.

In the designation Post-Mendelsohnian, "post" means also
"propter." It was that gentle yet forceful spirit that sent the first
rays of light into the darkness which had settled, for centuries past,
over the Jews and their religion. He knocked at the door of the
Jewish mind, barred and bolted against all intrusion, and, although
his rap was of the gentlest, it could not be overheard, nor be left
without some response. Here and there a sleeper awoke and (to use
Graetz's graphic phrase) rubbed his eyes, and, looking about, asked
himself: "Where am I?" "What am I?" "Why am I in this
slough of ignorance and social abasement?" Mendelsohn was, as it
were, the living, the visible proof that a strict observer of the Law, a
"Talmudjude," may be a modern man in thought, in literature, in social intercourse, may even take rank amongst the recognized leaders
in philosophy and literature. Like Maimonides, he appeared at the
threshold of a new era, fettered in his religious practice, but liberated
in his philosophical thought. Yet, although he, in his winning personality, could unite and harmonize the two, the conflict, as far as the
people at large were concerned, was inevitable. Mendelsohn pleading
for the civil emancipation of the Jews had to urge the Jews themselves
to acquire the speech, the manners, the culture of their surroundings.
Was it possible for his people to listen to him, and yet carry the
whole weight of the rabbinical Law with them? It was not long before
that question came to the front, and was openly answered in the
negative.

This explains the nature of the German Reform movement. It
did not begin as a revolt from ecclesiastical oppression ; it was not a
deflection from the faith on which the synagogue is built; it was
life itself that demanded relief. Problems more vital far and deeper
soon came to the surface. The Israelite should not be placed in the
dilemma of either foregoing the full enjoyment of his civil rights or
forswearing his religion, but just as little should he profess doctrines
or practice rites which he had ceased to believe in, or which conflicted
with his own widened sentiments. The following was the form in
which the last aim of the movement was mostly expressed :

" Den innern Glauben mit dem äussern Bekenntniss und der

religiösen Uebung in Einklang zu bringen und das Leben mit der Religion zu versöhnen."

A great undertaking, truly, especially when dealing with a faith as old, as complex, as dearly bought, and as completely identified with the whole life of its professors, as Judaism. But the brave reformers did not shrink from it. With a heroic faith in the vitality of their religion, they addressed themselves to their task and faced the storm which their declaration provoked from the defenders of the established church.

The beginning was made, as was natural, with the question of authority in Judaism. Bible and Talmud, or rather the codes into which the multitudinous laws deduced from them had been petrified, held undisputed sway. The Reformers did not deny it. Their first propositions were still discussed on that; the written and the oral Law were invoked by both, advocates of reform and opponents. The abrogation of a ritual, the change of a prayer, the use of the vernacular in worship, the introduction of the organ into the synagogue, and similar innovations, were debated, not on their own merits, but on the grounds of existing legislation. As a matter of course the advantage was with the orthodox. So, by-and-by, the right of the Talmud or oral traditions to dominate all succeeding generations was challenged, and then denied. One of the strongest arguments for this dethronement was the charge, not a new one, that the oral Law obscured the light of the revealed Law, nay, is often found to contradict the clearest teachings of the latter. For the sake of restoring the Torah to its legitimate right as the only true word of God, the Talmud had to recede. But this restitution did not last long; for it was soon observed, as people began to codify the Mosaic Laws, that many of them were just as inapplicable to our time and condition and often as contrary to our present ideas as most of the rabbinical enactments; and, furthermore, that those usages that might still be observed, needed tradition for their interpretation and application. At that stage Spinoza's distinction between the political and moral parts of the Law was recalled and insisted upon. The former by their very nature must be subject to changes, and could, therefore, never have been intended by their author as binding for all times; the latter only might be so considered and accepted as the abiding doctrine of Judaism and the ground-work of its theology. In the meanwhile, however, the critical or historical school of Bible students had arisen, with its theory of a gradual evolution of the Hebrew literature. Shunned and even ridiculed at first, that view gradually gained the scholar's ear, and many of the Jewish

reformers openly avowed their acceptance of the new method of
" Torahstudium." The Scriptures themselves, then, became part of
Jewish tradition; in point of time, the oral record preceded the written even from the beginning; all Judaism, from first to last, is the
product of the Jewish mind, or, to use the phrase now in vogue—of
the peculiar genius of the Jews for the religious life. The adoption
of that view was and is of the utmost moment to the Reformer; for
it puts an end to all discussions as to his right of changing the transmitted forms of worship or stating anew the ancient principles of
faith. If all came from the people, to the people belongs the rule over
it, if the experiences, the trials, the triumphs, and defeats of the nation furnished the training by which the native endowment of the
Hebrew mind was educated for, its peculiar mission to the world—that
training has never ceased and should, therefore, produce new results.
Verbal revelations were no longer received, prophets fell silent, when
the days for that mode of teaching passed away; but neither revelation itself, nor prophesying itself, can have vanished from the Hebrew
mind. What was true of the spirit once, is true of it always; if men
concede a Divine economy in the unique guidance of Israel, that
economy must continue as long as that guidance preserves its character. Hence, concludes the modern Reformer, the duty rests upon
us to give our ear to what God is still revealing to us, to try to understand it, and lay it to heart, and to withhold it from no one that
would listen to us. This principle adopted, we are no longer answer-
able because we still hold to the Old Testament, for every thing the
book contains concerning the nature of God, or His providence, or
His justice, or in regard to the soul, or our duties to men, or the
rights of the Gentiles, and so forth; we place these things at their
historical value. Neither can they hinder us from receiving light and
inspiration from other sources. All our literature is for guidance, not
for dominion over the spirit. The following are the most essential
changes in the tenets of Judaism that have come to pass under the influence of Reform principles.   .

1. The Unity of God, that chief corner-stone of Judaism, is conceived of more in its inclusive than exclusive bearing; it is no longer,
as it has been, a cause of separation and estrangement from people of
other faiths, but the opposite, a stimulus for seeking their fellowship
and co-operation in all things good, true, and right. Faith in the One
Father in Heaven imposes upon us the obligation to bring all his human children into the bond of one common brotherhood. Rituals intended exclusively to keep the Jew apart from his environments we
abandon for that very reason; all traces of hostility to any one section

of mankind, no matter what their religion, no matter what justification the compilers of our liturgies had when they called for vengeance on their persecutors, are expunged from our prayers and hymns.

2. The idea of a "chosen people" has for us no other meaning than that of a people commissioned to do a certain work amongst men; it implies, in our sense, no inherent superiority of race or descent, least of all preference and favoritism in heaven. The word that came from the Jewish mind thousands of years ago, "God is no respecter of persons," is not contravened by us either in our belief or in our prayers, or in our feelings toward non-Jews; and that other word from the same source, "Love thy neighbor as thyself," forbids us to countenance the least restriction of right or of duty based on a difference of race, station, culture, or religion. Whatever there is yet in our liturgies or in our ceremonials, even if it only seems to conflict with that great truth, will disappear when the new Order of Service, now in preparation, shall become the accepted ritual expression of the Reformed Judaism in America.

3. Palestine is venerable to us as the ancient home of our race, the birthplace of our faith, the land where our seers saw visions and our bards sang their holy hymns; but it is no longer our country in the sense of ownership, ancient or prospective; that title appertains to the land of our birth or adoption; and "our nation" is that nation of which we form a part, and with the destinies of which we are identified, to the exclusion of all others. Israel is a religious community only; even the feeling of identity of race is weakening. Restoration to Palestine forms no part of our prayers; neither does the lost sacrificial service, connected with that hope, because:

4. The substitute, the worship of prayer and praise and of the devout reading of the Scriptures, had already won the affections of the Jewish people a century and more before the Christian era; in the regions of the diaspora, long before that time. The people's meeting-house or synagogue, that glorious creation of the Rabbis, as Claude Montefiore calls it, the venerable mother of every church or mosque on earth, of St. Peter in Rome, St. Paul in London, and the Tadsh in India, became the People's Temple, and the pious and informed leader in devotion became the priest of the future. Only because it was violently wrenched from the nation and by the same stroke that ended its life, the loss of the sacrificial Ritual continued to be bewailed and its restitution prayed for so long and so fervently. The sorrows of the exile hid from the Jewish mind the true significance of the interdict of sacrifices by the inexorable edict of fate. But light came with the new day of liberty; Israel "fell, we say, but fell upward;"

and we have no desire to seek our way downward again. The adoption of the word "Temple" for our modern houses of prayer, in preference of "Synagogue," is one of the landmarks of the new era. It is a public avowal, and, as it were, official declaration, that our final separation from Palestine and Jerusalem has deprived us of nothing we can not have wherever we gather together for the worship of the One and only true God and the study of His will.

5. The tragic question of the Messiah has ceased to be a question for us; it has been answered once for all, and in such wise that we have no controversy on that point with any creed or church. Has come, is come, or to come again, all difference in time, is meaningless to us by the adoption of the present tense: Messiah is coming now, as he has been coming in all past ages; as one of the Talmudists distinctly taught: ימות המשיח מאדם הראישון עד עתה "Messiah's days are from Adam until now." That form of the idea about which the dispute has hitherto been waged between synagogue and church is clearly a creation of the needs of a certain period of Jewish history fashioned in the likeness of the minds that testified of it; that we leave to history what was temporal in the conception; and keep only that which is spiritual, and, therefore, above time. That part consists in the belief that mankind will outgrow and overcome all causes of evil in its midst; that peace and not war, love and not hatred, freedom and not bondage, joy and not pain, knowledge and not ignorance, trust and not fear, hope and not despair, are the ends toward which the Ruler of the world is guiding mankind; and that Israel was chosen to make this proclamation to the world, and to labor and to suffer in the fulfillment of that mission. About things of the past, we dispute not, believing with Goethe that

Alles Geschehende
Ist nur ein Gleichniss,

let every one construe these events or what goes for such as he sees fit. What alone and always concerns us is its influence upon the present. And when the Reformed Jew says: Messiah means progress, means betterment all around, means peace, means redeeming of the fallen, means equality of rights and good will toward all men, means, in short, the best which the best minds could ever think of as *not* too good for the humblest brother or sister—how far is he in this hope and faith from the hope and faith of the best Christian? What matters it how the movement began or who began it—so we only agree that we must move on and upward in the same direction. Has it not been said in both Testaments that in the end God shall be all in all? Then shall the death of creeds be swallowed up in the victory of God's own eternal life.

6. With the development of the Messianic idea came the change in the conception of Israel's dispersion. As in all calamities, so in the final catastrophe that ended his national life, there was punishment for sins; but it was not that alone, nor chiefly so; how *else can we account for the heroism displayed by the people and the magnificence of Judea's death scenes? The flames that consumed Jerusalem's splendor and the temple's treasures were his magnificent funeral pile. Can sin, can crime be so glorified? And has he not received a thousandfold for all his sins? I say: this is the mercy of God that His punishments are meant for good and not for evil, for blessing and not for curse; and he that curses the sinner curses God, as he that mocketh the poor, mocketh his maker. We deplore no more our dispersion, wish for no ingathering. Where God has scattered us, there also is His vineyard into which we are called as laborers; and well will it be with us if we are numbered amongst those that were found faithful unto the Common Master.

These, in brief and general outline, are the changes of ideas that have come to pass since Mendelsohn. Within this framework others of less vital importance, though not less notable, occurred, which, however, it is impossible to mention without trespassing the limits of time allowed; as the Sabbath and the Sunday services, the position of woman, and others. They will, however, appear in the complete treatise. If it be said:

" But yours is no longer the Judaism history knows; it is virtually a new Judaism," we answer: " Be it so, as long as it is Judaism; and where is the man or body of men that have the right to say it is not?" We stand for the sacred privilege of every man to name his religion as he chooses, and to affiliate himself to any creed or church with which he feels himself in sympathy. Will any one dare to question the fidelity of the modern Jew to his brethren, or his independence in avowing his religion and race? A new Judaism. This is precisely what the movement aims at. It does not wince before the accusation. It is not the first time that Judaism is taking on a new form of expression and rises to a wider reach of conceptions. It has passed through several crises and come forth in better health and with a stronger constitution. Our inspiring thought is, that this wonderful faith, withal so simple, so free from mysticism—this faith, with obedience to God's law as its main artery, and righteousness for its soul—should have passed through its evolutions without losing its identity; that it did

not perish under the ceaseless strokes of a world that has emptied all
the vials of its wrath upon it. Think of it, what it means. A religion of that hoary age and that long and varied experience, so soon as
it feels the breath of the new day, bestirs itself, girds up its loins, and
begins the work of fitting and adjusting itself to the needs and requirements of the present time. Why, the mere will and purpose and daring, even if nothing came of it, prove that it can not be a dead or
dying faith. But look about you, and see the fruits of the departure
on every side. Here we are, in these great and holy days, amongst
you, brethren of all the earth, followers of many prophets, disciples
of many masters, children of many churches, gathered together from
the East and from the West, from the North and from the South.
Here we are, a community, oldest in time, but smallest in tale, with a
record of trials that must touch every feeling heart. Here we are,
with our old message still on our lips, seeking your fellowship, pledging
our good faith to the best things you stand for, asking nothing but
what you yourselves declare to be due to every child of God. Will
you reject our hand, or, accepting, help us to make God's covenant
with his ancient people a covenant of peace between all peoples and
the everlasting Father in heaven ?

THE SABBATH IN JUDAISM.

By DR. B. FELSENTHAL.

The desire has been expressed that some one belonging to the Jewish community and confessing the Jewish religion should come forward on this platform and speak on the Sabbath-question from his Jewish standpoint. In compliance with the kind request that I should do so, I appear before you and offer you a few thoughts on this highly interesting topic.

The Sabbath, conceived as a day of rest and of sanctification, is undoubtedly of a Jewish origin, and to the Jews the Christian world is indebted for this grand institution. It is true enough—and we admit it without hesitation—that the Semitic nations, among them the Assyrians especially, celebrated in their own way and manner one day in each week, long before the Israelites did so. But with them the day was not a day of rest, giving recreation to the body; not a day of pure and innocent joy, refreshing to the soul; not a day of thoughtful meditation, enlarging the mind. It was with them either a day of fasting, of wailing and lamentation, or a day given up to sensual excesses and to low and degrading revelry. And, furthermore, it was dedicated to the god Saturn, a god whom the prophet Amos mentions under the name of Kiyyun, or to some other of the gods worshiped by these heathenish nations. From Western Asia the belief in the seven planetary deities, ruling the seven days of the week, came to Egypt, from Egypt to Rome, from Rome to Gallia, Germania, the British Islands, and other European countries, and in the English language the name of the seventh day of the week, viz., the name Saturday, is still bearing witness to the fact that the seventh day in the week was dedicated in ancient times to the god Saturn.

While among the Assyrians and a few kindred nations the day celebrated in each week was devoted either to fasting and mourning or to sensual and dissolute pleasures, the celebration of the Sabbath among the Israelites was decidedly and essentially of quite a different nature. With them it was, or at least it became in the course of a few centuries, a day of joyful rest from wearisome labor, a day of holiness, of elevating the mind, of cleansing the heart, of purifying the will. It became a means for lifting up the Israelite religiously and morally, and for placing him, religiously and morally, on a higher plane. In this connection it deserves especially to be noted that by the Sabbath the Israelite was lead to a humane treatment of all his fellow-beings—of *all* his fellow-beings, including the sorrow-laden stranger and the afflicted slave, including even the toiling and otherwise helpless cattle. For thus it is repeatedly said in the Law, "Thy man-servant and thy maid-servant shall rest on the Sabbath-day *as well as thyself*, and the stranger within thy gates also, and thy ox and thy ass likewise." And this day was not devoted to Saturn or to some other pagan deity, but it was *Shabbath la-Jehovah Elohekha*, a Sabbath devoted "to the Lord thy God;" it was *Kodesh*, sanctified, or set apart, to the service of the Lord, to the One-God of Israel and of all the world, to the Ruler of the nations, the Father of mankind.

In the first centuries, following the times of Moses, the masses of the people had not risen to the heights of the pure and lofty conception of the Sabbath-idea as it was taught by the divinely inspired prophets. From the words of warning and admonition and exhortation falling from the lips of several of these prophets, we must conclude that there were large numbers of people who disregarded or profaned the Sabbath, and who did not keep it in the sense desired by these prophets and incomparable teachers; by these teachers who were teachers not only for their contemporaries, but for all subsequent generations, and not only for Israel, but for all the world. Still, nearly a hundred years after the return from the Babylonian captivity, Nehemiah bitterly complained about the profanation of the Sabbath, and from the Biblical book bearing his name, we learn how he insisted upon certain measures in order to bring about a better observance of the day. But in post-Nehemian times, a stricter observance of the Sabbath became general, and since the fifth century B. C. until the middle of the present century, the Jews, as a community, rarely, if ever, desecrated the Sabbath by physical labor or otherwise. On the contrary, a spirit of extreme rigor in the manner of keeping the Sabbath grew up rapidly, and a tendency prevailed to extend to the utmost limits the practice of abstaining from labor, and to follow the deductions from this law and the ramifications of the same in all possible directions. But there was a danger lurking in this tendency, the danger that thereby the higher character of the Sabbath and its power for sanctifying the soul-life of the observant Jew might be forgotten, or might at least be pushed into the background. Happily— thus impartial History teaches us—these apprehensions proved to be groundless. The Sabbath retained its sanctifying power and influence even among the extremest of the strictly law-abiding Jews, with whom each of the numerous precepts of the so-called Oral Law or Traditional Law was a *noli me tangere*. With a majority of the people at least, the essence of the Sabbath was not considered to exist in the observance of the innumerable negative, talmudical, and rabbinical precepts, telling us what a Jew must *not* do on the Sabbath, and the higher character of the Sabbath did not disappear and did not become lost among the Jews. Nevertheless, there is no doubt that the great teacher of Nazareth was perfectly correct when he upbraided a certain class of his Jewish contemporaries for their laying the main stress and accent upon the negative side of keeping the Sabbath. His words regarding the Sabbath were golden words. And he was in full harmony and accord with other Jewish teachers living in his time or soon after him, when he maintained that not in the Sabbath ceremonials and not in the scrupulous abstaining from physical labor consists the holiness of the Sabbath; and when he said that, "the Sabbath was made for man and not man for the Sabbath." Rabbinical sayings which have come down to us from the Apostolic age and which are clothed almost in the very words in which the corresponding New Testament sentences are expressed, we meet frequently in the various parts of the Talmudical literature. *Ha-Shabbath mesurah lakhem velo attem mesurim la-Shabbath;* "the Sabbath is handed over to you, but you are not handed over to the Sabbath." *Kol saphek nephashoth do'he eth ha-Shabbath;* "if the remotest danger to health or life is to be apprehended, the Sabbath must be disregarded and the Sabbath laws must be deviated from." Such and similar sentences could be quoted from the Jewish literature of yonder times in considerable number. The regulations of the Pharisees in the times of Jesus, the laws laid down by the dialecticians of the Talmud and their followers in later centuries, by the casuists of the post-talmudical period, they could not and did not deprive the Jewish Sabbath of its higher and holier character. They contributed rather to a certain degree to enhance the holiness of the Sabbath, and to give to the day a still greater power for sanctifying the inner and the outer life of the confessor of Judaism.

But, in briefly outlining the history of the Sabbath institution among Jews, should we restrict ourselves to merely looking up the old Jewish law-books? No live institution can be fully understood if we study merely the written laws and ordinances concerning the same. The life of any great institution and its real character manifests itself independently of the words of books, of the letters of laws, of the sayings of old authorities. And if we now ask history, we shall soon

learn that the Sabbath proved to be an institution of the greatest
blessing for the Jews. It was for them, in the first place, one of the
means, and a very powerful one, by which the preservation of the
Jews as a separate religious community was secured. The Sabbath
endowed them with an unshakable confidence in a Divine Providence,
and gave them every week new strength to withstand the almost
unceasing cruel and pitiless attempts to exterminate the Jewish people
and to extinguish the Jewish religion ; and it kept them united as one
religious denomination despite of their having been dispersed over so
many parts of the world and despite of their having no ruling hie-
rarchy and no other centralizing authorities. The Sabbath, together
with a few other strong bonds, effected this almost miraculous per-
petuation of Israel's existence.

And what a great bliss and happiness did the Sabbath bring to
the family-life! The more the storms raged outside, the closer and
firmer became the mutual attachment of the members of the families to
each other and of the families among themselves. And while the Jews
during the week days had to go out into the world and to see where
they could find the scanty bread for themselves and their families, and
while in doing so they had to experience so much humiliation, so
much malice, so much hatred—when the Friday evening came and
they were again within the circles of their families, they were joyful,
they lighted the Sabbath lamps, they sang their Sabbath hymns, they
chanted their Psalms, and they forgot, once in each week, all the sorrows and cares of every-day-life, and all the affronts and insults which,
without pity and without mercy, were heaped upon them, and at least
on the Sabbath they felt released in body and soul from troubles and
burdens.

The Sabbath proved also a great blessing to the Jews in another
regard. To the observance of this day the Jews owe the conspicuous
fact that ignorance never spread among them as far as among many
other nations and sects. With the Jews education and learning were
at all times kept in high esteem. To this came now the deep-rooted
usage that in each city and town where Jews were living, discourses
were delivered and learned debates were held on the Sabbath days in
schools, in the synagogues, in the meeting rooms of societies of various
kinds and in consequence of the instruction received by these discourses and debates the audiences were more or less enlightened in the
principles of their faith and in the doctrines and precepts of their religion. And thus to the Sabbath, too, we can partly ascribe the fact
that, in that period of history called "the Middle Ages," a period
which was characterized by the deep darkness of ignorance and super-

stition prevailing almost every-where among the Christian nations in
those times, numerous poets and philosophers and scholars arose and
flourished among the Jews.

We must, before we close, not forget to remark that the Jewish
Sabbath had at all times the character of cheerfulness and delight.
In the Old Testament already we read the words of the prophet by
which he reminded the people to "call the Sabbath a delight." And
in the post-biblical literature of the Jews we find evidence that for the
Jews the Sabbath was a day of cheerfulness and of bright sunshine, a
hundredfold and a thousandfold. Other sources of Jewish history
corroborate more than fully the fact that the Sabbath among the Jews
had such a serene and cheering character. On each Friday afternoon,
when the Sabbath was approaching—so we read in the Talmud—Rabbi
'Hanina clothed himself in his festive attire and went into the fields
with his disciples and friends, saying to them: "Come, let us go to
meet becomingly and in a festive mode the queen Sabbath." Rabbi
Jannai acted likewise, and he was accustomed to receive the Sabbath
joyfully by saying: "Be welcome, O bride! Be welcome, O bride!"
Rabbi Josua, another great authority of the Talmud, said: "Let the
celebration of the Sabbath be divided into two parts; one half to be
devoted to God, the other half to your own enjoyment." Rabbi Jose
said: "Whosoever keeps the Sabbath in a joyous manner, will be
richly rewarded." Rabbi Jehudah added: "Whosoever keeps the
Sabbath in a joyous manner, will have all the desires of his heart fulfilled." And how—thus the Talmud continues to ask—is the Sabbath
to be kept in a joyous manner? To which question one of the rabbis
answers: "By having better meals than usually and the like." Let it
also be added here, that it was a law antedating the rise of Christianity
to open the festive celebration of the Sabbath on Friday evenings by
Kiddush, that is, by praising God, the giver of all good things, over a
cup of wine, and by the drinking of wine during the Sabbath meals,
and every one of the family partook in this wine drinking. Without
doubt, this law concerning Kiddush was piously observed by Jesus and
his friends, as he, whom millions of our Christian brethren adore as
their "Master" and as the divine founder of their religion, himself
has declared that he had not come to destroy the law, but to fulfill it.
This law just mentioned is still strictly observed among so-called orthodox Jews, by those who have the means to do so.

Sad and serious contemplations were not permitted on Sabbath,
nor were fasting, or mourning, or supplications in behalf of sufferers.
While the reading and study of Sacred Scriptures and of other good
books was certainly highly recommended, it was prohibited to read on

Sabbath certain parts of them, as *e. g.* the Lamentations of Jeremiah and other portions of a similar sad character. For no gloom should fill the heart of the Jew on the Sabbath, and no other sentiment should dwell therein than of pure joy. It is well known that the precepts of Judaism laid great stress upon the sacred duty of visiting the sick and of consoling the mourner. While such acts of kindness, of sympathy and mercy were not to be neglected on the Sabbath day on account of the Sabbath, yet the Sabbath joy should be disturbed thereby as little as possible. Thus, when one visited on a Sabbath a sick person, he had to refrain from the common methods of consolation, and he had to say to the sick and his friends: "It is Sabbath to-day, and it is not right that on this day we should send up to God our supplications to restore the suffering brother; but health and strength, let us hope, will speedily come, and you, you keep your Sabbath in peace." Similar words were spoke on Sabbath to those who were in mourning for a dear departed one.

Much more could be said on this subject. Hours could be filled without exhausting it. Yet I feel that this is not the place nor the time for doing so. One thought, however, I can not refrain from expressing before I close. We live, God be praised, in the freest land of the world, in the United States of America, in a land where Church and State are entirely separated, and where every one can follow the dictates of his own conscience and the precepts of his own religion, as long as he does not thereby infringe upon the rights and privileges of his neighbor. Let now the Jew, who desires to keep his Sabbath in his own way, have the undisturbed right to keep it when and how he wishes. And let no unholy and sacrilegious hands attempt to attack the sanctuary of American freedom. May the dark day never come on which it shall be decreed by any legislative or executive power in America that one certain day for keeping the Sabbath and one certain manner of keeping it be *forced* upon unwilling minorities. The Sabbath is a grand and sacred institution—we all agree in that. But its celebration must be left to the individual; it belongs to the category of his eternal and inalienable rights. American liberty, I venture to say, is a still grander and a still holier institution, and the maintenance of it is intrusted to each and every American citizen. We praise the weekly Sabbath, we are sure that from it immense blessings will spring forth—blessings for the mental and for the moral life of individuals, of families, and of society at large. But what the laws and statutes, enacted or to be enacted by the legislative authorities of our American States, can do for the Sabbath, is this, and only this: They can protect and ought to protect every congregation assembled on their Sabbath for divine worship in a church, or a chapel, or a synagogue, or a mosque, or any other place, against being disturbed in their worship; and they can guarantee and ought to guarantee to each person in our land, and be he the poorest laborer, one day of perfect rest in each week of seven consecutive days. All further Sabbath legislation by the State powers is unnecessary and would be un-American. But let us, let all the friends of the great and sacred Sabbath-institution trust in the power of public opinion. Relying upon this great power and upon the divine blessings of our Heavenly Father, we, all of us and all the friends of the holy Sabbath-institution, can look hopefully toward the future and can rest assured that the land in all times to come will have a Sabbath, a real, genuine Sabbath.

WHAT THE HEBREW SCRIPTURES HAVE WROUGHT FOR MANKIND.

By DR. ALEXANDER KOHUT, NEW YORK.

To them who cradled in the infancy of faith, rocked by violent tempests of adversity, and tried by passion-waves of lurking temptation; who seeking virtues, find but vice; who striving for the ideal, gain but the bleakest summit of realism; who sorely pressed by rude time and ruder destiny, encounter but shipwrecks upon shipwrecks in the turbulent oceans of existence: God is the anchor of a newborn hope, the electric quickener of life's uneven current, drifting into His harbor of safest refuge from the hurricanes of outward seas, wherein no ship, no craft ever founders, drifting into the tranquil Bible streams.

Faith is a spark of God's own flame, and nowhere did it burn with more persistence than in the ample folds of Israel's devotion. There worship and sacerdotal lights of virtue glowed with mellow unpretentious ambition, fanned by prophetic admonition and timely advices. No exterior luster of transient hue could effectually diminish the chaste, unrivaled radiance of Israel's ever luminous belief in Him and His all-guiding providence. With faith as the corner-stone of the future, the glorious past of the Jew, suffused with the warmest sunshine of divine effulgence and human trust, reflects the most perfect image of individual and national existence. Faith—the Bible creed of Israel—was the first and most vital principle of universal ethics, and it was the Jew, now the Pariah pilgrim of ungrateful humanity, who bequeathed this precious legacy to Semitic and Aryan nations, who sowed the healthy seeds of irradicable belief in often unfertile ground, but with patient, inexhaustible vigor infused *that* inherent vitality of propagation and endurance, which forever marks the progress and triumph of God's chosen, though unaccepted people.

This then, to begin with, is Judea's first and dearest donation to mankind's treasury of good!

Israel also gave the world a pure *religion*, a creed undominated by cumbrous tyranny, unembarrassed by dogmatic technicalities, unsustained by heavy self-sacrifice and over-extravagant ceremonialism—a religion sublime and unique in history, free from gaping superstitions, appalling idolatries and vicious immoralities; a pure, taintless, lofty, elevating, inspiring and love-permeating faith, originating in a monotheistic conception, and culminating in that indestructible edifice, which no waterfall of time, no stratagem of destiny, no shrewd device of man, no whim of circumstance, no hatred, no bigotry, and no harsh excommunication from civilization, could ever degrade into intellectual slavery, beguile into infidelity, or corrupt into treachery. A religion at whose sparkling fountain wells of ethical and cultural truths the world's famed pioneers in art, science, literature, politics, philosophy, architecture and kindred attainments of learning, so eminently wielded by classic Greece and boastful Rome, slaked their thirst.

In religion, Hebrew genius was supreme. It is no rhetorical extravagance of sentiment, nor misplaced eulogy, to assert, that " in the ancient world Israel attained an eminence as much above all other peoples of the circum-Mediterranean world in religion as did Greece in art, philosophy and science, or Rome in war and government." In fact, *the Hebrews drank of the fountain, the Greeks from the stream, and the Romans from the pool.* Those majestic Hebrew seers are reproduced in worthy prototypes in modern Judea to-day, only in them the national force was strongly impelled upward. "They grasped heavenly things so vividly, that even their bodily senses seemed to lay hold of God and angels. Spiritual presences faced the bodily sight in wilderness, or burning bush, or above the ark of the covenant. The earthly ear caught tones from the other world in some still, small voice, or pealing from a bare mountain peak. And here it is that the Jew has accomplished his most extraordinary achievement. His faith furnished the stock upon which two other religions have grafted their creeds. And all this national magnificence, religious superiority and unparalleled historic grandeur is recorded in the Sacred Annals—that unsurpassed standard for man's moral and mental government—*the Book.* Every unprejudiced mind gladly acknowledges now that the Bible, the divine Encyclopedia of unalienable truths and morals, belongs to the world, like the sun, the air, the ocean, the rivers, the fountains—the common heirloom of humanity.

No need to ask who first bequeathed its treasures of law, religion, truth, morality, righteousness, equity, brotherly love, not to speak of its literary and scientific merits; who first diffused its luster, disseminated its doctrines; who first planted so extensively and cultivated so highly this flower-garden with its diverse variety of luscious fruits and blooming lands? Was it not Moses charged by the Lord:

"Gather the people together, and I will give them water!" and was it not Israel that sang this song:

"Spring up, O well, sing ye nations unto it,
The well which the nobler of the people delved
With the scepter and with their staves."

Chaldea wrought magic; Babylonia, myth; Greece, art; Rome, war and chivalry;—of Judea, let it be said, that she founded a hallowed faith, spread a pure religion, and propagated the paternal love of an all-father. His omnipresence feeds the lamp of the universe, speaking in all its voices, listening in all its silence, storming in its rage, reposing in its calm; its light the shadow of His greatness, its gloom the hiding-place of His power, its verdure the trace of His steps, its fire the breath of His nostrils, its motion the circulation of His untiring energies, its warmth the effluence of His love, its mountains the altars of His worship and its oceans the mirrors where He beholds His form "glassed in tempest." Compared to those conceptions, how does the fine dream of the pagan myths melt away—Olympus with its multitude of stately, celestial natures, dwindles before the solitary, immutable throne of *Adonai.* What is all the poetry and philosophy of Greece, all the wisdom of the entire heathenish world, compared with the one sentence : "Hear, O Israel, the Lord our God, the Lord is one," or held before any of those ten majestic commands hurled down amid lurid blaze from above, in a halo of divine revelation ! The revealed Mosaic Law. with its unequaled mastery of detail, its comprehensiveness of character, its universality of human right and rigid suppression of wrong, its enthusiastic championship of truth, justice, morality, and above all righteousness, is the most unique marvel of lofty wisdom and divine forethought ever penned into the inspired records of authentic history. Righteousness, from its patriarchal primitiveness to full-blown glory of prophetic instinct, is the choicest pearl of Biblical ethics, and together with the fervently advocated brotherly love, pleads most eloquently Judea's claim as the *first moral preceptor of antiquity.* "As long as the world lasts," declares a modern Bible bard—Matthew Arnold—"all who want to make progress in righteousness will come to Israel for inspiration, as to the people who have had the sense for righteousness most glowing and strongest. The Hebrew race has found the revelation needed to breathe emotion into the laws of morality and make morality religion. This revelation is the capital fact of the old Testament and the source of its grandeur and power. For, while other nations had the misleading idea that this or that, other than righteousness, is saving, and it is not; that this or that, other than conduct, brings happiness, and it does not; Israel had the true idea, that righteousness is saving, that to *conduct* belongs happiness." . . .

Let us now briefly demonstrate to what degree humanity is indebted to Hebrew Scriptures for some other gifts not so generally accredited to Judaism by the envy of modern skeptics.

On Judea's soil, that green oasis in the desert of yore, first blossomed and flourished the lilies of actual culture and civilization. There blossomed the bud of polite arts, of the so much boasted sciences of later Greece and plagiarizing Rome. The flowers of stately rhetoric, thrilling drama, captivating song, lyric poetry, fervent psalmody, and rhythmic prose, not to speak of legend and fable, myth and parable, metaphor and hyperbole, wit and humor, sarcasm and allegory, and minor subdivisions of graphic and sentimental love—all thrived and matured in its fertile grounds. Greece and Rome, of classic art and pagan splendor, with their skilled adepts in letters and all manner of research, with their magnetic orators, powerful rhetoricians, world-famed poets, and romantic historians, were indebted to humble Israel for that reputed familiarity with profound philosophy and cognate learning. Imbued with a spirit of hero-worship, the archaic visionary is wholly lost in the alluring vistas of Greek and Roman genius, and is but with pardonable reluctance argued into discarding his fixed and cherished convictions as regards the superiority of Hellenic and Augustan culture. Can, however, Plato, Demosthenes, Cato, Cicero, and other thunderers of eloquence, compete with such lightning-rods of magnetic power as Moses, David, Isaiah, Jeremiah, Ezekiel, and other poet-orators of Bible times? Who wrote nobler history, Moses, Livy, or Herodotus? Or are the'dramas and tragedies of Sophocles, Æschylus, Euripides, worthy of classification with the masterpieces of realism and grand cosmogonic conceptions furnished us in the soul-vibrating account of Job's martyrdom? In poetry and hymnology, the harp of David is tuned to sweeter melody than Virgil's Æneid or Horace's Odes.

Strabo's accurate geographical and ethnological accounts are not more thorough in detail than Scriptural narratives and the famous tenth chapter of Genesis. The haughty philosophical maxims of Marcus Aurelius, Epictetus, and Seneca fade into insignificance before the edifying discourses and moral chidings of Koheleth, whose very pessimism, in contradistinction to heathenish levity, failed not to inspire and instruct. Compare the ethics of Aristotle with those pure gems of monition to truth, righteousness, and moral chastity contained in the Book of Proverbs, and confront even the all-conquering intellect of Socrates with Solomonic wisdom. "The zephyrs of Attica were as bland, and Helicon and Parnassus were as lofty and verdant, before Judea put forth her displays of learning and the arts, as after wards." Yet no Homer was ever heard reciting his vibrating strains of poetry until David, Isaiah, and other monarchs of genius and soul-culture, poured forth their sublime symphonies in the Holy Land; yet none of all the muses breathed their inspiration over Greece till the Spirit of the Most High had awakened the Soul of Letters and of Arts in the nation of the Hebrews. Not to Egypt, Phœnicia, or Syria do Greece and her disciple, Rome, owe their eminence in the entertaining and refined branches of learning. They flourished at a period so remote that fable replaces fact, and no authentic records—chiefly obtained through a comparatively new field in modern exploration—are extant, which establish an impartial priority of culture and science before the Hebraic age.

Egypt is accredited with far too much distinction in knowledge, which she never possessed in any eminent degree. Recent excavations and discoveries from ruins of her ancient cities tend to corroborate our view. A mass of inscribed granite, a papyrus roll, or a sarcophagus bears the tell-tale message of her standard in taste and her progress in art. "They prove," says an erudite commentator, "that if she were entitled to be called the *Cradle of Science*, it must have been when science, owing to the feebleness of infancy, required the use of a cradle. But when science had outgrown the appendages of bewildering and tottering infancy, and had reached matured form and strength, Egypt was neither her guardian nor her home. Many of Egypt's works of art, for which an antiquity has been claimed that would place them anterior to David and Solomon, have been shown to be comparatively modern; while those confessedly of an earlier date have marks of an age which may have excelled in compact solidity, but knew little or nothing of finished symmetry or grace."

Architecture, the boast of Greece and the pride of Assyria, whose stately palaces of Nineveh are to this day the marvel of the world, attained its loftiest summit of perfection in the noble structure reared by Israel's mighty king in Jerusalem, of which the holy tabernacle mounted by the Cherubim of peace and sanctity was the magnificent model. No one acquainted with the history of the Hebrews can question their pre-eminence in this noble art. The proof of it is found in the record that endureth forever. Though the Temple at Jerusalem was destroyed before Greece became fully adorned with her splendid architecture, the plan which had been given by inspiration from heaven, and according to which the peerless edifice was built, remains written at full length in Hebrew Scriptures. The dimensions, the form and proportion of all the parts, are described with minute exactness. Every thing that could impart grandeur, grace, symmetry, to

the art palace of worship, and which made it to be called for ages
"the excellency of beauty," was placed in the imperishable volume,
to be consulted by all nations and in all ages.

Wherever we turn, in fact, we are forcibly reminded of Israel's
precious legacies to mankind in almost every department of industry.
We must ever return and sit at the feet of those Hebrew bards, who,
as teachers, as poets, as truthful and earnest men, stand as yet alone—
unsurmounted and unapproached—the Himalayan mountains of mankind.

And why not strive through the coming ages of mortal eternity,
in fraternal concord and harmonious unison with all the nations of
the globe? Not theory but *practice*, deed not creed, should be the
watchword of modern races, stamped with the blazing characters of
national equity and unselfish brotherhood. Why not, then, admit the
scions of the mother religion, the Wandering Jew of myth and harsh
reality, into the throbbing affections of faith-permeating, equitable
peoples, now inhabiting the mighty hemispheres of culture and civilization?

It was at Jacob's historical well, we feel constrained to remind
the waverers, that three herds clamored to allay their burning fever-
thirst for the water of rejuvenating life—quenched by the timely assistance of the patriarch "Israel," who with firm, unhesitating force
removed the heavy stone obstacle resting on its mouth. Three religious—Judaism, Christianity, and Islam—imbibed the liquid of enlightenment from that virgin spring of truth, and yet they are distinct,
estranged from each other by dogmatic separatism and a fibrous ac-
cumulation of prejudices, which yet awaits the redeeming champion
of old, who, with the Herculean grasp of irrevocable conviction,
should hurl far away the lead-weight of passion and bigotry, of malice
and egotism, from the historical streams of original truth, equity, and
righteousness. Three religions and now many more gathered at the
sparkling fountain of a glorious enterprise in the cause of truth, con-
gregated beneath the solid splendor of a powerful throne, wherein
reclines the new monarch of disenthralling sentiment—a glorious sovereign of God-anointed grace—to examine and to judge with the impartial scepter of Israel's holiest emblem—justice—the merits of a
nation who are as irrepressible as the elements, as unconquerable as
reason, and as immortal as the starry firmament of eternal hope. The
scions of many creeds are convened at Chicago's succoring Parliament
of Religions, aglow with enthusiasm, imbued with the courage of ex-
piring fear, electrified with the absorbing anticipation of dawning
light. The hour has struck! Will the stone of abuse—a burden

brave Israel has borne for countless centuries—on the rebellious well of *truth* at last be shivered into merciless fragments by that invention of every-day philosophy—the gunpowder of modern war—rational conviction; and finally—O, blessed destiny!—establish peace for all faiths and unto all mankind? Who knows?

THE DOCTRINE OF IMMORTALITY IN JUDAISM.

By RABBI JOSEPH STOLZ, OF CHICAGO.

Man's personal immortality was always an established belief in Israel. Throughout all his long history we search in vain for a period when this doctrine was not affirmed, believed, or defended by the Jew. The voluminous literature of Judaism is unanimous on the subject. It has the sanction of priest and prophet, bard and sage, Rabbi and people. It is confirmed by precept and by ritual practice. It is supported by the testimony of nearly two hundred generations.

This assertion, so positive and unequivocal, would not require substantiation were it not for the oft-repeated statement that the Jews believed not in eternal life. Yet, if modern researches prove that all ancient nations and tribes believed in a personal immortality, and if ethnologists tell us that no tribe so savage has yet been found but has some conception of a life after death (v. Tylor's Primitive Culture, vol. II, p. 21), it would indeed be surpassingly strange that the Jews alone should have been ignorant of the deathlessness of man, when their fundamental conception it was, that man is a duality, and that what constituted the essence of man was the נִשְׁמַת חַיִּים, "the breath of life," which God, The Eternal One, Himself breathed into the body of clay (Gen. i, 27), hence a חֵלֶק אֱלוֹהַ מִמַּעַל, "a portion of God Himself," a force as deathless as God; wherefore death could not possibly have meant annihilation, but simply a separation of body and soul, as it is said in Ecclesiastes, "and the dust returns to the earth as it was and the spirit returns unto God who gave it" (Eccles. xii, 7; cf. also Gen. xxxv, 18, and Jer. xv, 9). If, as is demonstrated in the Anthropological collection at Jackson Park, the primitive American Indians and the wild inhabitants of Australia and the Pacific Islands believe that death is not the end of man, how much the more should they have nursed that belief who could conceive of the One, Absolute, Most Holy God, the loving Father of all mankind, who could think of revelation, prophecy, prayer, and providence, and who could dream of the day when there would be no more war and all men would be united by the bonds of love and truth and justice; yea, could dream of a World's Parliament of Religions (Micah iv). If the

4

primitive Chaldeans, Assyrians, and Babylonians could not believe that death ends all conscious existence (v. Sayce's Hibbert Lectures, 1887, pp. 358, 362, 365), how could their Semitic brethren * who felt that the soul was capable of infinite possibilities, and could and should rise on the wings of holiness from the creature to the child of God, ever have believed that death puts a sudden and lasting stop to the development of man, no matter whether like Esau he despised his birthright and ate and drank, for on the morrow he might die, or whether like Jacob by dint of supreme self-denial and a struggle with powers, divine and earthly, he rose from a spoiled, crafty, selfish boy to the dignity of a prophet, a champion of God?

Starting out from general principles, it is simply impossible to think that they who conceived God as the Righteous Judge of all the earth (Gen. xviii, 25), the moral Ruler of the Universe who rewards righteousness and punishes guilt (Ex. xxxiv, 6, 7), the Supreme Governor to whom all nations and individuals are responsible (Exod. xviii, 11), the All Good One whose mercy endureth forever (Ps. cxviii, 1), did not at some period of their history arrive at the conclusion that there must come a day when all the injustices of this earth will be righted, when the righteous who suffered and the wicked who prospered will be rewarded or punished according to their individual merits.

We must consider the broad, unifying principles of Scriptures and not bind ourselves hand and foot to isolated texts and disjointed metaphors, a slavery which has long been the curse of religion; for even tyranny has found texts to engrave upon her sword, and slavery has carved them upon her fetters, and cruelty has bound them to her faggots, though freedom and love and mercy are fundamental principles underlying the whole system of Biblical ethics.

If God, the Father (Mal. ii, 10), is eternal (I Chron. xx, 10), an oft-recurring Biblical idea (Exod. xv, 18; Deut. xxxiii, 21; Isai. xl, 28; Ps. xc, 2), then it is self-evident that man, the son of God (Deut. xiv, 1), can not perish like the flowers of the field. If God, the Creator, is eternal, then the child of God that is spirit of His spirit (Num. xvi, 22), life of His life, and light of His light (Ps. xxxvi, 10), that can commune with Him, speak to Him face to face,

---

That the primitive Semites believed in the deathlessness of man is evident from their custom of making incisions into the flesh, cutting off the hair, and rending the garments, by means of which the living entered into an enduring covenant with the dead. v. W. Robertson Smith's Lectures on the Religion of the Semites, pp. 304, etc., 317, etc.

understand His divine message, behold His glory, walk in His ways, and become holy like Him, must be as deathless as is the Source of this power.

The Bible does not in so many words draw this inference. It takes it for granted as a self-evident truth, as it takes for granted the existence of God, without ever attempting to prove it by any philosophical or scientific arguments. Of this there can be no doubt, even though, for reasons that will appear later, the Old Testament maintains a discreet and commendable silence about the future life; for like fossils that reveal to us the condition of things that existed when none are left to tell of them, are there imbedded here and there in the old Scriptures, traces of a popular belief in life after death that reach down to the very dawn of Hebrew life.

When the Pentateuch says that "Abraham went in peace to his fathers" (Gen. xv, 15), though he was not buried in Ur of the Chaldees, and that Aaron and Moses were "gathered unto their people" (Numb. xxvii, 13), though their bodies were not interred in Canaan, these words can only signify that death had not annihilated their ancestors. Saul would never have asked the witch of Endor to conjure up the spirit of Samuel, long after he had died, and he would not have said to Saul, "To-morrow thou and thy sons will be with me" (I Sam. xxviii, 19), had immortality not been a general belief among Israelites. Nor would Moses have prohibited " inquiring of familiar spirits and communing with the dead" (Deut. xviii, 11; cf. Isai. lxv, 4; Ps. cvi, 29) and Saul have found it necessary to enforce the law (I Sam. xxviii, 3), had the people not believed in a conscious existence after death. Were not a belief in immortality current, the people would not have told of the dead children Elijah and Elisha re-animated by bringing the departed soul back into the lifeless body (I Ki. xvii); nor would they have repeated the story that Elijah went alive into heaven (II Ki. ii, 19); nor would David have said to his servants: "I shall go to him (his dead child), but he shall not return to me" (II Sam. xii, 23).

"It is not true that the concept of immortality is unknown in the Old Testament," says Schenkel in his Bibellexikon (5, 579); and in his Bampton Lectures on the Psalter (1889), Cheyne corroborates the statement (pp. 383–409). The story of " the tree of life" (Gen. iii, 22) attests a belief among the Israelites in the possibility of escaping death (ibid., p. 383). In his last song Moses makes God say, " I kill and I make alive, I have wounded and I heal" (Deut. xxxii, 39); and Hannah says, " The Lord killeth and maketh alive, He bringeth low and also lifteth up" (I Sam. ii, 7); Isaiah declares, " He hath swallowed up death forever " (*i. e.*, life is eternal), (xxv, 8); and again he says, "The dead shall live, my dead bodies shall rise. Awake and sing ye that dwell in the dust, for thy dew is as the dew of the herbs and the earth shall cast forth the dead" (xxvi, 19). Hosea (vi, 2) and Ezekiel (xxxvii) refer to a national resurrection (which of course implies the possibility of the resurrection of individuals), and many Psalms (16, 17, 49, 73) unmistakably advance the idea of a personal immortality and resurrection, from the motive of moral compensation. In Proverbs (xii, 28) we find the word "Al-Maveth" (אַל־מָוֶת), " immortality ;" and Job speaks of a super-mundane Justice which will one day pronounce in favor of the righteous sufferer not only in this world (xvi, 18, 19; xix, 25; xlii), so that all may recognize his innocence, but also beyond the grave, the sufferer himself being in some undefined way brought back to life in the conscious enjoyment of God's favor (xiv, 13, 15; xliv, 26, 27; v. Cheyne's Psalter, p. 442). As time advanced, the immortality idea became more and more pronounced and definite. Koheleth says: "And the dust shall turn to dust as it was and the spirit to God who gave it" (xii, 7), which Daniel explains further in the words: "And many of them that sleep in the dust of the earth shall wake, some to everlasting life and some to shame and everlasting contempt" (xii, 2).

But the development of Judaism did not stop with the last page of the Bible. Judaism is a religious force penetrating the ages, and no man, no book, no Temple, no Synod, no national catastrophe, and no persecution or oppression could ever stem or destroy it. The final word was not spoken when Malachi closed his lips, and there is more than a fly-leaf between the Old and the New Testaments. The interim is pregnant with development, and many an idea that was only embryological in the Old Testament period, then reached a fuller and more pronounced growth. Particularly is this the case with the immortality-idea. Influenced by contact with the Parsees and Greeks as well as by the untoward political events that brought so much undeserved suffering upon the righteous and pious, great stress is henceforth laid upon the future life, and the first real attempts are made to define and describe it and give it a philosophical expression.

The Apocryphal book, the Wisdom of Solomon, is a "gospel of immortality." " The sinner falleth and shall not rise, but those that fear the Lord shall rise unto eternal life and their life shall be in the light of the Lord and shall not fail" (iii, 13, 16). " The Lord's ' Hasidim ' shall inherit life in gladness; the inheritance of sinners is Hades and darkness and destruction" (xiv, 6, 7). " The sinners shall perish in the day of the judgment of the Lord forever, but those that fear the Lord shall find mercy and shall live by the compassion of their God" (xv, 13, 15). "They shall 'live forever' not by tasting ambrosial fruit or following ritual practices, but by 'walking in the law which God commanded us'" (xiv, 1, 2), a principle embodied almost literally in the second Benediction over the Law.

The Book of Enoch, which in the main is of pre-Christian origin and belongs to the second century B. C., not only expresses a belief in immortality, but even describes quite minutely the future lot of the righteous and the wicked. (Ch. xxii, 102, 103; cf. Cheyne, ibid., p. 413; Schwally's Das Leben nach dem Tode, p. 148). The second and the fourth books of the Maccabees tell how the seven martyred brothers "live unto God" and "now stand before the throne of God and lead the happy life."

And then to cap the climax, Josephus tells us that already in the second century, the doctrine of immortality was so prevalent that three sects quarreled about it. The Pharisees believed in future rewards and punishments, and the continuance of the soul; the Sadducees, who lived in the visible present and not in an imagined future, denied this; while the Essenes believed that the spirits of the righteous would no more be burdened with bodies, but would rejoice and mount upwards (Ant. xviii, 1, 3; Wars ii, 8, 14; cf. Wise's Judaism and Christianity, p. 71; iii, 5, 8). Passages in the Targum, Midrash, and Talmud, which are undeniably early traditions, the Apocalyptical Books, the writings of Philo and Aristobul, the second of the eighteen Benedictions, the second benediction over the reading of the Thora, the oldest funeral service and funeral rites, all furnish positive proof that a belief in immortality existed in Israel prior to the time of Jesus: yes, the fact that Jesus and his apostles teach the doctrine of immortality in the very words of the Pharisees, shows that it was from Israel that they derived this doctrine, and that even if an innocent man crucified and pierced with a spear, had not arisen after the third day, it would still have been known that death is not the end of man. (v. Wise's Second Commonwealth, p. 260, and Proselytizing Christianity, p. 34). The resurrection-story never had a particle of influence upon the Jew or Judaism, and yet the rabbinical writings, from beginning to end, are full of allusions to the future life. Maimonides codified the doctrine in his Yad Hahasaka (H. Teshuba, ch. viii), and embodied it in his creed; the medieval philosophers coined a new word for it, and, without exception, defended and defined it; the Kabbalists reveled in pictures of the life to come; Moses Mendelssohn proved it from his own philosophical standpoint; and to my knowledge, there is not a nineteenth century Jewish, orthodox, or reform preacher, teacher, or author of a catechism or prayer-book that has denied it. It runs through the whole history of Judaism, through every phase of its development, from the very beginning down to the Pittsburg Conference, which declared (Art. vii): "We re-assert the doctrine of Judaism that the soul is immortal, grounding this belief on the divine nature of the human spirit which förever finds bliss in righteousness and misery in wickedness."

Just as unanimous, however, is the Jewish idea that the canon of ethics and worship must not be based upon the doctrine of immortality. "Be not like servants who serve their master for the sake of the reward" (Pirke Aboth i), has never been disputed. That is not the highest morality which does the good for the sake of future happiness or out of fear for future punishment (v. Maim. II. Tesh., ch. x). Ethics must stand on a higher basis than that of selfishness. It must not be an insurance to bring one into heaven or a gate to keep one out of hell. That makes morals immoral and worship a blasphemy.

Nor must the center of gravity be changed from this world to another because there is a life after this. This life is not to be shunned and our duties here are none of them to be slighted because there is a hereafter. We have no right to separate ourselves from society and seek seclusion in deserts and caves; we have no right to mortify the flesh and make ourselves useless in this world because there is another world. The Rabbinical dictum is that "this world is the vestibule to the next" (P. Aboth iv, 16), and that "every righteous man will be rewarded according to his own merits" (Sab. 152 a). Our life here fashions our life hereafter. That explains the Mosaic silence. Moses, who was an eye-witness to the frightful inequalities and injustices sanctioned in Egypt because the whole stress of religion was there laid upon the other world, purposely ignored the hereafter, so as to inculcate the doctrine that man must perform his social and private duties in this world, and seek perfection here, and then the hereafter will take care of itself, for it is but a continuance of this life. Describe it no one can. "The secret things belong to the Lord our God only, the things revealed belong to us" (Deut. xxix, 28). Human intelligence can not comprehend a state of existence purely spiritual, wherefore human words can not define the nature of spiritual reward or punishment, nor describe the place where the souls of the departed abide; yet many Rabbis have pictured to us Heaven and Gehenna, with all their good and bad spirits, all their spiritual and material pains and pleasures. This was the special delight of mystic minds, and our literature is full of their queer musings, which, by the way, made a much stronger impression upon Christians and Mohammedans than upon Jews, because the Jewish rationalists were many that, like R. Johanan, repudiated them all as idle speculation, saying that "all the prophets prophesied about the future of the human family on earth, but as to the state of existence hereafter no eye has ever seen it but God's" (Ber. 34b). Vain is it to attempt a description of the future life, and Maimonides sums it all up well when he says: "In the future world there is nothing corporeal; every thing is spiritual; wherefore there can be no eating and no drinking, no standing and no sitting (hence no local heaven and no local hell). These phrases are but figurative expressions to make abstract conceptions concrete to childish minds" (II. Tesh. v.; cf. Ber. 17a). Future joy is all spiritual joy, the happiness that comes from wisdom and good deeds; future pain is all spiritual pain, the remorse for ignorance and wickedness. The joy is eternal, because goodness is everlasting; the pain is temporal, because "God will not contend forever, neither will He retain His anger to eternity" (Ps. ciii, 9).

The Jews never taught the eternity of suffering and chastisement. They know naught of endless retributive suffering. Sheol was simply the abode of the spirits of all who died. An eternal hell-fire was alien to them. Some denied the existence of Gehenna altogether (Ned. 8b). Others said the duration of its punishment was but twelve months (R. H. 15b). And others said there was but the span of a hand's distance between heaven and hell, so that it may be very easy for the repentant sinner to pass into paradise.

There was no authorized dogmatic Jewish teaching on the subject of endless punishment; the views of each Rabbi depended upon his interpretation of Scriptures and upon the results of his own reflections (v. Hamburger's Real-Encyclopädie, II, art. Vergeltung). All are agreed without exception that ‏הסידי אומות העולם י"ש‎ ‏להם חלק לעולם הבא‎ (cf. A. Z. 10b), all of clean hands and pure hearts, whether they are Jews or non-Jews, whether it is Confucius or Buddha, Socrates or Plato, Jesus or Mohammed, or Moses and Isaiah, all that feel and think and act to the best of their ability, will ascend the mountain of the Eternal and behold the eternal glory of God there, where all is not passive rest, but where the pious can rise from moral height to moral height until they approach the perfection of God (Ber. 64b)

JUDAISM AND THE SCIENCE OF COMPARATIVE RELIGIONS.

By RABBI LOUIS GROSSMAN, D.D., DETROIT, MICHIGAN.

— · —

I can not tell how others who have spoken here in this Jewish section have felt, and I will not take it upon myself to criticise in advance those of the other denominations who are likely to take the platform after us; but I imagine the most of them will be under the impression that they ought on this special occasion to say only such things as they believe to be final, and remembering that this Congress suggests a retrospect of four hundred years, they are probably disposed to emphasize those matters which they judge to be earnings of these Centuries and which they believe to be incontrovertible facts of religion up till now. Of course there is quite a latitude in the judgment of the mental, surely of the sentimental, coin of an age which circulates and sustains mental intercourse; I can not help feeling a mild degree of that same distrust against such a gratuitous undertaking which has caused so much mischief in less critical times; in fact, in all the history of religions. For who can determine what, after all, is only a vague desideratum, and who can say with any sort of precision what is felt and believed by a multitude? One of the most unsatisfactory things in the world is a snap-shot photograph of the world's mind. Thought is fluid, and when we speak of habits and temperaments, of convictions and principles, we ought to know that we are speaking of matters which are largely convenient fictions. There is a modern scholasticism which is not much less professional and which is as tradesmanlike as that of notorious memory. All that we know is history, biography, facts. Motives elude our detective philosophy to-day as they ever did, and the analysis of them is as abstract a piece of work just as regrettably to-day as it was a fatal piece of guess-work in the age of witchcraft. We still scent spirits everywhere.

We are not entirely helpless, however, to establish what are the subtle facts of society. We can not dig out of the bosom of people with all our theological acumen the ore of their precious life as miners dig from the bowels of the earth, but somehow all popular thought and all popular feeling become manifest. It is the same old story; mystery is a defiant giant. We close with it at first in an exasperated struggle, perhaps we succeed in manacling him, and we think we have overcome him because we have bound him; but we may have his body, we have not his will: we have his submission, not his co-operation; just as tyrants have the slavishness of their subjects, not their manhood. Neither compromise nor bribery accomplish much; persuasion, justice, and love are the final and real conquerors. The history of theology is a history of policy, of fight, of truce, of Jesuit-ism, of enslaving and of enslaved. The theologians arrogate to them-selves a precarious domination, but the word finally dominates them. The disengaged fiction is ungovernable; the haunting fancy is vin-dictive. None of us can afford to be positive. There are royal laws in this ordered world; but there are also imperial as well as imperious exigencies. Truth is administrative, not tyrannical, and all around us are myriad instances of adaptation and of accommodation, of com-promise, of the ideal, which ought to be, with a practice, which can be.

Institutions are precipitates of movements of mind. The sewing machine, the steam engine, the telephone, the altar, the temple, the church, the painting, the statue, and the pantheon, the flute of the shepherd, the church-choral and the oratorio, are historical facts of social psychology. The world needed more expeditious work, wanted to release many plodding laborers from employment as unprofitable as it was degrading, wished to beautify life for the multitude and to en-noble it and to add power to it, and to vitalize the communities, and the world got the labor-saving machines, the life-saving institutions and quickening and enriching inventions. The people supplied what the people needed. The history of want is implied into history of in-vention and discovery. Not that the people was conscious definitely of what it needed, but the subtle factors of society gave birth to the fact. The vague experimentalism of an epoch at last comes upon a thing it has dreamt of and for which it has yearned, and the presenti-ment, undefined yet strong, has its fulfillment like an oracle whose words grow out of mystery into sense.

Let us never speak of a religion as if it were a final thing, which the reason of man has established as unalterable. I fear the pretty notion of revelation has misled us. We have enlarged the primeval fancies, but we have not improved on them. As soon as we begin to gauge our sentiments, we depreciate them. It makes no difference whether we credit absolute value to our favorite religion or are more modest and content ourselves with a discreet contrast of it with other religions. We ought to tolerate neither a monopoly nor a tariff on truth.

Judaism can not be charged with ever having been extravagantly self-assertive. The spirit of assumption is foreign to Jewish thought. Throughout the extent of Jewish history, there is not one period of intense dogmatism. The policy of legislation which Moses pursued was in the interest of national integrity, more than for a domineering priest-religion. The origin of the new sect of Christianity right out of the heart of Judaism was attended with less throes than ever attended a like momentous birth. The contagion of medieval zealotry never could inoculate Jewish earnestness with more than a passing spasm of foolish dissentions of a handful of Talmudists against a handful of Maimonidians. Nowhere, neither in ancient nor in modern, not even in recent polemics, as soon as Jewish thought and life had assumed a character of its own, was there any division in Judaism as to what in dogmatic terminology we call articles of faith. The differences of opinion were rather as to system and classification than as to fact, and all sides deferred to the common tradition, that absolute truth may be stated, but must never be legislated. " I am the Lord thy God," the ten commandments declare, but do not enjoin. Perhaps, in no more distinctive matter than this, the difference between Judaism and Christianity is clear. The Bible in Judaism is a source of august legislation; to the Talmudists it was *the* source. To Christianity it is more; to all schools of its thought and in all its sects the Bible is the origin and the finality of thought-life. Not so among Jews. You will remember how the Talmud exercises itself over the problem of the resurrection of the dead, a problem at once sentimental as well as philosophic (as such theosophic notions generally are). But in all the desperate attempts there made to discover in, and even to import some suggestions of it into, the text, the Rabbis intimate that they would feel themselves amply content if they could procure the biblical prestige for the doctrine, they never aspire to arrogate to it authority by showing its biblical authenticity. We, who have been disciplined in modern ways of thought, may find it difficult to think ourselves into the economy of a sect which foregoes authority as to belief. Nevertheless, it is true, Judaism has never enforced faith. Jewish Ministers are often called upon to define Judaism, and the large number of them respond by giving the history of Jewish thought; but if we were frank, we would, without hesitation, confess that literally there is no such thing possible as a Jewish Catechism. Every codification of Jewish principles has met with opposition; every statement of them has been received with distrust by some if not with positive disfavor; and Jewish Synods have never established any thing except that which the laity had anticipated by self-assumed validity, tolerated too long to be dislodged. Perhaps the notoriety of the abortive Pittsburg Conference has its explanation in this.

It is interesting to notice how contemporary discussions among Jews between orthodoxy and reform (divisions which are as ancient as thought is) circle about practice—church-practice, temple-practice—and comparatively less about dogma and articles of belief, certainly with a lesser degree of severity and precision. The famous dispute between Gamaliel, the Nassi, and Rabbi Joshua, and that between the followers of Nachmanides and of Maimonides, if we lay bare the real facts which the denunciations now reported to us suggest; the impassioned rigor of Bernays in Hamburg and of Herschel in London; and most noticeably the vapid airings we are victimized by in the current Jewish press—all point not only to the fatal foibles incident to theological disputations, in which the Jewish instances share with the rest of denominational fanatics, but more so to the philosophical fact that there is in Judaism an entire absence of an accentuation by any mutually recognized authority what are and forever must be the incontrovertible and substantially absolute doctrines of our faith. The convenient, though otherwise quite unimpugned and of course decidedly reverend, " hear, O Israel, the Lord our God, God is one," smacks of controversialism. We are too unclear when and how it originated and what is its exact meaning, and we are not entirely agreed whether we can accept it as a satisfactory statement in any final way, either of Jewish transcendentalism or of the Jewish spirit of religiousness.

We have then here a phenomenon, the like of which we would search for in vain among the many religions which have been active in the history of the world with any similar degree of influence. We must remember that Judaism has exerted an undeniable influence on almost the whole world, and does still exert influence, at least by the proxy of Christianity, despite its aversion to system and catechism, and that it has thriven in the heart of the Jewish people with a vitality which is the wonder of the world. There is something instinctive about the Jewish temperament, and the domestic and social affiliations of the Jews. The solidarity of the Jewish people has been imperturbable, and this fact, eminent in itself, grows into proportions beyond conventional explanations, when we consider that this faithfulness to tradition and this sincerity and closeness of sentiment are supreme, though the dispersion of the Jews is as wide as the extent of empires and as diverse as the genius of nations, and that this unity has been accomplished and is maintained not by the administration from somewhere and by some one. What I wish to emphasize in keeping the thread of our thought is, that no prescription of belief has done this, that there has been, in fact, an unhampered freedom, a multifariousness of individual views, which would have wrecked many other denominations, and in fact has wrecked many. This diversity of opinions has been respected and has been deferred to with a readiness such as the Fathers of the Church would have chuckled over to the infinite felicity of their dogmatic souls.

Many a magazine writer has indulged a harmless sensation by provoking the discussion on "What is Judaism?" The probably well-meaning questioner, however, brings upon himself often the derision of the malevolent and the pity of the thoughtless. Frankness is often perverted and toleration is a burdensome virtue. The questioner is sincere enough and suggestive enough. Perhaps it is the glory of a denomination that it can constantly readjust itself to new conditions, that it can enfranchise itself readily in the new liberalism, when it hears the trumpet sound for fraternization with the family of the faiths with willing ear, perhaps, that, unincumbered by the burden of a pretentious absoluteness, it can naturalize itself as a citizen in the republic of thought. Perhaps, free from the exactions of a repressive despotism, it can feel the thrill soonest which shall some day send new vigor through the blood and tissue of natural associations. Perhaps Judaism, exactly in this and exactly at this time, when faiths are tested as never before they were tested, makes good the claim which it. has made for so many centuries, that it is the religion of priestliness and that all the people are priests. Lastly, perhaps just because of this felicitous absence of all preclusive and exclusive teaching, Judaism can offer proof of its true merit and its acceptableness now more than ever. For the faiths are dwindling away in numbers and in prestige; authority is taken from some because they abused it, from others because they might abuse it, from some because they have forfeited their right to rule, having shown that they are slaves themselves, from others because they manifest a lamentable lack of insight such as statesmen ought to have into social needs, social movements, and social exigencies. They failed because they leaned upon a reed which pierced their hands up to the very bone. Contracts were written so long as mutual confidence was impossible. To-day, bits of paper pass from hand to hand as matters of reliable honor, and integrity has made them into coin. So constitutions are written; the public conscience then takes them out of Magna Charta and writes them into the heart of nations. We do not need paper; we need blood. So also the sects needed the creed, to make possible a sectarian integrity. But we want a free religiousness. Dogmas are words, and words must never manacle reason. Freedom is never a risk. The coils of rhetoric have embarrassed men long enough. Dogmas are the ingenuities of unpractical pedants. Some day, perhaps, we shall classify transcendentalism as a delirious exhaltation, intense but morbid.

Definition is the death of thought. It has been said by those who take comfort from contrasts that Christianity has shown a wealth of accommodation in the history of its teaching, and in the way it has naturalized among divers nations and climates; and it has been cited as one of the evidences of its universality. Judaism, on the other hand, it has been alleged, is tribal. By that is meant that it has had potency in one people only; that its compass has never gone beyond that of the Jewish people, and that Judaism, from the beginning up to the present, and, as is evident from the peculiar tenacity of the race, it will likely forever persist to be an isolated phenomenon. And that, it is claimed, is a weakness, and not a strength.

It is true no Jew has ever shown eagerness for proselyting, though the first missionaries, and probably the most eminent among all missionaries who ever lived, were Jews. It is true, also, that Christianity presents not only an eventful but a checkered history. At no period during the centuries from the origin to the present has the Christian world been unanimous. There has been no time in which the Christian church was not disrupted by sectarian disputes. It is also true that the spirit of denomination has had a long-continued luxuriance, the noisome growth of which has been any thing but an unmixed benefit. The theologies of the church are as manifold as the national habitats in which they have thriven, and, in order to be fair, we must admit the fact that religion is often called upon to do political service in the furtherance of sociological aims. But we must remember that it is not Christianity which has promoted the intimacies between foreign nations, and that it is surely not to be credited with being the source of a modern spirit of internationalism. That did not come from the church, nor through the church, but in spite of the church. In fact, Romanism, ecclesiasticism and state churches were fatal, not only to individualism and the freedom, without which there can be no religiousness, but they have been a bar to a wholesome interchange and intercommunication in the open world of thought. Nothing contributes more toward keeping England insular than the Westminster Confession; and the Catholic Church, or the Protestant Church, or the Universalist Church, each in its degree, is a dissolvent of the body politic and of the great fraternity of the nations.

Judaism, it is said, depends for its life upon the solidarity of the Jewish people. Into what other soil would you plant religion, if not

into the affections and instincts of the people? From where else shall
come its vitality? What a force must that religion be, and how psy-
chologically correct, which maintains a bond of sympathy so strong
and indissoluble, and for so long, as the bond has been between Jews,
and which has sustained them through no elaborate organization or
centralized administration. I doubt whether in the whole range of
religious variations there is another denomination with so insignificant
an equipment for denominational government. We have to-day in
this country about a million of Jews, but no head for their ecclesiastical government, nor an authority over them to establish doctrine.
Some people are so imitative in their disposition that, observing all
around them that the churches and sects have each a complicated organization and a canonical government, and seeing that we Jews are
orphaned of the like, deplore it, and regret what they call the latitudinarian license rampant among us. But they do not understand Judaism. It has never tolerated task-masters, and its synods have never
originated a single doctrine. For, if they had undertaken to prescribe
and impose matters of belief, such is the moral health and mental acumen and the spiritedness of the Jew, he would have resented the med-
dling. The fact is, theological disputes never arise in a religious sect
save when there is a denominational crisis. Let us never forget that
when freedom is taken from some one, be it taken only from one, the
whole community is dishonored and enslaved. There is nothing which
the Jew has felt more keenly by an instinct which, I suppose, is too
natural to be accounted for, than that a man is inviolable, not only as
to the property of his goods, but also as to the possessions of his mind,
and to the integrity of his person. This guarded self-respect and
cheerfully rendered deference breeds mutual justice, and upon this rock
alone a church can be built.

We can estimate the value of a faith, and perhaps even its validity, by determining how much it contributes to the radical discipline
of the people, how it maintains the vigor of the national life.

Religion is a sociological fact, and the religious tension of a nation is one of its re-enforcing or depressing factors, according to the
quality of its soul-life. The day is gone by when we can settle the
validity of a religion by a rule in mathematics or by a pretty syllogism.
We have taken the crown from many heads, and we know, also, that
the world's pulses beat with a healthier logic than that of priests and
confessors. It is what a religion does for the world which validates it;
how it serves, not merely by the inspiration of its great men (though
the caliber of its geniuses and how many it has given to the world
ought to go for something), but by the plodding of its unpretentious

laity. Do not misunderstand me. I do not mean what preachers mean when they deliver unctious homiletics. In what degree the members of a sect live up consistently to the indoctrination of their church, is, of course, a matter of moment. Whether or not the moral system of a denomination is philosophically just and logically acceptable, and even practical and business-like, is decidedly an item of importance which none can afford to ignore, least of all the adherents of them. But beyond the question of reliability, beyond considerations which properly belong to students and to such as are pre-occupied with conventional standards of belief, is the item, what sort of social contribution does religion, or do religions, or does any specific religion, make to the life of the world? Religion, if it is any thing like a public factor, is ingrained into the moods and temperament of the people, and its peculiar spirit is organized in all the social establishments which it has built up. The architecture of Egypt is as distinct from the dignified architecture of Greece as the heavy and clumsy faith of the one is different from the bright and genial religion of the other. And the castes which divide off families there are not more indigenous to the soil along the Nile than are the Book of the Dead and the Sarcophagi in the Pyramids. The bravery of Mucius Scaevola is weird and madly faithful; but no less appalling and sinister is the Roman spirit in all other things. The legislation of the later republic has become fundamental in modern codices. The Romans had a keen sense for organization and order, which was nursed by every citizen in his home under the shadow of the Penates. The spirit of Judaism is manifested by the domestic virtues and the law-abiding sense of the Jews. Persecution cultivated a spirit of humility and the capacities of martyrdom, and emancipation and the deliverance from harrassing restraints freed the native brightness of the Jews and helped them at once to earn bread and fame. The same influences which endowed fathers and mothers with a sentimental purity, which nothing could taint, made the blood rush with quickened energy when the avenues of commerce, of professions, of public service, opened for employment and the ambitions were aroused.

We have too narrow a view of ethics. We are still in the arena of thought and sentiment when we talk of morals. The facets to a moral fact are many. Morals are the sum total of characteristics, not only as to how men conducted themselves when they had dealings with one another; not only when they in common gave expression to a common joy or to a common grief or to a common indignation or to a common enthusiasm; not only in national poetry or literature or game of war, but also by the silent facts of institutions and tools.

The knife, for instance, as a tool, is a chapter of the history of morals as well as industrialism. The sharp blade of the savage, our table knife; the straw matting, the downy bed; the turf-covered hut and the house with paneled walls and frescoed ceiling—report morals as much as convenience. We interpret archaeological finds in caves and mounds as suggestions of something besides mechanical ingenuity men had in the pre-historic days. The spade, the tool of the industrious, belongs to religious history as much as to economic. Conversely, every religious custom and ritual reflects the social status of the people; culture and worship are interdependent. You will never find sacerdotalism except when notions of right by the grace of God prevail; and the "Rights of Man" contravene as much the traditional sovereignty of the church as of the state. We can almost safely deduce from the specific tone of the Mosaic dispensation what must have been the political status of the Israelites, in which it had its birth as well as its life. Some day we may be able to construct from the data which we have in great amplitude of the rich and varied history of the Jewish people, ever since the dispersion out of Palestine into the world, a reliable soul-picture of Judaism. A given custom will furnish a more exact portrait of Jewish psychology, and disclose for us the mind and morals of the Jew with more relief, than would all the professional dissertations on the subject and scholastic analyses we have had as yet of it. The endless differences between reformers and orthodox, when sifted, amount to a disdainful deprecation on the one side, and unintelligent laudation on the other, of something, the exact nature of which neither conservatives nor radicals have grasped. A domestic right or a popular custom, or a Synagogue ritual, is an item of history, but it is also what the national or communal or denominational spirit has precipitated into some form or habit. What for want of a better word we call the religious sense unfolds itself into church-forms and civil customs. He who summarily brushes them away as meaningless, as well as he who sweeps them together as precious, is little aware how customs reveal a former living thought. The recuperative powers of the social organism depend upon such storage of the popular affections which has been laid away as hidden energy.

We shall have to revise our notions of revelation. I deem this an eminently felicitous occasion. We have for a long time clung to a too restrictive scope of the idea of revelation. The untutored man implied by it a guess of the grand. He had come upon many a thornbush all aglow with a mystic message, and dared not approach nearer to it. We, too, have profound visions; our legislation is a farce and insincere, unless we have as prototype a state of order and

a community in peace. Our theologies are impertinences, unless we
have the ideal of piety. Socialism, ethics, politics, all pre-condition a
sort of Utopian hope. Of course we fall short of these high aims. We
say God gave the ten commandments from the top of Mount Sinai.
But we know that the whole world is even at this late day far from
a complete obedience to them. The magnificent visions into the harmony of the universe, into the unity of the races, into the justice of
the world, into the moralness of fate, poets and legislators and the
popular instinct share alike. From the cleft of the rock, shaded from
the dazzling brightness of a divine illumination, each man sees a
vision of his own. The whole world is revealing and all men are
seers; you say this is pantheism. I hope we are out of scholastic
tournaments by this time. Philosophy, poetry, the songs of nations,
their frolic and their wails, and their mobs, and their armies, their
tranquillity, and their rebellions, all develop subtle facts. My neighbor is an artisan; he has made a piece of furniture, and he says: I
am nothing but a tradesman. But the whole nation speaks through
him. His trade, the work he is demanded to do, is a pulse of the
nation. His skill is the wit of the nation; his life is the wave of the
vast throb of the great social system. Plane and saw, inventions and
discoveries of the race, centuries of industry, have served him in the
single bit of work he does. The world-spirit gives birth to the
Homunculus.

Even speech, that second soul of man, that pilgrims across continents, making brothers of nations, reveals. The language of the
world is the most reverent symbol of life we have. Every sound
which now bridges mind with mind and fraternizes the world, is revelation. And there are so many languages. There is not one sentiment
which we share in common but is coined into speech and binds the
race more closely. That which makes manifest a common truth is
biblical. The oracle, therefore, is given us from many tripods.

I can readily understand how the natural instinct led the early
man to people the world with Gods. The Bible speaks of the Sun in
his majesty; Homer seats him upon Mt. Parnassus.

The presence of the inexhaustible overawes the mythology of a
people, is as logical as it always is beautiful. The contemplation of
the grand and the unusual is a synonym for revelation in the traditional sense of the word. To-day we must learn to perceive deliver-
ances of the world-spirit from the common and from that which passes
by us every day and every night. Not alone from rocks and woods,
from Sun and Moon. Schelling said that if we suppose that God
communicated religion to man, we would also have to suppose that

5

there was a time when man had no religion, and consequently that man was originally atheistic. It would then be hard to understand how an atheistic person could have been susceptible to such a revelation. Prof. Tylor tells us how by nature we are disposed to feel as if the whole world and every thing in it were alive. Sleep is filled with dreams; even the dead haunt us. Spirits are all around as, and we feel kinship with every thing that is drawn into touch with us; souls speak to us out of every thing. This may be coarse mythology, but man sees more than his eye does. There is mind behind the eye; the delicate fibers swoon when black night puts its leaden touch on them. The mind can not be killed off; nothing save vice and death can deaden it. Still there is something more tenacious even than mind. The dead may be gone and things may molder, but recollection and memory are preservatives, respect and fear last, even if life does not. Herbert Spencer and Lippert speak of the awe man has for the departed, of the apprehension and the love or hate to chiefs who are dead, and how this state of mind is the germ for the worshipful man. Fire, the flame from the matrix, the bolt from the cloudy sky, how did they come? asks the child-man, if not from God? The logic of man is always sound. We can not give any precise account of what we see. A residual quantity will always embarrass us. Every trifle is endowed with a defiant mystery, and timid fellows will fall upon their knees, being always on the threshold of the inscrutable. The river that flows forever, the winds that jostle each other overhead, the mountains hoary and high and solid, the forests thick and gloomy, in whose deep shade the serpents coil and lie in wait, and the lion with stealthy tread falls upon a victim to crush out its life, or slinks to the edge of the thick shrubbery—is he companion or foe; the broad sky and the myriad-eyed night; the golden or the firy Sun and the silvery light through the winter's gray-haze; and the day and the next day and ceaseless time; and this child coming into life; and the man moving in it and that one passing away; the ocean and the large seas and the murmuring waves and the tossing storm, and infinite expanse beyond the rocks that jut out with white foam above the crags up to the far distant sky—what is all this? The ancient man had thousand Sinais, thundering, whispering, revealing God.

I wish we Jews would give a hearty welcome to the new science of comparative religions. We can afford to do it, our faith does not contravene it, not even a single datum of it; we must indorse it, for it is a tradition with us that we feel GOD every-where, in the garden of Eden, before the tent of the Arab, on the mountain of Moriah, in the burning bush of the desert, in the tabernacle of the congregation, on bleak Sinai, in luxuriant Kenaan, to the king, to Isaiah at home, to Ezekiel in exile. If Judaism contradicts that which the psychology of the world does not warrant, nay repudiates, then Judaism performs only a duty. Religion must not only be logical, but also psychological. There is only one way to tell what is a true and what is a false religion, how far do a man's thoughts or a man's feelings or these both relate to his organic make-up. The national and the social conditions feed and shape the national mood. The religious polity is built by the facts of national history.

Mythologies are embodied fancies, but they are also embodied morals according as the national genius is strong or weak. Some say Judaism has no mythology, but we know better; for Judaism is a religion of disciplined instincts. Some say that Moses has dealt a death blow to art among the Jewish people; "Thou shalt not make unto thyself any graven image," but we understand Moses better. The spirit of Art demands a large latitude. This latitude can be and often is contracted by the arrogance of a fashion, but then the instinct for the beautiful suffers.

I love my distant friend though I never have seen him. I have nothing but what my imagination elaborates as to his person and appearance, but this fits every need; he is with me when I laugh and he sits at my side when I am sad, and he is a true companion. In tranquil hours my fancy draws curves in the air and they conform according to the throbbing of my pulse into a similitude of him, all my own; but show me his photograph and the fancy is gone and felicity with it. His face is never more the same, live and companionable. I see the immobile features fixed, not living. Art is like a spring, you can not stop it from flowing, not even the finest of marble is art, and even the blackest of ebony may be shaped exquisitely. Beauty must be living, the sense of the inexpressible is opulent. That which you see you will own, which you see now, which perhaps you will never again see so, how rich it is. The thought we have of God by nature is more poetic than the one which has been cultivated in us. Some day the prose of the church will be translated back into the poetry of Religion.

All religion is socialized wisdom. This the science of religion proves. I do not know whether even the combined contributions of Max Mueller, Tylor, Spencer, Chantepie de la Saussaye, Happel, Lippert, Steinthal, Bastian, and the rest have yet shown this fact. Some day the science of religion will go farther than simply to give an account of the origin of religion. The history of religions will have a broader compass. There obtains an intimacy between religion and politics. Catholicism has perverted this notion, and Protestantism, aware of the difficulty, has taken up the delicate relationship as a fisherman takes up a lobster, fearing the lacerating fangs. But the dispute between Church and State is not after the features which they share in common, but as to those in which they seem to be irreconcilable. I do not wish to approach an unpleasant theme. I would rather suggest that which goes beyond issues. A religion prevails, has followers, makes converts, establishes a government, and exerts an influence only and so far as it is a social factor, and to the degree in which it serves to sustain the community. This gives it its economic, its political character, and gives it legitimacy.

The question has been often asked, do the Jews constitute a nation? The question implies vagueness as to what is meant by nation, and it shows also a lamentable want of information as to what Judaism is; in fact, an intelligent judgment of what religion is, is required if we should dispose of the question properly.

That which establishes and maintains a community partakes of the religious. In this experimental country of ours we often attempt to meet exigencies by statutory enactments; legislation, however, never goes to the radical facts of social affairs. Habits can not be dislodged by the police; no sort of formalism can touch temperament; there must be a common term either in the interests of occupation and employment or in experience and history. The churches aggregate not through any radical congeniality of the votaries, but because there is a metaphysical parallelism of the believers, and for this reason the modern sects have failed to contribute much to the real good, surely little to the discipline of the world. There can be no such thing as a formal faith or catechismal confession, if it shall be a force in the world unless it be allied with the household of the people. The Jew has never tolerated a divorce of belief from character. Christianity has fostered this precarious duplicity. To the Jew the divine in man is at once absolute and creative.

It is true, every religion has its own way to express itself, it has its peculiar terminology, it has its own ritual, which is a mode of expressing its profound conceptions, it has its sectarian physiognomy; but the language of a religion, this manifold speech by which it reveals what it is, is most noticeably conveyed by the degree of intensity of its communal spirit. It is not centralized authority that makes a people solid. We have before spoken of the interesting fact that there is lacking in Judaism a supreme government. But the Jewish people have an identity of interests as they have an identity of mind.

The functions of religion have organized themselves into the Jewish family, into the Jewish community. The religion has become socialized. There is no point at which the Jewish spirit ceases to constrain obligation. Even the ancient Hebrew language, aside of the interest which it has from the standpoint of philology, is most engaging to the student of psychology. The subtlest facts of the national soul reappear in language. The idiom of a nation is its mirror. We respect the ancient Bibles because they report soul-life, which is neither ancient nor modern, but always the same. We respect the ancient Bible of the Jews because it reports not only the status of ancient Jewish life, but because it reveals the exceptional fact that at a time least encouraging to, and least susceptible to, a conception of pure morals, the Jews transcended the legitimate expectation with high credit. The Prophets are famous for their genius, but so ought also indeed have become the Jewish people for its genius in morals.

Perhaps orthodoxy and reform might have to fight their battles upon quite another ground if their acrimony would leave them enough of consideration so that they would ascertain what after all the real issues between them are. There might be a new apology for customs and rites, perhaps even for traditional customs, perhaps also for the kind of religious worship, both domestic as well as congregational, by which Judaism has up till recent times been so plainly marked. The laical practices, whether private or public, have served to discipline constitutionally and morally. The practices were minute and refined, and tinged the life and conduct of each member of the community. A man's life had become as it were politico-religious. The life of the individual was turned into an arm for the organization of the social unit. The legislation of Moses might be called an embodiment of social philosophy. It would be impertinent to readjust and to reform unless we in turn had in mind as thoroughly constructed an economic ideal. So long as we can not show that that which we wish to put in place of the old is relevant to a social policy, we have no title for our reformatory attempt. There is an interdependence between abstract notions, such as religion and faith have always been understood to be, and the practical or economic facts of the state. But the true religious facts are operative in the thousand-fold phases and incidents of the community. It may be supposed that I mean to say that the religious thought of a people, and its political practice are bound to one another only in the sense of ratio, that is true, but I mean more. Secular and sectarian mean at bottom the same thing, only from two different aspects. Where there was despotism in government there was also fatalism in religion, where life was easily sustained there was optimism, where life is cheap there is no industry, where talents are rare there is no enthusiasm, where there is phlegma there is pessimism, where there is artificiality there is transcendentalism. The origin of Christianity might be studied anew, the politics and the social status of that epoch ought to be more closely regarded. Palestine in the first century is not like Europe in the middle ages, nor are the ideals of the first likely to have been the same as those were of the second. A period of disruption can not breed a state of mind such as a period of organization does. The ascetic interpretation of the Christian faith is a distinct phenomenon ; so also is the crude unformed state of Europe at the invasion of the Goths. It is sociology that tells the story of the origin of every movement, and also of the fate of each. Superficial observers call us a people, a nation, a race; we, however, know that ours is an exemplary instance and the only instance of a religion thoroughly political and social.

If there is one thing which Jewish teachers, ever since Jehuda Halevi, have insisted upon, it is that Judaism respects history; that history is religion in solution. This we will persist to teach. Dogmas are losing their prestige. The nations have been weaned of that sort of violent discipline. The age of individualism has come. We need another method with which to organize the world-life ; the church-principle is doomed not only because there is a multiplication of sects and a disintegration in each, but because each of them is in the main a school of metaphysics, with a bit of ritualism thrown in, without any relation with the vital influence and factors in national progress. Besides, the constituency is coerced by a certain prescriptive code in belief. Out of the very seat of social necessity must come its constitution. The law of gravitation holds throughout the world. The social organism will bear its church. Nature brings forth with pain out of her great lap. The martyrdom of saints, the disappointments of the hopeful, the grief of dreamers, the anguish of saints, broken hearts—over graves the spirit of life moves with reverent but firm step.

There is much gossip about the identity of Judaism and Unitarianism. I am sorry that there are Rabbis who are so eager for a premature universalism that they will hurry to engage in any sort of companionship. Not even the last form of the Christian church can ever be any thing else than Christian, and that which is a link (let us say the last link) in the evolutionary chain of Christian philosophy, is radically, I say radically Christian. The difference between Judaism and every phase of Christian theology is clear enough. Judaism is not a chapter in the history of thought, not in the history of zeal; it

is the soul of the community which breaks out into all the moods and
movements of the body politic, just as the soul of a man breaks
through his flesh and bone. Judaism is not a protest against any
school of thought. It is as peaceful as light, as germinal as life, as
true as God.

THE FUNCTION OF PRAYER ACCORDING TO JEWISH DOCTRINE.

By RABBI I. S. MOSES.

"To appreciate the poet, one must go into the poet's land," is a German adage. To understand the character of a religion, one must study its prayers; to know the nature of a religious community, one must enter into the sacred precinct of their liturgy. Were to-day the history of Israel wiped out from the memory of men, were even the Bible to be obliterated from the literature of the world, the student of the science of comparative religion could reconstruct from a few pages of the Jewish prayer book the lofty faith of Israel, the grandeur of his moral teachings, and the main points of his historic career. What kind of men were they who would pray every morning: "Be praised, O God, King of the world, who hast not made me a slave?" They certainly had no reference to the poor creature bought and sold like merchandise; for neither in old nor in later Israel was slavery so extensive nor so abject as to call forth such a self-complacent benediction. During the long night of persecution, the position of the Jew was such as not to compare favorably with that of a slave. The slave at least enjoyed the protection of his master, but the Jew during the middle ages was at the mercy of every ruffian who chose to insult him. Yet would he pray with grateful devotion to his Maker and rejoice that he has not been made a slave. Compared with his tormentors, he felt himself to be the free man spiritually and morally, far above those who thrust him into misery. Indeed, *freedom* is the first note of Jewish worship; a song of freedom was the first prayer which liberated Israel attuned to his God. "They shall be my servants;" this divine assurance included the behest, not to be servants of men, not to fear their frowns, not to fawn their favor, but to obey the will of Him alone who has manifested Himself in Israel. The divine will is not hidden; the divine law has been revealed and intrusted to the keeping of Israel. This consciousness of being the possessor of divine truth in the form of the *Torah*, is a source of unspeakable joy for the soul of the Jew; from it he drinks ever new inspiration and new strength. *Truth*, therefore, or the Torah, is the second great element in Jewish worship. Amidst all changes of fortune, in the face of direst distress, even in the agony of death, the Jew would look upon his lot as specially favored by God; thanking Him for the great boon of having received the burden of the Law. In this law and in his obedience to it, he beholds his chief distinction, or election, before all other nations. Again and again the gladsome tone is struck that God has given the law to Israel. A few sentences from the evening service will be sufficient to illustrate this deep, intense love of the Jewish people for their sacred heritage. "With eternal love Thou hast guided the house of Israel; law and commandment, statutes and judgments, Thou hast taught us. Therefore will we constantly think of Thy law and rejoice in Thy teachings; for they are our life and the lengthening of our days, and in them we will meditate day and night; so may Thy love never depart from us."

And even so in the morning service the chief petition is for illumination in the law. "Our Father, our King, as Thou hast taught our fathers the statutes of life, so graciously teach us. Enlighten our minds in Thy law, and unite our hearts to love Thy name. Enable us to understand, to appreciate, to listen, to learn, to teach, and to practice the words of Thy law in love."

This, then, is the great longing of his soul, this the substance of his prayer, this the hidden fountain of his joyousness: to be able to understand and to carry out the law of his God! If we did not know from history what the Jew has done and endured in his steadfastness and fidelity to the law, such prayers would reveal the fact. But the law is only the outward expression and examplification of a deeper truth, which is the center and soul of Jewish thought and life. That truth has been formulated at the very incipiency of the people, and has become the watchword and battle-cry, the sign of recognition and the sound of confession, for all the members of the Jewish faith; it forms the central part of every divine service, private or public, and will cease to be uttered only with the last breath of the last Israelite on earth. The Sh'ma or the profession of the *One God*, is the formula of that truth which Israel first announced to the world; the truth which inspired the souls of the Prophets, winged the imagination of the Psalmists, set aglow the hearts of the sages in their longing for a righteous life, which gave birth to two grand systems of religion professed to-day by the civilized nations of the earth. This truth is no mere theological postulate; it is an *ethical movement;* for the declaration of the Oneness of God necessarily produces the idea of the oneness of humanity, or the brotherhood of man. "Thou shalt love the Lord, thy God," and "thou shalt love thy fellow-man as thyself," are only two different forms of expressing the same thought. In this thought, then, lies the mission of Israel, this is the reason of his great joy when thinking that he has been deemed worthy to be the bearer of that mission. Therefore he exclaims: "Happy are we, how goodly is our portion, how pleasant our lot, how beautiful our heritage; happy are we who proclaim: Hear, O Israel, the Lord is our God, the Lord is One."

To freedom, law and truth is thus added a fourth element of worship—Love! Love to God and love to man.

Among no other class of people has the sentiment of love found such a rich expression as among the Jews; an expression not in words but in deeds. Filial love and reverence, honor and obedience, conjugal love and fidelity, brotherly love and charity, are virtues to which the Jew has furnished the noblest illustration. From the depth of such a sentiment rose that portion of the Service which, because of its importance, is called "the Prayer." It is unique in form and sublime in its suggestiveness: "Praised be thou, our God, and God of our fathers," our fathers' God—this expression is the noblest testimony to the tender and grateful heart of the Jew—"Thou art great, mighty and awe-inspiring, O God, Most High." To the Jewish mind God is not a mere sentiment, but an overpowering reality, in whose presence the soul is awed to adoration, and can find but superlatives to clothe into words what stirs within: "Thou rewardest the good, rememberest the love of the fathers and bringest redemption to the children's children out of love. Thou alone art mighty and in Thy mercy givest life unto all: Thou sustainest the living in Thy grace, supportest the falling, healest the sick, loosest the bonds of captives, and keepest Thy faithfulness to those who sleep in the dust." What a tender and touching expression—"they who sleep;" not departed, not dead, only sleeping in the watchful care of God!

And now, rising to the highest conception which the finite creature can form of the Infinite and Eternal, the worshiping soul can but repeat the solemn words which the prophet Isaiah reports to have heard in his first vision; the "Threefold-Holy" of the angels worshiping the divine presence: Holy, holy, holy is the Lord of Hosts; the whole world is full of His glory!"

What God is to the myriads of worlds encircling His throne, we know not; but in the heart of man longing for virtue, and to the mind searching for the light of truth, He is revealed as the Holy One, who loveth righteousness and leadeth man to holiness. Or, in the words of the Law: "Ye shall be holy, for I, the Lord your God, am holy;" a strain modulated by a later Teacher—whom to-day, in this Parliament of Religions, we are proud to call one of Israel's noblest sons—in the words, "Be ye perfect, even as your Father who is in heaven is perfect."

This is the purpose of all religion—this especially the object of Jewish worship—to lead man to holiness, to perfection. The function of prayer, therefore, is not to persuade God to granting us favors, or by our hymns and praises influence His will, but an opportunity for man to learn to subject his will to the will of God; to strive after truth; to enrich his heart with love for humanity; to ennoble the soul with the longing after righteousness. To the Jew the house of prayer is not a gate to heaven, not an instrument for gaining celestial rewards, but simply a gate to righteousness (*Shaare Zedek*) through which he enters into the communion with the larger life of God. Holiness, or the obligation of virtue, the sacredness of duty, is the fifth element of Jewish worship, the indestructible foundation of Jewish morality.

To some it may seem strange to find so little of the personal, or individual element in the Jewish service. Even in that prayer which by long usage has become associated with the idea of immortality, in the *Kaddish* prayer, no reference to personal grief or personal reward is found. It contains nothing but the praise of God, the sanctification of His great name. But this fact again reveals only the lofty idealism of the Jewish mind. The consciousness that above all fleeting things God is; that He is the only reality; that His life is the life of all. This thought has sufficient cogency to uplift and console the heart of those sorrowing over the loss of their loved ones.

This thought of God is also parent of another sentiment, the sentiment of gratitude, forming an essential element of Jewish worship. I know of no more spiritual, noble and dignified thanks-offering than the one of the old Jewish service, known as the "*Modim.*" What is the Jewish worshiper most thankful for? For the thought of God, for the knowledge of His works! It may not be amiss even for Jewish ears to listen to this prayer once more. "We gratefully acknowledge, O Lord, our God, that Thou art our Creator and Preserver, the Rock of our life, and the Shield of our help. From age to age we render thanks unto Thee for our lives, which are in Thy hands, for our souls intrusted to Thy care, for Thy marvelous works by which we are surrounded, and for Thy boundless goodness, which is revealed unto us at all times, morning, noon, and night. We bless Thee, All-Good, whose mercies never fail, whose loving-kindness is without end. In Thee do we put our trust forever."

To unite all men unto a band of brotherhood, and thus establish peace on earth, is the aim of all religion. *Peace*, therefore, is the chief blessing for which the Jew prays to his God. In no liturgy does the word peace occur so often as in the Jewish, or those patterned after it. He, the hero of a thousand battles, the warrior in the service of God, the martyr in the service of truth, the undaunted, uncompromising defender of liberty of conscience, has no sweeter melody, no more soul-stirring song, than when he prays to God for the blessing of peace. This prayer has found a place in the liturgies of church and mosque. The threefold benediction of the ancient Hebrew priest foreshadowed humanity's prayer for universal peace.

We need no statistics to prove that the Jew is a loyal, law-abiding citizen of the nation whose social and political life he shares. He who breathes such a prayer for peace is certainly a lover of peace.

They who were wont to decry the Jews as selfish, narrow, exclusive, should take the trouble of examining the Jewish prayer-book as to the sentiment of universality, of human brotherhood. In the prayers for New Year and Day of Atonement, the days when his soul is most attuned to vibrate in response to noble sentiments, the Jew prays: "O God, let the fear of Thee extend over all Thy works, and reverence for Thee fill all creatures, that they may all form one band and do Thy will with an upright heart, so that all manner of wickedness shall cease, and all the dominion of the presumptuous shall be removed from the earth."

Still more clearly is this idea of the brotherhood of all men expressed in the grand concluding prayer of every service, the prayer known as "Alénu" or "Adoration." "It behooves us to render praise and thanksgiving unto the Creator of heaven and earth who has delivered us from the darkness of error and sent to us the light of His truth. Therefore we hope that all superstition will speedily pass away, all wickedness cease, and the kingdom of God be established on earth; then will the Lord be King over all the earth, on that day shall God be acknowledged One and His name be One." Again let me emphasize that these prayers and hopes for the coming of the kingdom of God rehearse in theological terms the grand and ever-recurring theme of the one humanity built upon the rock of righteousness and ruled by truth and love.

One more element of worship must be mentioned, as without it the circle of Jewish ideas would be incomplete, viz.: The idea of sin. To the Jew the thought of sin is no metaphysical conception, but a personal experience: the consciousness of his own shortcomings burdens his soul, not the concern for the evil doings of some remote ancestor. The orthodox Jew feels his responsibility for the sins of his people, in the past as well as in the present; to them he attributes his national misfortunes. But these sins are not inherent in his nature; they are remediable. The time is near, he hopes, when the measure of his suffering shall be full, and when God will lead him back in glory to his own land. The modern, liberal Jew, who has discarded from his heart as well as his liturgy all longing for a national restoration, but considers his native or adopted land his Palestine, still feels the moral responsibility for the sins of all his brethren in faith, but this feeling does not carry with it the thought of divine punishment. According to Jewish conception man is responsible only for his own sins; forgiveness of sin can be obtained only by thorough repentance. The Jewish worshiper feels " there is no wall of separation between God and man." In him lives the consciousness of being a child of God. The Father will not reject the prayer of His children. This assurance of divine forgiveness explains the spirit of joyousness and cheerful trust that prevails throughout the Jewish service. For this reason, too, the Jew reserves confession of sins and prayers for forgiveness for the great Day of Atonement. On that day he is bidden to examine his conduct, to make amends for his wrongdoing, to seek forgiveness of his offended brother, and thus be reconciled to himself and his God.

The words of the concluding prayer of the Day of Atonement will express more clearly this sense of intimacy with God, which animates the Jewish worshiper, than any lengthy exposition could do: " Thou reachest Thy hand unto him who is astray, and Thy right hand is outstretched to take up in love those who turn again unto Thee. Thou hast taught us, O Lord, to acknowledge all our sins before Thee, to the end that we may withhold our hands from unrighteousness. For Thou knowest, Lord, that we are but dust and ashes; therefore dost Thou forgive us much and often. But Thou hast chosen weak, fragile man from the beginning, and hast exalted him to know and reverence Thee. For who should dare say what Thou shalt do? And were man yet righteous, what avails it to Thee? In Thy love also hast Thou given us this Day of Atonement, as a day of forgiveness and pardon for all our sins, that we cease from all unrighteousness, turn again to Thee, and do Thy will with the whole heart. Have pity upon us, therefore, in Thine infinite mercy, for Thou desirest not the destruction of the world, as it is written : Seek ye the Lord while He may be found, call ye upon Him while He is near ; let the wicked forsake his ways, and the unrighteous his thoughts, and let him return unto the Lord who will have mercy upon him, and unto our God, for He will abundantly pardon."

Yet in all these prayers and supplications no reference is found to

future punishment or reward; no dread of everlasting torment over-
shadows the Jewish mind; no selfish longing for eternal pleasures is
an incentive to his repentance.

These are, in brief, the elements of Jewish worship; they give
sufficient answer to the question: What is the purpose of prayer according to Jewish doctrines? It is to imbue the worshiper with
the spirit of freedom and truth, with the love of God and of man;
with reverence for the past and trust for the future; with the
feeling of the sanctity of life and sacredness of duty; of gratitude
and peace; it is to inspire him with the larger thought than his own
individuality, with the thought of the universal brotherhood of man
and the all-embracing, all-pardoning love of God. These ideas of the
Jewish liturgy are at the same time a truthful testimony to the character of the Jewish people.

A REVIEW OF THE MESSIANIC IDEA FROM THE EARLIEST TIMES TO THE RISE OF CHRISTIANITY.

BY DR. I. SCHWAB.

The hope of the Messiah, that is, the hope of a restoration of dispersed Israel to a prosperous and glorious national independence under their own king, is ancient. How far back in history it dates can, however, not be decided with certainty. Professor Fürst, the erudite author of the "History of the Biblical Literature," traces it back to the early period of the division of the Israelitish empire, after the death of King Solomon. This event, he maintains, had so seriously weakened the Hebrew government and country, and occasioned so many hostile onsets by neighboring nations, that the better part of the Israelites began already then to long for a restitution of the Davidic dynasty, which they expected to be after the pattern of the first. The ideal God-favored "branch" of the house of the beloved and renowned King David would, so the vision was, fill the present gap, and establish again a mighty, large, and unified empire. As eloquent exponents of that fervid longing for a reinstatement of the Davidic empire, Fürst suggests, the Hebrew prophets, alike of the northern and southern kingdoms, came forward in their respective times. And that learned writer adds, that those very prophets raised the Messianic hope at the same time from its narrow scope to the expectation of the universal dominion both of Israel over other nations and of the religion of Jehovah over the false beliefs of the Gentiles.

Fürst is followed, to mention one more Jewish scholar, by Weiss, in his "History of the Traditions." He holds about the same position. We do not here propose to enter upon a discussion of its merits. Let us state that we strongly incline to a divergent opinion. We prefer to coincide with the Jewish historian, Herzfeld, who very plausibly proposes that the manifold older Messianic predictions, some of which reach as far back as the ninth century B. C., lay dormant in the body of the transmitted Hebrew literature, and were not made use of for doctrinal objects or for sentimental vehicles of expectation until the period of the Babylonian captivity.

When at the commencement of the sixth century B. C. the deportations of captive Judeans to the lands of the Babylonian conqueror began, which ended with the total destruction of the State of Judah, comforting words and efforts of reassurance were needed for those unfortunates. At that epoch Jeremiah, the stanch and foresighted prophet, puts forth a course of encouraging and cheering speeches, opening out to the exiles brilliant perspectives of restoration. In the period of the exile fall also the comforting discourses of Ezekiel and Isaiah, the latter called by the critics the Great Unknown or Unnamed. All of these holy men aimed to arouse in the hearts of their downcast and distracted countrymen glowing expectations of a felicitous return to their native land.

The prophets, Jeremiah and Ezekiel, connected this prospective restitution of the exiles with the reappearance of a Davidic, that is, Messianic reign. Jeremiah pointed out a coming reign of a "branch of David," whom God will at his appointed time cause to grow up (xxiii, 5; xxxiii, 15). He even calls this future ruler of the line of David by the specific name of David (xxx, 9). Likewise does Ezekiel designate in his predictions the future "king and shepherd of Israel" as Jehovah's "servant, David" (xxxiv, 24; xxxvii, 24). This denotation of David proper for the promised king of Israel, was most probably not intended to be construed literally. At any rate it was commonly in the time of Jesus, as well as among the later rabbis of the Talmud, conceived to refer to none other than a descendant of David.

The Messiah to come was in popular parlance styled the "son of David." This title was already well and firmly established in the New Testament times, as appears unquestionably from the Gospels.

If we inquire, further, how have Jeremiah and Ezekiel as well as some older prophets pictured in their own minds the nature and form of the government of the ideal Davidic king—Christ—the answer will be, that they conceived it to be *theocratic*, after the pattern of the reign of King David of old. The Messiah was to be, like David, God's viceregent or viceroy, carrying forward, on behalf of the Almighty Sovereign, an administration of "judgment and justice."

There are many evidences from Scripture corroborating our assumption that the ideal Messianic king was held eminently vicarious of Jehovah. It may be reluctant to our advanced sentiment to admit that the Davidic kingship, alike past and to come, should have been extolled so egregiously. But the fact nevertheless remains that the Hebrews of the pre-exilian and exilian times were as susceptible of exalting kings as were other nationalities. One need only compare

Pss. ii, and cx, 1, to be convinced of the accuracy of our assertion. As to the ideal Messianic king it is no less true that his government was prophetically conceived to merge into that of Jehovah and become in every sense and bearing, except that of religious worship, identical with it. It is this consideration that accounts for the easy interchange, in many Jewish writings of old, of the phrase "Kingdom of God" with "Kingdom of the House of David"—the latter in the view of Messiahdom. That interchange made the phrase "Kingdom of God" or "of Heaven," in its relation to the Messiah, very popular in course of time. So familiar was, indeed, in the subsequent era of the Roman dominion in which the hope of Messiah had to be cautiously veiled, the expression Kingdom of God to every Israelite, that, when John the Baptist and Jesus heralded its near approach, every Jewish hearer readily understood it in the Messianic meaning, which both previous custom and present political fear had put and fixed upon it. All this can be explained to be originally due to that Hebrew concept of anterior times, a concept merging the divine government and that of his temporal viceregent into one another.

After this diversion we have to pass over to the before-mentioned third prophet of the exile, Isaiah II. A more enthusiastic prophet Israel never had. His zeal for the cause of his captive brethren exceeded all measure. In the airy sweeps of his lofty imagination, he sought to set up the waning confidence and flagging courage of his brethren of the captivity. He became in reality the prophet of consolation proper.

At last, after about fifty years from the destruction of the State of Judah, the hour of restoration struck for the wretched exiles. When Cyrus approached Babylon with his gigantic army of sturdy Persians, our fiery prophet, overcharged as he was with pious patriotism, proclaimed that eastern conqueror as Jehovah's gentle "shepherd and liberating Messiah" (ib. xliv, 28; xlv, 11), who would dismiss the exiles to their former homes and rebuild Jerusalem (ib. xiii). He makes no mention whatever, though, of a Hebrew Davidic king being in any way instrumental in the act of restoration. Cyrus was to him evidently a good enough organ of salvation for Israel. He was in his eyes fully qualified to act the part of Christ-emancipator. What mattered it, in very fact, whom Jehovah would appoint as national savior and redeemer. All that Israel craved for in the desert of the exile was reinstatement into their inheritance. This granted and about to be accomplished, the rest of previous Davidic predictions could fairly be waived or at any rate held in abeyance as to their dog-

6

matic force. Moreover, our prophet was, to judge from his various compositions, more engrossed by the religious than the political feature of Israel's restoration. His chief concern was, that it should be attended with the stamping out of idolatry from Israel and the abolition of false worship in general, as well as the universal recognition of the Unity of God. (See xlii, 6; xlv, 6; lvi, 3, 6.)

If now we come to consider whether the many encouraging and uplifting predictions of the prominent prophets of the exile became true, we will find that they were only partially realized. It can be proven without any difficulty that all of them fell considerably short of the wide range those inspired men had given them. Were the hopeful anticipations uttered in, and aroused by, their writings for this reason vain and futile? Not at all. They served their purpose at the time. They rekindled the dispirited hearts of the people of the captivity, held them together in a bond of union, and guarded them from losing their identity in their scattered condition among the heathens. Were these not objects well worthy of the highest efforts of spirited eloquence? Will we find fault with them for depicting the future in too bright, even dazzling, hues, and thus awakening too high-flown expectations in the minds of the exiled brethren? No, our historically sympathetic hearts are too indulgent for that. Moreover, it has to be borne in mind that those prophets were inspired idealists. They would figure less on the natural evolution from the complexities of the stern and sad present than on a supernatural flashing out of divine help for their people. In their idealism they would leave out of the account the practical consideration—to use a phrase of a modern writer—that "liberty is a matter for the statesman to define rather than the poet to invoke." Persian statesmanship was, as events proved, not willing, despite scores of Hebrew oracles to the contrary, to surrender the dominion over its Jewish subjects into their own hands. Was it not favor enough that Cyrus gave the exiles permission to return? This message of emancipation was, indeed, received by them with jubilant applause. Their sore-tried hearts broke forth in high strains of rejoicing. Yet, alas! the sudden exultation was soon toned down again by many adverse events. All their high hopes of national bliss were blighted by stubborn untoward reality.

We can not here venture to describe even briefly the condition of the returned colony in the Jewish land in the two centuries of the Persian period. On the whole, it has to be said that it was almost invariably precarious, depressed, and dismal. Their hoped-for greatness proved an abortive dream; their fancied glory a delusive mirage. Their material lot became hard in many ways while under Persia.

But what grieved and vexed them most was the very condition of foreign servitude itself. The hearts of the Jews in the new settlement were never at ease in view of their tributary dependence on foreign, heathen powers. (See Neh. iv, 36. 37; Ezra ix, 8. 9.) To be such tributaries mortified them to the core. In their strong feeling of themselves as a nation and one with a God-given, hereditary territory, they were continually irritated at a state of such dependence. They could not but regard it as actual slavery. And slavery it essentially was. They would bear it submissively, though, as long as it was not too oppressive and degrading. But as a reproach and disgrace it nevertheless appeared to them at all times. For a redemption from that dependence they craved and prayed with devout hearts. This national consummation was, as they expected, to be reached through the arrival of its central personage—the God-appointed King—Messiah.

A vague notion of the realization of the Messianic hope in the person of their leader, Zerubbabel, may indeed have struck the returned congregation of exiles. This grandee who headed the caravan of liberated Jews on the return march toward the loved Jerusalem, was really descended from David. Yet how grievous must have been the subsequent disillusion, had they really indulged such a notion. For they soon found out that their governor was not even powerful enough to carry on and complete the building of the Temple. It remained unfinished for twenty years. So little was Zerubbabel subsequently regarded as the Messiah, that the prophet Zechariah had to predict another "branch" (iii, 8; comp. Jer. xxxiii. 15) for accomplishing the work. Far from being an independent Jewish sovereign, Zerubbabel was no more than a commissioned functionary of the Persian crown. His political dignity consisted mainly, we suppose, in being the responsible revenue deliverer to the satraps of Persia. Nor was the office of Jewish governor hereditary in his family.

There may, indeed, have existed in Judea during the second State a line of titular princes whose descent was from David. But if there were such distinguished personages, we are confident that they were not invested with any political authority. Furthermore, it is historically certain that the incumbents of the chief magistracy of the Jewish nation during the second Commonwealth were, at all events from the Greek period forward, the high priests, and not any secular princes. Josephus knows of no other heads of the nation than the high priests, even from the beginning of the second State. But even these high priests, we contend on well-based research (against Schuerer and Wellhausen), were not independent rulers. It was the national council, the Sanhedrin, which the Jewish people regarded as their only rightful supreme authority. The high priests derived their title from that representative national body. Whatever autonomy the foreign masters left to the nation was vested in the Sanhedrin. From this supreme council emanated all the power and prerogatives enjoyed by the high priests. For the new state was in approximate accommodation to the theory of Mosaism, a democratic theocracy. Accordingly, it was the senate alone that held the national judicature. The high priest had no judicial competence of his own. All the prestige by which he excelled the other senators was, that he passed for the diplomatic and fiscal representative of the people before the foreign governments to which the Jewish nation was subject.

Passing now from the Persian to the Greek period, we have to say that when Alexander of Macedon made himself "master of all Asia," the Jews of Palestine submitted voluntarily to him. They hailed this European conqueror with genuine, hearty confidence. In it they were not disappointed. The two centuries of dreary and hopeless national life under the Persian reign were with the new Macedonian epoch succeeded by a comparatively long term of peace and fair and intelligent dealing on the part of the Greek rulers. The favors which Alexander showed to the Jews generally, and the privileges he accorded to those of Alexandria, are known from history.

The rule of the Ptolemies over Palestine after the division of Alexander's empire was, on the whole, mild and pacific. The Jews bore their tributary relations to them very probably without murmur. They always acquiesced submissively in this dependent condition under judicious and humane government.

That the traditional Messianic expectation was during those earlier centuries of Greek dominion as much alive as before can not be doubted. But there were, we judge, few, if any, occasions for any sudden stir and excitement of the national feeling toward an independent Messianic government. The Palestinian Jews may have suffered periodically from the wars carried on between Egypt and Syria since the death of Ptolemy Philadelphus. Yet they bore this fate patiently as long as their sacred rights were not invaded, their honor not assailed, and no violent attempts made upon the security of their lives and interests. That their Messianic hope will have in that century, as ever before and afterward, varied in degree of fervor according to the complexion of the times, may be taken for granted. The logical postulate that what lives at an earlier and exists still at a later point of time can not have died out in the meantime, holds good with the Messianic hope as with all other objects. But aside from this unfailing truism we can bring positive proof that there never was any cessation of the hope of the Messiah through the entire length of the second Jewish State. Our information comes from the ancient liturgy. By turning these early compositions to account, we will find that much as the historical records have left us in the dark as to the question of the later pre-Christian Messianic expectations, there is at least one source which, if properly viewed, diffuses sufficient light upon it. This source is the original type of daily service handed down to us from the earliest days of the reorganized Judean community.

A detailed consideration of the old liturgical passages bearing on Messianism is precluded on this occasion. Briefly we will say in this place that our oldest forms of the prayer have as their substantial keynote Israel's national hope of salvation. Those forms we hold to date essentially back, not only to the Men of the Great Assembly, but to the sages of the earlier national councils. Those wise representative men—Scribes as they are called—will have composed, soon after the completion of the Temple, suitable types of service for public and private occasions. The year 500 B. C. may have already witnessed the institution of that liturgy which has come down to us with the stamp of antiquity. We invite students of our liturgy to cast a glance at the two benedictions preceding and the one following the Shemachapters. The two former have significant Messianic clauses, the last is exclusively Messianic. We call their attention further to the traditional eighteen forms of daily prayer. Upon close research they will discover that the theme of the present forms 1, 2, 7, 10, 11, 14, 15, and 17 is either entirely or partly Messianic. Even one of the three extant formulas of the third benediction, the Kedushah, has a Messianic reference.

It may perhaps be inexact to apply the epithet Messianic to the contents of all those prayers just noticed. We know that it is more correct to say that their theme is that of "salvation." The word salvation comprehends more aptly the various points into which the hope of national-religious restoration is divided. But as custom has attached to such restoration the general term Messianic, we too may use it here indiscriminately as to the various relations of Israel's latter-day expectation.

Let us, in addition to the foregoing specimens, mention, yet, two out of the four benedictions of the traditional Thanksgiving Prayer after meals. That the original character of this prayer has not been altered in its run through successive ages, we may assume with some degree of certainty. It is safe to say that all the Jewish stock prayers dating back to the ages of the Men of the Great Assembly remained, in regard to type and even order, the same during the whole Persian, Grecian, Maccabean, Herodian, and Roman periods. Those two thanksgiving benedictions are, as will be borne out by an examination of their tenor, Messianic, too. Even our popular Kaddish prayer was originally meant to be no other than an invocation of God to let his Kingdom, the Messianic, come speedily. Our ancient liturgy offers us then, as can be clearly seen, a direct and eminent illustration of the Jewish thought and feeling concerning Messianism or national futurity, as maintained for the four hundred years preceding the Syro-Greek rule over the Jewish land.

History has, accordingly, not been so envious as to foreclose for us a tolerably clear view of Israel's national hopes during that long stretch of time. It has in any case not withheld from us the opportunity of making out, by the way of close investigation, the attitude which the patriotic and pious Jews of those ages held toward the inherited Messianic expectation. We have from our transmitted ancient liturgy abundant evidence to prove that this expectation was incessantly alive during the whole existence of the second State. We learn to satisfaction that what the prophets had foretold as to the reinstatement of Israel to their own land, government, and sanctuary, was not inanimately imbedded in obscure minds of literature, or only silently embodied in the spiritual songs of sacred bards, but made up an integrant, solid, and living part of their soul's innermost hopes and aspirations.

We have now to pass to a brief review of the Syro-Greek dominion, from about the beginning of the second century B. C. With the entrance of Antiochus the Great on the scene, the Jewish affairs took a decided turn for the worse. The fierce persecution of the Jews by his son, Antiochus Epiphanes, is amply known to readers of history. Despair had in those days seized upon the faithful when they were by that mad tyrant forced to abjure, for the first time in their national existence, the God of their fathers, and embrace the pagan worship, a worship which was in their eyes "an abomination of desolation." The Maccabee uprising and struggles to avenge those unheard-of Syrian attempts of profanation of their sacred institutions and all the atrocities committed against their nation by Antiochus, his menials, and his army, are set forth in the annals of history. In those troublous days the cry for speedy delivery, the prayer for the arrival of Messiah, the son of David, will have gone up from the heaving breasts of thousands of the pious Jews. How long that dire fatality would hang over the nation, no one could tell. There was

no prophet who could forebode the future. Prophecy was then believed to be extinct. Yet there was a would-be prophet who came
forward to make known the end of the national sorrows. His assumed
name was Daniel. His book, which made a powerful impression upon
the mystically inclined of all after times, contains, among other matter, four prophetical visions (in chapters vii-xii). All of these alleged
oracles aim to point out, as modern criticism has established, the early
downfall of the fanatical tyrant, Antiochus Epiphanes. This downfall would, the seer advances, be accomplished miraculously by the
God of Heaven, Israel's God. The prophet tells us that he was translated to Heaven where God held court with his angels, pronouncing
the sentence of destruction upon the arrogant beast. But this aveng-
ing doom alone was not sufficient to our visionary. He felt himself
called upon to offer yet greater consolation to his hearers or readers.
In a nightly vision he " beholds one like the son of man coming with
the clouds of heaven. . . . And there was given him dominion
and glory, and a kingdom that all people, nations, and languages
should serve him ; his dominion is an everlasting dominion which shall
not pass away."

This apparition, the subject of which is a nebulous quasi-son of
man, had an astounding effect upon the minds of Messianic believers
during that second century. The author of the apocryphal book of
Enoch has copied and adopted for his spiritualistic Messiah that very
title " son of man," leaving out, however, the particle of comparison,
"like." He uses it alternately with the name " son of God " for the
same supernal personage of his. Likewise has Jesus, as the gospels
show, called himself, in his capacity of Messiah, by the name " son of
man," and that much more frequently and seemingly in preference to
the other title " son of God."

Nay he emphasized his real Messianic claim under the form of
that Danielic vision. His reapperance about the end of this world to
perfect his Messianic Kingdom which he declared to be accomplished
at an early date, Jesus repeatedly enunciated to be in or with the
clouds of heaven. In that incontestably authentic gospel account,
that of his trial before the high priest, in which he avows himself " the
Messiah, the son of God," he further asserts of himself, "hereafter
shall ye see the son of man sitting on the right hand of power (God)
and coming in the clouds of heaven." The stupendous influence exercised by that Danielic image is clearly recognized from this and kindred circumstances.

There are critics, let us remark, who insist that the author of
Daniel never thought of foreshadowing a personal deliverer and ruler

to come. They argue from the sequel of the description of that vision, that the "kingdom" was not really promised to one man, but to the people of the holy ones in heaven, that is, to' the saints in Israel whose guardians the angels in heaven are.

Ambiguous enough that Danielic vision is in very truth. Yet in spite of all this ambiguity, were the great majority of past and present expositors not frightened from accepting that relation as typifying a Messianic one-man rule.

To return once more to our would-be prophet. By the way of mystical calculations, he brings out the revelation that the stereotyped seventy years which Jeremiah had set down as the term of the desolation of Jerusalem, mean not years, but weeks of years, that is, seven times seventy years. By this prodigious stretch, the extent of Israel's entire national suffering could be approximately brought down to Daniel's own, really the Maccabean, time.

The end of that suffering he predicts in a sort of veiled oracle. The sum and substance of it no doubt was, that with the death of the hated persecutor, Antiochus, a real glorious and golden era would be ushered in for the faithful of Israel. They would receive the government from the God of heaven and possess it forever more. Now let us ask, was this prediction fulfilled? Did the anticipated salvation come to pass? Was independent government, with or without a king—Messiah—vouchsafed to Israel after the death of Antiochus, the terminus laid down by Daniel for the cessation of Israel's misfortune? By no means.

Judas Maccabeus accomplished, indeed, the reparation of Israel's religious institutions. He vindicated most successfully, together with the holy warriors who followed him, the honor of his country and the purity of the ancestral religion. But political independence from Syria he did not achieve.

From 161 B. C. on, when Jonathan, his brother, had succeeded him, a sort of free government with fair political privileges was established. His brother Simon secured, nineteen years later, even total political independence from Syria. But it was not of long duration. Judea became afterward again tributary to Syria. From this condition it was not ultimately freed till about the year 128 B. C., under John Hyrcanus.

What were the Messianic expectations of the Jews since the growth of the Maccabee dominion? Scarcely can it be supposed that the cry for a Messiah burst forth with loud accents while the Maccabee prince, Simon, ruled over the country. The nation, recognizing his merits, chose him in a collective assembly " high priest and chief forever until a prophet would rise" (who might, namely, give, in the name of God, different directions about the government).

The latter clause suggests to us that that Jewish assembly were diffident in their minds as to their liberty in designating popular rulers without a direct divine authority. Prevalent, we presume, was in their thoughts the possibility of a sudden, authoritative proclamation, through an accredited oracle, that the ideal king of the line of David was coming to take charge of the divine government—the theocracy of the Jewish nation.

Provisionally, however, it is reasonable to believe that the Jewish people were then content with the prevailing order of things. If, further, it be true what the author of the first book of Maccabees avers, that in those days "every man was sitting under his vine, and under his fig-tree," we can not for one moment suppose that, under such realizations of Messianic bliss, there should have existed an impulsive yearning toward another ruler, the imagined Messiah of the family of David. A tone of calm religious waiting for him will have, we allow, even then pervaded the souls of the pious. But that it should have had the character of an impatient longing, we can not consistently with reason presume.

The set prayers for national restoration were doubtless continued to be offered then as before, in public as in private. The hopes of Israel's futurity, once cast in a fixed mold by the venerated Scribes, enjoyed a popular respect and awe which consecrated them into inviolable canons. Devotional formularies, sanctioned by anterior authority and age, obtained always a strong, tenacious hold over orthodox people, however meaningless and soulless they may have become through the change and progress of the times. But for all that, it is impossible for us to believe that there was any particular pathetic force to the prayers for restoration recited in the days of the Maccabee ruler, Simon.

The same may be said of the prosperous reign of his son, John Hyrcanus, B. C. 135–105. Under him almost a Davidic splendor, greatness, and power prevailed. By the side of proud national self-consciousness the morbid sigh for an unknown and unknowable royal personage who should yet improve upon the present common happiness, can not well be imagined to have burst forth.

The Messianic vision, it must be admitted by all, was originally born of gloom. It was always expressed, with more or less demonstrative force, under somber aspects of the times. Its "reason of existence" was either the dreary night of oppression or the dim twilight of a dubious destiny. In the serene radiance of the light of freedom and peace, or the lucid gleam of temporal bliss, however, the motive for its being is only hypothetical. If it nevertheless exists under such favorable conditions, it is due to a mere emotional attachment to the past and a pious repugnance to part from the wonted track cut by venerated ancestors and trodden all along in subsequent ages. That, therefore, the Jews were under the prosperous reign of the high-priestly prince, John Hyrcanus, little troubled about the Messianic future, may be set down as a reasonable conclusion.

Yet, while all this seems natural in the common point of view, and even obvious from a general glance at the outward aspect of the Jewish affairs of that time, we must not conceal a counter-view inevitably thrust upon us in the present consideration.

This contrary impression results from the fact that a serious and far-reaching religious disturbance entered the Jewish life at some juncture of that prince's reign. It was when he deserted orthodox Pharisaic Judaism and joined the Sadducean party. That the Sadducees were, for their rejection of the traditions, the disavowal of resurrection, and a latitudinarian mode of religious life generally, regarded by the Pharisaic votaries and the people at large who adhered to them as their teachers and guides, as heterodox, later even as heretics, is notorious. From the time, therefore, that John Hyrcanus introduced Sadduceeism and raised it to the throne, till Pompey made an end to the domestic Asmonean government, there must have sprung up among the orthodox masses a decided discontent with that ruler and a strong revulsion of their innermost sentiments, which interfered seriously with their feeling of happiness, otherwise secured by the strength and success of his reign.

But it was not only Sadduceeism on the throne that aggravated the pious sensibilities of the people. There came to it yet the bold attempt of absolute monarchy, of kingship symbolized by the diadem. Hyrcanus's son, Aristobulus I., was the first Asmonean prince who put on the regal diadem. This was to the Jewish people of those latter days—so vast a transformation had been wrought upon their minds in the post-exilian period—an odious emblem of irresponsible absolutism.

Against such domination of mastering rulers their hearts rebelled. They even denounced it openly as irreconcilable with their national destiny. We meet in Josephus with two accounts of such open deprecations of formal kingship by the representatives of the nation; the one in Pompey's time, which was directly aimed at the Asmonean prince, Aristobulus II., and the other about sixty years later, after the death of Herod. That the feverish nation broke forth into vigorous demonstrations against crowned royalty on both those occasions is very suggestive to us.

What we venture to derive from those marked expressions of sorely agitated national sentiments is, that the cry for the "Kingdom of God" is associable with, and dates back to, the early days of detested Sadducean-Asmonean rule, if not already to the earlier period of the Maccabee struggles. We mean to say, that that phrase, old-established as it was in its *affirmative*, theocratic and theological bearing, came prominently forward in an additional *negative* sense as early at least as the hated ruling Sadduceeism usurped the insignia of overpowering tyranny, especially its most repulsive sign, the royal diadem.

As a true and devout exponent of those combined meanings attached to the expression, "Kingdom of God," appears to us the author of the apocryphal Psalms of Solomon. These compositions were, in our opinion, written by the son of a Pharisaic fugitive from the fury of Alexander Janneus, about the middle of the first century B. C.

At the time of his writing, there had already passed over the nation the twenty-seven years of the rule and atrocious misgovernment of that most corrupt Asmonean prince. Also the fierce contention between his two sons had already brought on the armed arbitration by Pompey, who subdued the Jewish land into tribute to Rome. The lamentable havoc made by this triumphant conqueror at the capture of Jerusalem, as well as the great suffering and near partial exile attendant upon the later invasion of Cassius, were fresh in the memory of our psalmodist.

Open the book of his Psalter and read. You will meet most touching Messianic outcries and invocations. The ring of his Messianic sighs is as forcible as it is melancholy. We can not here enter upon a particular estimation of that most invaluable collection—invaluable the more because it is the only Jewish literary product of the later pre-Christian ages which treats of the Messiah in a common-sense style and does not wrap up its expectations in unintelligible hints or entangle us in a labyrinth of impossible imagery and confusing ciphers.

Summarily let us observe that its author betrays at once an invincible loathing and rankling hatred for the degenerated and impious Asmonean dynasty, and a strong, patriotic, religious antipathy against the newly established foreign supremacy, the Roman. As an unholy power, for its image worship, moral corruption, and brutality, the world-conquering Rome was already then viewed by the serious-minded sons of Israel.

A relief from the state of misery and degradation into which the nation had fallen at the time of our psalmodist, he could expect but from God. Him he implores, indeed, as the only savior of Israel, to let His mercy soon appear over them and to send as ruler his own Messiah, the son of David, thus verifying His ancient oath that the kingdom should not part from the house of David forever.

Did his tuneful and pathetic strains, let us inquire, meet with Providential response? Did the anticipated Messiah come? No. There was even a worse fate in store for the Jewish nation than the one our poet had witnessed and reflected on.

It was the crushing and insupportable misrule of the Idumean usurper, Herod, which lasted for forty long and weary years. Herod "filled the country with poverty and iniquity and inflicted more suffering on the nation during his reign than they had sustained through all the five centuries previous"—this was the bitter complaint which a Jewish senatorial deputation brought before the Emperor Augustus in the year 4 B. C., after that blood-thirsty monster had passed from the living.

It was on this occasion, too, that these Jewish representatives begged that their nation should have no more kings. Their official protestation against kingship was, as we suggested above, the negative side of Israel's constant watchword, the " Kingdom of Heaven,"

They pleaded further " for liberty to live by their own laws," avowing in all other respects profound loyalty to the imperial sovereign. They asked that their land be joined to the Syrian province, rather than be held longer under the thraldom of a domestic tyrant like Archelaus.

It was in this very year, too, and in the absence of that delegation, that a violent revolt broke out in the Jewish land. The popular uprising took its start on the Pentecost feast in Jerusalem. The whole nation from one border of the country to another, seemed to have been seized by an instantaneous impulse to make a bold strike for liberty. The insurrection spread all over Judea, Galilee, Perea, and Idumea. The inflamed and infuriated masses who besieged the fortress of Jerusalem had to deal with the pitiless and rapacious procurator of Syria, Sabinus. They were even, for all that we can learn to the contrary, without any commander.

During those convulsions which shook the Jewish land to its center, there occurred a characteristic insurrectionist movement which deserves special notice in this place. Josephus tells us that the insurgents of Galilee had as leader, Judas; those of Perea, Simon; and those of the valley of Judea, north-west of Jerusalem, a shepherd named Athronges.

The last two leaders he lets put on kingly diadems. Of Judas of Galilee he only says that he had the "ambitious desire of the royal dignity." Kings were, he informs us, moreover, created on all sides.

We are of opinion that those kingly agitators were Messianic pretenders. As would-be Messiahs they have possibly succeeded in drawing mobs after them by miracles of liberation. For all those "false prophets" whom Josephus introduces here and there as pretending liberators of the nation in the Roman times, were such as claimed "divine inspiration," finding credit with the vulgar by performing first some "signals of liberty" and setting out afterward on their martial deeds of deliverance.

We venture to believe that the kingly pretenders in question were of about the same type as those "false prophets." Scarcely, we think, could those adventurers have succeeded in attracting mobs for their designs, had they not joined with their presumptuous boast of kingship the transcendent claim of supernatural endowment for their alleged office of liberation. This presumed call from Heaven they would doubtless manifest by performing some magical feats.

It is needless to inquire into the condition of mind of those agitators. In excited days, impulsive men with an adventurous spirit rarely fail in finding a following. An ignorant and easily seducible rabble can be mustered almost in the twinkling of an eye. To win their confidence by some luring methods of imposture is an easy matter. The crafty and fanatical leaders know how to improve upon their susceptibilities and use them for their selfish or vain-glorious schemes. In pursuing them, the designing deluders affect greater and greater superiority over their dupes, till at last they become themselves, many of them, a prey to the frenzy of indomitable egoism, to the point even of believing themselves in the paroxysm of their conceit, extraordinary beings, gifted with powers inapproachable to all the rest. That an overwrought egoism possessed also the minds of those kingly agitators, whether they passed themselves off for Messiahs or not, is not to be questioned. Their movement, we have to add, was unsuccessful. The whole revolt was indeed soon quelled. Varus's mighty forces had little difficulty in crushing the revolting multitudes who had attempted to shake off the Idumean yoke.

Before concluding we have yet to mention another, much more important and momentous pre-Christian movement. It is that of the same Judas of Galilee who raised an insurrection after Judea had been incorporated into the Roman empire as a province and annexed to Syria, in the year 6 A. D. With this act, the political autonomy of the

Jewish State came, strictly considered, to an end, to be restored no more while Rome held its sway over it.

A year after that annexation, the Roman authorities introduced a system of direct assessment on the property and persons of the Judeans. It bore the Latin name census. This census enacted by Quirinius called forth a violent irritation and resistance on the part of the entire Jewish people. They held it an "awful thing" to have to obey the foreign dictation of enrollment for taxation. It was not so much the unheard-of direct taxes levied from individual inhabitants, or the chafing burden of the new taxation imposed on them, as the coercion into the despotic will of the Roman masters, that made the census so repulsive to them and aggravated their resentment to the highest pitch. Yet the excited multitude was soon prevailed upon to calm down and subside into the inevitable with loyal subordination.

There were, however, enough Jewish people, and those mainly of the younger class, who would not consent to endure the new harsh enactment without a forcible attempt at redress. They were those who held, to use an expression of Lecky's, "non-resistance incompatible with political liberty." They found a ready leader in the person of the heroic Judas of Galilee, the same who had previously acted as head of the Galilean revolters.

This time Judas came forward as the champion of all the insurgents of the land, to lead them forth to victory or death by open and defiant armed resistance.

Did he set up for a Messiah at this juncture? From a relation in the Acts of the Apostles (v, 37), it would almost seem, by implication at least, that the present venture was of a Messianic sort. But for us it is impossible to form such an idea of that gallant Gaulonite. His memorable watch-word, "God is the only Ruler and Lord," by which he threw the gauntlet at every form of human despotism, precludes positively any royal and, consequently, Messianic aspiration having taken hold of his mind.

That declaration was a bold manifesto thrust out against any foreign restraint, no less than against domestic tyranny.

Different from the Pharisaic rabbis and the larger body of the common people who waited idly, though eagerly, for a miraculous manifestation of the Kingdom of God, which would bring to an end forever all native and foreign tyrannical sovereignty alike, the adherents of Judas concluded to be their own Messiahs, and help forward the independent self-government of the nation, under God, in accordance with the Mosaic constitution.

Did those zealotic Independents, then, not cherish the hope of a coming personal Messiah at all? We can not tell. What we know from the invidious Jewish historian, Josephus, himself is, that they had "an inviolable attachment to liberty." For it they would, indeed, hazard life, substance, and all. For it they would buckle on their armor and enter into a desperate struggle with the Roman colossus, fully aware, as they must have been, that they could be no match for it.

Their revolutionary attempt was the noblest contest for liberty and God ever undertaken by any body of men. It was at once an assertion of the cause of the people against human autocrats, and of God, the King of king, against what Thomas Paine has styled the "little paltry dignity of earthly kings."

It was further in its high aims and principles, in many respects at least, the antetype of the American republican independence. It differed from it only in this respect, that Judas's movement was ineffective, issuing in disaster then and ending, in the later revolution which it had spiritually and organically engendered, in the ruin of the whole Jewish State. But the American war of independence led to a signal conquest over tyranny and the brilliant achievement of liberty.

The one failed of bringing on the Kingdom of Heaven on earth, the dominion of pure religion, law, and justice administered by the people's own representatives, without interference by domestic or foreign potentates.

The other brought in its train the reign of the Messiah—the union of the American republic upon the foundation of freedom and equality. Under the guidance of this Messiah, impersonal, yet all-sufficient for the happiness of men, the American nation has since that memorable struggle for independence continued to proclaim to the whole world the "everlasting creed of liberty."

Of this nation we, the Jews, feel proud to be members. To it we are bound by the sacred ties of love of country and unshaken devotion. In this "promised land that flows with Freedom's honey and milk," we have our safe refuge, feeling ourselves exiles no more, nor yearning in the least degree toward a repatriation to the land of Israel of old. In it we will continually strive, in common with all the other citizens of different extractions and creeds, to enhance its welfare and help forwarding all peaceful arts, higher culture, generous, mutual sentiments, and true religion.

ETHICS.

THE ETHICS OF JUDAISM.

By RABBI I. M. WISE.

What Aristotle called Ethics, Cicero called Morals. The two terms are synonymous also with Moral Philosophy, *in re*, different in method only. Any one of these three terms designates the science of man's free will, motives, volitions and actions, rights and duties, in his relations to man and accountability toward God. Man's duties to God, being of a religious nature, belong properly to Theology.

The principle of ethics is in human nature. Every self-conscious human being feels and knows that the Good and the Right, the True and the Beautiful, are desirable and ought to be chosen, and the negatives thereof are objectionable and ought to be shunned. We call this conscience, an innate and unconscious judgment, which distinguishes man as such.

The Moral Law, the *Categoric Imperative*, mustnecessarily be in man, No moral laws, no ethics of any kind, could possibly be evolved or developed in the human race if the moral capacity was not there originally.

Evolution or Development signifies the production of a succession of facts, phenomena, or things similar to their fundamental element. None can evolve gold from iron or rocks from clouds. Experience and education can only develop that which is elemental in man; it can but evolve qualities from capacities, and render them constant in consciousness and character. So the unconscious and innate conscience may evolve virtue, which is the flower of the plant.

What is good and right? What is true and beautiful? These are problems of quiddity which experience and judgment define, and have defined differently in different generations, nations, climates, natural or artificial environs which differently affected the experience and judgment of the original reasoner, who established in any particular case this or that definition of the good and right, the true and beautiful. The difference between Ethics and Æsthetics is formal only.

Therefore, the Moral Law is one in the whole family of man, the moral laws are multifarious, not seldom contradictory, unstable, and unjust. Slave holding nations consider slavery perfectly moral; we do not. Despotism is considered moral in despotic countries; we consider it immoral. Slaying dumb animals is a moral sport to habitual hunters, and a barbarous crime to sensible people, who would punish their boys for destroying a bird's nest or maltreating a cat. It is right to slay many innocent men on the battle-field of contesting nations and a capital crime to slay one. Every act which the Decalogue prohibits was considered just and right somewhere and at some time, and it is partly the case to-day, even outside of the homes of the savages and semi-barbarians. Auto dafes, torture, and pyre applied to punish heretics, was for many centuries considered right, perfectly moral; ostracizing, persecuting, and expatriating persons under the same plea, is considered right and moral in certain regions of civilized society; and we condemn both practices as unjust and immoral.

It is evident, therefore, that history offers no fixed code of moral laws, and can produce no canon and guide to all, either by speculation or evolution. The conscientious individual could be guided only by the maxim of his own judgment, viz., that which I to the best of my knowledge consider to be right, good, and true, is moral to do, and the negative thereof is moral to shun. No man can be better than he knows how to be. But it is insufficient in two directions: 1. No man can stand still to consider at every problem in practical life, whether to do or not to do is moral to the best of his knowledge. 2. Any deed, action, or volition, to be moral, must also be beneficial, or at least not injurious to society, of which every person is a mere individual. That only is good which is good for all the good, only that is right which is right to all the righteous, as only that is true which is true universally. No man can stand still to consider at every problem in practical life, whether to do or not to do so is beneficial or injurious to society; few possess the ability so to do.

Therefore, philosophers like Baruch Spinoza and his numerous followers, denying moral freedom to man, advanced the moral maxim of authority. They maintain it is moral to do or to shun that which the existing authority, the highest power, commands or forbids to be done or shunned. Obedience is the highest virtue; it is Stoic submission to the inevitable. If such submission is sinful according to the inherent Moral Law, the individual is not accountable for it; it is the sin of that authority or that highest power.

This maxim, which, indeed, is the underlying principle of all despotic governments of state, society, military, and semi-martial organizations, is factual, but not ethical, because it is not from man's free will, volition, and action. It makes a virtue of necessity, and necessity is no virtue. Moral laws can be advisory only; if they become a compulsory necessity, they are moral laws no longer.

Still, moral laws, which are the definitions of the true and the good in general and in particular cases, being necessary to man for the sake of certitude, must come from a higher or highest authority, and can be advisory only. This is the case with the Ethics of Judaism, as laid down in the Five Books of Moses, expounded by prophets and sages these three thousand years, and actualized completely or partly in the history of civilization. Let us consider this system of ethics.

1. THE MORAL LAW IN MAN.

The Book of Genesis is teleological. It contains besides other doctrines the narrative of the successive development of the God idea in man—natural revelation—from the elementary conceptions of the first self-conscious man to that God-cognition in the fourth generation of the family of Abraham; and the progress of the ethical doctrine developed and cultivated in man by this progressive God-cognition, as finally actualized in the life of Joseph, in which the moral imperfections of the prior patriarchs disappear. In this book, at the very start of man's history, we find the Moral Law in man.

In Genesis i. 27, it is stated that God created Adam in his image, as explained in ii. 7, by permeating the body of clay with the breath of life, which made that body a living person, a physical body enlivened with a God-like spirit, the spirit of wisdom and understanding the intellectual capacities (Exodus xxxi, 3; Isaiah xi, 2). Then (verse 28) we are informed: "And God blessed them (the male and female alike) and God said to them, Be fruitful and multiply and fill the earth, and subdue it, and have dominion over the fish of the sea, the fowl of heaven, and over all that creepeth upon the earth." The same blessing is repeated (Genesis ix) as bestowed on Noah and his sons as conditions of the covenant of God with mankind.

Blessing in Hebrew, *baruch*, signifies "bestowing of some additional good" (הוספת טובה); in this case it signifies, after the Creator had bestowed upon man the breath of life, the God-like spirit, he bestowed on him additionally the Moral Law as a part of his nature: for these words of blessing contain the main elements of all moral laws in the following order:

1. THE PRESERVATION OF THE HUMAN FAMILY BY SELF-PRESERVATION AND PRESERVATION OF THE RACE IS THE FUNDAMENTAL MAXIM OF ALL MORAL LAWS. Also, according to the Talmud, this is the first divine commandment given to man, and this is not commanded; it is bestowed on human nature as a blessing. It obligates

him by his own nature to perform all the duties which tend toward the preservation of the race, the preservation and protection of life, limbs, and health, together with the means and conditions of sustenance, and forbids him to do the contrary thereof, as is evident from the additions to this blessing in Genesis ix. Here is the broad basis of all moral laws upon which state and society primarily rest, expressed in numerous commandments in the Mosaic legislation, and in the legislation of all other civilized nations more or less perfect up to the climax of "Thou shalt love thy neighbor as thyself," "Thou shalt love the stranger as thyself," "Thou shalt not return the fugitive slave to his master," all of which, the whole category of commandments, including the laws concerning alms, support of the poor and needy, and protection to the weak and helpless, have this one aim, the preservation of the human family, and rest upon the broad basis of man's innate Moral Law.

If we take into consideration the feebleness and long helplessness of the human child, the feebleness and helplessness of man in his primeval condition, opposite not only the powerful quadrupeds, but also the lower animals from the serpent down to the venomous insects, and add to it the peculiar difficulty of man to secure a livelihood and protection against the inclemency of the elements; it must appear miraculous that the human family still exists and has increased to over fourteen hundred millions of individuals, when so many of the much stronger races are extinct and many more nearly extinct. The words of the divine blessing solve this mystery by pointing out the means and methods for the preservation of the human family, first by the term (וכבישה) "Thou shalt or wilt subdue the earth" to yield sufficient sustenance for all, which man only can do. The earth is subdued by labor only, thus this blessing contains:

2. THE DUTY OF LABOR CONTAINED IN THE INNATE MORAL LAW OF MAN. As it is every person's duty to contribute his share to the preservation of the human family, it could be no less his duty to contribute his part for the production of the means of its sustenance. He who contributes naught to the household consumes the bread of others, and counts in the *minus* class of humanity. This also is outlined in Genesis ix. Labor is a necessity of human nature. None besides the sick, the old, and feeble can live happily without it.

Here then is the broad basis in the innate Moral Law to a category of moral laws most minutely expounded and expanded in the Mosaic legislation. The duty of labor found its way into the decalogue, "Six days shalt thou labor and do all thy work." The genius of the Hebrew language coined the term *Malach* for angel, which is identical with

Melachah (work or labor), so that angel and working factor are identical. Numerous are the Mosaic laws for the protection of the laborer and the fruits of his labor up to the admonition, "Thou shalt not keep over night till morning the wages of the hired man, on the very day thou shalt give him his wages." More even than this is ordained in Deuter. xv, when the person sold for theft is set free before the year of release, "Thou shalt not let him go away empty; thou shalt furnish him liberally out of thy flock and out of thy floor, and out of thy wine press, of that wherewith the Lord thy God hath blessed thee thou shalt give him." This is more than wages. As to the social position of the laborer, the Law calls him invariably "thy brother," and knows generally of no distinction between man and man. All work, all must work, the priest at the altar, the Levite at music and song, the judge and the bailiff in the temple of justice, the teacher and the author, the musician and the singer, the husbandman and his help, the mechanic and the wage laborer, all must work; the Law has no room for idlers; all must contribute to the subsistence and progress of the human family, for such is the dictum of the Moral Law in man. "For not upon bread alone liveth man, but upon all that cometh out of the mouth of the Lord man liveth," as we shall see next. This accounts for the industrious habits of the Hebrews in all parts of their history.

The next term of divine blessing is וּרְדוּ "thou shalt or wilt have dominion over the fish of the sea, the fowl of heaven and the creeping things upon the earth," viz., also those living beings which apparently are beyond the control of man. So the human race will not be exterminated by the animals superior to it in strength and combativeness. Man exercises his authority, maintains his dominion over the brute creation by his superior intelligence only and exclusively and in exact ratio to the height or lowness of his intelligence. Thus his blessing contains:

3. THE DUTY OF MENTAL CULTURE CONTAINED IN THE INNATE MORAL LAW OF MAN. It is not labor alone, it is intelligent labor which subdues the earth, arrests the fury of the elements, and renders forces of nature subservient to man's purposes. It is not physical strength, it is the power of intelligence which holds dominion over brute creation. Therefore like labor the mental culture, the growth and progress of intelligence, is every man's duty as his contribution to the preservation of the human race. It is by the ideality and inventive genius peculiar to man; that education and progress of the race are possible, nd these rise or decline with the progress or retrogression of mental culture. So his inherent *Categorie Imperative* urges to mental culture as

it drives him to labor. Without mental culture as without labor one belongs to the *minus* class of the race.

Here we have with the broad basis in the innate Moral Law another category of moral laws most minutely expanded and expounded in the Mosaic legislation, the only legislation of antiquity which urges the education of the young as a solemn duty (Exodus xiii, 14 ; Deuter. vi, 7), and makes it every one's duty to learn to read and to write, not exempting even the king and the priest—the only legislation of antiquity which made wisdom and intelligence the ideal of the nation, as Moses verily told them : "And ye shall observe and do them (these laws), for this is your wisdom and your understanding in the eyes of the peoples, who will hear all these statutes, and they will say only this great nation is a wise and intelligent people" (Deut. iv, 6). It has been advanced by wise expounders of the Law, that Moses denounced all pagan practices, all idolatry, all superstition of any kind, so rigorously, not so much to the greater glory of God, but to the advancement of mental culture, because those superstitions and practices corrupt and cripple human reason, and retard its progressive development ; and that his rigid spirituality in his presentation of the monotheism which phantasy can not depict and reason can not define, was specially calculated to set his people to think, to reason on the highest ideal, to stretch the reasoning power to the unlimited universal, thus training and urging the reasoning faculty to dive into the fathomless deep of universal reason and redeem it from the bondage of narrow superstitions and crippling fetichism ; to advance mental culture as the path to the *summum bonum*. This accounts for the liberal reason of the Hebrews in all parts of their history, in the literature of their prophets, their sacred bards, their rabbinical, philosophical and poetical sages in all ages, and the rationalistic *Psyche* of the entire people although profoundly religious.

This triangle, whose sides are the preservation of the human family, the duty of labor and the duty of mental culture, with the center of the innate moral law, comprises the whole system of ethics. With the growth of the God-cognition in Israel its provisions became more definite and more intensified, but no new principle was added. The moral attributes of God were revealed to the people, such as holiness, love, mercy, grace, loving kindness, benevolence, benefaction, long suffering, justice, equity, forgiveness of sin, iniquity and transgression, preservation of the good and the true to the thousandth generation, and neutralizing the effects of evil doing in the third or fourth generation—not indeed to advance a new principle of ethics, but to furnish man with the highest ideal of all ethics, the ideal of perfection, and to connect therewith:

4. THE DUTY OF MAN TO STRIVE CONTINUALLY TO BECOME GOD-LIKE, TO COME AS NEAR AS POSSIBLE TO THE HIGHEST IDEAL OF DISIN-TERESTED GOODNESS, LOVE, MERCY, JUSTICE, HOLINESS, AND ALL THE OTHER VIRTUES WHICH THE INNATE MORAL LAW URGES AND OUR GOD-COGNITION DEFINES. This is expressed in the commandment given to Abraham. " Walk (conduct thyself) before me and become thou perfect " (Genesis xvii) ; in the admonition of Moses, " Thou shalt become perfect with the Lord thy God " (Deuter. xviii. 13) ; and according to the Rabbinical sages, also in the words. " Ye shall walk after the Lord your God " (Deuter. xiii, 5) ; to which we might add the injunction, " Take heed and hearken to all these words which I command thee ; that it may be well with thee and thy children after thee forever, if thou wilt do the good and the right in the eyes of the Lord thy God " (Deut. xii, 28)—if thou strivest to do as God does, and to be as He is, holiness and goodness for the sake of holiness and goodness.

II.   THE MAXIM TO REGULATE THE ACTION.

The maxim to regulate the doings of man must also be in the innate Moral Law. This is evident from the whole tenor of the Mosaic legislation, which is based upon Freedom. God, according to Mosaic revelations, is absolutely free. He created heaven and earth from His own free will. He preserves and governs them by the forces of His free will, which He can suspend or change at His will. He made man a free being, that can choose good or evil as did the first human parents, and as Moses often announces in unmistakable words (Deut. xi, 26-28 ; xxx, 15-20). The very fact that reward is promised for the observation and punishment threatened for transgression in all parts of the Thorah shows that man is free in the estimation of the Mosaic legislation. This is most unequivocally expressed in Deuteronomy v, 25. 26. The nation which God constituted is free. Its form of government is the theocracy, not a theocracy with a reigning priesthood, but with a reigning law, a most outspoken free democracy. God is the king, which means His law and His truth reign by a council of elders and the heads of the tribes chosen by them. Freedom is the underlying principle every-where, in God, state, and individual, hence there must be moral freedom limited only by the dicta of reason. This accounts for the spirit of freedom which never and no-where left the Hebrews.

If freedom is the principle, it must be certain that man possesses it also in his moral life, in his innate Moral Law. Therefore any person who conscientiously regulates his volitions and actions to the best of his knowledge in obedience to the Moral Law in him is a righteous man, however different his doings may be from those ordained in the Law of Moses. He is one of the class whom the Rabbis of old called חסידי אומות העולם. "the pious conscientious non-Israelite, whose reward in life eternal is secured to him—something which all gentile creeds refuse to admit. The blessing of the Lord which contains the Moral Law was not bestowed upon Israel only or any other nation especially; it was not conditioned by any creed, faith, law, or institution; it was unconditionally bestowed on man, on Adam and Noah prior to and independent of all creeds, faiths, laws, or institutions; it is the heritage of the entire human family, the peculiar treasure of every human being who expounds the innate Moral Law to the best of his knowledge, and thus conscientiously regulates his volitions, motives, and actions. Therefore the prophet said: "He hath told thee O man what is good," and not O Israelite, O Greek, or O Roman. To all of which the triangle of duty is an infallible guide.

III. THE ADVISORY AUTHORITY FOR THE SAKE OF CERTITUDE.

The Thorah was given to Israel for the sake of certitude. It defines with precision what is good and right, true and beautiful in all cases of human affairs, national, social, and individual. It reveals to man the ideal of moral perfection and prompts him to rise in the moral scale toward this ideal with the conviction that it is the Eternal God who is so, does so, and teaches us so to do. It was given to all conscientious men for their satisfaction, that they might know with certitude what is good and right, true and beautiful to be chosen, and what being the contrary thereof is to be shunned, "What the Lord thy God requireth of thee." Still it is advisory only, there is no coercion, there can be none, for this same Thorah teaches the principle of freedom and the duty of reason and reasoning. The same Thorah teaches that the moral value of any performance is commensurate with its motive. Coercion is an imposition, no inner motive at all, certainly no virtue, whatever action it produces is morally indifferent. The laws of the Thorah are definitions of the quiddity of the good and the right, the true and the beautiful, and also the contrary thereof. The Israelite is expected to know them, and they are to him the definitions coming from the highest authority. If he is conscientious in interpreting to himself the innate Moral Law to the best of his knowledge, he must be guided by the Thorah which is the best of his knowledge in moral matters. If he fails to do so, he fails.

This to the best of my knowledge is a true synopsis of the Ethics of Judaism, higher than which I know of none.

ETHICS OF THE TALMUD.

By DR. M. MIELZINER.

Ethics is the flower and fruit on the tree of religion. The ultimate aim of religion is to ennoble man's inner life and outer life, so that he may love and do that only which is right and good. This is a biblical teaching which is emphatically repeated in almost every book of Sacred Scriptures. Let me only remind you of the sublime word of the prophet Micah: "He hath showed thee, O man, what is good, and what doth the Lord require of thee, but to do justice and love kindness and to walk humbly with thy God" (Micah vi. 8).

As far as concerns the Bible, its ethical teachings are generally known. Translated into all languages of the world, that holy book is accessible to every one, and whoever reads it with open eyes and with an unbiased mind will admit that it teaches the highest principles of morality, principles which have not been surpassed and superseded by any ethical system of ancient or modern philosophy.

But how about the Talmud, that immense literary work whose authority was long esteemed second to that of the Bible? What are the ethical teachings of the Talmud?

Although mainly engaged with discussions of the Law, the civil and ritual Law, as developed on the basis of the Bible during Israel's second Commonwealth down to the sixth century of the Christian era, the Talmud devotes also much attention to ethical subjects. Not only is one treatise of the Mishna (The Pirke Aboth) almost exclusively occupied with ethical teachings, but such teachings are also very abundantly contained in the Agadic (homiletical) passages which are so frequently interspersed in the legal discussions throughout all parts of the Talmud.

It must be borne in mind that the Talmudical literature embraces a period of about eight centuries, and that the numerous teachers whose ethical views and utterances are recorded in that vast literature rank differently in regard to mind and authority. At the side of the great luminaries, we find also lesser ones. At the side of utterances of great, clear-sighted and broad-minded masters with lofty ideas, we

meet also with utterances of peculiar views which never obtained
authority. Not every ethical remark or opinion quoted in that literature can, therefore, be regarded as an index of the standard of Talmudical ethics, but such opinions only can be so regarded which are
expressed with authority and which are in harmony with the general
spirit that pervades the Talmudic literature.

Another point to be observed is the circumstance that the Talmud
does not treat of ethics in a coherent, philosophical system. The Talmudic sages made no claim of being philosophers; they were public
teachers, expounders of the Law, popular lecturers. As such, they did
not care for a methodically arranged system. All they wanted was to
spread among the people ethical teachings in single, concise, pithy,
pointed sentences, well adapted to impress the minds and hearts, or in
parables or legends illustrating certain moral duties and virtues. And
this, their method, fully answered its purpose. Their ethical teachings did actually reach the Jewish masses, and influenced their conduct of life, while among the Greeks, the ethical theories and systems
remained to be a matter that concerned the philosophers only, without
exercising any educating influence upon the masses at large.

Furthermore, it must be remembered that Talmudical ethics
is largely based on the ethics of the Bible. The sacred treasure of
biblical truth and wisdom was in the minds and hearts of the rabbis.
This treasury they tried to enrich by their own wisdom and observation. Here they develop a principle contained in a scriptural passage,
and give it a wider scope and a larger application to life's various conditions. There they crystallize great moral ideas into a pithy, impressive
maxim as guide for human conduct. Here they give to a jewel of biblical ethics a new luster by setting it in the gold of their own wisdom.
There again they combine single pearls of biblical wisdom to a graceful ornament for human life.

Let us now try to give a few outlines of the ethical teachings of
the Talmud. In the first place, teachings concerning *man as a moral
being*:

In accordance with the teaching of the Bible, the rabbis duly emphasize man's dignity as a being created in the likeness of God.[1] By
this likeness of God they understand the spiritual being within us, that
is endowed with intellectual and moral capacities. The higher desires
and inspirations which spring from this spiritual being in man, are
called *Yetzer tob*, the good inclination; but the lower appetites and desires which rise from our physical nature, and which we share with

---

[1] Aboth, III, 14.

the animal creation, are termed *Yetzer ha-ra*, the inclination to evil.[1] Not that these sensuous desires are absolutely evil ; for they, too, have been implanted in man for good purposes. Without them man could not exist ; he would not cultivate and populate this earth.[2] Evil are those lower desires only in that they, if unrestrained, easily mislead man to live contrary to the demands and aspirations of his divine nature. Hence the constant struggle in man between the two inclinations.[3] He who submits his evil inclination to the control of his higher aims and desires, is virtuous and righteous. "The righteous have their desires in their power, but the wicked are in the power of their desires."[4]

Man's *free will* is expressed in the sentence : "Every thing is ordained by God's providence, but freedom of choice is given to man."[5] The ground of our duty, as presented to us by Talmudical, as well as biblical teachings, is, that it is the will of God. "Do his will as thy own will, submit thy will to his will."[6]

Although happiness here and hereafter is promised as reward for fulfillment, and punishment threatened for neglect of duty, still we are reminded not to be guided by the consideration of reward and punishment, but rather by love and obedience to God, and by love to that which is good and noble. "Be not like servants, who serve their master for the sake of reward."[7]

As a leading rule of the duties of *self-preservation* and *self-cultivation*, and, at the same time, as a warning against selfishness, we have Hillel's sentence : "If I do not care for myself, who will do it for me? and if I care only for myself, what am I ?"[8] The duty of *acquiring knowledge*, especially that knowledge which gives us a clearer insight in God's will to man, is most emphatically enjoined in numerous sentences : "Without knowledge there is no true morality and piety."[9] "The more knowledge, the more spiritual life."[10] But we are also reminded that "the ultimate end of all knowledge and wisdom is our inner purification and the performance of good and noble deeds."[11]

Next to the duty of acquiring knowledge, that of *industrious labor* and *useful activity* is strongly enjoined. It is well known that among the ancient nations in general, manual labor was regarded as degrading the free citizen. Even the greatest philosophers of antiquity, a Plato and Aristotle, could not free themselves of this deprecating view of

---

[1] Berachoth, 61a and Midrash Bereshith. IX.   [2] Midrash, ibid.
[3] Kiddushin, 30b ; Berachoth, 5a.
[4] Berachoth, 61b ; Midrash Bereshith, ch. xxxiii.   [5] Aboth, II, 15.
[6] Ibid., II, 4.   [7] Ibid., I, 3.   [8] Aboth, I, 14.   [9] Ibid, II, 5.
[10] Ibid., II. 7.   [11] Berachoth, 17a, Aboth, III, 17.

labor.[1] How different was the view of the Talmudic sages in this respect! They say: "Love labor, and hate to be a lord."[2] "Great is the dignity of labor; it honors man."[3] "Beautiful is the intellectual occupation, if combined with some practical work."[4] "He who does not teach his son a handicraft trade, neglects his parental duty."[5]

Regarding man's relation to his fellow-men, the rabbis consider *justice, truthfulness, peaceableness,* and *charity* as cardinal duties. They say, "the world (human society) rests on three things—on justice, on truth, and on peace."[6]

The principle of *justice* in the moral sense is expressed in the following rules: "Thy neighbor's property must be as sacred to thee as thine own."[7] "Thy neighbor's honor must be as dear to thee as thine own."[8] Hereto belongs also the golden rule of Hillel: "Whatever would be hateful to thee, do not to thy neighbor."[9]

The sacredness of *truth* and *truthfulness* is expressed in the sentence: "Truth is the signet of God, the Most Holy."[10] "Let thy yea be in truth, and thy nay be in truth."[11] Admonitions concerning faithfulness and fidelity to given promises are: "Promise little and do much."[12] "To be faithless to a given promise is as sinful as idolatry."[13] "To break a verbal engagement, though legally not binding, is a moral wrong."[14] Of the numerous warnings against any kind of deceit, the following may be mentioned: "It is sinful to deceive any man, be he even a heathen."[15] "Deception in words is as great a sin as deception in money matters."[16]

Peace is considered by the Talmudic sages as the first condition of human welfare and happiness, or as they express it: "Peace is the vessel in which all God's blessings are presented to us and preserved by us."[17] As virtues leading to peace, those of mildness and meekness, of gentleness and placidity, are highly praised and recommended.[18]

The last of the principal duties to our fellow-men is *charity*, which begins where justice leaves off. Prof. Steinthal, in his great work on General Ethics, remarks, that among the cardinal virtues of the ancient philosophers, we look in vain for the idea of *love* and *charity*, whereas, in the teachings of the Bible, we generally find the idea of love, mercy,

---

[1] Arist. Polit viii, 3.   [2] Aboth i, 10.   [3] Gittin, 67a.
[4] Aboth ii, 2.   [5] Kiddushin, 29a.   [6] Aboth i, 18.
[7] Ibid. ii, 12.   [8] Ibid. ii, 10.   [9] Sabbath, 30a.   [10] Sabbath, 45a.
[11] B. Metzia, 45a.   [12] Aboth i, 15.   [13] Sanhedrin, 92a.
[14] B. Metzia, 48a.   [15] Chullin, 94a.   [16] B. Metzia, 58.
[17] Mishna Oketzin iii, 12.
[18] Aboth ii, 10; iii, 12; v, 11; Taanith, 20; Gittin, 6a.

and charity closely connected with that of justice.[1] And we may add, as in the Bible, so also in the Talmud, where charity is considered as the highest degree on the scale of duties and virtues. By words of charity man proves to be a true image of God whose attributes are love, kindness, and mercy.[2] "He who turns away from the works of love and charity, turns away from God."[3] "The works of charity have more value than sacrifices; they are equal to the performance of all religious duties."[4]

Besides these principal duties in relation to our fellow-men in general, the Talmud treats also very elaborately of duties concerning special relations, as the conjugal duties, the parental and filial duties, the duties toward the old and aged, toward teachers and scholars, toward the community and the country, and even of duties in regard to animals. But the time limited for this paper does not permit us to enter into details.

To these short outlines of Talmudical ethics, let us add only a few general remarks: Being essentially a development of the sublime ethical principles and teachings of the Bible, the Talmudical ethics retains the general characteristics of that origin.

It teaches nothing that is against human nature, nothing that is incompatible with the existence and welfare of human society. It is free from the extreme excess and austerity to which the lofty ideas of religion and morality were carried by the theories and practices of some sects inside and outside of Judaism.

Nay, many Talmudical maxims and sayings are evidently directed against such austerities and extravagances. Thus they warn against the monastic idea of obtaining closer communion with God by fleeing from human society and by seclusion from temporal concerns of life: "Do not separate thyself from society."[5] "Man's thoughts and ways shall always be in contact and sympathy with his fellow-men."[6] "No one shall depart from the general customs and manners."[7] "Better is he who lives on the toil of his hand than he who indulges in idle piety."[8]

They strongly discountenance the idea of *celibacy*, which the Essenes, and later, some orders of the Church regarded as a superior state of perfection. The rabbis say: "He who lives without a wife is no perfect man."[9] "To be unmarried is to live without joy, without blessing, without kindness, without religion, and without peace."[10]

While, on the one hand, they warn against too much indulgence

[1] Steinthal. Allegemeine Ethik, p. 108. [2] Sota, 14a.
[3] Kethuboth, 61a. [4] Succah, 49a; B. Bathra, 9a.
[5] Aboth ii, 4. [6] Kethuboth. 11a. [7] B. Metzia, 86a.
[8] Berachoth, 8a. [9] Yebamoth, 63a. [10] Ibid. 62a.

in pleasures and in the gratification of bodily appetites and against the insatiable pursuit of earthly goods and riches, as well as against the inordinate desire of honor and power; on the other hand, they strongly disapprove the ascetic mortification of the body and abstinence from enjoyment, and the cynic contempt of all luxuries that beautify life. They say: "God's commandments are intended to enhance the value and enjoyment of life, but not to mar it and make it gloomy."[1] "If thou hast the means, enjoy life's innocent pleasures."[2] "He who denies himself the use of wine is a sinner."[3]

"No one is permitted to afflict himself by unnecessary fasting."[4] "That which beautifies life and gives it vigor and strength and even riches and honor are suitable to the pious, as agreeable to the world at large."[5]

Finally, one more remark: The Talmud has often been accused of being illiberal, as if teaching its duties only for Jews toward fellow-believers, but not also toward our fellow-men in general. This charge is entirely unfounded. It is true, and quite natural, that in regard to the *ritual* and *ceremonial* law and practice, a distinction between Jew and Gentile was made. It is also true that we occasionally meet in the Talmud with an uncharitable utterance against the heathen world. But it must be remembered in what state of moral corruption and degradation their heathen surroundings were at that time. And this, too, must be remembered, that such utterances are only made by individuals who gave vent to their indignation in view of the cruel persecutions whose victims they were. As regards *moral* teachings, the Talmud is as broad as humanity. It teaches duties of man to man without distinction of creed and race. In most of the ethical maxims, the terms *Adam* and *Beriyoth*, "man," "fellow-men," are emphatically used. In some instances, the Talmud expressly reminds that the duties of justice, veracity, peacefulness, and charity are to be fulfilled toward the heathen as well as to the Israelites."

"Thou shalt love thy neighbor as thyself;" this is, said R. Akiba, the all embracing principle of the divine law. But *Ben Azai* said, there is another passage in Scriptures still more embracing; it is the passage (Gen. v, 2): "This is the book of the generations of man; in the day that God created man, he made him in the likeness of God."[6] That sage meant to say, this passage is more embracing, since it clearly tells us who is our neighbor; not as it might be misunderstood, our friend only, not our fellow-citizen only, not our co-re-

[1] Yoma, 85a.   [2] Erubin, 54a.   [3] Taanith, 11a.   [4] Ibid. 22b.
[5] Baraitha Aboth, 8.   [6] f. i. Gittin, 61a.

ligionist only, but since we all descend from the common ancestor, since all are created in the image and likeness of God, every man, every human being is our brother, our neighbor whom we shall love as ourselves.

The liberal spirit of Talmudic ethics is most strikingly evidenced in the sentence: "The pious and virtuous of all nations participate in the eternal bliss,"[1] which teaches that man's salvation depends not on the acceptance of certain articles of belief, nor on certain ceremonial observances, but on that which is the ultimate aim of religion, namely, *Morality*, purity of heart and holiness of life.[2]

[1] Siphra on Lev. xix, 18.

[2] Tosephta Sanhedrin, ch. xiii; Maimonides Yad Hachazaka, H. Teshuba iii, 5; H. Melachim viii, 11.

8

SYNAGOGUE AND CHURCH IN THEIR MUTUAL RELATIONS, PARTICULARLY IN REFERENCE TO THE ETHICAL TEACHINGS.

BY DR. K. KOHLER.

Among the wondrous exhibits of this World's Exposition, the Religious Parliament just opened justly claims the greatest attention, for no matter what it may actually accomplish, it is in itself the token and pledge of the approaching realization of the glorious dream of Israel's lofty seers, the time of universal brotherhood of men and of the acknowledged universal Fatherhood of God.

The Executive Board of this Religious Congress have manifested a high sense of justice in according the place of honor to the ancient Synagogue, the Sons of Abraham, who since the dawn of history have been intrusted with the charge of proclaiming the one God every-where in order to be a blessing to all nations on earth. Not only as mother of the Church, but as holding forth this great promise of peace to united mankind, the Synagogue stands here the first in the race. Well, then, speaking on behalf of the Synagogue, I wish to bring the message of peace and good will, the sincere offer of fellowship to all religious bodies represented, but especially to the Christian Church, flesh of our flesh and spirit of our spirit, and emphasize the fact, too often overlooked, that Synagogue and Church represent but the different prismatic hues and shades, refractions of the same divine light of Truth, the opposite polar currents of the same magnetic power of Love. Working in different directions and spheres, Synagogue and Church supplement and complete one another while fulfilling the great providential mission of building up the kingdom of truth and righteousness on earth.

The erroneous impression of most people, learned or laymen, is that Judaism is identical with the Old Testament, which represents the rigidity and harshness of the law, while Christianity, founded on the New, holds forth the sweet and gentle sway of love. The German schools of Hegel and Schleiermacher went so far even as to set it down as an axiom, that whatever is liberal, cheerful, and humane in Christian thought and culture, is due to the genius of Hellas, and whatever is fanatical and austere emanates from the Semitic or Hebrew source.

Semitism against Aryanism was the watchword of David Friedrich Strauss and Ferdinand Christian Bauer before young Renan found the scientific formula which, under the baneful name of Anti-Semitism, has done such great harm when once thrown as a battle-cry and a fire-brand among the masses. Thank Heaven, historical research has begun to bridge the wide gulf and to realize that the Synagogue holds the key to the mysteries of the Church. For after all, Jesus and his Apostles were both in their life and teaching Jews. From the Jewish Synagogue they caught the holy fire of inspiration to preach the coming of the Kingdom of Heaven, for which they had learned to pray, while sending up their daily incense of devotion to the "Father in Heaven." The Synagogue was the center of their activity. There they went from Sabbath to Sabbath to offer the gospel to their Jewish brethren, and from there to enlist the attention of the pagan world around. In the Synagogue they found the sick and sorrow-laden in wait of their work of relief and miraculous cures. From times immemorial, every Jewish town or settlement throughout the vast Roman, Syrian, and Persian empires had its meeting-place for common worship and study of the law, and last, not least, for the support of the poor, the sick, and the stranger, yea, a feature which has thus far escaped the notice of writers, also for the reception, instruction, and protection of the Jewish Proselyte. These Synagogues, called by Philo schools of wisdom and virtue, prepared and plowed the soil for Christianity to reap the harvest with the large means and forces at its command. " I was hungry and ye gave me meat; I was thirsty and ye gave me drink; I was a stranger and ye took me in, naked and ye clothed me; I was sick and ye visited me in prison; and ye came unto me; for whatever ye did to the least of my brethren, ye did it unto me." In these beautiful words of the Son of Man, who as a Judge of the nations addresses the good ones in the future Judgment, Jesus refers to the organized charity work done under the roof of the Synagogue by the Essene brotherhood, and the idea expressed corresponds exactly with the Talmudical word: He who receives a stranger with Abraham-like hospitality, receives the majesty of God, the Shechina.

The entire institution of the Synagogue, unlike the Temple with its priestly sacrifice, is the creation of the Chasidim and Anavim, "the pious" and "humble ones," in the exile who first poured forth fervent prayers to God as ABINU ("our Father"); who composed the world's matchless treasury of inspiration, comfort, and devotion, the

Psalms; from whose circles emanated works of such lofty ethics as the books of Job and of Jonah, Tobit and the Testament of the Twelve Patriarchs.

It is a pity that the Essene traditions and records have not yet received the full attention they deserve, or else there could be no longer any dispute whether the claim of priority for the Golden Rule is due to Jesus of Nazareth or to Hillel, the Jewish master, forty years his anterior. Two centuries before Hillel, Philo, and Josephus, we hear already the maxim inculcated by the sons of Jacob, the Twelve Patriarchs: "Love God, thy maker, with all thy life, and love thy neighbor with all thy heart. Forgive him if he has insulted thee, and if he plots evil against thee, pray for him and do him acts of kindness, and the Lord will redeem thee from all evil." Love for God, love for man, and love for virtue and fortitude or self-consecration—these were the three rules after which the Essene brotherhood fashioned their lives while striving for the attainment of the Holy Ghost and for that perfection which was to open for them the gates of bliss in the Kingdom of Heaven. They corresponded with the trio of virtues given in Micha vi, 8: "Thou hast been told, O man, what is good and what the Lord, thy God, requires of thee: To do Justice, love Mercy, and walk humbly as an Essene (zena') with thy God," or with the three virtues singled out by the Psalmist: "Who shall ascend the hill of the Lord and who shall stand on His holy ground? He that hath clean hands and a pure heart and lips not defiled by profanity."

How remarkable, then, to find John the Baptist as he stood on the shore of the Jordan to invite all the sinners to wash off their sins in the river, and cleanse their souls by repentance, in preparation for the Kingdom of Heaven that was near, preaching, according to Josephus, the same three rules of Essene life: Love of God, love of man, or righteousness, and love of virtue or fortitude of holiness.

There was undoubtedly the power of a great originality felt when this re-risen Elijah had raised the cry of the speedy coming of the Messiah while hurling his bitter execrations against the hypocrites, those Zebuim or chameleon-like vipers that shine in all colors of piety, relying on Abraham's protection at the gates of hell. Jesus, the young Galilean, was seized by the same prophetic impetus, at first using almost the identical words of his forerunner or master. There was no reason why he should antagonize the teaching of the synagogue any more than John the Baptist did. Was not the very prayer, the so-called Lord's prayer, he taught his disciples according to Luke, prompted by a similar prayer John the Baptist had taught his followers? But he was far from rejecting the old morning prayer of the synagogue. When asked what he took to be the foremost commandment, he began like any Jew, used from boyhood up to begin the day with the benediction for the light and the law, followed by the SHMA, with that ancient watchword: "Hear, O Israel, the Lord our God, the Lord is one, and thou shalt love the Lord thy God with all thy heart;" and then he declared as the next one: "Love thy neighbor like thyself." But we have the emphatic declaration from his own lips: "Think not that I came to destroy the Law or the Prophets, I came not to destroy but to fulfill, for verily I say unto you, till heaven and earth shall pass away, one iota shall in nowise pass away from the Law till all be accomplished." Never was the so-called Sermon on the Mount intended to supplant the Law of Sinai, as the gospel of Matthew would have it. According to the far more exact report of Luke, it was the solemn consecration of the disciples to their great task of living in a state of poverty, privation, and contempt while going forth to preach the Kingdom of God. It was the Torath or Mishnath Chasidim, a code of ethics not intended for the many, but for the few elect, for those forming a holy congregation within the Congregation of Israel, the ideal servant of God, who gives his back to the smiter, only eager to be the light, and the lasting covenant of salt to humanity in the midst of decaying earthly life. "The lovers of God take insult and contumely and resent not, knowing that when they depart this earth they will shine like the sun in its full glory." This is the Talmudic version of the same Essene teachings as were couched by Jesus in the well-known words: "If you love only those that love you, if ye only reciprocate kindness and love when you are sure of its return, what are you more than the *Amme Hiaretz*, the careless and sinful people of the land (not Gentiles as the Greek writers put it). "You who desire to be sons of the Most High and to have God as Father dwell in your midst, you are expected to love your enemies, to do good to those that hate you, to bless those that curse you, and pray and fast for those that insult you. Let people in general, the men of little faith, the *Ketane Emunah*, be anxious, saying: "What shall we eat? What shall we drink? Or wherewithal shall we be clothed? As for you who ought to be heroes of faith, *Baale Emunah*, who read daily the chapter of the manna, the bread which rained daily in the wilderness for the good and for the bad, take no thought for the morrow. Behold the birds of heaven. They sow not, neither do they reap, yet your Heavenly Father feedeth them. Behold the lilies of the field, whose exquisite purple color reminds us in their very name, 'King Lilies,' of all the splendor of King Solomon's robes, and they

eclipse it, yet. Has not each hair on your head its own channel of
nurture in order not to interfere with the others? How much more
is every human being provided for in God's paternal care!" All these
beautiful sayings dropped from the lips of the Jewish Essenes of the
Talmud as well as from Jesus. Before the maxim, "Lay not up
treasures on earth, where moths and thieves may take them, but lay
up treasures for yourselves in Heaven," was penned in the New Testament, Monobaz, King of Adiabene, the Jewish proselyte, son of
philanthropic Queen Helen, in the time of Jesus, preached it to his
own greedy brothers. Let others guard against the transgressions of
the commands: "Thou shalt not murder. Thou shalt not steal, nor
swear falsely!" You who wish to ascend the hill of God and not go
down to hell's pit, beware of anger, of calling your brother by names,
of keeping sheep and goats that do the stealing for you, of swearing
in vain or profaning the name of God. "Let thy yea be yea, and
thy nay nay." This is the rule of the *Chasidim*. It was the boast and
constant prayer of these Pious Ones that neither they nor their beasts
or property should ever cause others to stumble. Hence the declama-
tion of Jesus: "Woe to the man through whom stumbling cometh.
It were better for him to have a millstone hanged about his neck and
be sunk into the bottom of the sea." Oh, how the blood curdles in
our veins as we hear Jesus cry forth: "If thy right eye, or thy right
hand cause thee to stumble, cut it off and cast it from thee; for it is
profitable for thee that one of thy members should perish and not thy
whole body go to hell." Yet the Galilean preacher was not the only
one who used this phrase. R. Tarphon has the identical saying in the
Talmud, and even the threat of Gehenna's fire against him that lusts
after another one's wife by the mere clasping of hands, is derived from
Scriptures.

THE TRUE CHARACTER OF JESUS.

These instances, which could be greatly multiplied, may suffice to
show that Jesus was a true son of the Synagogue. Still, it is a mistake on the part of Jewish scholars to place him alongside of or even
beneath Hillel, the liberal schoolman, and Philo, the mystic philosopher. Jesus belonged to no school. He was a man of the people.
In him the Essene ideal of love and fellowship took a new and grander
form. Unlike John the Baptist, he felt by the magic power of divine
love drawn to the very lowest of his fellow-creatures. With true
greatness of mind, he sat down with those shepherds, publicans, and
sinners, who, in the eye of his brother-Essenes, were doomed, and
whose very touch seemed to them to be polluting, and ate and drank
with them, saying: "I have come to save the lost sheep of Israel, not

the healthy but the sick are in need of the physician." There were Essenes who would not mind pollution while teaching the Law, saying: "Can the law be defiled? As well may fire or the great ocean, the fount of purity, be contaminated." In similar manner, Jesus asserts: "The heart that engenders evil thoughts is impure, not the hand. O ye Pharisees, ye cleanse the outside and leave the inward parts filthy with wickedness. Of you hypocrites, Isaiah well said: 'With their lips they draw near me, but their hearts are far from me.'" This is the language of a prophet, a bold reformer. There was at least one school of the Pharisees, that of Shammai, who discountenanced arbitrariness and licentiousness in regard to divorce. Among them, R. Eliezer said: "The altar of God is covered with tears when the wife of man's youth is divorced, for 'I hate the putting away,' saith the Lord through Malachi." Jesus goes straight to the bottom of the truth, saying: "God spoke: The twain shall be one flesh. What God has joined together, let not man put asunder." The same sweeping force of a great truth is voiced by him in regard to the adulterers. The ancient saints of Jerusalem would release the woman suspected of adultery from the ordeal prescribed in the Law, when the husband is not perfectly free from blame. Jesus put it in still bolder form: "Let him that is without sin first cast a stone at her." Did not the Essene, Simon ben Jochai, declare the Law of the prodigal son in Deuteronomy xxi, 18, to be but a symbolical lesson, yet of no practical bearing? Jesus, in his profound sympathy with the erring, went farther still and suggested in his parable that the prodigal son might turn out the better one after all.

And with the same courage of true love with which he reclaimed the sinner, he solicited the company of woman, the very target of Satan's arts and tricks in the eyes of the Essenes, and broke the power of her doom. At his awe-inspiring presence, Mary Magdalene, whose long hair-locks were the very network of evil spirits to entangle men into adultery, according to Talmudical tradition, melted into tears of repentance, to become his most faithful follower to the very grave and the first witness of his resurrection.

With the same freedom of the spirit, he loosens the fetters of the Sabbath laws. To be sure, the Essene brotherhood had turned the somber and austere Sabbath of priestly tradition into a day of festive cheer and thanksgiving, of social and spiritual elevation and comfort. Still the schools clung fast to the letter, forbidding even the caring of the sick, until the saints of Jerusalem, of whom Simon ben Menasea was one, declared: "The Sabbath was given to you, not you to the Sabbath." Yet how in a case of ailment without danger? Quick to

penetrate into the principle of Essene love, Jesus pursued his work of
healing on the Sabbath, saying: "The Sabbath is given to man, not
man to the Sabbath." And so in regard to the plucking and eating
ears of corn in the week preceding the Omer or thanksgiving sacrifice
of corn (the second Sabbath or week of the First Month—the term in
Luke being misunderstood).

Here certainly was a master mind, a great individuality, a religious genius, while at the same time a true Essene, the paragon and
acme of the order of Chasidim. But Providence had designated him
to be more than preacher and saint. He died as martyr of the Essene
principle. He was not the first to denounce the greedy house of the
High Priest Hanan. The Talmud has preserved the prediction of an
Essene father to the effect that "strife and greed will be the ruin of
the second temple, just as murder and idolatry were that of the first,
but (according to Jeremiah xxxi, 6), there will the *Notzrim* (watch-
men), come from Mount Ephraim, under the cry: *Yahee Hosha*,
"Lord save the people of Israel." Did these remarkable words ring
in the ears of Jesus of Nazareth, as he, bursting forth into a fire of
just indignation at seeing Jerusalem with its temple turned into a
poultry and cattle market and money-exchange for the priestly house
of Hanan, raised the cry that shook the temple to the very core: "Is
is not written: 'My House shall be called a House of Prayer for all nations;' but ye made it a den of thieves." Surely, the moment he seized
the tables and chased money changers out of the temple precincts, a new
spirit must have taken hold of him, he must have realized something like
a Messianic calling of his. And who can tell whether at that moment, so full of awe, he may not, while referring to that ancient prophecy of the Notzrim in Jeremiah, have spelled forth the holy name
of Jehovah, combining it with his own name. Joshua of Nazareth, so
as to fill the very air about him with sights and visions of the Son of
Man in the clouds and at the same time shock and alarm the bystand-
ers with the blasphemous word or act of a "seducer," corrupter,"
"blasphemer" and "magician." From that hour, on, he knew that
he would be, as he said, "delivered to the high priest and Sanhedrin
to be condemned to death, and then handed over to the Gentiles to be
mocked, scourged and crucified." He fell a victim of his Essene zeal
for the true sanctuary of God at the hands of his Roman executors
and his cowardly Sadducean judges. There was no reason for the
Jewish people at large nor for the leaders of the Synagogue to bear
him any grudge or to hate the noblest and most lofty-minded of all
the teachers of Israel. It was the anti-Semitism of the second century Church that cast the guilt upon the Jew and his religion. Jesus

died praying for the forgiveness even of his cruel murderers—a true Essene Jew.

THE EARLY CHURCH.

Before the church turned into a persecutor of the innocent Jews, the followers of Jesus, the crucified Christ, were perfect Jews themselves. Let me call special attention to the remarkable fact, not noticed as yet, as far as I can see, by any theologian, Jewish or Christian, that the entire order of prayers for the evening, for the morning and the Sabbath, was word by word taken from the Synagogue and preserved in the last two Books of the Apostolic Constitutions, a collection belonging to the second century. These early Christians never dreamed of beholding in their departed Messiah any other than a human being, lifted by his saintly martyrdom as the pure white lamb of God up to the throne of heaven, working, by his very death, as the Man of Sorrow, the ideal saint and sufferer of the 53rd chapter of Isaiah, atonement for their sins. And if they saw him in spiritual garb right near them as companion and brother at their Essene love-feasts, they beheld in him only the first among the children of God, the embodiment of all Essene virtue and holiness, the very ideal of greatness and tenderness, yet still a man and a brother, in heavenly luster shining like the sun. There is nothing in the oldest Apostolic teaching and Church manual for proselytes that was not directly taken over from the Essene tradition. Only when the simple life of Jesus was no longer remembered as a grand human pattern of purity and love, but from an atoning high priest or Passover lamb turned into a metaphysical principle of the world, the *Logos* or creative word of God; when he, who in his great humility declined even the title of "good master" because it belonged to none but God alone, was lifted above the reach and ken of humanity to be the inborn Son of God turned flesh; when finally all the mythological and gnostic elements of Egypt, Syria and Alexandria were blended with the nature of the man Jesus, then the leaders of the Synagogue apprehended danger for the pure monotheistic faith in the keeping of Israel and rejected the Church as one of the many gnostic law-destroying heretics or *Minim*. Still the intercourse was not broken off altogether, neither the anathema of the Synagogue nor the Sunday service with its hailing of the light of the first day as symbolical of the newly-risen Sun of righteousness, could eliminate the Jewish character of the Church and Sabbath worship. With the downfall of Jerusalem's temple and the final overthrow of Judea, however, the prediction of Jesus seemed fulfilled. The victory of Rome established also the triumph of the Christian cause. The Church, making peace with Rome or Babel, the beast of Satan of the Apocalypse, while disowning the mother Synagogues, set out to win the world for the man-God, while the Synagogue with its untrammeled idea of the one God and Father, spiritual and holy, with its historical past and hope for the future, clung all the faster to the Law as its center and citadel. The Church rose like the sun over the nations, while amalgamating the Pagan elements. The Synagogue protested against such compromise, while waning like the moon before the daughter religion, only hoping for a renewal. The Church, pointing to the temple ruins as the death warrant of ancient Israel, became aggressive; the Synagogue was pushed into defensive, scattered and torn into shreds. The Church became the oppressor, the Jew the martyr; the Church the devouring wolf; Israel the lamb led to the slaughter, the man of sorrow from whose wound the balm of healing was to flow for the nations.

The roles seemed exchanged. Sixteen hundred years of persecution, however, could not exterminate the remnant of Israel. The Synagogue proved its safeguard, its fortress and shield. Judaism remained, because its soul, the Law, was indestructible.

MISSION OF CHURCH AND SYNAGOGUE COMPARED.

Here, then, we come to the real issue between Church and Synagogue. It can not and ought not to be denied that the ideal of a human life held up by the Church is of matchless grandeur. Behind all the dogmatic and mystic cobwebs of theology there is the fascinating model of human kindness and love, a sweeter and loftier one than which was never presented to the veneration of man. All the traits of the Greek sage and Jewish saint are harmoniously blended in the man of Golgotha. No ethical system or religious catechism, however broad and pure, could equal the efficacy of this great personality, standing, unlike any other, midway between heaven and earth, equally near to God and to man. He was the ideal representation and symbol of the Essene brotherhood, nay, the perfect brotherhood of man personified. And if the organizations of charity connected with his name were not new to those brought up under the shadow of the Synagogue, they became the marvel of the Gentile world and accomplished wonders there. Jesus, the helper of the poor, the friend of the sinner, the brother of every fellow-sufferer, the comforter of every sorrow-laden, the healer of the sick, the uplifter of the fallen, the lover of man, and the redeemer of woman, won the heart of mankind by storm. Of what avail was the proud philosophy of the sage, or the depraved religion of the priest to a world longing for God and for redemption from sin and cruelty? The time was ripe for a social upheaval, for a millennium, in which the proud ones would be humbled again and the little ones become great. Jesus, the meekest of men, the most despised of the despised race of the Jews, mounted the world's throne to be the earth's great King. Was this not a victory of the Jewish truth, the triumph of the humanity and philanthropy taught and practiced in the Synagogue?

There were three radical effects in the system of the Church. First, all the salvation preached, the love and charity practiced, were all made dependent upon the Creed. The rich treasures of the love of the Father in Heaven were all withheld from those who failed to recognize the sonship of Christ, the sole distributor. The world was divided into believers and unbelievers; hence, all the fanaticism and cruelty toward heretics and dissenters. Secondly, to be a true follower of Christ, one had to shape life after the pattern of the Sermon on the Mount—to renounce wife, wealth and comfort, and lead the life of a monk or nun, offering no resistance to acts of injustice, and forget the claims of home and country, of state, and society, the demand of justice and manhood, of intellectual progress, and of industrial enterprise. There was no room left for civic virtue. The Church had to create a double code of ethics, one for the privileged class of monks and priests and another for the laic world; one for the faithful and one for the infidel. Here was the door opened for every vice, to the eradication of which Jesus had devoted his whole life.

And the third fault of the New Testament ethics is that it turns the human gaze too exclusively to the life beyond the grave, forgetful of the duties of life here on earth. True enough, the symbol of the cross had lent to human life a deeper pathos, and to sorrow and suffering a holier meaning. It has robbed death of its horrors and lifted the soul from an unsatisfactory existence into the realm of a richer and higher life. Hence, the sweetest strains of music, the sublimest flights of art and poetry emanated from the Church. What power of inspiration moved a Michael Angelo and a Raphael, a Palestrino and a Bach, a Dante and a Milton! What a crown of real saintliness adorns the brows of the Sisters of Mercy or the Brotherhood of Misericordia! What a nobility of sentiment is there in a Father Damien or in a La Casas! And to the asylums for orphans and waifs, to hospital and poor-house, Protestant Christianity added the school-house and the reformatory, the family Bible, and individual freedom. Still, amidst the exclusive cultivation of the emotional side, the intellectual culture of mankind was neglected. Blind faith laughed knowledge to scorn. The simplicity of ignorance became a virtue, and science a snare and a sin of the devil. Reason fell into disuse. *Credo quia absurdum* became the rule; the free-thinkers were cast out as heretics. The consequence was that the Church of Christ was finally split into Churches. The New Testament was found insufficient to serve as basis for the social structure of mankind. The Reformation, in the endeavor to establish greater freedom and broader manhood, went back to the Old Testament, to the Mosaic Law. And even in our days, we saw Henry George, and before him, Proudhon, point to the Mosaic system of land and labor division as a pattern or suggestion for their socialistic ideas and plans.

It was the Synagogue that, before and with the Mosque, held up the light of culture and learning, the torch of science, at the time when there was densest darkness round about the Church.

The Synagogue made study the first religious duty of the Jew. It was the father's pride ever since Josephus and Philo to have his sons trained well in the Law. The entire life of the Jew was soldier-like drilling for the sacred battle in behalf of truth. Let Temple and State sink into ruin, the school-house will save Israel from shipwreck, was the consoling word of Johanan ben Zakkai, the witness to the destruction of the Temple. True, the Synagogue had no life, no ideal of human greatness to point at, as uplifting and inspiring, as was presented by the Church in her Christ. All the greater scope was left for each individual to work out his own salvation. Instead of offering one perfect pattern of humanity, Judaism holds forth as maxim: "God is the only pattern of holiness; men are but strivers after the ideal." But while Judaism fails to offer a perfect human model of individual greatness, it presents a far safer basis of social ethics than the Church does. The Decalogue is a better foundation to build on than the Sermon on the Mount. Society can not be reared on mere love, an element which is altogether too pliable and yielding. Justice and law are the pillars of God's throne. Love is but the shining countenance of the divine ideal. The stability of life rests on immutable law. The tablets with the eternal Thou Shalt! and Thou Shalt Not! lend to the right and the true its awe-inspiring authority. Justice implies the right of every being. Altruism is fallacious if it disregards the claims of the *ego*. Saints are proper people for heaven; the earthly life demands men of sterner stuff, of good sense and self-respect.

Judaism is the embodiment of a noble contest for righteousness, independence, and truth. The Law rendered the Jew sober, practical, and self-reliant. Church charity often pauperized the masses. The poor Jew was upheld and uplifted by discretion and good judgment combined with love.

In the Synagogue, reason dominated over the mysteries of religion. Ceremonialism was after all a good school of temperance and privation for the Jew to concentrate his mind on the practical objects and aims of life. Dogma never became a fetter to winged thought, nor was the shadow of the dark beyond allowed to obscure the view of life. Whatever harsh things are said concerning the rigor of the law, the chief feature of the religious life of the Jew was its cheerfulness. The Sabbath meant joy for every home, nay, for every heart, even for the homeless. In the midst of all the gloom of the Ghetto, the optimistic view prevailed. "No evil but works for the good" was the general maxim. Consequently there was a willingness on the part of the Synagogue to recognize also the soul of truth in every error instead of condemning the same. I wonder whether any father of the Church ever showed such good will to the Synagogue as the leading authorities of the Synagogue, Moses ben Maimon, the great thinker of Cordova, and the Castilian poet and philosopher, Juda Halevi, displayed toward both Church and Mosque when declaring that both Jesus and Mohammed are God's great apostles to the heathen, intrusted with the task of bringing the nations of the West and East ever nearer to God, the universal Father? And which of the Churches has a word to match the grand declaration of the rabbis made at the very time when the gospels were composed, that "all the good and the just among the heathen have as good a share in the bliss of the world to come as the descendants of Abraham"—a view which became the general recognized dogma of the Synagogue.

Thus, in the great battle between Moslem and Christian, between faith and reason, between love and hatred, the Jew stood all through the ages pointing to a higher justice, a broader love, to a fuller humanity, ever waiting and working for the larger brotherhood of man. While standing in defense of his own disputed rights, the Jew helped, and still helps, in the final triumph of the cause, not of a single sect, or race, or class, but of humanity; in the establishing of freedom of thought and of conscience, in the unfolding of perfect manhood, in the rearing of the Kingdom of Justice and Love, in which all creeds and nationalities, all views and purposes, blend like the rainbow colors of the one bright light of the sun. Judaism begins and ends with Man—"Not unto us, O Lord, to Thy name belongs the glory." Not a single man, however great, not a single Church, however broad, holds the key to many-sided Truth. Like this great parliament—humanity voices the truth in many forms and tunes.

Sinai, cloud-enwrapped, stands out lonely in the desert, crying forth: Move onward, ye wandering shepherds. Golgotha, with its golden aureole around the brow of one single saintly sufferer, forms a high peak in the promontory of truth and love, but fails to offer standing-room for all God-seeking tribes of mankind. But Zion, with all the hills of God and all the worshiping nations and ages round about, towers far higher yet. When life's deepest mysteries are once all spelled forth and God is sought and found, revealed and felt everywhere, when to the ideals of sage and saint that of the perfect lover of man has been joined, the seeker after all that is good, beautiful, and true, then Church and Synagogue, Jew and Gentile, the pursuer of love and the pursuer of righteousness and truth, will have merged into one Church Universal, into a humanity in the likeness of God, into the city whose name is. "The Lord is there."

UNIVERSAL ETHICS OF PROFESSOR HEYMANN STEINTHAL.

By RABBI CLIFTON H. LEVY.

We have before us the work of a modern Jewish Philosopher, in whose absence we must look to his written self for light and instruction. Let it be our task to find the "objectified spirit" of Steinthal in the thoroughgoing, lofty-minded pages warm from his brain and heart. What follows is presented as the digest of his work, in as faithful adherence to his words and spirit as possible.

INTRODUCTION.

Ethics teaches wherein the perfection and destiny of man consist—treats of character, freedom, duty, and accountability. It is practical philosophy; *i. e.*, the philosophy (theory) of practice or the practical life of man. Superadded to the science must be the impulse to goodness. In Germany, ethics is relegated to the church, is considered tiresome, and lacks the interest belonging to natural science, historical research, and anthropology. But Schiller and Goethe have shown the need of esthetics and ethics, so that no poem or picture lacking these may look for favor or immortality.

Back of all theology and philosophy lies ethics as the moral consciousness manifest in moral life and proverbs. Primitive men include morality in religion as the command of God. In times of unbelief, noble spirits are needed to restrain those who think there is no morality, no duty, no virtue.

The task of ethics to-day is to implant idealism in the mechanical methods of the world—ethics alone can redeem us from mechanicalism.

The scientific form of ethics is in the treatment of the eternally moral laws of commerce, of labor, of ends and means, of good and duty, of socialism in good doing.

No new categories are found in logic, no new virtues in ethics, but the principles lying behind these virtues must be improved and classified. Ethics takes its place among the sciences first in the light of freedom. The measure of freedom is the first step forward. It is deductive in all its methods and distinct from the history of morals. Ethics is the theory of conscious judgment, is purely formal, and expresses itself in the praise or blame of deeds.

We feel ourselves as feeling, we ourselves are the only object of all possible feelings, which are modifications of ourself. Perception and thought are transitive, feeling is intransitive or reflexive. Only the soul feels, but there are feelings of sense and of spirit—these are not subjectively distinguished but by the cause either bodily or spiritual—they depend on whether we feel a stone or a thought. The ego is the center of these feelings which are altogether a matter of relation. We have the following classes of judgment according to the relation of feeling :

1. Is any thing pleasant? Judgment of feeling in narrower sense.

2. Is a means useful? Practical judgment.

3. Is a given knowledge true? Logical judgment.

4. Is a given form beautiful? Esthetic judgment.

5. Is a given deed moral? Ethical judgment.

Ethics seeks the eternally valuable and humanly necessary, the moral may however be pleasant and useful. Ethical feeling is not awakened by the merely useful or pleasant, but by the beautiful and good. Something of the objective is superadded. Being not pathological but objective, a criticism is possible, as in logic. Their existence is proven in facts—they are unified, and are not pathologic. Since what separates objective feeling from the pathologic connects it with knowledge (perceptions), it is not egoistic, not furthering or limiting life, not helping or harming, but only awakens feeling. It is not egoistic or egotistic, but omitting the *we* pronounces a deed good or bad, *i. e.*, it is objective. Moreover it is absolute fixing the worth and universal value. In simple feeling we destroy the pleasant by enjoying it—in esthetics the pleasure of the beautiful is indestructible. Their reproductive force is greater than mere sensation by the addition of logical thought, *e. g.*, axioms, principles, abstract laws, but bodily action exhausts force. The ethical-esthetic is altogether objective, dealing with *forms* of the object. Hedonism is not ethical, dealing with matter. The objective feelings are formal, seizing upon relations, not matter, as there is esthetically a pure form, so is there ethically. Form is the unity of the many. The esthetic and ethical differ from the scientific, logical, and psychological, because they are without activity for the power of existence. The statue may be material, but it is artistic in form only—form is the unity of the many, a synthesis making an ideal object only. Pure form is the idea, therefore formal feeling may be termed ideal. Colors harmonize by the unity, not the quality of the separate colors. The separate syllables of a verse are immaterial, but the verse as an artistic whole has an ideal existence, ideal and objective in esthetic feeling. This formal feeling may awaken the pathologic, the *ethos* has its *pathos*. Pathologic feeling is practically weighty—the formal is purely theoretic, a knowledge-feeling. Ethics is the highest human dominion. The deed does not make the ethics (ethos), it is practice and belongs to reality ; ethics comes from ethical feeling only which judges the will and begets the deed.

Then considering *Ideas in general and the idea of good in particular* the opposition between Idea and precept, law and concept, must be noted. There is no generally accepted definition of idea, but it may be said that the idea *is a category of judgment*, not of perception. Ideals precede ideas in human consciousness. Before the idea of virtue is conceived the father is a model to the son, the teacher to the pupil. The idea-content of virtue was at first only thought in this form of different models or types. Then the qualities were abstracted from a number of types. As it seems impossible to combine all beauties in a single face, so we have various ideals. The idea is the one creative thing, the one active power in mankind. The original model is the idea which man has, the existence of which he recognizes in later life. Any thing is beautiful or good because it corresponds to the model. The model is thus and so, because the idea furthers it. Formal feeling announces immediately the acceptation or rejection of any thing, the ground of which is *criticism*. The theory of criticism is the exposition of the content of the idea. The idea differs from concept and law in being the object of formal feeling—not lying in things, but in their relations. Laws contain material determinations, ideas only formal, therefore formal feeling is also called ideal. Neither is the esthetic idea a mathematical proportion or a law. The ethical forms a real unity of the various parts, not a mere combination of them, this being reached by intuitive procedure, not by discursive.

The idea of a picture differs from the concept, one knowing it as beautiful, the other as an actuality. The ear furnishes esthetic unities, almost purely—the polysyllable presents a spiritual unity when heard. The special concept conceives a thing as actual, the esthetic makes an intelligible mode, *e. g.*, a picture, a pure form. The idea needs homogeneousness and reciprocal penetration of the members of relations; tone combines with tone, color with color—there is a sort of spiritual chemistry. Categories are the forms of processes which, like ideas, are creative. The ethically good is objective in and for

9

itself, and not relative to any one or any thing. Its province is to teach what is good or bad. Good and bad are the categories of ethics on which ethical feeling lays hold for the will. The will is good or bad objectively, not subjectively only. The good will is good only for the ethical feeling of approbation—it may be absolutely good. The will, not as power, but according to conscious relations, is good—forms the ideal picture.

When *the form and structure of ethics is to be considered, its character must be fully stated*. In speaking of the doctrines of virtue, good, and duty, we come to the consideration of their development. At first man sought favors of God by piety and morality, aiming at happiness, and this is the germ that is still in process of development. It was found that the most pious were not always the most happy, and it was concluded that the highest happiness lies in the possession of virtues. Ethics became the teaching of virtue, and then of the highest good. Is the highest good virtue? Is duty virtue? Then ethics is duty. Good, virtue, duty form a circle lying in the formal feeling of morality. Hedonism is impossible for ethics, because it is empiric. The popular doctrine of salvation is a refined doctrine of desire. Goods and duties are also empiric, furnishing facility only. Ethics teaches the good relations of will-ideas. Ethics resembles esthetics, in being the idea of the good, as the latter is the idea of the beautiful.

We shall *divide ethics into four parts* for treatment. First, the essence of a good will; second, a full presentation of ethical life in human consciousness; third, of individuals, virtue, duty and character, freedom, obligation and responsibility, the " phenomenology of morality." Then the depths of ethics, the basis of obligation, of ethical furtherances, the metaphysics of ethics.

As to the *style of ethics*, it is not sermonic, but treats of the relation of idea and reality, that ideas are relations of will—they are nowhere and every-where. It depends upon history, as it is filled with the past, and lifts humanity to a higher plane. It presents what is eternally good, praiseworthy and true. There is a distinctly ethical judgment, and the difference in morals does not impugn the absolute character of ethical ideas. No one can develop ethics *a priori*, losing sight of man's struggles in morality; it analyzes morality. We trace the psychological processes of ethics, holding in view, not the individual, but (as seen in the fourth part) the ideal essence of humanity, without ignoring experience. But ethics is formal and history is material; it can deal with the abstract only. Moral laws are mere ideas with no relation to power or matter. Ethics teaches with consideration of what has been, what should be; it teaches the eternal form of will with the inner *ought*, not considering *must* or *can*. The law of freedom is the content of the moral command of ethics. We should speak of moral commands, not of moral laws. Freedom is not real—a must, but a should, a command, a holy obligation.

So much by way of introduction.

PART I.

The first part treats of the *ethical doctrines of Ideas*. The ethical ideas must treat of all possible objects of the will, not as psychologic, but as facile and quiescent. and also of the relations between wills. The ideas may be thus enumerated :

1. The idea of ethical personality on which rests the adjustment of every will to ethical ideas. That the judgment of self so trained pleases, and the non-performance displeases.

2. The ethical personality bears a similar relation to others of the same kind, including them in itself, and aiming at furthering them. Well-wishing.

3. Two, several, many combine their wills into one, produce the idea of unity.

4. Each ethical personality gives like regard to the other, that the will of others for their own will is so far limited that it does not thwart it, but is acknowledged and sanctioned. The idea of Righteousness.

5. The idea of perfection finally lies in the grade in which the ethical personality establishes ethical ideas in controlling force over its will. Each idea is independent, no one derived from the others, only in the form of will or mind. This form supports the will as the essence of *intelligible* rule. The ideas are in so far dependent as they complete or supplement one another. Each idea presents all morality from one side, all being synonymous to one another and morality. The three ideas, well-wishing, union and righteousness, are the three possible accords of movements of the will.

As man reasons without knowing logic, so unconsciously he judges ethically. Ethical science aims to raise this ethical consciousness to clearness and precision, as logic does speech and thought.

The first point concerning the moral personality is that ethical character demands judgment and it demands not only the harmonizing of the will with the ethical model, but must finally develop the will. The will must be subserved under an ethical idea. We can not think of the idea without thinking of the will. Ethical insight must compel the will to act, and impel to the formation of resolution. The first ethical idea is thus formulated. "That will alone is satisfactory to man (be it what it may, according to ethical examination), which is in harmony with ethical insight; and *vice versa*, the will which man resolves upon (notwithstanding ethical examination) in opposition to ethical insight is unsatisfactory. The will and ethical insight must be homogeneous.

Ethics is the doctrine of mind—the will is only the active means of mind. Mind is the ethical peasonality, and it is by morality that a man becomes an intelligible person, citizen of the intelligible kingdom. He must be veracious and conscientious. Man has the facility for ethics and the relation of the individual to his idea makes character. Man is his own moral creator, artist and picture in one, the essential to character being morality. He must be in harmony with others, for egotism and lust are barred out of ethics.

The second idea, well-wishing, is taught first and best in the Bible. Love is sought in vain among the four cardinal virtues of the other ancients. The Bible gives two forms of well-wishing—righteousness and love. Well wishing consists in a relation of feeling between two persons, binding them together. One takes the other into his consciousness. His essence and activity are absorbed, joy and care are superadded. This may be partial in energy or depth. It is truest in benevolence to all, in love and self-sacrifice—giving hope or alms. Its opposites are revenge, jealousy, envy, or vexing of any sort. The will, wish, thought of the interest of others should be the motive of our will. It is not like righteousness, a movement of character, but it is a dedication of the entire personality, helping others toward moral life. Thought and feeling are also ethical, in forming relations between personalities. Well-wishing is more than doing good, feeling is essential and primary,—will is secondary and accidental. The spirit of man is full of character—it is moral, because permeated by moral will, thinking, and feeling. The spirit is proportionate to benevolence. It differs from sympathy, as it does not wait for evil to show itself, and the latter is without will, psychological, pathological, and unethical. We may be filled (and should be) with benevolence for the wicked with whom we have little sympathy. Sympathy is a natural gift, well-wishing is an ethical idea.

God is the living absolute goodness. Therefore man should serve Him with all thoughts, feelings, and efforts—that is the meaning of loving God with heart, soul, and might—this ethics furthers. Righteousness will show what man owes to man—so much that nothing remains for benevolence. These two go hand in hand.

The Biblical command to love our neighbors displays the idea of legal equality, and Lev. xix presents our duties in an ascending ethical scale. It commends kindness to the poor and the stranger—forbids stealing, lying, robbery; forbids the keeping of the pledge over night, taking advantage of weakness; enforces to righteousness in judgment, forbidding slander, hatred, oppression, even of enemies. As monotheism perfected right, it also deepened right.

The third idea—*Union*—is the essence of all construction—the foundation of society as a community for working together. Not merely similarity of spirit or moral essence, but a union is formed for a common purpose. We have the objective relation of will forming an idea distinct from well-wishing. Union is for an end, not merely mutual like benevolence. Union destroys egotism, making each for all and all for each. The combination must be for good ends or it is out of harmony with the ethical idea. From good men only does good come. The bad want what they do not need, and do not want what they do need; but they know what they are doing. A band of robbers is bound by egotism, not by the *idea* of union. Those unions are good which are formed for lasting, future benefit, and are not a fortuitous coming together like those in a car.

Race hatred, class hatred, religious hatred, impede and prevent true unity. The copartnership for gain is no higher ethically than the single merchant. A factory is an ethical unity only when culture has changed its character from mere money making to a real unity. In political and religious bodies lie greater possibilities for thought of *all*. The spirits of many should be unified to the spirit of a unity. The adherence to our native land, our people, our religion, is the highest evidence of this idea in the moral life of men. Confirmation in a religion makes a man religious, not being born into it. A man is a citizen only when he does something for the state. The unity of spirits is no quiescent relation, but is a moral deed. The union of idea may be formulated thus: "The single will and common will are forthwith absorbed into one another."

The fourth idea—*right and righteousness.* Judicial and ethical right are very different, but right is never against good morals. The jurist condemns the thief for breaking the law; the ethical man censures him for being immoral. Ethically, we refrain from wrong, not because it is against the law, but because it is immoral. The jurist omits feeling—he regards the overt act, considers the act by rule, not by idea. Right assists well-wishing by giving it room and removing hindrances, and therein it is moral. Right may be defined as "*the system of conditioning by restriction, by which social, moral ends are made safe.*" The stream of morality guides the right, which, as the science of right, is non-ethical, and becomes ethical only when motives are considered.

Methods of trade are often selfish and not for the common good, instead of being guided by the idea to live and let live. Right and duty should be conceived as one. Peace is the cradle of right—the proper peace which flows from the triumph of right, not might.

Rights are innate; we love rights because we are. *Not right in itself is ethical, but righteousness—considering the rights of others. The only positive right is the right of recognition of human worth, i. e., our ethical personality, by considering our moral will. Righteousness consists in recognizing the worth of others, the value of their will, whereby the righteous become of value to others.* The contest, not for right, but for the recognition of right, is in the highest degree moral—the striving for the recognition of right in the community is a highly moral task. Is right derived from the feeling of right, or *vice versa?* Codified law is built upon custom—even unwritten law is not to be violated. It is immanent in commerce and is developed with ever increasing complexity. The essence of right is threefold: it is objective in the law book and commerce, subjective in the spirit of those constituting the society of right, and last, moral.. Man is within his right always by the recognition of right. The objective and subjective may disagree in the application, producing wrong right. Ethics is the judge above laws and maxims, is the feeling for right in the community—according to it, all history is the development of morality or of intelligible rule.

When we view the right of punishment or coercive force, ethics censures its wrong use, giving no absolute rule of punishment. Ethics forbids the return of ill-will for ill-will. Punishment is warranted, only for betterment. The state has no right to do this, while society may. We may even have the combination of right wrong in exceptional cases. Right, being purely formal, could not unfold itself freely without having been written down, so that improvement is possible. Laws are needed, to be fixed and certain. The ideal of just punishment is that the violator punishes himself by weakening his consciousness of right. In the life of a nation, the ethical personality is broadened and made intelligible. In Rome and England, where there was greater freedom, great characters were developed; in Germany, where the development of right has been checked, the feeling of right is weak, while that of well-wishing is stronger. Right, unlike benevolence, is or is not—but is not graded.

The fifth idea, *perfection,* contains the final effort of ethics, and is synonymous with morality. Man should be more and more a moral personality. *Becoming more perfect in morality is pleasing (to ethical feeling). Retrograding or standing still is displeasing. Equality displeases.* Ethics is not merely interpretative and analytic, like esthetics, but announces man's duty to be the objectifying of the ethical ideas in consciousness in ever higher degree. *Activity is demanded of every one.* Perfection must be of moral harmony; the perfection of evil is like a glass, full of emptiness. In practice and morality, the one changes circumstances, the other changes the will and causes harmony. As the wicked perfect evil, they deserve blame; their perfection is the greatest imperfection. Imperfection may be in ethical insight or in will—either without the other is imperfect and unethical.

Blind obedience is will without insight, unintelligible and unfree; tyranny alone demands it. Strength and power are differentiated thus: as the former works, the latter rules; one is mechanical, the other ethical. Ideas have no strength, are not strong—but they may have power. For the idea of perfection, they reach the grade of the power which the ethical insight has over the will. The power of ethical insight over bodily powers forms the moral character. Perfection is proportionate to the love of goodness—the perfect man works for moral ends with all his powers, he seeks for opportunities, and brings others to morality. The intensity of the love for the moral is the full power of the rule of ethical insight over the will. This insight must be broadened and intensified. Thought and doing are higher forms of benevolence—*e. g.*, the advance from caring for the individual sick to the building of hospitals, etc. This idea rules the understanding for correct judgment and methods, industry, order, etc. Not character alone is furthered by the idea of perfection, but individual character. "That is like him," should be said of each and all. Any dogma that is ethical must not oppose what morality sets up. "God alone is Lord in heaven and on earth" means the good, the moral, is the only power by which human life is regulated—and there is no consideration of paradise or hell (Ps. lxxiii, 25). Progression or retrogression expresses merely the relation, progress is relative. Ethical insight should grow in loftiness of ideas and all clearness of view, in rule over the will—the means of presentation and morality should grow, just as physical means increase in the technique of art. The means of presentation of morality is as a whole called culture or civilization. All should work morally to further the rule of the intelligible spirit. Helping others is morality. The development of language and writing, the telegraph, the railroad, science—all are aids to this end. What is the Intelligible Rule? Its first element is a self-conscious, free spirit, dealing with all the activity of thought. By it only we live a spiritual life. It is the objective morality of the highest thought of man, and its real deed, its absolute and highest worth. Man enters it, not by fate, as he enters nature, but by his moral activity. Science and labor assume a new meaning. Man perfects nature by cultivation (Ps. viii). The unified product of the human race is the combination of subjective morality and the objective moral regulation of the world. Ideas are the forces working in and behind all—they become objective as realized in each.

PART II.   PRESENTATION OF IDEAS OR THE FORMS OF NEW LIFE.

Morality, like the soul, is in every body; the upbuilding of morality is our highest good and our solemn duty. Desire is the feeling of power, and spirit has no other possession than activity. The house, state, etc., are the establishments of morality; are objective morality, established by moral work, and make moral life possible.

The Family and the Home.—The home is the moral cell, the smallest structure of the moral organism, its heart and pulse, the hearth of benevolence. Marriage forms the smallest community. "It is not good for man to be alone;" it is impossible for a man to be good, true, fully human alone. There are four principal tendencies of morality—benevolence and gratitude, right and duty. In true marriage these melt imperceptibly into one another; their claim is granting, their granting is the claim. It is one life divided into two persons. The two concerned first know each other in married life. They grow toward resemblance in character, temperament, habit, and even in appearance. The passion of youth is soon over, furnishing no inspiration. Passion does not make the exact choice—"only thee and none other." The happy man or woman tries to be worthy of his or her happiness; the unhappy one searches for the defect and tries to remedy it. Divorce is the most sorrowful of necessities if the ethical end of marriage is impossible—if moral generalness and general morality can not be established. Children give to marriage a wider, moral task—make the full ethical school of life. Duty is proportionate to education both for parents and the community. The first human, moral feeling of the child is gratitude. The more feeling bond is between child and mother; the more earnest between child and father.

The relations between brothers and sisters are a most important source of development, a preparation for life. The idea of right is freely developed: partiality does not arouse jealousy, but a sense of wrong.

Labor, though mechanical, prepares for the ethical. Prudence distinguishes men from animals. It is derived from labor, as is breadth of view. A man's occupation has considerable influence in forming his character; a farmer is apt to be higher morally than a shepherd or hunter. The last merely destroys, the second preserves, the first produces, and from him comes the division of labor, of produce, protection, and the founding of a permanent home. At first men sacrificed to the gods to gain their good will, but as their judgment developed (keeping pace with occupation), they formed the consciousness of the duties of benevolence and right; duties to God and men were considered as laws of God. The ideas of clothing and dwelling seem to have aroused the ethical ideas of shame and modesty. Man is ashamed to be an animal. Shame is not foolish; man is no animal any more than a statue is a block of stone. Men cover the flesh to forget it. Good morals are a product of shame and modesty, or rather these are the guards of morals. True speech is that which praises the good and censures the bad. As physical existence is necessary for ethics, bodily purity is of importance; the shelterless and unclothed lack and need morality. The house and clothes correspond to the person—show individuality.

The *community and its organization* show moral tendencies developed from the home. It is not a mere number of houses, but a unity. Want leads to labor, labor to the unifying of powers; new wants are then awakened. Man is not simply a pleasure seeker. The prudent man is never satisfied, and can always be happy, both according to the idea of perfection. The source of all advancement is not the desire for pleasure, but for work. Where one generation (the parents) is satisfied, the next generation (the children) is dissatisfied. History is an account of the self-elevation of man to constantly increasing morality. As the animal functions are developed to ever higher activity, so are the spiritual powers; there is a sharper individualization. The division of labor makes men more dependent on one another. Every series of needs and activities is objective morality constructing the rule of spiritual manhood over natural existence. Science is needed for art and religion, industry and trade, forming the perfection of labor. Babylon, Phœnicia, and Egypt were first scientific. Science itself is not moral, but the desire for it is moral. Parents, teachers, and schools are needed for instruction. There should be a younger *community*, while parental or parochial schools make the differences in station too distinct. They should learn human similarity and equality, and the schools should give that universal human and practical religious teaching so much needed. The church and school should be kept apart. Men are in so far irreligious as they are irrational and benighted. The test of the schools is in the citizens. Press and libraries are needed for further culture.

Labor.—It becomes ethical by conscientiousness alone. Work as *well* as possible! Commerce works ethically in binding all men together for honesty, the unity of mankind becomes an active unified society. The ethical essence of trade lies in the confidence in honesty. There can be no business without credit. Confidence is good-willing, and rests in doing what is promised, keeping faith. The settlement of debts contains no ethical idea any more than price; it is altogether material and needs no good will. Self-preservation is the nerve of trade. Trade demands *no deceit.* The general interest must be considered and unified with self-interest. Commerce is the most complex of machines, demanding industry, order, punctuality, honesty, conscientiousness, trust, and self-sacrifice. It is the state of birth and school of morality. The ethical view of trade may be thus stated: 1. General and private interest may and should coincide. 2. The idea of self-preservation and satisfaction do not exclude ethics. 3. The ethical view of commerce is the generalization of self-preservation and pleasure through right and truth. It becomes artistic and scientific.

Art makes us *see* the ideal truth of all appearances, forces us to recognize the ethical worth of circumstances in life for the rule of morality. The artist has his truth and objectivity, his morality as an artist. Music and the drama influence the formal feeling and draw us from egoistic interests toward interest in universal human fate. Luxury is not the true aim of art, but the moral is; it tries to make beautiful the unfortunate of the earth. In public museums it gives pleasure to all the people, teaching them to love the good and the beautiful; this is its true sphere.

Religion has the highest place, and is proportionate to benevolence, righteousness, honesty, conscientiousness, and truth. It is nothing or all. Insight needs inner power (will), love for the good; religion is their inspiriting for all that is good, true, and beautiful. This may hold even for atheists, since belief is only a form of religion. When we recognize the source of goodness, truth, and beauty in God, religion becomes the inspiriting of man for God. For the atheist it is an animation toward the "intelligible rule of all humanity." Religion is a special force in the whole of ethical life and of great power. The religious community is a union for its end. There have been errors doubtless, but the church has done much for morality, science, art, and civilization. It influences and permeates all of life, the real personality. It keeps us in purity, lifts us up, gives us power and trust in the moral battle of life, trust in sorrow, moderation in joy and good fortune, and makes us active in all the affairs of life.

Recreation is activity for no end but for itself. Play is the curse of ethical earnestness in life. It is warranted for assisting the recovery of the sick, or when it is employed to lift us to higher thoughts (Ex. xxiii, 1 ; xxxi, 17). The Sabbath seems to be given for spiritual recovery.

State.—Rights and duties are always for ends in the community ; the state and laws always for their overseeing. Right is the end of the state, the state is the means. It must be either a social state or a rights state. It must watch over and not order, and should do nothing which individuals or corporations can do well. That state is ethically best which furthers the morals of its citizens, which awakes all the powers of the community and gives every man opportunity according to his power. It is ever striving to make positive right ideal. There should be an inner peace—not such as one would break if he had the power. Control by right means for high ends is ethical, so that a war may be ethical. The state has both the duty and right of compulsion. The good citizen must obey laws, even those that he considers bad. The *Citizen* has the right to life, even as an unborn child—the right also to nurture and education. The child has the right to prove himself moral, by bringing himself to ethical activity. It is moral to consider a person as a person, not as a thief ; each must judge the other ethically as a member of the state ; lies are outlawed. there is harmony between the person and society. The citizen is a free person, sacred in thought and religion, free for union and free in speech. Foolishness is sufficient punishment of the fool. Freedom of speech and press give religious freedom. Besides, he has the right to the choice of home, of wife, and of representatives. The duties corresponding to these rights are those of obedience to law and payment of taxes. The schools should teach these duties and also admiration of the state. National unity comes from the equal ensouling of all society ; the same well-wishing, feeling of duty, and consciousness of right, taste for the beautiful, sense of truth, efforts for good. The similarity of ethical ideas in individuals forms a harmonious figure of all national life. The unity of national spirit finds expression in its classic literature.

Property is ethically indifferent. Occupation or possession signifies a relation of person and thing. Property is a relation of a person to a community in regard to a thing. The right to property is only conditional, and the common weal takes precedence of right to property.

All property is only a *fee*, of which the community is feudal lord. The ground of property is labor; what a man produces is his.

Excursus on Socialism.—It may be traced historically from Thomas More. Things are of no value, save as supplying a demand, through labor and difficulty of production or talent needed. The *worth* can not be paid, as ideal only pays for ideal. There is no difference whether the state or individual pays in money or material. There is no ethical activity as to mine and thine, no opportunity for objective right, no opportunity for benevolence in material Socialism. He will breathe a purer spiritual air without egoism. Man does not change his nature, but his circumstances in higher socialism. The amount paid for a great work buys ink and paper; appreciation is the real payment: science will be helped. There will be no weakening of the powers of genius by need. The socialistic tendency of human life is an ideal to be desired ethically. 1. No moral consistency may be intentionally destroyed; immorality destroys itself. Socialism is not to be made, but is to born of society. It is not a mere question of clothes. 2. State socialism is a contradiction in terms. It should be a free community of citizens, and should flow from our free united life. 3. It is no self-delusion, no mistaking of the present, no false hope for the future. The future will grow from the present; all good tends to this end. Absolute equality is foolishness. Be free within, despise vanities, fight distress, are the watch-words.

Relations between Persons should be actuated by sympathy first, by well-wishing afterward. Those between master and servant are in the department of right, not good-will. Conscientiousness is a necessary quality of service, whether recognized or not. Honor seems to be needed for merchant, mechanic, and citizen, as well as the ideal of faithfulness and skill. Consideration for the rights of others is also commendable and necessary, as evinced in giving room on the street, or apology for unintentional injury. The ethical idea of friendship is strengthened by putting aside the ego. Careless criticism of another is unethical: gossip is not even criticism. Well-wishing should not expect gratitude. Gratitude is good-will for good-will and a good deed, while envy needs no deed.

The two Sexes.—Though woman may not equal man in bodily or spiritual strength, yet many women surpass many men, though their power is not alike in quality on account of the differing organs through which the strength works. She has a peculiar spiritual place, and applies general ethics well. The male and female spirit are mutually supplementary. She has the smaller and probably finer brain; her power is smaller and weaker, but fine: man's is large and strong, but coarse. She is the more sharply individualized. It is unethical to consider woman as a slave. The realm of ideas is divided between man and woman. Marriage is the feeling of individuality in the individuality of another. Monogamy is the only moral form of living together. Free love is not free, because liberty is not the right to wish different things at different moments. Love is the fruit of moral effort and labor. Man and woman are alike designed for marriage, which means personal surrender. No socialism can put aside marriage. The child needs love most in its bringing up, and the mother understands this well. It would be the destruction of family life for man and woman to have the same work to do. Man works with his arms and hands, woman with her fingers; she becomes a good teacher only by womanliness. We need first healthy mothers, not weakened by attempts at philosophic thinking. Her thinking is intuitional; man's logical; her sphere, purification. Woman is not limited to the home, but has an equal right in society. She purifies the home and human intercourse. She compels the observance of the social rules. While righteousness seems to be the natural principle of man, benevolence belongs to woman; she is and should be foremost in charitable work.

Culprits. – The criminal should surrender himself and repay the community, but (ethically) the community should not exact payment. The state as society must remember well-wishing. Capital punishment is useless; but as long as man holds it to be necessary, it is so.

Our Dead.—The corpse should be considered, like the picture of of the man when living; we should respect it for what it has held.

Remarks.—Exert yourself to carry out the good even against the will of others, but with good will and persuasion, not force. Our duties are empirically given, not *what*, but *how* is ethical. Good consists simply in the harmony of ideas. A system of ethics can not cover every incident in life, but man should be prudent, examine his powers and limitations, and help on the good. Are there higher and lower duties? Yes, there is a system of ends forming the " Intelligible Kingdom." By system and love the small may become great; therefore, the small is not to be neglected. Revolution or well-wishing by dynamite is an ethical, logical impossibility; it is ethical disharmony. Without the transmutation of formal feeling into pathologic feeling, there can be no good. The end does not justify the means.

PART III.   THE PSYCHOLOGICAL MECHANISM OF ETHICAL PROCESSES.

The whole moral condition of men is a completely determined product of nature. Mind is dependent upon body, for man sees through the eyes, thinks through the brain. As the central organ (brain and spine) works through nerves on other parts of the body, so does the soul work through the body on the outer world. Sensory, sympathetic, and motor nerves are the ground elements of our soul-life. Consciousness and the unity of our sensations are regulated by certain laws. The sympathetic nerves convey sensations of health or sickness; feeling and perception lead to motion, then this same motion becomes feeling and perception. Movements may be thus divided: 1. Movements following bodily feeling. 2. Imitating perceptions arousing movements. 3. Spiritual feelings causing movements. 4. Perceptions arousing actions, seizure, keeping time, etc. 5. Reproduction of feelings may cause reproduction of movements. 6. Imitative actions. 7. Volitional actions. The first three are called reflex-unvolitional, the three latter impulse actions. The will is also a spiritual impulse. Reflex and impulse actions are teachers of the will—show what may be willed, as does a teacher or instructor. Members may incite to actions, either of fear or bravery, witness a panic or an assault. Suggestion by example is almost overpowering, even compelling murder in certain cases. Within the presentation lies a strong impulse for the will, a motor power. Man leaves the animal impulses behind by soul development. Motive and resolution must accompany the deed to its conclusion, while the animal merely seeks food. A natural aid to the will lies in the law that repetition of activity makes dexterity or habit. Habits make tendencies or inclinations, of which the noblest is love.

Prudence and Will.—Herder called prudence the distinctive mark of man. It is the checking of inclinations or impulses. By prudence spirit is made lord of the body and nature. Culture is the instrument by which we control the feelings. Muscular reflex-action is controlled by will-action. The uneducated can read letters aloud only. We need prudence and self-control. Prudence is reached by attention, labor and will, directed to presentations, *e. g.*, tone-production by a singer. He who reflects, acts prudently. The immoral must not be yielded to, even in part, or reflex movements may compel action in weak moments.

Freedom and Culture.—Freedom is no psychologic fact. Health of soul is distinct from it. It may be asked, why be the slave of morality and not of desire or passion. Man must be bodily sound to be free, but it must be in *moral* society. Freedom presupposes spiritual health, while the most talented may be the greatest scoundrels. That freedom means that man is *free* from something is not the real signification. But philologically, from its root meaning, free means beauti-

ful, lovely.   There are five classes of freedom.   1. Mechanical freedom
from bonds or chains.   Being according to law, is freedom; it is not
slavery that we can not fly.   2. Physiologic freedom, according to the
laws of body, no illness.   3. Psychologic freedom, according to the laws
of mind, consciousness clear.   4. Free citizenship; free from unlawful
checks.   5. Moral freedom; free from selfishness and passion; bound
to the furthering of morality.   We may be free in wishes, but not in
will.   We should not want the false, the untrue, the immoral.   The
spirit is bound by unculture; freedom is the synonym of morality.   It
is no power, but a category of the judgment.   Rightly do we term the
spirit a free power, although dependent on the body, and always determined, for freedom is the rule of the spirit over the body and matter.   It works not without brain, but in no way through it.   How free
we are in dealing with abstract thoughts!   Freedom is a psychologic
power.   We define it, "Determinateness of our psychical and corporeal powers, through moral motives, by ethical ideas."   Thought is
willed; as opposed to presentation, it is free and comparable to artistic
culture.   The determination of presentations is the mechanical foundation of freedom, the ethical group of ideas being predominant.   It is
our duty by culture and training to enlarge freedom.   Freedom is
only relative—is to be constantly developed.   It is autonomous, not
capricious or heteronomous, the worm of our well-being dictated from
without.   The motor force of ideas depending on the feeling can be
checked.   Freedom by inner necessity and the consciousness that this
necessity flows from known eternal law, which is held as our innermost
peculiar essence and our highest power, forms the moral autonomous
character.

Character is a determined habit, facility and sureness in the willing
itself.   Maxims, laws, traits of character, express the moral ideal.   A
complete man is he whose will, feelings and thoughts are actuated by
ethical motives.   Every deed is then moral and every thought a deed.

PART IV.   THE ETHICAL VIEW OF THE WORLD.

We now need a broader statement, found in the combination of all
the preceding.   The mortal and the absolute soul, according to metaphysics, is not ethical.   Theological ethics treats of the relations between God and man, philosophic of those between man and man, e. g.,
not marriage itself, but the form thereof, may be civil or church.
According to philosophic ethics it is no sacrament, but a moral good.
The grave or the church is consecrated by feeling.   Ethics knows no
sins, only bad or blameworthy acts.

I. *Nature and Moral Spirit.*—Accident is the contradiction of willing a conscious end—the *all* is worthless (mechanical) save as through us and our morality. Shapes and forms are ever changing—nature is an endless sea of restless matter. In the struggle for existence as many fixed kinds of forms or types as possible are formed in the sea of matter and force. There is no *end* in the mechanism of the universe—earth was not built for man, but is purposeless—nor were plants for animals, or *vice versa*. Man brings purpose into the world—he saw the light and it was color and harmony.

II. *The Cosmos.*—The true, beautiful and good. These three ideas are the star builders in the heaven of humanity. Art raises us above egoistic, material pleasures. The artist makes us see nature without fear; we gain an ideal feeling. The feelings are purified by art; but, while the artistic sense is limited, goodness is for all and is the duty of each. Truth and art are more external—goodness is only within. Through his will man is good—it is *he*. Knowledge and art are dependent upon it. Yet all are different: they form the three sides of the idea of humanity.

Scientific knowledge is the prerequisite. We make the *all* as we *think* it. We need the conceptions of order, necessity, connection and eternity to give symmetry to all. Appearances are conditioned by, and correspond to, realities. The spirit is an appearance or the place of appearances. The thing is true if the spirit is truthful. (We are daily less and less frightened by accidents. Industry is moral.) We feel truth as beauty through art; it presents the ideas of nature, of history, of spiritual life. Spirit, humanity, idea, morality, are synonymous, all tending toward the perfection of spirit. Life is moral. All culture and civilization contain the idea of perfection; the higher these are, the higher the grade of morality. Man is true, as moral motives underly knowledge, feeling and will. The development for intelligible rule is a lofty idea, and while purely a formal feeling, the feeling of religion is sublime. It is not the mother of all moral feelings (ideas), but includes them all. It is another expression for the idea of perfection.

III. *The Rule of the Intelligible or Objective Spirit.*—Truth, the eternal ideas and laws are not in the objects, but in mind or spirit. They are in the state of work and birth of ideas. The soul is in neither space nor time. As the spirit works in individuals it is called subjective; in concept, picture, and deed, it is objective. As the wood is a table, it is spirit. The outer half of each separate subject is an objective spirit, as the sum and system of the objects of combined subjective spirits which have lived. This is our morals, laws, and religions: The objective spirit rules and makes the subjective. The subject is bound up in the present condition of objective spirit. Ancient heroes would be as children to-day. The objective spirit is the medium of life (the air) for the spirit of the subject. The joint (universal) spirit is the sum of all the united spirits of all nations and all time. Objective spirit grows out of itself. It makes ever new presentations. The objective spirit is the historical human rule of the intelligible, the place of ideas and of all truth, beauty and goodness,—the medium of life for the subject, the everlasting environment and content of all being and doing,—the developed content of mind (of morality and humanity).

IV. *People--Humanity.*—The spirit of a people is objectified or corporealized in institutions and churches, in their common language and labor, their literature and art. Mankind is a mere abstract concept,—there is no real unity, as there should be. It should form an organism with the nations as organs. The beginning has been made in the laws of war, in international postal laws. Peace should be furthered by ethics. A real worthy form of moral life is needed for the enrichment of humanity. Nations are too egoistic. They seek power, and patriotism is made the opposite of humanity instead of its synonym. Peoples make history, and history makes peoples,—and the objective spirit of mankind is the all real. We give thanks to the dead for what they have given to us, by working for posterity. Morality is a historical product; the spiritual instinct is therefore spirit, because it develops in history.

V. *The Individual—The Ideal, its Power and Actuality; The Ideal and its Realization.*—Individual spirit is the active principle. Ideas are ideal, but lack power, and the objective spirit is a material mechanism—the individual *can be an ideal man*. Through a right deed the subject makes objective right, ideal actuality. The ethical institutions, marriage, home, union, state became alive through the individual. The individual is the point at which ideal spirit becomes open and energetic, and the same is true of society. It is our duty through the united spirit to present ourselves as spirits. Man is a product not of nature, but of morality. *He* is the real ethical life. He owes all to the common spirit. Be real, perfect thyself. This duty is his intelligible being. The common spirit is himself—as he owes all to the common spirit he should be humble. Therefore he should so conduct himself that others will honor the spirit in him. He should preserve himself for others; care for himself and serve the community thereby.

VI. *Sorrow and Desire—Evil and Good Conscience—The Obligation to Morality.*—The good is not what we are ready to desire. It is

10

useful, but not all that is useful is good. Good music is not merely that which gives pleasure. Joy is not the good, nor pain. Hold the mind and heart open for the true, the good, and the beautiful,—and have the hand ready with love ; assist the sorrowing. Natural wickedness and evil are accidental, so is desire. Some men, like animals, seek pleasure and flee from pain, but ethical conscience must come into play. We should give pleasure to others by our labor. Why is it good to further the health and joy of others? Joy is the symptom of health. The highest morality is to elevate the morality of others. Each in case has more power for morality. Therefore advance the intelligible life and joy will follow. Pain does not make us unworthy or worthy. If we look into the intelligible we must choose morality.

VII. *The I and Self, We—Accountability and Responsibility.*—The I, self is to be developed. Every man has his own world. I am I and my world. The I or self is the real back-ground of our freedom. The immoral are without the ethical ego, without character or aim, and being bad is only negative, destructive. *We* is the consciousness of a number of heads, or ethically, of the might of ideas, and *we* is the objective spirit. Therefore there is one we—spirit of mankind. We attribute no *I* to the wicked (ethically), but the judicial finds responsibility in all. Morality is teachable and learnable like mathematics, according to capacity. The cultured possess morality of a higher order than the uncultured, and repetition is the best training. The idea of perfection contains the command to watch ourselves. No one may say that he can not learn morals. This is the basis of responsibility. Freedom rests on health, but is only accompanied by it.

No one should say that he has had no chance to be free. Freedom, morality, should be reckoned as the deed and self-creation of a person. The moral character is always humble. A man should not excuse himself for debasement, as he has the power of self-elevation. As the I benefits the we, "as they deal morally with one another, they thank the we, humanity, and mankind, out of which they were bodily and spiritually born."

Thus have we followed the outline of the system of ethics propounded by a Jewish philosopher—and these ethics are the ethics of Judaism. His frequent references to the Bible show whence he drew the basic principles of his system, as lofty as true, as universal a presentation as can be conceived to-day. We may well be glad that we can count so clear a thinker, so profound a philosopher as Dr. Heymann Steinthal among the firm adherents to our inspired and inspiring faith, the religion of the Jews.

REVERENCE AND RATIONALISM.

By MAURICE H. HARRIS, A. M., PH.D.

In the Hebrew tongue we have but one word for reverence and fear, and in all languages we seem to use the words interchangeably. Where does the fear that is terror leave off, and the fear that is reverence begin? Terror seemed to be the chief element in the beginnings of all religions. For fear is the child of ignorance, and knowing nothing, primitive man feared all things. Nature and God were not then two distinct ideas, but all the forces and phenomena of nature were conscious beings that could help, but that also might injure. The tempest was a devouring dragon, an eclipse was the moon pursued by blood-hounds, the rainbow was a serpent, and sickness was "possessed of demons." Every stock and every stone had its indwelling spirit that would wreak vengeance if not appeased. Man himself could enter into leagues with these imps of darkness through witchcraft, necromancy, and the evil eye to cast blight upon his fellows.

But as experimental knowledge began to prove these fears groundless—they may have been succeeded by a higher sensation—awe—which is a supreme admiration mingled with mystery for that which is beyond us, but a glimpse of whose glory we already see. Fear pictures the unknown as terrible, awe pictures the unknown as sublime, but character as well as knowledge decides the difference of sensation.

The Hebrew Psalmists looked upon nature from its sublime side, not from its terrible side, to them "the heavens declare the glory of God."

Religion is sometimes defined as our conception of the universe—Weltanschauung. But cold scientific observation does not become religion until translated into the language of the soul, it distills through the feelings as reverential awe. It needs that touch of emotion of which Matthew Arnold speaks. The heavens do not declare the glory of God to every body. Our impressions are susceptible rather than objective; they reflect the self within rather than the world without. Some remain cold and unmoved before majestic scenery that would thrill and inspire others. While a man of vivid imagination and strong emotion looks up to the stars studding the blue vault of Heaven and thinking of their distance and their magnitude, of the suns that are beyond them and the forces that maintain them, the grandeur of the universe overwhelms him and he feels uplifted in holy ecstasy.

I think we may say, without laying ourselves open to the charge of glorification of our own, that the controlling influence in Judaism has never been fear, but always reverence. Hell has never played any figure in Jewish theology. A Jewish Dante would be as unthinkable as a Jewish John Ward, preacher. And while the Rabbis did not deny Gehinnom, they always touched upon it half playfully. While if a modern Rabbi, however orthodox, were to dwell on the tortures of the damned, he would either expose himself to ridicule or be censured for preaching not so much against the doctrine as against the genius of the Jewish religion.

I think the key to our faith is rather found in the injunction, "Ye shall reverence my sanctuary." This command is not exclusive, but intensive, the Sanctuary being the center of worship, the school of modern education, the home of religion, or even a fine metaphor for religion in general. "The heaven is my throne and the earth is my footstool, where is there a house that ye can build unto me and where is the place of my rest?" The universe is the House of God. Natural laws are throne laws, the book of nature is the Word of God. Those who do not recognize God outside the Sanctuary can not hope to meet Him within it.

Now, while none have understood this better than our own ancestors, since they took special pride in reminding themselves that the Synagogue was not consecrated ground, that any meeting place with ten worshipers became a House of God, still, we too have made the mistake of restricting our reverence to the tangible sanctuary, and giving to this behest a mechanical obedience by fulfilling it only in external demonstration and artificial formula. Not that we can doubt for a moment the sincerity of reverence expressed as ceremonial, but we must not confuse it with the feeling of reverence itself. Removing the shoes because the ground is holy, covering the head or uncovering it in the Sanctuary, are but outward demonstrations of reverence, just as black garments and crape are outward demonstration of sorrow. Reverence is a command issued to the soul only that can be expressed in feeling rather than in form, though feelings seize upon formulas of movement at last for their outlet. We might almost translate the command, "Ye shall reverence my sanctuary"—"realize the sanctity of all that is, and see in every place a possible Temple of God."

That outward forms of reverence for the tangible Sanctuary did not always imply inward regard for the principles which that Sanctuary only typified, is indicated time and again in every Hebrew prophet.

Says Amos: "They lay themselves down beside every altar upon clothes taken in pledge, and in the house of God they drink wine of such as have been fined." "When will the New Moon be gone that we may sell corn and the Sabbath that we may set forth wheat, making the ephah small and the shekel great, and dealing falsely with balances of deceit."

Says Hosea: "For I desire kindness and not sacrifice, and knowledge of God more than burnt offerings."

Says Micah: "The priests teach for hire and the prophets divine for money, yet will they lean upon the Lord and say: 'Is not the Lord in the midst of us?'"

Says Isaiah: "When you come to appear before me, who hath required this at your hand to trample my courts? Your new moons and your appointed feasts my soul hateth. When you make many prayers I will not hear. Your hands are full of blood."

Finally, Jeremiah, speaking with still greater directness, bluntly says: "Trust not in lying words, saying the Sanctuary of the Lord, the Sanctuary of the Lord, the Sanctuary of the Lord are these. Will ye steal and murder and stand before me in this house, which is called by my name, and say we are delivered?"

We must reverence not so much the House of God as the Word of God, was the later cry, and all religion was concentrated in the Law as containing the whole duty of man. But even here the worship of the Word led to a lessening of the Spirit. Indeed, it was difficult to reduce the sublime teachings of humanity and that spiritual fervor born of the soul's yearning toward the Highest to the codification of law and the dry formulas of legal enactments, without losing a something of their spirit and their essence. The Book itself came to be worshiped as a fetich, even to its externals, so that the ink with which it was written must be prepared with almost the care of the oil for the continual light in the Sanctuary. The blind worship excluded discrimination, and the names of Esau's wives were to be regarded with the same reverence as the Ten Commandments.

Once the principle accepted that all religion can be reduced to law, the Rabbis zealously endeavored to codify a rule for every minute duty of life, thus cutting off the opportunity for spontaneous religious outburst, and the free play of holy emotions, either in prayer or action. So, while they cried to hallow every moment of life, and blessed be their memory for it, this noble ideal, of which we can not speak too highly, was defeated by the unfortunate method.

But we must discriminate here as every-where, and not rashly decide that, because ceremonialism, that legitimate and helpful side of organized religion, has been abused in the past, that therefore it is in itself an abuse. The prophets just quoted must not be understood as despising all ceremonial. Nor is it fair to interpret them too literally, when carried away by righteous indignation. For we have only to turn a few leaves to find in other chapters a refutation of that mistaken but popular supposition. The subtle influence of religious symbolism upon character will surely be recognized by the thoughtful, who acknowledge that morality is complex and needs many springs to feed it.

But it is hard to formulate faith and feeling without their degenerating into grotesque symbols, which escape all likeness to the original idea. But if the Hebrews of the middle ages lost the spirit of reverence in ceremonial, they were entirely free from what I can only describe as artificial reverence, which was perhaps the corresponding error of the Church. They always shrunk from make-believe in religion.

But by artificial reverence I mean this: The officials of the Sanctuaries thought it necessary to give external evidence of their appreciation of its holiness. Hence the straight-laced countenance, the sanctimonious tone, the unctious manner, the frequent pious quotation so that the whole bearing breathes the very aroma of the Sanctuary. I do not mean that officials were necessarily impostors, like the Roman augurs who could not look into each other's faces without laughing; but that when such forms of reverence have removed their impression and are mechanically continued by force of habit, that the pious phrases become cant, and such officials fall into hypocrisy so gradually as hardly to be aware of it themselves.

This mere semblance of reverence for the Sanctuary has brought the Sanctuary into discredit and reverence too. Awe is beautiful, but the pretense of awe is contemptible. The actor in the Sanctuary playing the rôle of reverence is the last extreme of blasphemy. The priest in the temple practicing upon the superstitious fears and the ignorance of the people, giving them a sham to worship while comfortably consuming their sacrifices, believing only in his solid comfort and his substantial salary, deserves no mercy at the hands of an infuriated mob when his fraud is discovered. I say the same, be he a priest ancient or modern, pastor, Rabbi, or Church deacon. Such impostors have injured the cause of religion, have shaken the very foundations of morality.

The revolt against organized religion that began at the end of the last century with the French Revolution and the spread of skepticism, were the natural consequences. Every thing religious was regarded with suspicion. The Sanctuary was no longer reverenced, it was mistrusted. The Church, the Synagogue, religious ceremony, the ministry, even the Bible, became favorite subjects for ridicule, for ribald jest, and coarse jibe. From the one extreme of the worshiper trembling with bowed head before his Maker with an awe that was almost superstitious—there followed that other extreme of turning Houses of Worship into granaries and fortifications, and insulting and defiling their hallowed belongings. Men jumped from blind faith to blind atheism.

The storm of upheaval has somewhat subsided. We are gradually readjusting ourselves to better conditions. We are reverencing the Sanctuary again, but in a new and more enlightened way. The dim religious light has been succeeded by a flood of sunshine. Reverence does not require darkness for its background. We need not create by theatrical effect artificial suggestions of mystery to feed the imagination, the real mysteries of God, the World, and the Soul are so vast and so profound.

But again mistrust has followed this temporary reaction. The skepticism of the nineteenth century is deeper than the skepticism of the eighteenth. We are appalled at our own discoveries, and alarmed at the bewildering infinities that our researches have conjured up. The conscientious and thoughtful are full of misgiving. They declare that, if fear is the child of ignorance, then doubt is the child of knowledge; and that reverence is further away than ever. Evolution has revealed to us a much vaster universe than was pictured by the unaided imagination of our ancestors. But if theoretically God has been brought nearer to us, practically he is further away from us. Natural selection and the survival of the fittest have almost explained away the need of Providence and have made the universe well nigh automatic. Has not evolution magnified creation as a whole, but minimized man in particular? they ask in dismay—forcing him to the conviction that he is deposed from his proud position as the center of all creation—that he has been robbed of something of his dignity, something of his importance. There is no longer a gap between him and "the brutes that perish." Perhaps he is brute that perishes himself.

Furthermore the far-reaching application of cause and effect, that has been so minutely elaborated by scientific study, is robbing him of freedom of the will and hence personal responsibility. Some disciples of the Utilitarian School even explain away conscience, worth, and merit. And the general spread of such theories among the masses at large would be far more disastrous to the moral future of the world than that loss of dignity just referred to.

All this new conception of the universe has made him less sure of his immortality, or even of his soul. Even the teaching of Antigonus of Socho that we do good for its own sake, and not for the hope of reward, that punishment is subjective, may be carried too far; and the old fear of punishment in the future may be followed by the still more awful fear that we and our doings are entirely ignored by the powers above. The thought of punishment may have its terrors, but the thought of neglect is still more terrible. Man hopes when he fears less. Take from the future its consequences, you take from life its enthusiasm. Half light encourages romance and mystery; full glare dispels illusion, but sentiment too, and clips the wings of imagination.

Is it true that we feel less because we know more? Does knowledge make us cold? Does the fact that we have learnt the causes of so many things lessen our feeling of reverence? Is science the enemy of religion after all? Do faith and inquiry stand at opposite poles? Is ignorance necessary to faith? Is skepticism the necessary outcome of knowledge?

If all this were true, the conclusion would fill us with melancholy. We would be progressing backward. The ignorance of savagery would have been the golden age. The tree of knowledge would indeed be the disenchanter, driving us from the garden of hope and ideals to the gloomy desert of a despairing reality.

Let us hasten to reassure ourselves at the outset. Reverence is not the measure of our ignorance. They are not mutual conditions. In certain respects they are natural contradictions. The reverence of the ignorant is not the result of their ignorance, any more than the materialism of the scientist is the consequence of his science. Atheism antedated evolution, and theism has survived its dissemination. It has even deepened the faith of some. To many an explorer its results have made God greater, life grander, and duty holier. We need not be afraid whither our researches may bring us, for we can never exhaust the glories of the Infinite, nor fathom the source of the Everlasting God. Our reasoning faculties are the gift of our Maker, and we would be showing poor gratitude for his gifts by neglecting or mistrusting them. God's perpetual revelation unfolds before us as fast as our expanding souls can drink it in. Let us not earn the reproach of Isaiah, that having eyes we should see not, and having ears we should hear not. If the age is not religious, it is not because the age is wise. And he who knows only enough to be irreverent, only enough to deny—he knows little indeed, and is not less ignorant because he dis-

claims it. Many a fool hath said in his heart there is no God. Never
is the proverbial "little knowledge" so dangerous as in the realm of
religion, and heaven save us from the newly fledged college graduate,
who has heard a few chapters from Herbert Spencer's "First Principles," and thinks "he knows it all."

And yet there is a something in this charge against the times,
one-sided and half-truth though it be, that bids us pause. This is
the age of rationalism. It has made as its motto: "The voice of
reason is the voice of God." The worth of all things in the heaven
above and in the earth beneath must be tested in the crucible of logic,
and be capable of experimental demonstration. This spirit of rationalism has reached religion too. Our beliefs and doctrines must admit
of almost mathematical deduction. The pulpit busies itself with
proofs and evidences, and appeals to the intellect of the congregation.
A scientific lecture will often replace the simple homily of olden days.

Of course, it would be childish to deny that this spirit of investigation has not done good service to religion. It has cleared it from
error and misconception; it has checked unbalanced sentiment; it has
broadened and deepened its principles in the light of the very latest
knowledge. But our enthusiasm has carried us too far. In our admiration for mind, we have neglected the claims of emotion. But remove emotion from religion, and you reduce it to a cold philosophy.
Man is something more than a thinking machine. The intellectual
and the emotional react on each other and become mutually helpful
by revising and supplementing each other's deductions. A certain
kind of knowledge is revealed through feeling that cold thought failed
to discern. Intention, to which we owe so much, is perhaps a compromise between feeling and knowing—a conviction of the soul that
evades demonstration through mind.

Reason is not *the* voice of God, but *a* voice. Is it "the still small
voice?" must be religion's supreme question. If God speaks to us in
a thousand different voices, or, as it has been poetically put, "God ful-
fills his will in many ways," let rationalism dispel our illusions by all
means, but let it not rob us of the sanction of sentiment, or we will
be paying too much for it. Because religion no longer fears science
as an enemy, it need not go to the other extreme and regard it as all-
sufficient, and neglect its own inheritance.

> Let knowledge grow from more to more,
> And more of reverence in us dwell.

Religion is not a mere matter of argument. The gathering of
priests and rabbis by some stupid mediæval kings to prove publicly the

merits of their respective creeds, fill us with horror and disgust. The
best that is in religion escapes demonstration, is perhaps degraded by
demonstration. " Words, like nature, half reveal and half conceal the
thought within." We get flashes of it here and there in moments of
inspiration, but " no man can see God's face and live."

So I believe that when one is tried for heresy, the essence of religion is gone. A man's conception of God is a something sacred to
himself. To tamper with his faith, to strive to force it by physical
violence, is irreverence carried to the extreme of blasphemy. For it
must always be borne in mind that creeds follow religions; they do not
precede them. First the Prophets and then the Law was the real
order. They are simply the result of looking back upon beliefs after
the religion is fully developed, and is followed by a critical stage,
usually a time, too, when religious fervor has so cooled down that man
can leisurely pause to codify his theories and take stock of his doctrines. It is, therefore, never the most spiritual period of a religion.

We persist in going to science and philosophy to find out God, in
spite of their calm and positive assurance that it lies beyond their
province either to prove or disprove divinity, their deductions only re-
sulting in antinomies. Religion begins where science ends. I venture to say that even the proof of a First Cause through the cosmo-
logical or the ontological argument has no value for religion. It is no
more likely to inspire to worship than mathematics. It is approaching
God from the wrong side. " Can we by searching find out God?"
No. Religion must teach man to reach God through the soul. When
we must needs sit down to prove God, our faith is in a desperate condition. The Psalms can hardly be said to contain proofs of God, yet
they breathe his whole spirit. It is not a book of proofs, it is a book
of faith. I am fully aware of the abuses to which blind faith has led
man, just as well as I am aware of the dreary and dispiriting results
of science unaided by religious imagination. Intelligo ut credam, we
must understand to believe, is a good maxim, but credo ut intelligam,
we must have faith to understand contains a more subtle truth that
touches a vital principle in religion. And yet there is a fear that the
modern rationalistic preacher fails to appreciate the value of faith in
religion. They feel that doing and being are so much better than believing, that man can be saved by works rather than by faith, which
is certainly true. but here, too, they have carried a virtue to the extreme of a fault. We point with a little too much pride and a little too much positiveness to the absence of dogma from Judaism. We
should not forget that some kind of faith must underlie works; that a
belief is implied in every reasonable deed. The grandeur of our

ancestors as the religious teachers of mankind lay in their implicit
faith in the power of a righteous God, whose nearness to us varies
with our moral worth. To cry for morality and to despise faith is to
cry for flowers and despise roots, and is as unreasonable as to expect
our flowers to continue blooming after they have been severed from
the root on which they grew.

Indifference to doctrine and loss of faith have been followed by a
lack of appreciation of prayer, by a lowering of ideals and a loss of reverence for the sanctuary. I use the expression "reverence for the
sanctuary" in the broad sense, that there is nothing holy for us. Our
lives are becoming more secular, and we are losing what I can only describe as spirituality, and which is the bloom of that very morality of
which we preach so much.

Spirituality is a word easier uttered than defined. It is a species
of moral refinement that comes from a vivid realization of the soul's
kinship with divinity—a sense of entering into communion with God.
In our craze for rationalism, and in our decline of faith, we have wan-
dered so far from the spirit of our ancestors, that that yearning of the
Psalmist, "As the heart panteth after the water brooks, so my soul
panteth after thee, O, God. My soul thirsteth for God, for the living
God," must sound strange, indeed, almost incomprehensible to the
ears of the modern, practical, prosaic Jew, as though this were the
phraseology of some other creed instead of the very spirit of the ancient Hebrews. I can almost imagine a smile at reference to these
soul yearnings, because from the material standpoint it seems that
these expressions must either cover hypocrisy or are the result of
weak-mindedness and maudlin sentiment.

But the rationalist will tell us that we need above all things the
truth; that we must boldly and fearlessly say what we believe regard-
less of consequence; that evil can not possibly come from the utterance of truth; and the word is written in big capitals.

But there is danger here, too, in the manner we may present
even what we believe to be absolutely right. For since we can never
get more than fragments of truth at best, since so much is left to the
inference of imagination in which feeling plays so large a part, therefore must we, the guardians of religion, realizing the solemnity of our
trust, strive, with painstaking and conscientious care, so to present
the little that we think we know to those who look to us for guidance
in the highest and holiest of life's duties, that it may inspire them
and lead to their spiritual awakening, and not in a way to shock their
moral sensibilities, producing religious apathy or hopeless despair.

If Biblical research has led us to the modern school, there is less difference between the old theory of the plenary inspiration of the Scriptures and the new school of higher criticism than there is between the possible ways of presenting the latter for the purpose of cultivating faith and reverence. We may, like Ingersoll, see in the Pentateuch nothing but the mistakes of Moses, and give it forth to the public in a caricature, as Schleiermacher presented the Talmud. Or, on the other hand, even in discrediting the miracles as miracles, we can show the intense morality behind the very legends and the exquisite trust of our ancestors in a perpetually present Providence that slumbers not nor sleepeth—that has made the Bible the book of power it always will remain. The touch of reverence with which we present the truth as we understand, makes at times more difference than the truth itself.

Even our doubts can be expressed with that reverential awe that the perpetual mysteries around us inspire, or can be made the occasion for mockery and levity. Reverence does not always vary in the ratio of belief. There are people who never doubt because they never think, while " there (may be) more real faith in honest doubt, believe me, than in half the creeds." Again, we can feel reverence for the religion of another. This is the highest form of liberality—perhaps the only liberality. So much depends upon the attitude with which we approach the Holy of Holies—whether we recognize it as holy, removing our shoes, so to speak (כי אדמת קדש הוא), or whether as fools we rush in where angels fear to tread, and vandal-like rudely tear aside the veil, to gratify a vulgar curiosity.

For mockery is a vandal that ruthlessly shatters our hallowed sentiments enshrined in the temple of our hearts and by its coarse jeers tears in shreds the living garment of God, in which the labors of all humanity are interwoven. Mockery makes the sacred profane tainting the soul with its venom, and the holier the theme the more revolting becomes the caricature for "corruptio optimi pessima." The variation of a tone changes a prayer into a sneer and may do more to upset the honest faith of an honest soul than twenty solid arguments; for though it be but a step from the sublime to the ridiculous, from the ridiculous to the sublime, is a gulf impassable.

Therefore, in the religious education of children, the manner of presentation should give us much concern. A parent may encourage certain religious observances in the home and yet present them in a matter of fact way that robs them of all religious value. Prayer without reverence is worse than nothing. We give perhaps too much consideration to the question: Teach us what to pray, and not enough to the question: Teach us how to pray. We are so afraid that our prayers might not be logical or that an anthropomorphism might creep in. As if the feeling were not every thing and the words nothing.

Without teaching children any doctrines of dogmas at the outset, we must strive diligently and lovingly to cultivate their sense of reverence, not necessarily for any particular object, but reverence as such, as a quality of character. Open to its young soul the perpetual mystery and the perpetual sublimity of all that is. It will then of itself look upon life and the universe from its sublime side, and the idea of God will be intuitively suggested almost before it is distinctly taught. In this way the very frame-work of religion is already laid in the heart of the child ready to be clothed with the particular faith of its ancestors. The perpetual wonder of a child for every thing around it may be discouraged into sober matter-of-fact, may be darkened into fear, may be deepened into awe. Here is the parent's supreme opportunity and supreme responsibility. The child's boundless and sensitive imagination—one of its greatest charms—must not be allowed to run wild, but should be directed to religious uses. They should be taught to regard their parents as invested with divine authority for them, to disobey whom is sacrilege; and they should be led to look upon the home as their first Sanctuary, for if they desecrate that Sanctuary, no spot can be holy for them—no shrine can be sacred in their eyes. "Ye shall reverence my Sanctuary"—"Ye shall reverence, every man his father and his mother."

I have said that religion is our conception of the universe. The child's universe is very small indeed, but we can make it sweet and pure and beautiful, or we can make it dreary and rough and common. For life for all of us is what we make it—material or sublime—and reverence is the dividing line.

I am not calling upon my people to preach a new gospel, but simply asking them to go back to their own first principles. Since it was their privilege to bring to man the first message of righteous divinity, let them resume their ancient birth-right. And in an age that would worship reason only—like some new idol—let them vindicate the claim of the soul. "There are more things in heaven and earth" than we can ever hope to explain. Such knowledge is too wonderful for me, I can not attain it. But faith begins where knowledge ends. The senses have been developed to their utmost, but the endless capacities of the spirit, in which are hidden divine possibilities, are still almost untested. The realm of the soul is still an undiscovered world, yet all the greatness of the coming man lies there—all our Messianic hopes and grandest ideals. Let religion then return to its neglected inheritance, and perhaps, like unto Moses, the glory of God may pass before us.

THE GREATNESS AND INFLUENCE OF MOSES.

By RABBI G. GOTTHEIL.

Last Monday morning it was the day of our church new year, a festival of great solemnity with us. About this very hour of the day, I and my brethren, over the face of the earth, read this prayer:

"Our God and God of our fathers, reign Thou over the whole world in Thy glory, and be exalted in Thy majesty over the whole earth, and shine forth in the excellence of Thy supreme power over all the inhabitants of the terrestrial world, and may every thing which has been made be sensible that Thou hast made it, and every thing formed understand that Thou hast formed it, and all who have breath in their nostrils know the Lord God of Israel reigneth and His supreme power ruleth over all. And thus also extend the fear of Thee, O Lord our God, over all Thy works, and the dread of Thee over all that Thou hast created, so that all Thy works may fear Thee and all creatures bow down before Thee, so that they all may form one bond to do Thy will with an upright heart, for we know, O Lord our God, that the dominion is Thine, that strength is in Thy hand, that might is in Thy right hand, and that Thy name is to be reverenced over all the earth."

Just at that moment this great Parliament of Religions was opened, and we could not but point to this great manifestation as a sign that our prayers and our sufferings and our labors have not been in vain—that to this free country it was given to show that the Word of God is true, and that not one of His promises can fall to the ground.

Now I am to speak on the greatness of Moses. I believe that is the most striking testimony, that he always remains Moses, the man of God, the legislator; and that he so instructed his people and so infused his own spirit into their constitution that never, at no time and under no provocation, was the attempt made in the Jewish Church to raise him above his simple humanity. Although they have proved their fidelity to him—their belief in his law by every possible testimony that can be applied—yet he was Moses, the servant of God, until the highest praise bestowed upon him, which, I may say, is the

canon of the Jewish Church in regard to the legislator, is taken from
the pages of the Scriptures themselves, where it is said: "Never was
in Israel a prophet like unto him, and beyond Israel where shall we
look for his equal?"

I am not speaking in the narrow spirit of rivalry; far be that
from my theme. Veneration for Moses has not yet hindered me to
see, to admire, and to learn from other masters—the sun has lost
nothing of his glory since we know that he is not the center of the
universe, and that in other fields of the infinite space there are like
suns unto him. What shall hinder me to learn from the masters
which you honor? I can well understand, I can honor the man that
said: "All must decrease that Christ may increase." But no true
Christ ever said: "All must decrease that I may increase." And I
remember the fine saying ascribed to Buddha: "I forbid you," said
he to his disciples, "I forbid you to believe any thing simply because
I said it."

Where shall we find one that combines in his personality so many
greatnesses as Moses, if I may say so? He was the liberator of his
people, but he spurned crowns and scepters, and did not, as many
others after him did, put a new yoke on the neck from which he had
taken the old one. To every lover of the American constitution that
man must be a political saint. And his republic was not of short duration. It lasted through all the storms of barbaric wars and revolutions—hundreds of years, down to the days of Samuel, that all-stout-
hearted republican who could endure no kings. That man that saw
so clearly what royal work would do; that man who is so wrongly
judged by our Sunday-school moralists; he fought with his last breath
for the independence of his people, and when the king they had
chosen showed he was not the right man, he spared him not and looked
for one that should be worthy to rule his people.

But the republic he founded stands unique in the history of the
world, for it was altogether based upon an idea—the idea of the unity
of God and the righteousness of His will. Think of it! Among a
nation escaped from bondage, too degraded even to be led to war, that
needed the education, the hammering, as it were, into a people for
forty years, to go among them with the sublimest truth that the human mind can ever conceive and to say to them: "Though you are
now benighted and enslaved, any truth that I know is not too good
for you nor any child of God." Whence did the man derive that inspiration? If from the Almighty, then may we not say there arose
not another like him? And can we wonder that when he came down

from the mountain, the light that shone from his face was too much for the eyes of his people and he had to cover it?

Did he learn that grand idea from Egypt? We know that he was learned in all the wisdom of the Egyptians, but if he learned any thing there he learned there how not to do it. For so complete is the contrast between Egyptian conception of state and the Mosaic. All honor to that nation of torch-bearers of antiquity! And here we now recover the whole literature of that people, and there has not been found a single sentence yet that could be given to mankind as a guide in their perplexities. And not a name has come down to us that was borne by one who labored for mankind. As a teacher of morality, why need I praise him? As a teacher of statecraft in the highest and best sense, who surpassed him? The great wonder is that that man speaks the language of to-day. The problems which we have not yet succeeded in solving were already present to his mind, and he founded a nation in which the difference between the poor and the rich was almost abolished. The laborer was not only worthy but sure of his hire. No aristocrat could rule over his subjects and no priesthood could ever assume the government which, alas! according to history, means the opposition of the nation. How did that man of that vast mind, how did he combine all these great talents? And yet that man, how tender his heart was! Why, friends, it is a thousand pities that you can not hear the deep sorrow, the sadness that is to be heard in his original words. When an over-zealous disciple came to him and told that they were prophesying in his name, and they said: "Hinder them, master, hinder them. Why, if they prophesy what will become of thine own authority?" I fancy I see his venerable head sink upon his breast and he saying: "Indeed art thou zealous for me! Would that all the people of God were prophets, and that God gave His Spirit to them."

Follow that man to the top of the mountain, where he is alone. See the man who could stretch forth an iron hand when it was necessary, stretched on the face of the earth and seeking forgiveness for his people, and when his prayer was not answered, "O, if Thou wilt not forgive my people then blot me out of the book that Thou hast written." So tender! And another instance: Before his death he, as you know, admonished the people in words that are immortal. After forty years of such labor as he had expended he admits that his people have learned almost nothing, and I must quote Emerson, who says, "It is in the nature of great men that they should be misunderstood." But with the tenderness, with the thoughtfulness of a father

11

he did not scold his people before the shadow of death fell upon him. Why, he says, not "you are ignorant," "you are hard hearted," "you are blind," "you are stubborn." Listen! "But God has not yet, my dear people, given you a heart to understand nor eyes to see nor ears to hear." Do you hear that tenderness in these words? "God has not given you the light you need."

They say that that man was not a man at all, but it is the simple creation of the nation's fancy. Glorious fancy! We should worship him, for where has the nation's love and veneration ever produced a picture like it? It appears to me as if it had been painted in three great panels. The first period, the period of storm and stress, where he undertook the delivery of his people, but God was not in it and so he failed. And then the second period of retirement, of solitude, of self-absorption, of preparation for the great path; then the final picture shows us the man of action, the man of energy, the man of insight, and the picture closes with the words, "No man knows his grave to this day." Lonely he was in life, lonely he was in death; but though no man knows his grave all the world knows his life.

Here, briefly, I will say something, as part of my duty, on his influence. I can not circumscribe it. I know not where it ends. Every Christian Church on earth and every mosque is his monument. Peace is the foundation stone, the historic foundation stone on which they all rest, and that cross over the church on which the man is hung, which to the Christian is the symbol of deity itself, where he said that he must die so that the law of Moses be fulfilled. And the Arabian's great master, Mohammed, why, he is overflowing with praise when the son of Amram comes to his mind. Five hundred millions, at least, acknowledge him their master. Five hundred millions more will bow to his name. I know not what human society can be or become and allow that name to be forgotten.

Are his doctrines to be abolished? For two centuries, the first two centuries of the Christian Church, no other Bible was known but the Old Testament, and to-day in every synagogue and temple, and on every day and occasion of prayer, when his own followers come to the sacred shrine, the whole mystery hidden there is the law of Moses. And they take it in their hands, and, Oh, how often I have seen in my youth that scroll bedewed with the tears of the poor suffering Jew, and they lift it up again and say, "This is the law that Moses laid before the people of Israel." It is done so at this very moment, at this very hour of our Sabbath, and I thank God from my whole heart, and I feel inclined almost to say, " Now let thy servant go," that from the Jewish synagogue I could come here among you followers of other masters, disciples of other teachers, pilgrims from many lands; that I could stand up in your midst, and feeling that your heart and your soul and your sympathy is with me, simply repeating, " This is the law that Moses has laid before us Israelites."

HUMAN BROTHERHOOD AS TAUGHT BY THE RELIGIONS BASED ON THE BIBLE.

By DR. K. KOHLER.

To Chicago belongs the credit of having rendered her World's Fair a World's University of arts and industries, of sciences and letters, of learning and religions. Humanity, in all its manifestations of life and labor, in all its aspirations and problems, is there exhibited and finds a voice. And the grandest and most inspiring feature of the unique spectacle is the *Religious Parliament*, which, in trumpet tones resonant with joy and hope, peals forth the great truth of the Brotherhood of Man based upon the Fatherhood of God.

(a) THE BROTHERHOOD OF MAN.

Thanks to our common education and our religious and social progress and enlightenment, the idea of the unity of man is so natural and familiar to us that we scarcely stop to consider by what great struggles and trials it has been brought home to us. We can not help discerning beneath all differences of color and custom the fellow-man, the brother. We perceive in the savage looks of the Fiji Islander, or hear in the shrill voice of the South African, the broken records of our history; but we seldom realize the long and tedious road we had to walk until we arrived at this stage. We speak of the world as a unit—a beautiful order of things, a great cosmos. Open the Bible and you find creation still divided into a realm of life above and one below—into heaven and earth, only the Unity of God comprising the two otherwise widely separated and disconnected worlds, to lend them unity of purpose, and finally bring them under the sway of one empire of law. Neither does the idea of *man*, as a unit, dawn upon the mind of the uncivilized. Going back to the inhabitants of ancient Chaldea, you see man divided into groups of blackheads (the race of *Ham*) and redheads (*Adam*); the former destined to serve, the other to rule. And follow man to the very height of ancient civilization, on the beautiful soil of Hellas, where man, with his upward gaze (*Anthropos*), drinks in the light and the sweetness of the azure sky to reflect it on surrounding nature, on art and science, you still find him clinging to these old lines of demarcation. Neither Plato nor Aristotle would regard the foreigner as an equal of the Greek, but consider him forever, like the brute, fated to do the slave's work for the born master—the ruling race.

Let us not forget that prejudice is older than man. We have it as an inheritance from the brute. The cattle that browse together in the field and the dogs that fight with each other in the street, will alike unite in keeping out the foreign intruder, either by hitting or by biting, since they can not resort to blackballing. They have faith only in their own kin or race. So did men of different blood or skin in primitive ages face one another only for attack. Constant warfare bars all intercourse with men outside of the clan. How, then, under such conditions, is the progress of culture, the interchange of goods and products of the various lands and tribes brought about, to arouse people from the stupor and isolation of savagery?

Among the races of *Shem*, the Ethiopians have still no other name for man than that of *Sheba—Sabean*. Obviously, the white race of conquerors from the land of Sheba refused the blackheads found by them on entering Ethiopia the very title of man, not to mention the rights and privileges of man. Yet how remarkable to find the oldest fairs on record held in that very land of Sheba, in South Arabia, famous from remotest times for its costly spices and its precious metals! Under the protection of the god of light, the savage tribes would deposit their gold upon the tables of rock and exchange them for the goods of the traders, being safe from all harm during the festive season of the fair. Under such favorable conditions, the stranger took shelter under the canopy of peace spread over a belligerent world by the scepter of commerce. What a wide and wonderful vista over the centuries from the first fairs held in the balsam forests of South Arabia to the World's Fair upon the fairyland created by modern art out of the very prairies of the Western Hemisphere! And yet the tendency, the object, is the same—a peace-league among the races, a bond of covenant among men!

It is unwise on the part of the theologian to underrate the influence of commerce upon both culture and religion. Religion is, at the outset, always exclusive and isolating. Commerce unites and broadens humanity. In widening the basis of our social structure and establishing the unity of mankind, trade had as large a share as religion.

The Hebrews were a race of shepherds, who were transformed into farmers on the fertile soil of Canaan. In both capacities they were too much attached to their land—being dependent either upon the grass to pasture their flocks or upon the crops to feed their households—to extend their views and interests beyond their own territory. When, therefore, Moses gave them the laws of righteousness and truth upon which humanity was to be built anew, he did not venture to preach at once in clear and unmistakable terms the great fundamental principle of the unity and brotherhood of man. He simply taught them: "Hate not thy brother in thine heart! Bear no grudge against the children of thy people, but that thou shalt love thy neighbor as thyself; I am the Lord!" He would not tell them: "Love all men on earth as thy brethren!" for the reason that there could be no brotherhood so long as both the material and religious interests collided in every way, and truth and justice themselves demanded warfare and struggle. Monotheism was more than any other religion an isolating power at first. It was in times of prosperity and peace, when Jews were first brought into contact with the great trading nation of Phœnicia, that the idea of man widened with the extension of their knowledge of the earth, and they beheld in the people of the hot and the cold zone, in the black and blonde-haired men, in the Caucasian and African races, offspring of the same human ancestors, branches of the same parent stock, children of *Adam*. At the great fairs of Babylon and Tyre, where the merchants of the various countries and remote islands came with their worldly goods for their selfish ends, a higher destiny, the great hand of Divine Providence, was weaving the threads to knit the human race together. And in one of these solemn moments of history, some of the lofty seers of Judah caught the spirit and spelled forth the message of lasting import: "All nations of the earth shall send their treasures of gold and spices, and their products of human skill and wisdom on horses and dromedaries, on wagons and ships to the city of Jerusalem; yet not for mere barter and gain, but as tokens of homage to the Holy One of Israel, whose name shall be the sign and banner of the great brotherhood of man." This is the idea pervading the latter part of Isaiah. No sordid trading after the fashion of the Canaanites, but truth and knowledge will be freely offered on the sacred heights of Jerusalem. Such was the vision of Zechariah prompted by the sight of the fairs held in the Holy City. (See Movers, Phönizier II 3, 145.) It was the idea of a great truce of God amidst the perpetual strife of the nations which they conceived of and forecast when announcing the time when "swords shall be turned into ploughshares and war shall be no more."

Never would the tenth chapter of the book of Genesis, with the lists of the seventy nations, have been written to form the basis for the story of Adam and Noah, the pedigree of man, and at the same time the Magna Charta of humanity, had not the merchant ship of the Phœnicians opened this wide world-encompassing view for the Jew to cause him to behold in the many types of men the one and the same *man*. It was on the Tarshish ship that the prophet Jonah had, amidst storm and shipwreck, to learn the great lesson that the heathen men of Ninevah have as much claim on the paternal love and forgiving mercy of Jehovah as the sons of Israel have, as soon as they recognize him as their God and Ruler. Who dares ask the question: " Who is my neighbor ?" after having once read in the grand book of Job the words: " Did I despise the cause of my man-servant or maidservant when they contended with me? What then shall I do when God riseth up? Did not he that made me in the womb make him, and did not he fashion us in the same mold?" (Job xxxi, 13. 15.)

The Talmud contains an interesting controversy between Rabbi Akiba, the great martyr hero of the time of the last Jewish war with Rome, and his friend Ben Azzai: The former maintained, like Hillel and Jesus before him, that the Golden Rule, " Love thy neighbor as thyself" (Levit. xix, 18), is the leading principle of the Law. Ben Azzai differed with him, saying : "This does not explicitly state who is included in the law of love," and he pointed to the first verse of the fifth chapter in Genesis: "This is the book of creation of man ; in the likeness of God has he created man." Here he said the principle is laid down : " Whosoever is made in the image of God is included in the law of love."

No better commentary can be given to the Mosaic commandment than that furnished by Ben Azzai. Cut loose from the rest of the Biblical writings many a passage concerning God, and man still has an exlusively national character, betraying narrowness of view. But presented and read in its entirety, the Bible begins and ends with *man*. Do not the prophets weep, pray, and hope for the Gentiles as well as for Israel? Do not the Psalms voice the longing and yearning of man? What is Job but the type of suffering, struggling, and self-asserting man. It is the wisdom, the doubt, and the pure love of man that King Solomon voices in prose and poetry. Neither is true priesthood nor prophecy monopolized by the tribe of Abraham. Behold Melchizedek, Salem's priest, holding up his hand to bless the patriarch. And do not Balaam's prophetic words match those of any of Israel's seers? None can read the Bible with sympathetic spirit but feel that the wine garnered therein is stronger than the vessel containing it ; that the Jew who speaks and acts, preaches and prophesies therein, represents the interests and principles of humanity. When the Book of books was handed forth to the world, it was offered, in the words of God to Abraham, to be a blessing to all families of man on earth. It was to give man *one* God, *one* hope, and *one* goal and destiny.

(b) THE FATHERHOOD OF GOD THE BASIS OF MAN'S BROTHERHOOD.

We can easily discern the broadening influence of classical culture exercised upon the Jews that spoke and wrote in Greek. Under the invigorating breeze of the philosophy of Alexandria, Moses was made to teach in the manner of Plato, and Noah and Abraham to practice all the virtues of Pythagoras; Philo, Josephus, and St. Paul endeavored alike to batter down the walls separating Greek from Jew, the unwritten laws of Athens being identified with the Noachian laws of humanity, the practice of which opened the gates of eternal bliss for the Gentile as well as for the Jew. All the more stress I lay on the claim that only the monotheistic faith of the Bible established the bonds of human brotherhood. It was the consciousness of God's indwelling in man, or the Biblical teaching of man being God's child that rendered humanity *one*.

Even though the golden rule has been found in Confucius as well as in Buddha, in Plato as in Isocrates, it never engendered true love of man as brother and fellow-worker among their people beyond their own small circles. The Chinese sage, with his sober realism, never felt nor fostered the spirit of self-surrender to a great cause beyond his own state and ruler. And if the monk Gautama succeeded, by his preaching on the world's vanities, in bridling the passions and softening the temper of millions; planting love and compassion into every soul throughout the East, and dotting the lands with asylums and hospitals for the rescue of man and beast, he also checked the progress of man, while loathing life as misery without comfort, as a burden of woe without hope of relief, dissolving it into a purposeless dream, an illusion evanescing into nothing. And what were, after all, the great achievements and efforts of man, to the proud Greek, if the rulers of heaven only looked down with envy upon his creation, and Prometheus, the friend of man, had to undergo a life's endless torture as a penalty for having stolen the spark of fire, the secret of art for the mortals, from the jealous gods. Neither Pindar nor Plato ever conceived of a divine plan of the doings of man. No Thucydides nor Herodotus ever inquired after the beginnings and ends of human history or traced the various people back to one cradle and one offspring. Not until Alexander the Macedonian with his conquests interlinked the East and the West, did the idea of humanity loom up before the minds of the cultured as it did before Judea's sages and seers. Only when antiquity's pride was lowered to the dust, and philosopher and priest found their strength exhausted, man, suffering, sorrowing, weeping, sought refuge from the approaching storm, yearning for fellowship and brotherhood in the common woe and misery of a world shattered within and without. But then neither the Stoic, in his overbearing pride and self-admiration, nor the Cynic, with his contemptuous sneer, could make life worth living.

It was the Bible offered first by Jew, then by Christian, and, in somewhat modified tones, by Moslem, that gave man, with the benign Ruler of the ages, also a common scope and plan, a common prospect and hope. While to the Greek—from whom we have borrowed the very name of ethics—goodness, righteousness, virtue, were objects of admiration, like any piece of nature and of art, beautiful and pleasing, and life itself a plaything, the Bible made life, with all its efforts, solemn and sacred, a divine reality. Here at once men rose to be co-workers with God, the successive ages became stages of the world's great drama, each country, each home, each soul, an object of divine care, each man an image of the Divine Father. True enough, this conception of the God-likeness of man is as much Platonic or Pythagorean as it is Biblical. Still there the relation is all one-sided. There is no more mutual response in the Greek system than there is between the string of the musical instrument and the great orchestra, between the citizen and the law of the state. There no deep calls to the deep, no spirit answers the spirit. Man follows the magnetic pole of the right and the good, but lacks courage to fling fear and fate to the wind and take fast hold of life, with all its tears and sorrows, trusting in a great God who leads man through toil and trial to ever higher paths of righteousness and goodness. It was the Bible which, holding God up to mankind as the pattern of a great worker for truth and justice, furnished life with a living ideal, with a propelling power, a forward-moving force, rendering man a toiler after the likeness of God for living aims and lasting purposes. Take the word *Goodness* in Plato. It is not the outflow of a paternal heart that finds blessedness in love. It is a fountain that works beneficently, but knows it not. Take the Platonic term *Righteousness*. It is a plan of equity and symmetry that rounds off every thing to perfection in the wide universe, yet not a power that enriches while taking, that comforts while exacting and demanding sacrifice. The Biblical idea of God's Fatherhood renders the very inequalities of men the basis of a higher justice. Just because you are endowed with a strong arm, the feeble brother claims your help. Just because you are richer than your brother, God holds you to account for his wants and feelings. Do you possess a better faith, a higher truth? All the more you are enjoined to enlighten, to cheer, to befriend him who is in doubt and despair.

There is no partiality with God. The weaker member in the human household, therefore, must be treated with greater compassion and love, and every inequality readjusted as far as our powers reach. "If thou seest one in distress, ask not who he is. Even though he be thine enemy, he is still thy brother, appeals to thy sympathy; thou canst not hide thine eyes; I, thy God, see thee." Can, alongside of this Mosaic law, the question be yet asked, Who is my neighbor? Thou mayst not love him because he hateth thee. Yet, as fellow-man, thou must put thyself into his place, and thou darest no longer harm nor hate him. Even if he be a criminal, he is thy brother still, claiming sympathy and leniency. Sinner or stranger, slave or sufferer, skeptic or saint, he is son of the same Father in Heaven. The God who hath once redeemed thee will also redeem him.

Are these the principles and maxims of the New Testament? I read them in the Old. I learned them from the Talmud. I found their faint echo in the Koran. The Merciful One of Mohammed enjoins charity and compassion no less than does the Holy One of Isaiah, and the heavenly Father of Jesus. We have been too rash, too harsh, too uncharitable, in judging other sects and creeds. "We men judge nations and classes too often only by the bad examples they produce; God judges them by their best and noblest types," is an exquisite saying of the Rabbis. Is there a race or a religion that does not cultivate one great virtue to unlock the gates of bliss for all its followers? Hear the Psalmist exclaim: "This is the gate of the Lord, the righteous enter into it." No priest nor Levite nor Israel's people enjoy any privilege there. The kind Samaritan, as Jesus puts it in his parable; the good and just among all men, as the Rabbis express it (Sifra Achre Moth, 13), find admission. No monopoly of salvation for any creed. Righteousness opens the door for all the nations. Is this platform not broad enough to hold every creed? Must not every system of ethics find a place in this great brotherhood, with whatever virtue or ideal it emphasizes? Is here not scope given for every honest endeavor and each human craving, for whatever cheers and inspires, ennobles and refines man, for every vocation, profession, or skill; for whatever lifts dust-born man to higher standards of goodness, to higher states of blessedness?

Too long, indeed, have Chinese walls, reared by nations and sects, kept man from his brother, to rend humanity asunder. Will the principles of toleration suffice? Or shall Lessing's parable of the three rings plead for equality of Church. Mosque, and Synagogue? What, then, about the rest of the creeds, the great Parliament of Religions? And what a poor plea for the father, if, from love, he cheats his children, to find at the end he has but cheated himself of their love. No. Either all the rings are genuine and have the magic power of love, or the father is himself a fraud. Truth and Love, in order to enrich and uplift, must be firm and immutable, as God himself. If truth, love, and justice be the goal, they must be my fellowman's as well as mine. And should not every act and step of man and humanity lead onward to Zion's hill, which shall stand high above all mounts of vision and aspiration, above every single truth and knowledge, faith and hope, the mountain of the Lord? There, high above all the mists of human longings, the infinite glory of Him dwells, whom angels with covered faces sing as the *Thrice Holy*, and whom all the mortals praise as the God of Truth—*El Emeth*, as the Rabbis put it; *Aleph*, the beginning; *Mem*, the middle, and *Tav*, the end—the *Alpha* and the *Omega*, the first and the last.

HISTORY.

THE SHARE OF THE JEWISH PEOPLE IN THE CULTURE OF THE VARIOUS NATIONS AND AGES.

By GOTTHARD DEUTSCH, PH.D.

There exists a tendency in our age to belittle every merit. The very spirit of criticism soon degenerates into hypercriticism. The latter word being a popular expression of the orthodox clergy of all denominations who, not willing to refute their opponents' argument, content themselves in denouncing it, it will have to be explained. Hypercriticism is criticism misled by the desire to produce surprising results. Just as orthodoxy is pre-occupied by the desire to establish what it believes without any further proof, so the hypercritics are convinced beforehand that what for centuries was believed to be an established fact, is a mere illusion. The same spirit which delights in the denial of Shakespeare's poetical genius will rejoice in the denial of the influence which the Jewish spirit has produced in the world from the time when the Greek-speaking nations first learned of the wonderful treasury in the biblical literature up to our time, where there is no realm of science to which Israel has not contributed to a considerable degree. While there is a zeal in discovering a similarity of thought between Indian, Persian, or any other remote folklore, and our own thought, be it as insignificant as it may, traceable to accidental causes or even questionable in its meaning, there is the same zeal active to disprove Jewish literature and thought as sources of our culture. While I undertake to show the remarkable participation by the Jews in all branches of human work, I shall carefully abstain from all assumptions and resort to facts only.

When we wander through the vast field of Jewish history, we are at once struck by the remarkable influence of the Bible. The numerous editions of the whole book and its parts, since when in 1477 the first edition of the Psalms and in 1488 when the first edition of the whole book appeared, the fact that the number of copies of the Hebrew Bible and its translations distributed by the bible societies since the beginning of this century are calculated to amount to one hundred and fifty millions, the fact that the greatest poets of all civilized nations, viz., Milton, Racine, Goethe, and numberless others,

drew their inspiration from the Book of Books, the further fact that
this book exists in more than two hundred translations, would suffice
to prove that the influence of Jewish thought on humanity can hardly
be overestimated.   From the time when R. Joshua den Hyrcanos made
Job's (xviii, 15) words, "though he slay me, yet I will wait for him,"
the ideal of piety (Sotah 27b) up to the day when Grace Aguilar,
that example of noble womanhood, uttered these words of consolation
on her death-bed, how many souls have been elevated and strengthened, consoled and comforted, cultivated and rendered better by the
words of this immortal book !

Another great historic fact by which Judaism turned over a new
leaf in the development of humanity, is the rise of Christianity.
However different the standpoint of the critical historians may be, in
this they agree that Jewish thought formed the bulk of Christianity.
It was F. Ch. Baur who showed the affinity of the doctrines of the
Essenes and those of the early Christians.   We find the principal
features of the new doctrine, celibacy, asceticism, contempt of worldly
pleasure and abstinence from politics.   More consistently than Baur,
we find D. F. Strauss, his disciple, advocating the idea of the connection of Jewish lore with early Christian literature.   Mostly guided
by Lightfoot's "*Horae Hebraicae et Talmudicae*," Strauss proclaimed
the principle that the miracles of the New Testament and consequently
the whole history of the life of Jesus can only be explained by the
midrashic rule of R. Berechjah (Koheleth rabba i, 9) כגואל ראשון
כך גואל אחרון "the savior of the future shall act like the savior
of the past."   However, Strauss, although very reticent in regard to
positive results, still believes in a historical Jesus, the son of Joseph
and Mary of Nazareth, who died on the cross for his broad views in
regard to the obligation of the Mosaic law.

More advanced are the ideas of the Dutch theologians, headed by
A. D. Loman, whose "*Quaestiones Paulinae*" make the Jesus of the
gospel a mere personification of the Jewish martyr-ideal, and even
deny the authenticity of any of Paul's epistles.   In the same direction
wrote the anonymous Englishman, the author of the book "*Antiqua
Mater, a Study of Christian Origins*," and the Swiss, Rudolph Steck, in
"*Der Galaterbrief, etc.*," both of whom took up the half-forgotten views of
the eccentric Bruno Bauer, with the only difference that they explain
Christianity from Jewish ideas, while the latter derived it mostly from
Seneca's Stoic philosophy.   To characterize the difference between the
principles laid down in Strauss's "*Life of Jesus*" and those of the mod-
ern Dutch scholars, we would say that, according to Strauss, the

writers of the gospel acted like Lord Byron in composing his "*Man-fred*," taking a remarkable historic personality as a subject of their picture of an ideal life, permitting themselves all the liberty of a poet: while Loman and his followers would ascribe to the Gospel the same character as to Goethe's "*Faust*" or Robert Hamerling's "*Ahasverus*," where the popular myth is the only essence of the history, notwithstanding its details and the trustworthy witnesses who testify to its facts.

There is a series of New Testament ideas which can be explained only by the talmudic sources, as, for instance, the personification of the Holy Spirit, the רוח הקדש which the rabbis, in order to avoid anthropomorphism, placed instead of God. That the spirit of God appears in the disguise of a dove is also a frequent rabbinical figure of speech (Math. iii, 16; Berakhot 3a). Undoubtedly a rabbinical reminiscence is the explanation of Pentecost as the day of revelation. There is no trace of this in the Old Testament scripture (or rather to the contrary), since Shabuoth has no fixed date, and therefore can not have been celebrated in remembrance of a historic fact. And besides, even the form in which the story of Pentecost is given in the Acts (ii, 3) reminds us of rabbinical fiction. According to the rabbis, the Thora was revealed in seventy languages, or, as the Midrash puts it, in seventy tongues. It was only natural that the new doctrine should not be short of its predecessor in any of its miraculous concomitants. Just as the idea of revelation was transplanted into Christianity in its midrashic garb, so were a great many other theological concepts. The term "gehenna" for hell is of purely rabbinical origin; the so-called Lord's prayer is a selection of rabbinical phrases from the invocation אבינו שבשמים to the end. Only in adopting this view can we escape the difficulties in the chronology of the last supper, to the solution of which Prof. Chwolson recently dedicated a whole book. The difficulty, briefly stated, is this: While according to the first three gospels Jesus on the first day of the feast of unleavened bread commanded the disciples to make preparations for the Passover (Mt. xxvi, 17; Mk. xiv, 22; Lk. xxii, 7), we find in John (xiii, 1) that it was *before* the first day of the Passover, and to remove every doubt, it is expressly stated later on (xviii, 28) that on the following morning the Jews would not enter the praetorium, lest they should defile themselves and become unfit to offer the Pascha.

All expedients to explain away this difficulty remain futile; the only possible solution being that, just as the early Christian church transformed the Jewish account of revelation into a Christian narra-

12

tive, so the same men transformed the idea of the covenant into Christian shape. Had God made a covenant with Israel when they left Egypt, it was necessary that He should renew His covenant, now that it had a different meaning; or, to explain it more clearly, the early Christians celebrated the old Jewish Passover until they became aware that it was for them meaningless. On the other hand, this festival was too deeply rooted in the hearts of the Judeo-Christians to be dispensed with entirely. So it became necessary to place it on a different basis. That the Judeo-Christian tradition made it more according to the old ritual, while the Helleno-Christian tradition wanted Jesus to depart from the Jewish custom as far as possible, is evident. By this explanation, we avoid the difficulty of explaining the words of Jesus: "take, eat, this is my body," etc. (Mat. xxvi, 26.29; Mark xiv, 22.25; Luk. xxii, 16), which, containing a prediction of the following events and expressions of a later and notoriously dogmatic idea, could not be understood when coming from the mouth of a mortal man, and not without accepting to a certain extent the dogmatic view which the church holds concerning the Lord's supper.

Thus we see how far Jewish custom, thought, and exegesis worked to produce the ideas which made the essential part of Christian belief, and we are not too bold in tracing the kernel of the gospel, "all things therefore whatsoever ye would that men should do unto you, even so do ye also unto them" (Mat. vii, 12), to the well-known saying of Hillel: דִּילָךְ סְנִי לְחַבְרָךְ לֹא תַעֲבִיד, "What is hateful unto thee thou shalt not do unto thy neighbor" (Sabbath 31a). Moreover, the addition in Matthew: "for this is the law and the prophets," shows the acquaintance with the original, זוּ כָּל הַתּוֹרָה כֻּלָּהּ וְאִידָךְ פִּירוּשָׁא, with the only difference that, instead of "the law and the rabbinical interpretation," the author said "law and prophets," which proves the secondary character of this reading, just as the change of the negative form of this sentence of Hillel into the affirmative is a proof of development.

It is very interesting to behold how in certain places the midrashic form of a sentence is the pattern of the evangelical form of putting it. In the gospel we read: "Thou hypocrite, cast out first the beam out of thine own eye; and then shalt thou see clearly to cast the mote out of thy brother's eye." One sees clearly that a beam in one's eye is so extravagant a figure of speech that it could hardly be original. Let us look, therefore, at the parallel expression in the Talmud. There (Arachin 16b; Bathra 15b) we read a complaint that in our time hardly any one is able to reprove, for if one would say, טוֹל קִיסָם

מכבין שנין, "take out a mote from between thy teeth," they would answer him, טול קורה מכבין עינין, "take the beam out of thine eyes." Here one can see clearly that the talmudic form is original. It is a common experience that one mildly reminded of a shortcoming in his character, a mote which remained between his teeth from a toothpick which he had used, will regard it as an offense, and say to his critic: "You have not a mote, but a beam, and not between your teeth, but in your eyes." Be it that some code had the word שנין falsely changed into עינין, or that it became corrupted in the mouth of the people, every body can see the fact that the Talmud has here the original and the gospel the secondary reading.

Let us give another evidence from the seemingly genuine Christian ideas of opposition to the obligatory character of the law. It is generally admitted that this main point of Christian doctrine was not clearly stated at its beginning. It passed, just as other ideas, through certain stages of development. In Matthew (v, 17.21), we find the theory of unchangeableness of the law expressed, while in 1 Cor. vii, 17, and 1 Rom. iii, 30, the keeping of the law is given to every body's choice; and finally, in Gal. v, 2.4, the observation of the law is a falling away from grace, which corresponds to the words of Luke xvi, 18, that law and prophets were only until John. The improbability of one man having taught in a career of not over three years so emphatically discrepant opinions forces us to the conclusion that first Christianity taught a more conservative doctrine, just as Luther, after having promulgated his ninety-five articles, still professed allegiance to the Pope; and John Wesley, after the disapproval by the authorities of his "method," would not sever his connection with the official church.

During this time, the liberal Christian view of the obligation of the law was shared by many prominent Pharisean teachers. When R. Jochanan ben Zakkai said, לא המת מטמא ולא המים מטהרין, "a corpse can not defile and water can not purify" (Tanchuma ad Num. xix, 1), it reminds us of the saying of Mark (vii, 15), "there is nothing from without a man that going into him can defile him." Furthermore, we find the disciple of R. Jochanan b. Zakkai, Eliezer b. Hyrkanos, expressing similar ideas, especially in regard to prayer. He says, "He who makes his prayer a formality, his prayer is no devotion" (Berakhot 38b), which is very much like the idea expressed in Matthew (vi, 7). The same R. Eliezer was indeed suspected of affiliation with the Christian congregation of Galilee. This

is the only sense we can make out of the confused talmudic legend
(Aboda zara 17a) of the report of his being banished by Rabban
Gamaliel (Mezia 59b), of Imma Shalom's, his wife's, disputation with
Christians (Sabbath 106a). Moreover, in Koheleth rabba (i, 9), we
hear about a disciple of R. Joshua, R. Eliezer's contemporary, and a
disciple of R. Jonathan, that they joined the Christian congregation.
And especially about the disciple of R. Joshua we are told that the
"Minees" induced him to ride on an ass on the Sabbath, which would
coincide with the tradition of the early Christian teaching that "the
Sabbath is made for man" (Mk. ii, 28), which is nothing but a rabbinical idea, לכם יִשְׁבַּת מְסוּרָה ואי אַתֶּם מְסוּרִין לְיִשְׁבַּת (Mechil-
tha Kithissa, ed. Weiss, p. 110). With this, we may duly conclude
our proofs that Christianity, as it was developed during the first century A. C., derived its doctrines, its thoughts, and its forms of expression from rabbinical Judaism, and Christianity is that form of
Judaism which has conquered the civilized world.

JEWISH-ALEXANDRIAN PHILOSOPHY.

Christianity is a product of historical development, and as such
it must have had more than one cause. We might say Judaism is its
mother, and Greek philosophy, especially Stoicism and Neo-Platonism,
is its father. And here we already observe the peculiar feature of the
Jewish spirit which we can find through all history, and which had
for its aim the combination of different opinions, not a mere eclecticism,
but rather a chemical ligation which created a new product. Such
was the work of the Alexandrian Jews. In Alexandria, Jews came
in contact with a superior mental culture; here they first encountered
an independent philosophy; here they found researches concerning
God and the world not based on any tradition; ethical doctrines not
relying on any authority; poetry whose authors wrote without claiming to be instruments of God. On one hand they were forced to
admit the truth of this scientific view; on the other hand they would
not give up the doctrines of their own faith, endeared to them by religious feeling and the weight of tradition. They did what at every
critical point in history is done when a new doctrine comes into light,—
they made a compromise, partly accommodating their views to that of
Greek science, partly retaining their own, always insisting on the superiority of their religion to the results of science whose true statements
they claimed to have been borrowed from the prophets and sages of
Israel.

The first movement in that direction was the translation of the

Bible into the Greek language, where they first met with the difficulty of explaining some terms and concepts which in the Hebrew original needed no explanation. Then they had to take into consideration the Greek public, before which they did not like to appear in an improper light, and finally they quite honestly introduced some ideas which they had accepted from Greek philosophy, believing them in fact not only not contradicted but even implicitly taught by the Bible. Thus we see anthropomorphisms avoided in this translation; so instead of "it repented the Lord that He had made man and it grieved Him in his heart," the Septuagint translated: "and God considered ἐνεθυμήθη, that he had made man and contemplated it διενοήθη." Thus we see a movement started which already in the second century B. C., and still more in the first, assumed the task of our philosophy of religion as it undisputedly existed up to the time of Spinoza; and even in some of the later systems which were not contented to explain the existence of religion and to classify the different systems but endeavored to harmonize religious conviction and scientific results. Such ideas occurring in some of the Apocrypha, as Sirach and the wisdom of Solomon, have been put forth more systematically by the greatest of all Jewish-Alexandrian philosophers, the one who closes this epoch of Jewish history as the light of the evening transforms a beautiful day in autumn. It is Philo, the Maimonides and Mendelsohn of the first century A. C. "who like an immense basin receives all the small channels of Alexandrian exegesis in order to shed its waters in manifold branches into the later exegesis of Judaism and Christianity." (Siegfried, Philo v. Alex., p. 27.)

Let me quote here what an orthodox Protestant theologian says concerning the great influence of this Jewish writer on the mental achievements of the world, which are the best characteristics of the man. "What Hebraism, says J. G. Miller, effected in life in ancient form, the belief in and the relation to the one God, this Jewish Hellenism, by the aid of Greek philosophy, was destined to introduce into the science of the world. Philo was called to be the first philosopher in monotheistic sense." The most important of Philo's doctrines is the logos idea. The origin of this idea was purely Jewish. It seemed irreconcilable with God's infinity, incorporeity and unchangeability that he should speak, act or even create the world. To solve this problem Philo invented the logos, the mediator between God and the world, who is the highest of all divine powers, the summit of the great series of intermediary beings. (De Cher., p. 112.) This logos idea shows manifold similarities with the Christian doctrine of Jesus, especially as it is given in the gospel of St. John, where Jesus is identified with the logos. Philo called the logos "second God" (Quaes. in Gen. ii, 265) and the "vicegerent of God" (De somn. i, 600), and although the logos is identified with God's wisdom he is not held to be one with the divine spirit πνεῦμα θεῖον. (De mundi opif. vi, 14. 30.) It is the logos who teaches virtue and punishes vice, and to him Philo assigns an important part in the divine guidance of human life, for he is the divine prototype of humanity. The logos is the eternal high priest and atoner, he is the ideal man living eternally with God in the invisible world of ideas." (De somn. i, 653, De opif. 32, Leg. alleg. i, 49. 62.)

Who could but be struck by the nearly literal identity of this idea with that contained in the fourth gospel: "In the beginning was the logos and the logos was with God." We can therefore hardly contradict the assertion of Bruno Bauer, who called Philonic philosophy the abridged kernel of evangelical history before it was brought into action, and the Philonic doctrine of the logos "a prologue to Christianity." The original work of Christianity therefore is the combination of the logos with the national Jewish messianic idea. Thus another phase of Judaism has passed by, which proved to be of unparalleled influence upon the history of the civilized world.

THE JEWISH-ARABIC PERIOD.

Another epoch in history where the Jews participated in bringing nearer to the world the best achievements of thought, is the Spanish-Arabic age. It was at this time that Semitic nations were again the teachers of humanity, the most active workers in the advancement of human culture, just as it was in the mystic ages when Cadmus (the man from the east), the father of Europa (the west), had brought the Alphabet to the Greeks. Christianity had abandoned philosophy; it had closed the academies where the science of the pagans was taught: it had become used to rely on the force of arms rather than on the strength of arguments. Besides, the Teutonic nations which were made converts to Christianity achieved preponderance over their former teachers, the cultivated Romans, and this was another strong reason for the downfall of science in that part of the world which for four hundred years before the Christian era, and still two centuries later, had produced those immortal monuments of human culture which still are the poll toward which our needle is pointing.

The Arabians had learned of Aristotle's work by the medium of Syrian translations which came to their hands when the Islam had extended its sway to the eastern shore of the Mediterranean. On these works they wrote commentaries and composed other philosophical books which partly by mistake of the credulous people of that time, partly by a fraudulent intention of the author, were believed to be genuine works of the founder of the Peripatetic school. When the dominion of the Islam was established on the Pyrenean peninsula, the Jews acted as mediators between the Mohammedan and Christian worlds, translating the Arabic works into Latin and bringing them within the reach of Christianity. But this is not their only merit. They were later on themselves influenced by the grand ideas of the Stagyrite, and adopted their religious views, and showed them not only to be in harmony with Aristotle's teaching, but even implicitly teaching the same ; and this method again stimulated Christian scholars to try the same with their own doctrines.

There are three names which are milestones in the path of progress of philosophical thought. They are Salomo ben Gabirol, Moses Maimonides, and Levi ben Gerson. The first of these had a great influence on the system of the most critical among the scholastics, on Duns Scotus, and in his book " *Fons Vitae* " is quoted by all the leading authors of the scholastic era as belonging to an Arabic philosopher by the name of Avicebron, whose identity with Gabirol has been established beyond doubt by Solomon Munk.

Moses Maimonides, the greatest of all Jewish philosophers, at the same time an authority in Jewish theology, was the teacher of Albertus Magnus, the "*doctor universalis*," and Thomas Aquinas, who up to our time is regarded as the mastermind of Catholicism. His chief work, " The Guide of the Perplexed," being translated into Latin shortly after the author's death, was not only frequently quoted by Albertus and Thomas, but even appreciated by modern philosophers as Leibnitz who made a synopsis of it for his own studies. Emile Saisset, a Catholic, says : " Maimonides is the forerunner of St. Thomas and the Moreh Nebuchim, announces and prepares the '*summa theologiae.*'" His demonstrations of the existence of God are those of Maimonides. Albertus again appropriates Maimonides' ideas of creation and prophecy, and if one compares Albertus' treatise on divination (tom. v, pp. 93–103) and his treatise on creation (tom. ii, pp. 325–334) with the corresponding chapters in Moreh (ii, 36. 37 ; i, 74 ; ii, 13. 14. 16. 17. 19), he will find analogies of such striking character, that he can not but admit that the great teachers of Christianity, who for centuries have been regarded the highest authority, and are still regarded as such among the largest denomination of Christians, have derived some of their best ideas from the book of a man whom Judaism reveres as its greatest teacher since the time of the prophets. When the present pope declared Thomas the patron of all studies because he had solved the greatest questions which perplex the soul of a Christian, he canonized partly the doctrines of a Jewish philosopher.

Next to Maimonides I have to mention Levi ben Gerson, whose commentaries on Averroes, the Arabic commentator of Aristotle, were highly esteemed, and in a Latin translation by Jacob Mantino made accessible to the Christian reading world. Besides, Levi ben Gerson had a celebrated name as astronomer. The part of his book wherein he treats on an astronomic instrument which he had invented, was translated into Latin by order of Pope Clement VI. Kepler once wrote to one of his friends he would be very thankful if he could provide him with a copy of this book. I can not speak of all Jewish men of science and literature of this age, and therefore chose only those who, by their works, exercised a remarkable influence on the development of the intellectual world. I therefore might conclude this part of my lecture by quoting the words of a competent writer on philosophy, Ueberweg, who says (Gesch. d. Phil. II, 169): " In the thirteenth and fourteenth centuries the philosophy of Arabic Aristotelians, persecuted by the Mohammedan potentates, found a refuge among the Jews of Spain and France, especially in the Provence, who translated the Arabic books into Latin and partly commented them. By the agency of the Jews, Arabic translations of books of Aristotle and Aristotelians were again translated into Latin, and formed thus the first communication to the scholastics of Aristotelian philosophy, who, stimulated by this, procured other translations of Aristotle directly from the Greek." Thus the Jews acted as agents in bringing the culture of the past and remote nations to their neighbors and contemporaries. They acted as missionaries of culture, just as did the great inventors and discoverers of the sixteenth century, being the messengers of one nation to the other.

BIBLICAL CRITICISM.

Although it is my intention to exclude from this treatise Jewish theology, it being rather my aim to show Jewish influence on science and literature in general, I see fit to mention one name whose bearer, although his merits lie within the limits of biblical exegesis, Hebrew grammar and poetry, deserves to be classed among the leading spirits of the world. I refer to Abraham Ibn Ezra, the first bible critic. It was he who, on rational grounds, first contested the Mosaic authorship of some passages in the Pentateuch, which, by reference to later events (Gen. xxiii, 7; xxii, 14; Deut. xxxiv, 1. 12), or by their explanatory character, give evidence of their later origin. It may be that he was prompted to this criticism by his antagonism to the Kara-

ites in the same way that the Catholics, Jean Astruc and Richard
Simon tried to overthrow the dogmatic foundations of the Protestants,
showing that the biblical authority is not established beyond doubt;
but he also frequently attacks the rabbinical interpretation of the
Mosaic law (Ex. xxiii, 19; Levit. xxiii, 40), and still more frequently ridicules the haggadic interpretation of some historical narrative in the Bible (Gen. xxiv, 1; xlvi, 27). Thus Ibn Ezra became a
pioneer of biblical criticism, a science which contributed very much to
the enlightenment of the world and to the purification of its moral,
philosophical and religious concepts. It was he who gave the first
hints to Spinoza, who, in his "Tractatus Theologico-Politicus," helped
to disseminate Ibn Ezra's teachings. The now prevailing doctrine of
the Graf-Wellhausen school, with its revolutionizing effect on the
theology of this country, is the fruit of the seed sown by this great
scholar who, expelled from his native country by religious fanaticism,
composed his great commentary on the Pentateuch while living the
life of a tramp—a picture of Israel's history!

The important turn in human civilization, when men broke loose
from the chain of scholasticism and began to think for themselves, to
believe in what was proven by the laws of evidence only, and to go
back to the sources of every tradition, this epoch-making age shows
again the contribution to culture by Jews. Just as the humanists
wanted to redeem the true Aristotle from the shackles of Averroes
and St. Thomas, so it was their goal to recover the true Bible from under the rubbish which misunderstanding, ecclesiastical dogmas, and
apologetic tendencies had heaped upon it. This they could successfully do only when they applied to Jews, who alone at this time possessed the knowledge of the Hebrew original. Here we find one of
the builders of modern thought, who put only one stone upon the
foundation of human knowledge, but this one little stone is very well
laid, and later builders in laying others upon it need not be afraid that
it will give way and endanger the whole structure. This comparatively unknown man is Elijah Levita, the teacher of Cardinal Egidio.
It was his merit to have proven beyond doubt that the vowel-points
are of late invention, and that in consequence thereof the Hebrew
text of our Bible, as it is before us, is of comparatively late origin.
This theory shook more than any thing else the scholastic doctrine of
the "Hebraica Veritas." But beside this literary merit, Elijah Levita
and many other Italian Jews deserve credit for the instruction of
learned Christians, amongst whom there is prominent the noble and
scholarly Johann Reuchlin, the forerunner of the Reformation, the
opponent of the inquisition which just at that time attempted to spread

the gloom of ignorance and intolerance over Germany, as they had
just succeeded in accomplishing in Spain. So it is to a certain extent
due to the Jews that the world was spared the pain of seeing the
misery repeated which was spread around the fagots erected by the
disciples of Thomas de Torquemada and Peter Arbues.

THE AGE OF REFORMATION AND KABBALA.

One might be justified in dividing the history of culture into
periods of rationalism and mysticism; two spiritual powers always
fighting each other and at the same time each one helping to amend
the one-sidedness of the other. Thus we find in the age of the reformation these two powers at work, the rationalistic criticism playing
havoc with baseless dogmas and the mystical power supplanting the
outward ideal of piety by the opposite devotion of feeling. A classic
example of this two-fold movement we find in Luther, who on one
hand cruelly destroyed the illusion of the sacramental character of
the priesthood, criticized biblical books, speaking of " hay, straw, and
stubble which are found amidst the best thoughts of the prophets,"
while on the other hand he fought the scholastic proofs of trinity by
the assertion of an inward certainty which does not need a proof at
all. We have seen that as to the critical movement there were Jewish guides who leveled the path before the reformers, and as for the
mystic inclination, although Jews were by their strict adherence to
the pitiless law rather opposed to all mysticism, their Kabbala exercised a great deal of influence even there. This quasi-science was
eagerly studied and recommended by Christians. Johann Reuchlin
in his defense of the rabbinical literature believed the cabbalistic
books the strongest arguments against the hostilities of the Domin-
icans and their worthy protégé, the converted Jew, Johann Pfefferkorn. Indeed there existed side by side with criticism, just as it is
in our time, a belief in occultism, a belief that ancient times and
remote countries had a perfect knowledge of the truth for which we
ardently seek.

One of the earliest writers in whose works we find an acquaintance with cabbalistic productions is the Spanish missionary, Raymundus Lullus (d. 1315), who invented a mnemotechnical method (*ars
inventiva, demonstrativa*, etc.), by which certain letters written in mathematical figures represented certain concepts. By turning these figures one could place letters in different connections so as to combine
two or more of these concepts to form theological or philosophical sentences. It is very probable, as Helfferich in his monography on Raymundus says, that the Jews initiated him into their cabbalistic system

and this suggested to him the idea to apply the same method to peda-
gogical purposes. This conjecture is supported by Raymundus himself, who calls his art Kabbala, and describes it as " *receptio veritatis
divinitus revelatae!* "

Next we have Reuchlin, whose interest in the Jewish literature
we already had occasion to mention. In his written arbitrament on
Jewish literature, which he had to give at the command of Archbishop
Uriel of Mayence, he expressly takes the part of Kabbala and says
that Pope Alexander VI had recommended the study of the Kabbala,
and Sixtus IV had three cabbalistic books translated into Latin.
Reuchlin says: " There is no art which can give more certainty in regard to the divinity of Christ than magic and Kabbala." Even before the time of Reuchlin it was Count Pico de Mirandola who, convinced of the strong support which the Christian dogmas could receive
from cabbalistic sources, announced a public disputation at Rome,
where he offered to prove this assertion (Graetz Gesch. viii, 243). It
was at this turn in history, at the end of the fifteenth century, that
mysticism became prevalent both as a reaction against the meaningless
formulas of Aristotelian scholasticism and as a foreshadowing of criticism which, dissatisfied with the old proofs for the ecclesiastical creeds,
sought refuge in the mysteries of Kabbala. There it was that the
civilized world found in Judaism an adequate supply for its temporary
wants.

SPINOZA.

The reformation with its heralds, the humanists, had destroyed
the foundation of medieval conceptions. This had to be supplanted,
and was supplanted by a new philosophy founded by Cartesius, but
consistently elaborated by the Jewish philosopher, Baruch De Spinoza.
We have already touched upon his affinity with Abraham Ibn Ezra,
and we may add that, though opposed as his views are to Judaism and
any revealed religion, he is greatly influenced by Maimonides. It was
the uncompromising monotheistic idea, says Kuno Fischer, wherein lie
the fundamental features of his doctrine which recognizes only one
real existence, one substance, of whom all other existences are only
limited manifestations. the difference being that he recognizes no purposes and designs, only causes and effects. His system stands at the
threshold of modern philosophy, and his negation of petty teleology
will forever remain an acquisition to human investigation, just as Aristotle's logic and Copernicus's planetary system form a part of the permanent treasury of human science. Instead of explaining his system
which would be beyond the limits of this paper, I may be permitted
to quote some of the greatest thinkers of later ages in their judgment

on the ideas which the lonesome philosopher has worked out in his
optical shop.

It was Lessing, the poetical genius of the age of the "Aufklä-
rung," who in his famous conversation with F. H. Jacobi a few weeks
before his death, said: "ἓν καὶ πᾶν One and all, I don't know of any
thing else. If I should name myself after any school, I know of nobody except Spinoza." The same Jacobi, the bitterest opponent of
Spinoza, confessed, if he would believe in metaphysics and its effi-
ciency, he would adhere to Spinoza for his only consistent system.
"Such a calmness of the spirit," Jacobi says; "such a heaven in reason as this clear and pure head has created for himself, few men have
ever tasted." And Schleiermacher, in his lectures on religion, pays to
him the highest tribute, saying: He stands the unique and unequaled
master in his art, but raised above his guild with no disciples, with no
birthright."

Next to Spinoza, we ought to mention his counterpart, Moses
Mendelsohn. While the former believed in effects only, the latter's
philosophy is based on design; while, according to the former, God
has no personal relation to man, in the latter's sytem providence occupies the foremost place; while Spinoza, although not formally ab-
juring his faith, remained indifferent to Jews and Judaism, Mendelsohn's life work was devoted to the elevation and promotion of his
co-religionists. It is no wonder, when we consider these differences,
that Mendelsohn abhorred Spinoza's philosophy: that pantheism and
atheism were to him identical; that he regarded it a gross insult to
the cherished memory of his friend when Jacobi called Lessing a
Spinozist. But what has Mendelsohn done for the world? Well, if
he had not done any thing but opened the way to civilization for millions of his co-religionists, and shown them by his exemplary life that
one could partake in the highest interests of the world and still remain a good Jew, if he had not done any thing but, by his translation of the Pentateuch, reached and uplifted the wretched youth who,
living among savages in the eastern part of Europe, was yearning
for light and truth, this would be, in my opinion, a great service done
to mankind, a service comparable to the emancipation of the slaves,
to the invention of the method for the instruction of the blind, to the
sanitation of an insalubrious country. In short, Mendelsohn's work is
equal to any service rendered to a part of humanity to which more or
less every service done to humanity has to be reduced. But one
might add in his life there was a service rendered to humanity at
large whom he delivered from their prejudices, especially from their
overestimation of Christianity; he was the model for "Nathan the

Weise," in whom German literature possesses one of its most precious jewels. Mendelsohn's "*Jerusalem*," his introduction to Manasse ben Israel's "*Salvation of the Jews*," helped to spread the ideas of mutual toleration, separation between ecclesiastical and civil affairs, and quickened the glorious ideas which this country had first enacted in its statute books as immutable, unchangeable laws of society.

Treating on philosophy, it would only be just to mention Mendelsohn's protege, Solomon Maimon, who, grown up among the semibarbarous Lithuanians without any school education and without any teacher and guide, mastered Kant's philosophy to such a degree that Kant himself was astonished to find such an able interpreter, and Maimon, although he never overcame his awkwardness of style, is still to be regarded one of the foremost philosophers of the Kantian school.

JEWS IN THE PRESENT AGE.

. In the year after Mendelsohn's death, Count Mirabeau wrote his essay, "*Sur Mendelsohn*," etc., wherein he recommended the unconditional emancipation of the Jews. Since that time the Jews have taken part in all branches of human culture, notwithstanding the obstacles which narrow prejudice put in their way. There is no department of human culture which Jews did not help to enrich. Turning to art, we find the painters, Philipp and Johann Veith, the grandsons of Moses Mendelsohn, Moritz Oppenheim and Leopold Horowitz; the sculptors, Moses Ezekiel and A. Antokolsky; the musicians and composers, Meyerbeer, Rubinstein, Jacques Halevy, Joseph Joachim, Jgnaz Moscheles, Jacques Offenbach; the actors, Rachel, Felix, Bogumil, Dawison, Abraham Dreyfuss, Adolf von Sonnenthal, Ludwig Barnay. Amongt he poets and writers, we have Heinrich Heine, Berthold Auerbach, Aron Bernstein, Moritz Hartmann, Julius Rodenberg, Fanny Lewald, Leopold Kompert, Hieronymus Lorm, S. H. Mosenthal, Adolf L'Arronge, Michael Klapp, Grace Aguilar (English), M. A. Goldschmid (Danish), Ludwig von Doczi (Hungarian), a list which could be greatly increased by prominent journalists, amongst whom I will only mention Jacob Kaufmann, Ignaz Kuranda, Albert Wolff, of the Paris *Figaro*, and Julius Stettenheim.

If we look at the scientific productions of our age, we might safely say that there is no department of science and no language of civilized nations in which Jews did not give evidence of their proficiency. Turning to medicine, we find L. C. Jacobsen (Copenhagen), Ludwig Traube (Berlin), Schnitzler (Vienna), Rosenstein (Leyden), See (Paris), Lombroso (Turin). Among the jurists, we have George Jessel (London), Goldschmidt (Berlin), Solomon Mayer (Frankfort),

Gruenhut (Vienna). Among the philologers, philosophers, and historians, we see the celebrated names of Gustav Weil, Theodor Benfey, Adolphe Franck, James Darmestetter, G. I. Ascoli, Jacob Bernays, Ph. Jaffe, M. Lazarus, and H. Steinthal, some of whom are laudable promoters of the religious interests of Judaism. Even among the great travelers and explorers, we find Jewish names. I mention I. J. Benjamin, H. Vambery, Emin Pasha, and Ed. Glaser.

The number of prominent statesmen is so much the more significant as Jews, only since a comparatively short time, are allowed to partake in the political life of the nation. We have in England David Salomons, Lionel Rothschild, F. H. Goldsmith, Worms, Montagu, and Lord Beaconsfield, who, although in his early youth converted to Christianity, always retained a strong love for his people. In France we have Achille and Benoit Fould and Adolphe Cremieux, who, during the hardest crisis which his country had to endure, helped in managing its affairs. In Germany we have Gabriel Riesser, vice-president of the first German parliament; Johann Jacoby, Kosch, Lasker, Bamberger, besides many others who rendered very valuable services to the different federate states of their country. In Austria, right at the beginning of constitutional life, a Jew was the most popular man in the empire. In the first parliament there were four Jewish deputies, two of whom were rabbis. Later on Ignaz Kuranda was one of the most influential members of the Reichsrath; four Jews were peers and two converts, Glaser and Unger, were ministers, as was Friedenthal in Prussia, which fact proves that a Jew, if left to his proper sphere, will be able to serve his country and mankind. In Hungary, Jews, from the beginning of the revolution, worked for the independence of their country, and are to-day prominent. I mention the secretary of state, Ed. Horn, Wahrmann, Franz Chorin, the son of the first reform rabbi, etc. In Italy, Senator Isaac Maurogonato and Luzatto, minister of finance, deserve due honor.

In connection with the statesmen, one might mention the numerous Jews who distinguished themselves in finance and commerce, although a great many people regard this rather a blemish on the Jewish character. But it seems to me that so long as the honest strife to increase one's fortune is no crime, so long as the desire to secure to his children so much as to enable them to resist the hardship of life is regarded a paternal duty, so long as people who have amassed a fortune understand the duty of the rich to be to take care of the destitute, so long as finance is regarded a science, I can not see how to be a successful financier shall be regarded as a crime in a Jew.

Finally we have to touch on the noble works of charity, in which the Jews every-where have won distinction. There are hardly more popular names in this respect than those of Moses Montefiore and Baron Hirsch, whose generosity has no equal in history. Besides, there is no Jewish settlement of any importance which would not testify to the truth of the rabbinical saying, that charity is one of the distinguishing marks of Jewish character. We can only mention very few of the Jewish benefactors: Jonas Fraenkel, the founder of the rabbinical seminary at Breslau, built a hospital, an orphan asylum and a home for the aged in that city; Joseph von Wertheimer established the first kindergarten in Vienna; Prospero Moses Luria bequeathed his fortune to the working classes; Salomon Heine, the uncle of the great poet, founded the great hospital in Hamburg; Jonas Freiherr von Koenigswarter built a school for the blind at Vienna; Hirsch Kollisch, a man in moderate circumstances, built by his untiring labor the institution for the deaf mute in the same city; Albert Cohn left, as almoner of the Paris house of Rothschild, eternal traces of his life work.

Judaism stands for religion, and not for race. Therefore all converts ought to be excluded from this treatise. On the other hand it can not be denied that early impressions have a great influence on the development of the character, even if one in maturer years changes his course entirely. Therefore such converts as Disraeli and Heine belong to Jewish History. How much the more have we to include in it the converts to other religions, who, by their Jewish education, first became conversant with religious questions and susceptible of this zeal which they used in the service of the new faith to which they became converts. Of such I may name Bishop Julian of Toledo (seventh century), who wrote a book to refute the Jewish argument that the Messiah would not come before the end of the fiftieth century of the world. Of more importance is Pablo Christiani, from Montpellier, the famous seat of rabbinical learning, who arranged the four days' disputation in the royal palace of Barcelona (1263), in which, on the Jewish side, was the greatest scholar of this age, Moses ben Nahman. Abner of Burgos, known under his Christian name, Alfonso, succeeded in his denunciation of the Hebrew prayer-book as containing anti-christian passages. Solomon Hallevi was, under the name of Paulus, Bishop of Burgos, and worked for the conversion of his co-religionists, one of whom, the grammarian, Profiat Duran Ephodi, ridiculed this effort in the biting satire אל תהי כאבותיך. Some Jewish converts, even in our time, acquired fame in the service of the church, as the venerable Liebermann, who is now "on the road to canonization;" the two brothers Ratisbonne, one of whom, Alfons Maria, is the founder of a religious order; Emanuel Veith, who is counted amongst the greatest German preachers of Catholicism, and finally, the recently consecrated prince, Archbishop of Olmuetz, by the unmistakable name of Theodor Kohn. Even the late English Cardinal Howard is, according to the hitherto uncontradicted statement of the "Bohemia," a native of the ghetto of Prague, known there under the name of Jacob Austerlitz.

In the Protestant world we have among the co-workers of the reformation, Tremellius (d. 1580), who first in Italy became a convert to Catholicism, afterwards an adherer of Calvin, whose friendship he enjoyed, and whose catechism he translated into Hebrew, which, like his Latin translation of the Old Testament, was highly appreciated in the reformed church. Besides a great many missionaries, as Chr. D. Ginsburg, de le Roi, Adolph Saphir, etc., the great scholar Paulus (Selig) Cassel, the illustrious church historian, August Neander, formerly David Mendel, who defended the orthodox dogma of Jesus against the attacks of David Friedrich Strauss, and finally the expounder of the idea of the Christian state, Friedrich Julius Stahl, are very prominent characters in the history of their church.

It would hardly be possible even to enumerate in this sketch all the scholars in the different branches of science; all the statesmen, artists, and benefactors of Jewish origin, and still less would it be possible to give the hearer an insight into the work done by them. I therefore may say, in the words of Isaiah: "Jacob shall not be ashamed, neither shall his face now wax pale but when he seeth his children, the work of mine hand; in the midst of him they shall sanctify my name; yea they shall sanctify the Holy One of Jacob, and shall stand in awe of the God of Israel."

CONTRIBUTION OF THE JEWS TO THE PRESERVATION OF THE SCIENCES IN THE MIDDLE AGES.

By DR. SAMUEL SALE.

The Jews have shared much the same fate both with regard to their religion and science. The more mankind have exploited them, the more they were persecuted and maligned. The greater the debt of gratitude due them, the less recognition they received. No one with but a passing knowledge of human history need be told that the religions of civilized mankind are founded on the principles that have come from Judea, and yet strenuous efforts have been made at all times, not excepting our own, to underrate and belittle, if not entirely to deny, their beneficial influence on the moral and mental uplifting of mankind. It is a stubborn fact that will not yield to all the untoward powers on earth, that Israel has been the heart of all mankind in a religious sense.

If in the realm of religion, wherein the Jew was original and creative and founded an ideal that has captivated the world, he was subject to neglect and discredit, we need not be surprised that he was curtailed of his just meed of recognition in a field where his services were less obvious and less open to the uninitiated. It is one of the commonest charges brought against the Jew that he has contributed little or nothing to the sciences and their preservation, and it was customary down to our own times for the profoundest historian to pass him by, either without any mention at all, or to speak only in derogation of him. Since the revival of learning and letters, however, which goes back to the days of Rappaport and Zunz, it is no longer possible to ignore the Jews as a factor in the culture of the sciences in the middle ages and their preservation for all times to come. Indeed, they were not only an important factor, but they were the only means and instrument by which at that time the philosophy of the ancient Greeks was transmitted to the European world. The Jews were the only people of whom we might say they had no middle age, an epoch of intellectual and moral decline. Notwithstanding their dispersion and oppression, by which they were deprived of all human rights, yea, often of the right to live, they busied themselves about their own literature and eagerly engaged in the study

13

of the wisdom of the Greeks, so that they preserved for others as well
as for themselves the foundation of their moral and intellectual life.
Had the Jew done nothing else than watch with jealous care and devotion his own sacred literature, which has found its way into the
thought and sentiment of all civilized man, we could not well over-
estimate the part he has enacted in the realm of science.

The Bible, naturally, was the object of deepest concern to the
Jew, and about it the intelligent labors of the learned were centered.
To their unremitting efforts of handing it down unharmed, and at understanding it, we owe its preservation. It is generally believed that
the science of Bible criticism is purely a modern product, but aside
from the fact that all subsequent work in this direction would have
been impossible without the Hebrew Bible, which the Jews had
preserved, it is moreover true that the learned commentators of the
middle ages had already begun to turn their minds upon problems
which have been solved in our own times. Exegesis, or the science
of a proper and thorough understanding of the Bible, had always been
a favorite occupation of the Jews, but it was only when the sages of
the middle ages cultivated it that we might say Bible criticism in its
real sense began.

In the sixth century, the genial Saadya, the powerful defender of
Rabbinical Judaism against the onslaught of the Karaites, translated
the Bible into Arabic. Unfortunately, we have but fragments of this
learned work, yet they enable us to appreciate the high estimate which
Mohammedan scholars put upon it. Saadya places reason above the
Bible and the Talmud and rationalizes the miracles of sacred literature. His contemporary, Chivi of Balk, may be classed among the
first and boldest rationalists, and we know to what length of liberalism
and even of infidelity he must have gone, when the enlightened Ibn
Ezra indulges of him the somewhat dubiously pious hope that his bones
may be ground to dust.

The religion of the Jews contains no ideas that run counter to
universal experience and common sense, and therefore it does not
quail before the inexorable consequences of exact science. It has
never set an interdict on free thought, and always admitted of the
greatest possible latitude in the exercise of reason.

It has never trembled before the disclosures of the boldest research, since into its essential constitution there enters no element repugnant to reason that might thereby be endangered or overturned.
It hails every discovery of the exact sciences, even the most startling,
as the sublimest revelation, destined to break down the obstacles and
partition-walls of sectarian prejudice and superstition, and by leveling

the artificial barriers which dogmatists have set up, to prepare the way for the ultimate realization of the grand ideal of its prophets, the fraternization of all men upon the solid basis of justice and love. If this is so, and no epoch of Jewish history furnishes more abundant proof of this assertion than the middle ages, in which the Jewish mind was all on fire with scientific thought, we need not be surprised to find even our rationalists of the last century forestalled by such men as Chivi of Balk, Jephet and Isaac Ibn Kastar, all of whom are mentioned by Ibn Ezra, their worthy successor.

Abu'l-Wahd, commonly called Rabbi Jonah, or Morinus, was the first to raise Bible criticism to the dignity of an independent branch of research. Ibn Janah has become the father of Hebrew lexicography; we might say that he created the syntax of the Hebrew language, and that every student and lover of the sacred tongue has sat at his feet. None before him and few after him, down to our own day, have so thoroughly penetrated the writings of the Bible in all their artistic delicacy as Ibn Janah. All preceding efforts in this department of science, from the first Karaitic Bible student down to Saadya, Menahem, Dunasch, and Hayyuj, seem the work of apprentices when compared with that of Rabbi Jonah. He was the first to study the Bible in its own light and to lay down principles of interpretation which have remained regulative in the realm of Bible science ever since. Among his predecessors were Judah ben Koreisch, who had already proved that Hebrew, Arabic and Aramaic were cognate languages; Menahem ben Saruk, who had made a dictionary of Hebrew roots which was enlarged by Dunasch ben Labrat; and last but not least, Judah Hayyuj, the father of Hebrew grammar, the first to prove that the roots in Hebrew were tri-literal. When we consider the magnitude of their contributions to Semitic philology, and their importance in making an exact study and understanding of the Bible possible, we can not put too high an estimate on their work. All the latter commentators of the Bible are dependent on them.

The daring yet shrewd Ibn Ezra, who wore the mask of traditionalism only to attack it with greater freedom and impunity, may be regarded as the first among the Bible expounders of the middle ages who came nearest to modern views and grounded the science on the strictest principles of hermeneutics. He recognized not only that the latter part of Isaiah could not have been written by the prophet who lived in the days of King Uzziah, but he also called attention to the fact that there were parts of the Pentateuch which had not been written by Moses, notwithstanding the trick that he has of condemning the book of Isaac Al-Kastar as worthy of the flames, because in it the latter had expressed his belief that the 36th chapter of Genesis was written in the days of King Jehosaphat. Nothing is more evident from almost every page of his commentaries on the Bible that none was less bound by tradition than he. Ibn Ezra did not believe in the Davidic authorship of the Psalms. It is needless in this cursory review of the activity of the Jews during the middle ages in the field of Biblical sciences to mention the names of all the most important commentators, but we can not pass over one who, though by no means the greatest in the realm of Biblical exegesis, yet on account of the simplicity and popularity of his commentaries exercised a great influence over the religious ideas of the non-Jews. We mean Solomon ben Isaac, commonly called Rashi. His writings were extensively translated and used by Christians. They were especially drawn upon by the Franciscan, Nicholas de Lyra (1300–1340) and through him Rashi's views and interpretations became current in the Christian world. It was through Lyra that Luther's ideas of the Bible were influenced and altered to such an extent that he felt himself called upon to undertake a new translation thereof, as an authority against the Vulgata of the Catholic Church. Luther was indebted to Lyra so largely that in the days of the reformation the words went round :

> "Si Lyra non lyrasset,
> Lutherus non saltasset."
> " Hätt' Lyra nicht geleiert,
> Wär' Luther's Tanzfest nicht gefeiert."

It may seem strange and exaggerated to hear this view expressed, but it is none the less true that without the precedent contributions of the Jews to the sciences in the middle ages the Protestant reformation would not have been possible. It was upon the Bible and the Bible alone, that Luther stood in the diet at Worms, or as he himself said : *Hier steh' ich, ich kann nicht anders, Gott helfe mir.*

It was the Bible as it had been preserved by the zeal and the learning of the Jews throughout the dark ages, and not upon the Latin version which alone was considered authoritative by the Church, but in direct opposition to it, that Luther founded his movement. The weapons which he wielded against the institutions of the Church were forged at the stithy of Jewish learning. Imagine for a moment that the Jew had been as reckless of his literary heritage as were the monks of the dark and middle ages of the classical treasures buried within the dust of their cloisters. Imagine if you can that the Jew had scrawled his prayers across the manuscripts of the Bible as the Catholic monks did their breviaries and the writings of the Church

Fathers, over the manuscripts of the classical authors of Greece and Rome; try to realize in thought a palimpsest of the Bible and your thought will fail you. In glaring contrast to the mental indolence of the world about him, the mental activity and unrest of the Jews of the middle ages remind us forcibly of a bee-hive in which all are busily at work storing away the precious honey of religious and scientific thought for the profit of mankind. The drones of those days were not found among the Jews, but the sting of prejudice from which the Jew has smarted came from those cells in which no honey at all was made. So far as the outward details of the lives of our great men of this age are concerned, they might have been shut up in cloisters. The Jewish celebrities of those days, both among the Muslims and the Christians, were barred from public life, and since they were always given over to the hatred and contempt of the reigning religion and threatened by the fanaticism of the populace, they sought peace and quiet in complete isolation and retirement. Ignored by society, the Jewish scholars devoted themselves to the culture of the sciences with a disinterested zeal which offered them neither honor nor emolument. The physicians were the only ones who were largely sought after and attained prominence on account of their superior skill and knowledge. The lives of the crowned heads, ecclesiastical as well as secular, were almost exclusively intrusted to their hands. To single out only one name from the many, we mention Isaac ben Suleiman Israeli (845–940) who was called to Kairuan by Ziadath Allah as his physician in ordinary, and when Ziadath in turn was overcome by Ubaid Allah, who founded a great empire in Africa, Isaac Israeli became *his* trusted physician. His renown spread far and wide, and he was always surrounded by students who came from a great distance to profit by his instruction. At the request of the Chalif he wrote eight books on the science of medicine, the best of which, according to competent judges, is that on fevers. He was never married, and when reproached for leaving no heirs, he replied that his work on fevers would preserve his name and fame better than children. His books were translated into Hebrew, Latin and Spanish, and were diligently studied by the votaries of Æsculapius. A Christian physician, Constantine of Carthage, the founder of the medical school at Salerno, filched his works and published several of them under his own name. It was regarded as an important religious obligation to maintain the health of the body, and it was enjoined upon the Jew to devote his services as healer to Jew and non-Jew alike. Thus we find that most of the rabbis of the middle ages were physicians. The beautiful prayer of Maimonides, written for a physician

who is called to the bedside of the sick, proves how conscientious the
Jewish physician was in the discharge of his duty and how exalted
was his idea of his profession. It has been said by the famous
Frenchmen, Astruc and Prunelle, themselves physicians, that until
the time when the schools of medicine at Montpellier and Salerno
were founded and mainly through the efforts of the Jews, the latter
were the only physicians in the then known world. It was only later
on that the Arabs followed their example, and when they were driven
from Spain the Jews again remained the sole representatives and cul-
tivators of the science of medicine. Their reputation in this department had taken such a deep hold on the minds of the people that
even the dignitaries of the Church and the rulers of the State who
shamefully plundered and persecuted the Jews, would have none other
as their medical attendants. Francis the 1st, famed by the field of
the cloth of gold, would not even trust himself in the hands of a converted Jew. It seems he had as much faith in the renegade as we
have to-day. It is worthy of note that Maimonides was called to
England as a physician by Richard, the Lion-hearted, but declined to
accept. Until the end of the seventeenth century, medicine and the
natural sciences had not parted company, and thus it goes without
saying that the learned Jews devoted themselves to the latter with
equal assiduity. There was no branch of inquiry that did not claim
their attention and devotion, and so eager were they in search of
knowledge that they traversed all countries to find it. We hear
of Petahyah of Regensburg, of Eldad Ha-Dani of Münchausen fame,
and especially of Benjamin of Tudela, who traveled for eight years
(1165–1173) and explored almost the whole of the then known world.
The account of his travels was translated not only into Latin but into
nearly all the modern European languages. In the voyage of discovery undertaken to East India the Jews were represented by Abraham
de Behia and Joseph Zapatero de Lamego, the same who had been
sent by King John the 2nd of Portugal to explore the coasts of the
Red Sea and the island of Ormuz in the Persian gulf. No one can
read the Psalms without being impressed by the fact that the Jews
loved nature and strove to look through nature up to nature's God.
They drank in the harmony of the spheres, and while they did not
sink to the level of nature worship, they were enraptured with the
beauty of the vault fretted with golden fire and all the forms of the
creation of God. Alexander von Humboldt thus speaks of this noble
sentiment of the ancient Jews: "Their lyrical poetry is more adorned
than their epic or historical narratives, and develops a rich and ani-
mated conception of the life of nature. It might almost be said that

one single Psalm (104th) represents the image of the whole Cosmos." He dwells upon their accuracy of natural description, and he declares that the book of Job propounds problems which in the present state of our physical knowledge we may be able to express with more scientific definiteness but scarcely answer more satisfactorily. "The heavens declare the glory of God and the firmament telleth His handiwork," and in all the ages the Jews were eagerly bent upon finding His glory as reflected in the heavens and established in His handiwork called nature. It is well known that our sages could never have fixed their calendar so accurately without an intimate knowledge of astronomy, and their method of calculation passed from them to the Arabs among whom they lived in Yathrib. About eight hundred of the common era, Rabbi Sahal Al-tabari was famously known as a physician and an astronomer; he translated the works of Ptolemy into Arabic and discovered the refraction of light. The pupil of Isaac Israeli, Dunash ben Tammim, was famous as an astronomer in his days, and was among the first to use the Arabic system of notation that had lately come into use. The works of Abraham bar Hiyya, an astronomer who lived about the beginning of the twelfth century, were translated into Latin and extensively used.

In Sefer ha-Ibbur, he proves the correctness and accuracy of the Jewish calendar. Maimonides, who was no mean astronomer and mathematician himself, wrote an elaborate refutation of astrology which seems to have been quite the fashion among Jews and Christians in those days. It is very remarkable, indeed, that the Zohar taught the revolution of the earth on its axis as the cause of day and night, long before Copernicus. About the middle of the thirteenth century, Alphonso, King of Castile, a passionate devotee of astronomy, had new tables prepared under the direction of Isaac ben Sid. Alexander von Humboldt supposes that the Latin term "nebulosae" for stellar clusters passed into these Alphonsine tables through the preponderating influence of this Jewish astronomer (Cosmos, Vol. IV, 294), who was not the chief Rabbi of the wealthy Synagogue at Toledo, as Humboldt has it, but only enjoyed the humble distinction of being the Hazzan of the congregation. Among many others I will only mention Levi ben Gerson, who, as philosopher and commentator, outshone all of his contemporaries. His attainments in astronomy must have been quite noteworthy, inasmuch as his description of an astronomical instrument invented by him was by special request translated into Latin for Pope Clement VI, and Keppler was very anxious to get it. Thus we find the Jews busily engaged in all of the exact sciences, but as yet we have not touched upon that department of thought in which the Jews

have enacted a most important part. The Arabs were the first to shed
a ray of light into the gloom which hung like a pall upon the nations
of Europe after the migration of the Huns and Vandals and the sad
havoc which they caused wherever they went.

But the works of the Greeks became known to the Moors through
the mediation of the Jews. In those days, in which the Jew was a
wanderer on the face of the earth, he seems to have been the only
linguist. There were whole families that were exclusively engaged in
translating, such as the Thibbons, through whom the works of Aristotle and of his foremost Mohammedan follower, Averroes, were translated into Latin, and thus made known to the occidental world.
Along with them the family of Kalonymos and of the Kimhis deserve honorable mention for fructifying the field of learning by means
of accurate translations of learned works. But the Jews were not
only translators; they were also original speculators in the realm of
religious thought and philosophy. It is true, they created no brand-
new systems of thought, but they popularized almost all the traditional
ones, and were chiefly instrumental in bringing them into the homely
thinking of the people by applying to them the test of religion, and
by attempting to reconcile them to their traditional faith. The Christian schools of the middle ages resounded with the praises of a philosopher celebrated as one of the profoundest thinkers, whose views they
feared to refute, and oftener adopted as their own. He was Avicebron. Who was he, and to what faith did he belong? These questions remained unanswered a long time.

Avicebron was a Jew. No name is more favorably known in
Jewish history—he is none other than the excellent poet-philosopher
whom we have just mentioned, ben Gabirol, a singularly gifted man,
and one who combined a depth of feeling and power of thought such
as have rarely been united in one person. He is the well-known author of "Kether Malchuth," a poem which alone would have established his fame, and also of a philosophic work known as "The Fountain of Life." It was the celebrated Jewish orientalist, Solomon
Munk, of Paris, who proved the identity of Gabirol and Avicebron.
Up to that time he was supposed to have been a pious Christian and
his works had been eagerly studied. It is doubtful whether he would
have been regarded as so great an authority had it been known
that he was a Jew, but, as it was, his book is frequently quoted in the
writing of Albertus Magnus and Thomas Aquinas, the two leading
school-men of the middle ages. Jourdain, the learned French historian of philosophy, equally versed in Arabic literature and the
scholastic writings, says that we can not get a sure and sufficient

knowledge of the philosophy of the thirteenth century, unless we analyze the "Liber de Causis" and the "Fons vitae," the one translated by and the other written by a Jew. After Munk had made his magnificent discovery, he committed it to the learned world in 1846. His article for the *Litteraturblatt des Orients* of that year was addressed to Professor Ritter, who, in his history of philosophy, had accorded no place whatsoever to the Jewish philosophers of the middle ages, but who, without being aware of it, had presented a Jew, this very Avicebron, as the most original mind of the entire period of Arabic thought, and as the one who had exercised a dominant influence in the Christian schools of learning down to the time of Albert the Great and Duns Scotus.

Ritter, as became a conscientious scholar, was not slow to acknowledge the mistake he had made. He admitted that a Jew was the first to give a lasting incentive and influence to the philosophic thought of the middle ages. We can better estimate the importance of Gabirol's services when we remember that he even preceded Ibn Badya or Avempace, the first of the Moslem philosophers. His work called "The Fountain of Life" had been translated into Latin even before it was into Hebrew, by the Dominican Archdeacon, Gondisalvi, by the aid of a converted Jew, Avendeath, about 1150. The Scotists and Thomists both seized upon it, the former as Platonists exalted and the latter as Aristotelians combated the views of Avicebron, but both regarded him as a Christian philosopher of the greatest importance.

Geiger has mentioned the names of Gabirol and Spinoza as worthy companions in mind, and we can hardly escape the belief that they were affianced spirits. It has been truly said that Gabirol's philosophy was so soon neglected and forgotten, because it was held to run counter to the teachings of Judaism.

I shall not mention the translators and commentators of the works of Aristotle, through whom alone his philosophy became known to the schoolmen and through them to the European world, but I shall conclude this very unsatisfactory sketch by referring to one whom Munk has called the greatest glory of the Synagogue, Moses ben Maimon, undoubtedly the greatest man among those to whom Mohammedan Cordova gave birth. His chief work, "The Guide to the Perplexed," was translated into Latin hardly a half-century after his death, and yet Rabbi Moses of Egypt, as he was called by Christians, was so well known in the Christian world that in all important matters bearing upon religion they appealed to his work as an authority. He was an Aristotelian out and out, like Averroes, the greatest of Mohammedan philosophers, but yet he was not bound to him slavishly, and he was the first to attempt with any success to refute Aristotle's arguments that the world was uncreated. In this particular he was closely followed by Albertus Magnus and Thomas Aquinas. There are, as Joel tells us, folio pages in Albertus's books on the subject of creation, which read like a translation of the Moreh. Thomas Aquinas was a still closer student of Maimonides. He accepts from him his exposition of the God-idea and his proofs of the existence of God. But the influence of Maimonides was not confined to the middle ages. The great Leibnitz, as we now know, studied him and extracted his books, chapter for chapter, and praised him in the following terms: " I find the book of Rabbi Moses, called ' The Guide of the Erring,' an excellent one and of much greater philosophical value than I had believed. I consider it worthy of attentive study." We can even assert that Leibnitz was indebted to him for the central idea of his most popular books the " Theodicy," a vindication of the justice of God in ordaining or permitting natural and moral evil. A comparison of the answers given by Leibnitz on this subject, with those of Maimonides in the third part of the Moreh, will prove this assertion.

Even Kant was not uninfluenced by Maimonides, we dare maintain, when we remember that he recommends as the only sure way of attaining a pure and worthy conception of God, is, not by predicating of him positive attributes, but denying of him every attribute that involves an imperfection. Maimonides was the first philosopher who clearly sets up this doctrine, and to him we owe the seminal and liberalizing idea that we can not say what God is, we can only say what He is not, and rest safe in the thought that He is. Indeed, we owe this religious inspiration to the Thorah itself, when it tells us that the most fitting name for God is, "I am that I am." It may be of interest to know that even Hegel had studied the Moreh.

The Jews have never been mere idle recipients of the liberal culture of others, but they have always been eager and earnest co-workers in every realm and department of knowledge. Their faith is founded on knowledge, and the fact that Jewish scholars have devoted themselves to science in the face of persecution and obloquy entitles them to the highest praise we can bestow on them, both for their nobility of character and their singular devotion to science. If the Jews of the middle ages have not been awarded sufficient recognition for the important part they have enacted in the enlargement and preservation of the sciences, it is due to the systematic and stupid attempts to suppress them and keep them and their religion in the background. The failure to give them their full meas-

ure of desert is but another colossal exemplification of the willingness
with which men forget their benefactors.   To the Jew as a vital factor
in the civilization of mankind more than to any other member of the
human family, the words of the world's master poet may be applied :
" Time hath, my Lord, a wallet at his back, wherein he puts alms for
oblivion—a great sized monster of ingratitudes."

HISTORIANS OF JUDAISM.

By RABBI E. SCHREIBER.

I.

While the number of writers on the history of the Jews is quite large, we do not yet possess a history of *Judaism*. This history must of necessity be a history of the development of the spiritual life of the Jew. The outward history has only the value of a substratum of the condition which acted favorably or unfavorably toward this evolution. "Not by might, not by physical force, but by my spirit, saith the Eternal." The history of Judaism is indeed a *Sefer milchamoth adonai*, a record containing the struggles in the cause of God. Truth is the seal of God. Just because Judaism developed independent of the destruction of its *national* and political life, it still exists. The history of the people of Israel and the history of the Jews, even in the period of their national and political independence, proves very little talent on their side for self-government, executive administration and statesmanship. Nor did the Jews exercise any important influence upon the political life of other nations, but the history of our spiritual life is in its grandeur, sublimity and influence without a parallel in the world's history.

The Jewish nationality was broken, the commonwealth destroyed, the Temple consumed by fire, and the priest's occupation was gone. Legend tells us that they threw the keys of the Temple toward Heaven, never to be returned again. New Messiahs and revolutions availed nothing against Rome's legions, and yet it was then, when the history of the Jewish nation was concluded, that the history of the Jewish spirit of Judaism proper began. Rome could never forget and never forgive the Jew that he had engaged for such a long time its military power. Rome instinctively felt not only hatred against, but fear and dread of, the spirit of Judaism. The Jew, although conquered physically, vanquished the haughty victor spiritually and morally. Well might the proud Roman sneer at the down-trodden Jewish captives who followed humbly Titus's triumphal procession; yet little did he dream that these same exiles would introduce into the city on the Tiber a spirit which ultimately destroyed Rome's temples and altars, and was instrumental in gradually converting the pagan world to the belief in ethical monotheism.

The Jew started on his sad pilgrimage of the Middle Ages, but he was permitted to erect tottering huts only, had to tear down to-day what he had built yesterday. Yet no matter of how short a duration his stay in a country, he never neglected to till the spiritual soil and to sow spiritual seeds.

It is a great mistake of many historians of our century that they dwell too much on the persecution and oppression of the Jews, and do not pay greater attention to the other and brighter side of the picture, namely, that while the Jew was oppressed, the spirit of Judaism could not be suppressed. Too many of our historians make our history simply a valley of sorrow, a tragedy, a tear-stained romance. Even at this late day, orators at conventions of our secret orders do not tire quoting Byron's well-meant verses:

> "The bird has its nest, the fox its cave,
> Mankind its country, Israel but the grave."

We do not care for the pity of the world, but we challenge its admiration and just appreciation due to the genius of Judaism, which was strong enough to endow the hunted Jew with the faculty of taking deep root in the spirit and character of the country in which his lot was even temporarily cast. As an instance in the case, I mention the fact that centuries after the Jews were driven from Germany, they have preserved the German language among themselves, and thus remained in touch with German culture and civilization. It is this genius which saved the Jews, even in the dark ages, from the curse of ignorance. At the time when dignitaries of State and Church were not initiated in the art of reading and writing, the dispersed Jew preserved a most astonishing aspiration to a spiritual development, which saved him from stagnation. He could certainly read and write one language. While science now and then took a crooked route, canonization of ignorance was never the rule in Israel.

At a time when the Jericho walls of superstition shut out every ray of light from the church, our priests sounded the bugle-call by proclaiming: "The Thora forces nobody to believe what is against reason;" or, "Reason is the only mediator between God and man." Gigantic works of darker and brighter times, productions of thought and spiritual activity, are before us, which contain an acumen and power of thought, a wealth of sound sense and salutary maxims, which must awaken the reverence of all those who appreciate them.

Judaism is not only the mother of Christianity, but stood likewise with its doctrines at the cradle of that new civilization, which in the seventh century sprang into existence within the boundaries of Arabia. The only fruit-bearing thought of Islamism, "There is no other God but the One in Unity," was taken from Judaism, and was garnished and adorned with Jewish views and tales. What is known as the civilization of the Arabs and Moors in the Middle Ages would not have exercised such a profound influence had the Jews not taken part therein. Through translations from the Arabic tongue into Hebrew, and from the Hebrew into the various European languages, the Jews scattered the seeds of the new culture far and wide. Well may the Jews be sneered at as peddlers with cast-off garments, but they carried the cast-off garments of ancient civilization and classical culture into the homes of European nations. They were not only business mediators, but mediators of the sciences.

It is impossible in the short time allotted to me to enumerate all the great Jewish minds who contributed so much to the philosophy, medicine, poetry, and other sciences in the Middle Ages. Prof. Schleiden did this in his *"Der Einfluss der Juden auf die Verbreitung der Wissenschaft im Mittelalter."* (Leipzig, 1879.) But suffice to say that all this bears testimony to the genius of Judaism, which, even under adverse circumstances, can not be broken down. The Renaissance newly awakened the European world by means of Hellenism and Judaism. It was the rediscovered Bible, made accessible to Christians by means of Jewish teachers, which brought about the great *reformation*. What is called "higher criticism" walks upon crutches borrowed from the Rabbis and Jewish exegetes of the Middle Ages (Chivi of Balk, Saadia, Gikatilia, Ibn Ezra, Mose del Medigo, Elias Levita, Asaria de Rossi, and others).

The originator of a new line of philosophical thought, the poor crystal cutter of Amsterdam, the creator of biblical criticism, Baruch Spinoza, was nurtured on the breasts of Judaism. He had been educated by the Jewish votaries of Aristotle, received many impulses from the Kabbala, and was greatly influenced by Maimonides, Ibn Ezra, Judah Alfakar, and Chasdai Crescas.

It is too early in the day to speak of the influence of modern Judaism on the world's history, but aside from the fact that the hue and cry of anti-Semitism proves that such an influence exists, thoughtful men will not deny that the Jewish reform movement, originated and fathered by Abraham Geiger and the German school, and devel-

The influence of the Jews upon the civilization of the Middle Ages. The pamphlet was translated into English (Baltimore, 1881) by Binswanger.

oped and forcibly carried out in this country, exercises a powerful influence toward liberalizing religious thought and advancing the interest of biblical science. Geiger's "*Urschrift und Übersetzungen der
Bibel*" (1854) has contributed largely toward a better understanding
not only of the Bible and of Judaism, but of Christianity.

II.

After these outlines it will be seen that "historians of Judaism"
are few and far between. Geiger's "*Judenthum und seine Geschichte*,"
in lectures held in Breslau, Frankfurt and Berlin (1864, 1865 and
1870), and Jost's "*Geschichte des Judenthum's und seiner Sekten*" (Leipzig, 1857, 1858, 1859), both in three volumes, came nearest to the
ideal. All the other histories are histories of the *Jews*, but not of
Judaism.

During the ages of persecution it was next to impossible for the
Jews to preserve and collect the vast memories of their glorious past.
They lost the sense for history. Outside of "Memmor-books" (so-
called "chronicles" of congregations, devoid of system and method)
only a few Jewish historians prior to the nineteenth century deserve
notice. I mention first the physician, astronomer, grammarian and
philosopher Profit Duran. His Jewish name was Isaac ben Mose, and,
as author, he is known under the name "Efodi"[1] (Ephodæus). His
"Memories of persecutions" (*Sichron hashmad*), contain the histories
of the Jewish martyrs from the time of the destruction of the Temple
to the fourteenth century.

Another Jewish historian was the physician *Joseph ben Joshua
Kohen* (born in 1496 at Avignon, died 1575). He published "Chronicles of the Kings of France and the Otoman House" (1554). The
title is: *Sefer dibre hayamim lemalche Zarfath umalche beth autiman hato-
gar*. The work was translated into English by Bialloblotzky under
the title: "*The Chronicles of Rabbi Joseph ben Joshua ben Meier the
Sephardi*."[2] His Hebrew style is excellent. Basnage calls him the
"greatest Jewish historian since Josephus." The author describes the
wars between the French and the Turks. It is in fact the history of
the struggle between Islamism and Christianity, beginning with the
destruction of the Roman Empire. The author relates, wherever the

---

[1] An abbreviation of *Omer Profiat Duran*. His letter, "*Igerath al Chi
Kaabothekha*" (Constantinople, 1854), is famous for its cutting sarcasm.

[2] It is a source of regret that this translation, which was issued in a
most elegant form in 1835–36, under the auspices of the "Oriental Translation Fund," is absolutely worthless.

occasion justifies it, the persecution of the Jews in the different countries. He writes not only with his pen, but with his heart, and shows God's providence in history; how wrong, cunning, and wickedness receive in the end their just punishment. The author bitterly attacks the tormentors of his co-religionists, a fact which is excusable, considering that he was himself a witness of the heartless persecutions.

His book "Emek Habacha," ("Valley of Tears") was commenced in Voltaggio in 1558 and completed in 1563. It was translated into German and supplied with very valuable historical notes by Dr. M. Weiner (Leipzig, 1858). This work is a martyrology of the Jews, and relates in detail the sad sufferings of Israel, caused by prejudice, calumny, artful tricks and false accusations. The author made use of a similar work of *Samuel Usque*, entitled, "*Consolacaem as Tribulacoens de Israel*" ("Consolation on account of the Tribulations of Israel," Ferrara, 1552), of which I shall speak later.

Another historical work of the same character, a martyrology, is "Shebet Jehudah" ("The Scourge of Judah"), also edited and translated into German by Dr. Wiener (Hanover, 1855). This book has virtually three authors—the father, son and grandson of the family *Ibn Verga, Juda, Solomon* and *Joseph Ibn Verga*—and was published in 1552. The Hebrew style is brilliant, but the work lacks system and method. Interesting are the causes which Salomon Ibn Verga gives for the persecutions of the Jews in general and of the Spanish Jews in particular. These are: 1. The excellence of the Jews, for "Whomsoever God loveth he chasteneth." 2. The punishment for the sin of the golden calf, which is not yet expiated. 3. The exclusiveness of the Jews; their separation from the tables of Christians have excited hatred against the former. 4. Jesus' crucifixion caused the Christians to take revenge. 5. Envy against the Spanish Jews. 6. Their immoral intercourse with Christian women. 7. Their false oaths. We see that Ibn Verga did not hide the faults of his contemporaries.

Elia Kapsali (born 1490, died 1555), Rabbi in Candia, was another historian of note. He published two historical works, one entitled "*Dibre Hayamim*," or "*Seder Eliahu*," on the Turkish dynasty and the Spanish Jews (Candia, 1523), extracts of which were made by Luzzatto for the translation of "Emek Habacha." The other is a collection of letters, entitled "*Sefer nam Vecholim*," Geiger's Zeitschrift III, 348. His Hebrew style is excellent and his history proves great talent.

Of less importance as a historian is *Abraham Zacuto*. King Emanuel of Portugal appointed him professor of history. His book, "Juchasin" (Chronicles), was finished in Tunis in 1502. The second edition was published, with many additions, in Cracow in 1850. The latest edition of the work came out in London in 1857.

But the most important and original historian of this period was *Samuel Usque*. His "Consolacaem as Tribulacoens de Israel" (1552, "Consolations in Israel's Tribulations") forms a dialogue between three shepherds, Icabo, Numeo and Zicareo, in which the first bitterly complains about the tragic fate of Israel in its checkered career in history. The other shepherds try to pour the balm of consolation into the wounded heart of the unfortunate shepherd by representing the sufferings of Israel as a necessary preparation for the fulfillment of a sublime mission. This work forms a historical poem, beginning with biblical times and coming down to his own period. He made good use of Latin sources, of French, Spanish, and Italian chronicles of the Hebrew writings and collections, and paid due attention to chronological accuracy. His main object was to raise the courage and the hopes of the Portuguese refugees from the persecutions of the Spanish Inquisition. They fled to Italy in order to remain faithful to the religion of their fathers. He, no doubt, succeeded in his noble task.

Since that time until the beginning of this century not even attempts were made by Jews to write a history of Israel. Christian historians, attracted by the grandeur of the subject, attempted the task, but even well-meaning and least prejudiced men, like Basnage, Gregoire, and Dohm, did not succeed in offering a true picture. To search the Jewish records as we would those of other nations was regarded "heresy," a dangerous outrage on the Christian religion.[1]

Of Christian writers on Jewish history, *Jacob Basnage*,[2] a French protestant clergyman, stands in the front rank. He was born in 1633 and died in 1723, and published a "History of the Religion of the Jews from Jesus Christ to the Present,"[3] in five volumes. He was the first to recognize that, notwithstanding the fact that Christianity had entered upon the historical arena and the national life of the Jews had ceased seventeen centuries before his time, yet their mission was not concluded. The martyrdom and literature of the Jews filled him with respect and awe. He plainly says that it must be more than an accident that the Jews, although oppressed and persecuted, still exist, while so many of their persecutors are laid away in their graves

---

[1] Stanley; History of the Jewish Church, Vol. I, Introduction.

[2] He fled to Holland on account of religious persecutions. He preached for the Wallonian Church in Haag.

[3] The title is: "*Histoire de la Religion des Juifs depuis Jesus Christ jusqu' a Present*" (Rotterdam, 1707–1711). It was translated into English in 1708 by Taylor.

14

or are at best ruins of former greatness (Introduction I, "*Plan de cette Histoire*"). The fact that Basnage, himself, owing to the religious fanaticism of Louis the XV. was compelled to eat the bread of exile in Holland made him just to the Jews. He had also the necessary knowledge to make use of Hebrew sources. Still he did not possess the historical tact for his important task. His division of the Jewish history into the history of the Orient and Occident was not fortunate because unnatural. The law of historical growth and development seems to have been unknown to him. In spite of his best intentions to be just, he saw the Jewish history through the lenses of church history. "The Jews were rejected by God because they rejected Jesus" is the leading principle of Basnage's work. And yet, his history has done great service to the cause of the Jews, who have been looked upon by the people as a horde of gypsies without a history. Christian Theophyl Unger, pastor in Silesia, and Johann Christophorus Wolf (born 1683, died 1739), professor of Oriental languages in Hamburg, were greatly influenced in their historical studies by Basnage. Many mistakes of Basnage were corrected by Wolf in his "*Bibliotheca Hebraica*" (four volumes; Hamburg and Leipzig, 1715, 1721, 1727, 1733). Of Jewish contemporaries, *Mose Chagis* was the only one who in his "*Mishnath Chachamim*" mentions and appreciates Basnage.

The Christian Friedrich *Dohm* (born 1751, died 1820), an able historian of Prussia, and a warm friend of the Jews, took great interest in Jewish history. He was an admirer of Moses Mendelsohn, and planned the publication of a "History of the Jewish Nation Since the Destruction of their State." In his memorable work on "The Civil Amelioration of the Jews" (Berlin, 1781) Councilor Dohm puts forth an earnest plea for the enfranchisement of the Jews. He points to the thrift and frugality which marks the Jewish race, and exposes the folly of debarring so valuable a class of population from the rights of the citizen. On the hand of history he defends the Jews against the charges always repeated against them, and appeals to the wisdom of the government to redeem the errors and injustice of the past. Reviewing the history of the Jews in Europe, he shows how they have been in possession of their civil rights in the first centuries of the Roman Empire, and how they had contributed to the culture and civilization of different lands, and that liberty and humane treatment would not only accrue to their advantage but to the welfare of the state in which they live.

The famous French priest *Gregoire* published an essay on "The Physical, Moral and Political Regeneration of the Jews," which was crowned by the Royal Society of Sciences and Arts, in Metz, August

23, 1778. In it he enthusiastically pleaded for the emancipation of the Jews. Yet he still believed[1] in the myth—that the martyrdom of the Jews is at least deserved, because of their rejection of the "Savior."[2] From the same point of view he treats Judaism in his "History of the Religious Sects" (*Histoire des Sectes Religieuses*, Paris, 1810).

The "History of the Jews from the Destruction of Jerusalem to the Present Time," by Hannah *Adams*, of Boston, was reprinted in London (1818) under the auspices of the "Society for the Propagation of Christianity Among the Jews." This society made so-called "improvements" to the book. In 1819 a German translation of the work in two volumes was published (Leipzig, Baumgartner). Basnage's "history," in English translation, 1708, Gregoire's "Essay" and "*Historie des Sectes Religieuses*," David Levi's "Ceremonies of the Jews," and Josephus' and Mosheim's "History of the Church" were the main sources of Hannah Adams. While the enthusiastic lady deserves credit for her earnest endeavors, it can not be expected to find in her work more than a feeble attempt. While she considers the Jewish "nation"[3] "chosen to proclaim the knowledge of the true God," she nevertheless sees in Christianity the fulfillment of Judaism. Every so-called "conversion" of a Jew is scrupulously chronicled by this historian. We look in vain for historical truth in this work, which for this very reason was taken hold of by the London missionary society. The true object of the book can best be seen by the following concluding passages: "The fulfillment of the prophecy of our Savior concerning the destruction of their city and temple, and of the misery undergone since their dispersion offers *the strongest proofs for the truth of the Christian religion*. . . . The Christian reader can not better conclude this book than with the purpose to pray often and zealously for the promised conversion of the Jews, and to subscribe to the Fund of the "London Society for the Furtherance of Christianity Among the Jews."

Such is the tendency of most of Christian historians of Israel, who, with perhaps one or two exceptions, close their histories with the beginning of Christianity. Even scholars like Heinrich Ewald, Milman, Stanley, and others who follow in their wake, form no exception to the rule.

Professor Heinrich Ewald's "History of the People of Israel,"

---

[1] Essay, "*Sur la Regeneration Physique, Morale et Politique des Juifs*" (1778).

[2] Ibidem, chapter 5.

[3] The fact is that there is no Jewish "nation" since 1900 years.

in seven large volumes (Goettingen, 1862), is justly considered a standard work. Ewald closes his history with the uprising of Bar-Khosiba in the time of Hadrian. This shows best his point of view, namely, that the Jews' history has lost in value since they have lost their *national* independence. Such a conception of our history is superficial. At the same time Ewald sees in Israel a missionary people, inasmuch as they prepared the world for the coming of the "Savior." But for Ewald this mission was ended by the appearance on the scene of Jesus. True, the history of the Jews is continued a century after Jesus, but only because the existence of Christianity was not firmly established before that time. Judaism is after this period for Ewald a corpse, a ruin, not worth mentioning.

Time has proven that Ewald and all his followers and disciples were wrong. For not only has Judaism been a living factor in history, but has proven its vitality and power by giving birth to another historical religion, namely, Islamism, and by influencing the great movement called "Humanism," which in its turn was the mother of the great Christian *Reformation*. Of the influence of Judaism in modern times it is needless to speak.

Ewald,[1] in spite of his stupendous scholarship and historical acumen, possessed neither the knowledge of the Jewish sources (Talmud and rabbinical literature) nor the want of prejudice so necessary for a thorough understanding and a clear conception and appreciation of the powerful forces at work within Judaism a century before and after the birth of Christianity. At the same time Ewald, although unable to read the Talmud, criticised it most arrogantly.[2] Since Ewald, Christian theologians have paid great attention to the study of the Jewish sources. [3] (Noeldeke, Merx, Dillmann, Kuenen, Renan, Stade, Hitzig, Haussrath, and a host of others.) As the short time allotted to us does not permit to consider all the works on the "History of Israel" by leading Christian scholars, such as Hitzig's, Haussrath's, and others,

---

[1] The following passage in Ewald's history is a gem and deserves to be engraved in letters of gold at the entrance of every synagogue. He says: "The history of this ancient (Hebrew) people is at the foundation of the true religion passing through all stages of progress by which it attained to its consummation; the religion which on this narrow territory advances through all struggles to victory, and at length reveals itself in its full glory and might to the end; that, spreading abroad by its own irresistible energy, *it may never vanish away, but may become the eternal heritage and blessing of all nations.*" (Vol. 1, page 9.)

[2] See Geiger's Zeitschrift F. W. U. L., Vol. VII, pp. 196-199.

[3] Geiger has done much to bring about this result. See his letter to Noeldeke. (Nachgel. Schriften, Vol. V.)

we therefore mention one of recent date, because the author's name is
familiar in the whole civilized world, namely, "The History of Israel,"
by the great Frenchman, Ernest Renan, of which three volumes are
published, and a fourth volume is ready for the press.[1] This most
brilliant writer, whose books are monumental as models of good
style, has all the virtues and faults of the French. He often sacrifices critical judgment for brilliancy of construction. The historical art is with Renan more of a poetic divinatory kind than a true
analysis of material presented. His "Life of Jesus" is a novel rather
than a history. Jesus appears as a visionary, vascillating, hypercriti-
cal "demigod," of whom we never know whether he was an enthusiast
or an impostor, more than mortal or less than moral. While we are
carried away by the vividness of its style, we find, when laying the
book aside, that its hero has dissolved into a mass of the most conflict-
ing tendencies. His other works in the same line, "The Apostles,"
"The Anti-Christ," "Mark Aurelius," although marvels of literary
art, can not be regarded as standard works on the origin of Christianity, if put to the test of critical scholarship.

But Renan was one of the few to whose mind it was clear that
without the proper knowledge of Judaism Christianity could not be
understood. Hence he wrote a "History of Israel," which displays
all the strength and weakness of the famous Frenchman. Of his
great appreciation of Judaism, the following passages give ample
proof:

"For a philosophical spirit," he says, "there are truly in the past
of humanity, only three histories of prime interest: Greek history,
the history of Israel, and the history of Rome. These three histories
united constitute what one may call the history of civilization, for
civilization is the result of the alternate co-operation of Greece, Judah,
and Rome. . . . Greece presents one great lack. It despised
the humble, and did not feel the need of a *just* God. Its philosophers
were exceedingly tolerant of the *iniquities* of this world; the idea of a
universal religion never came to them. It was the fire and *genius of a
small* tribe, established in a lost corner *of Syria*, which seems to have
been destined to supply this want in the *Hellenic spirit*. The prophets,
beginning with the ninth century before Christ, give to the idea of a
government by a just God the proportions of a dogma. These are the
fanatics of *social justice*, and they proclaim it loudly that, *if the world
is not just* or is *disinclined* to become so, it is better that *it be destroyed*.
. . . Rome represents *force*. As such, it has *conquered* the world

---

[1] The English edition was published in Boston. (Roberts.)

for the *ideas and ideals nurtured in Greece and in Judea.* Thus Rome,
Greece, and Judea have histories which are the pivots upon which
those of other nations turn, and these one has the right to call providential, because their place is marked in a plan superior to the *oscilla-
tions of all the days.*"

Now, while no Jewish preacher can better express our providential mission, we must not intentionally shut our eyes regarding the
great mistakes of Renan's peculiar notions on the religion of the
Semites. As far back as 1859, in his "Comparative History of the
Semitic Dialects," he advanced the bold theory that the Semite is particularly gifted with the monotheistic instinct, because, being a child
of the desert, which symbolizes monotony, he lacks imagination and
the gift of analysis necessary for the conception of a multiplicity of
natural forces and their deification. In short, the Semite's belief in
one God only is not a prerogative, a higher development of the religious idea, but the very opposite, the *minimum* of religious fervor.

The fact, however, is that it took many centuries, of hard struggle and patient labor on the side of the great prophets in Israel and
Judah, to supplant the polytheistic instinct by monotheism. With
this "race" theory Renan, against his will, became the spiritual father
of what is now called "Anti-semitism," the outgrowth of stupid nationalism and conceited chauvinism. I say unwittingly. For when the
poisonous seed sown by his hypothesis threatened to bear dangerous
fruit, Renan was among the first to raise his voice against this
"shame" of the nineteenth century. In his famous lecture before the
Société d'Etudes Juives, on "Judaism from the point of view of Race
and Religion," he corrected by uncontrovertible proofs from our history
the wrong impression, that the Jews of to-day were an unmixed
Semitic Race, and proved that the purity of our race is an untenable
myth.

Yet in his "History of Israel" Renan again harps on his exploded theory of original distinctive monotheism. In the three volumes of this in many respects great work can be noticed the same influences of his training in a Catholic Seminary, of his national French
bias, and of Rationalism, which are the main features of his "La vie
de Jésus." Many a tribal legend or Biblical myth is represented by
him as a clever trick of Moses and other leaders practiced on the people
for otherwise good purposes, on the principle that the aim justifies the
means. He reverses the idea of evolution in its application to the
Hebrews. Elohim is for him originally Universal God. "Jehovah,"
however, the "God of Israel," as taught by the prophets, is the
nationalization of the Deity, and a lapse, a retrogression from "Uni-

versal Monotheism." But the very opposite is the case. The religious evolution in Israel did not take place until the State fell and Judah was exiled. It was in the Babylonian captivity, where the prophets first emphasized that the "God of Israel," whose service consists in a righteous life, was also the creator of the Universe, the common God and father of the whole human family. The most prominent critics of Germany, Holland, and England subscribe to these ideas on Israel's history, Kuenen, Wellhausen, and others. But when it comes to a keen appreciation of Biblical poetry, Renan's "History of Israel" can not be surpassed. None other has so fully grasped the true function of the Hebrew prophet as a social reformer, as the preacher of a nobler morality, than Renan. None has ever so fully condemned the social system, which prevailed then and prevails now, as have the prophets, those men of fiery eloquence who preached in the name of God of righteousness who abideth with the humble and lowly, who could not tolerate oppression and high-handed robbery. To have brought out this glory of prophetism, is the signal merit of Renan's "History of Israel."[1]

From a secular point of view the history of Israel was treated by a number of historians of that time, I mention among others, *Duncker*, History of Antiquity, Berlin, 1852, and Karl Adolf, *Menzel*, "History of the State and Religion of the Kingdoms of Israel and Judah" (Breslau, 1853). They form a pleasant contrast when compared with Ewald's "History." Menzel said, in the preface to his work, that it was intended to free the educated Germans from their ignorance and prejudice concerning the history of Israel by means of an unbiased and scientific treatment of the important subject. Even men like Lessing, Herder, Bruno Bauer, Hegel, and Leo, had a most superficial conception of this part of our history. Both the infidel and the bigot have assailed the character of the Jew. Between the two the fate of the Jew has been not unlike that of the lion in the fable. A man called the attention of the grim king of the forest to a picture representing a lion vanquished by a man: "We have no painters," was his significant reply. In like manner the Jew's only answer regarding the falsifications of his history had been: We have no historians of our own.

---

[1] See Geiger, "Renan and Strauss" appendix to his Judaism and its history, vol. I (Breslau, 1854, Schletter); Slavet's criticism of Renan in Revue de Deux Mondes; also his "Le Christianisme ou ses Origines," and Emil Hirsch's lecture on Renan, Reform Advocate (1892, pp. 175-179).

III.

If it is true, that "Wer den Dichter will verstehen muss in's Dichter's Land gehen" (If you desire to understand the poet, you must go into his own country), then it is also true, that only a Jew can fully appreciate his own history. It was necessary to emancipate our history from the stamp of Christianity. The task was great, and most difficult, but it has been accomplished. The first attempt of this kind was made by a young man of Hungary, Solomon Loewisohn (born in Moor, Hungary, 1789, died there, 1822), who unfortunately died young, afflicted with insanity. His was a poetical nature, and his "*Lectures on the recent History of the Jews*" (Vienna, 1820), prove talent for historiography. He unrolls an attractive picture of our history from the beginning of the dispersion to his own days. Had he lived longer, he might have done great services to the cause of Judaism.[1]

Who are the historians of Judaism in the nineteenth century? The question can not be easily answered. It is just as difficult as to give a satisfactory answer to the question "Who has produced the scientific and religious progress of our age? Or who is the reformer of Judaism in our century?" Not any one man in particular, but hundreds of hands have been and are still active in this direction.

The "Hep-Hep" cry against the Jews in Germany in 1819 aroused them to the study of their historic past. To know what Judaism is and might be it was necessary to ascertain what it had been. The past would prove the index of the future. The Jews trusted that the image of Judaism, if presented in its proper light, would remove the odium which rested upon them. The ten years following the "Hep-Hep" excitement witnessed a series of literary achievements of greatest importance. Leopold Zunz, Nachman Krochmal, Solomon Rappaport laid the foundation to a "Science of Judaism" and discovered the thread by which they were enabled to wend their way through the labyrinth of Jewish literature. The dimness and vagueness that had hung over the history of the Jews was giving way, and the leading figures in the procession of past generations began to assume clear and distinct outlines. A band of worthy disciples followed Zunz's lead. M. Jost, Geiger, Frankel, Herzfeld, Dernburg, Lebrecht, S. and D. Cassel, Munk, Kirchheim, Carmoly, Graetz, Brueck, Brecher, Fassel, Heidenheim, M. Levy, Steinschnei-

[1] See his biography in the Literaturblatt of the "Orient," 1849, vol. 10, and Beth-El (1856, page 72).

der, Landshut, Fuerst, Dukes, A. Jellinek, Luzzatto, Reggio, Creizenach, M. Sachs, Franck, Wolf, Saalschuetz, P. Beer, A. Chorin, Jolowicz, Formstecher, Hesse, Kaempf, Joel, S. Stern, Wechsler, Prof. Weil, Mayer, S. Meyer, Abraham Kohn, Weil, I. M. Wise, Ritter, Jastrow, L. Loew, Holdheim, Neubauer, S. Sachs, Salvador, Zedner, Herxheimer, M. Bloch, Stein, S. and L. Adler, E. Gruenebaum, S. Hirsch, Rothschild, Einhorn, Kohler, N. Bruell, and numerous others in all lands and climes[1] have ever since added and are still adding valuable stones to the grand structure of a *History of Judaism and Jews*, which is not yet finished. If the "Hep-Hep" cry is the indirect cause of such stupendous activity within our ranks we may exclaim with Goethe, "This is the spirit which works for evil and creates the good." Let us hope that the modern "Hep-Hep" cry of Anti-semitism of to-day will be accompanied by a similar revival of Judaism.

Among those, however, who made Jewish historiography a specialty, are *Peter Beer*, who published a "History, Doctrines, and Opinions of the Religious Sects of the Jews" (in two volumes, I vol. 369, II vol. 459 pages, Bruenn, 1822–1823). The work gives proof of the indefatigable industry of the author and of his great familiarity with the Jewish and Christian literature of the middle ages. The author does not claim originality, but does not deserve the unkind, insulting criticism of Graetz.[2]

An attempt at Jewish historiography, a weak attempt at that, was made in the French language by Leon Halevy. Although the son of a Hebrew poet—his father, Elia Halevy, wrote a classical Hebrew—he did not understand the Hebrew language. No wonder that his "history" is no success. The title is, "*Résumé de l'histoire des Juifs anciens*," in two volumes (I, 1825; II, 1828).

Dr. Marcus Jost (born 1793, in Bernburg; died 1860, in Frankfurt on the Main) is the first historian of this century who undertook

---

[1] The names mentioned here belong to the Jews. There are many Christian scholars who have labored incessantly in this cause. I mention some: Delitzsch, Bertheau, Ewald, Hitzig, Olshausen, Renan, De Wette, Umbreit, Vatke, Staehelin, Bleek, Keil, Graf, George, Neander, Fleischer, Sylvestre de Sacy, Dillmann, Roediger, Merx, Noeldeke, Wuensche, Schenkel, Holtzmann, Kuenen, Strack, Hansrath, Haneberg, Gesenius, Hilgenfeld, Freytag, Chwolson, Benfey and others.

[2] History of the Jews, vol. XI, page 457. Peter Beer published also two volumes of Israel's history for schools (Prag, 1796; Wien, 1810, 1815; Prag, 1831; Wien, 1843), entitled: Toldoth Jissrael. The book was translated into Russian by B. Segall and A. Solonowitsch, and into Polish by Dr. Diankowitz.

the gigantic task to write a "History of the Israelites from the time of the Maccabees to our Day," nine volumes (Berlin, 1820–1828, Schlesinger). Jost was a pioneer in this work, without predecessors of any amount, and deserves the gratitude of not only every Jew, but of every friend of truth, justice, and science. As the name of the work indicates, it was not the intention of the author to give a history of the *growth and development of Judaism*, but to familiarize his co-religionists in particular with the fate and history of their ancestors. This work had a most beneficial effect on the Jewish community, not only of Germany, but wherever German was read (Austria, Hungary, Russia). Jost was not conceited. He calls the work a weak attempt,[1] and sees in Herzfeld's "History of the People of Israel, from the Destruction of the First Temple to Simon the Maccabee" (two volumes, Nordhaussen, 1847), a progress in the way of clearing up of obscure parts, a result of excellent research, ability, and love of truth. He appreciates Selig Cassel's valuable sketch on the history of the Jews in Ersch and Gruber's Encyclopaedia, and has a good word for Graetz. So convinced is he of the imperfections of his work, that he publishes a weekly periodical, "The Israelitish Annals for History, Literature, and Culture of the Jews" (Frankfurt on-M., 1839–1841), for no other purpose than to study history, "to exchange ideas on new historical discoveries and to find out the truth concerning doubtful facts." There is indeed great progress apparent between this work and Jost's later historical contributions. In the introduction to his "General History of the Israelitish People," in two volumes (Leipzig, 1850), Jost thanks not only for the appreciation of his first work, but also for the criticisms, corrections of the same, and particularly for the new material offered him by scholars. As a supplement to the nine volumes Jost added a "Recent History of the Israelites from 1815 to 1845" (Berlin, 1845–1847, Schlesinger), so that virtually his "History of the Israelites," contains twelve volumes.

The progress of Jost as a historian is best manifested in his scientific treatment of the "History of Judaism and its Sects," in three volumes (Leipzig, 1857, 1858, 1859, Doerflling and Franke). Here is given not a history of the Jews, but a historical development of Judaism as a progressive force, as a power that makes for righteousness. Jost attempts to answer the all-absorbing question: "What is Judaism as an essential moment of the world's history? What is its mission and its position in the history of the development of civilization?" He answers these questions impartially, free from any bias, on the

[1] *Stein*: Israelitischer Volkslehrer, vol. III, page 300.

hand of historical investigation, in a spirit of justice and truth. Many errors and mistakes in former publications are candidly corrected by the author, who was free of that dictatorial disposition and stubbornness of opinion so characteristic of not a few of our Jewish scholars. As *unum pro multis* I mention his change of opinion concerning the Talmud and Rabbinical literature. While in his "History of the Israelites," the Rationalist Jost had hardly a good word for this long misunderstood branch of Jewish literature; he takes the historical critical view of the Talmud in his "Judaism and its Sects"[1] (vol. II, p. 211). It must not be forgotten that the first impressions concerning the Talmud were gained by Jost from a dirty polish teacher in Wolfenbuttel, whose main arguments were the stick and the cudgel. No trace of a historical treatment was then known. Jost sees in the Talmud a work which, far from fettering thought, has stimulated profound mental activity among the Jews at a time when even bishops and knights were steeped in ignorance and superstition. This work may be justly designated as the "top stone of the great historical edifice which Jost had reared so perfectly from the outset."

It has been claimed, and not without some justification, that Jost's historiography is rather dry, pedantic, cool, and sober. But his very exactness and desire to be impartial "objective"—as the Germans well express it—to write with his mind rather than with his heart, are the cause of this failing. If it is a fault in a historian to lack the fire of enthusiasm, then certainly Jost must plead guilty in this respect. But nevertheless his heart beat warmly for the Jews, his mission and religion. His thorough knowledge of the classics greatly facilitated his work, which, even in style, improved with every new volume. There is nothing half-hearted, vacillating, inconsistent and unmanly in Jost's historiography. I doubt very much, whether in all the seventeen volumes on Jewish history written by Jost, one passage can be found which could give proof of intentional injustice done by him to any person. When we consider the vast amount of reading necessary for the accomplishment of such a gigantic task, and bear in mind that the sources from which he could derive information were scanty in his days, we are compelled to say that Jost's perseverance in the prosecution in his great work must have been wonderful.

After the labors of Jost, Herzfeld, Zunz, Geiger and others, the work of another modern Jewish historian was naturally made infi-

---

[1] I call attention to Goldschmidt's biography of Jost in the "Jahrbuch fuer die Geschichte der Juden" (vol. II, Leipzig, 1861, page 1—XXII), and *Zirndorf*, Jost und seine Freunde (Cincinnati, 1886).

nitely easier. We come now to Professor Hirsch Graetz, born at Ixions, Posen, 1817; died at Breslau, 1891. Prolific as a writer, it is the historian of the Jews who will occupy our attention. His "History of the Jews" was begun in 1853 with the fourth volume, followed in 1856 with the third, in 1860 with the fifth, and so on, until the eleven volumes were finished in 1876.

The nearest approach to a history of Judaism, as it ought to be written, is Geiger's "Judaism and Its History," in lectures, containing three volumes (Breslau, 1864, 1865, 1871, Schletter), but the work is too short and not complete.

Of Jewish historians who have treated special portions of our history, I mention Herzfeld, who has published the "History of Israel from the Destruction of the First Temple to the High-priest Simon the Maccabee" (3 volumes, Nordhausen, 1847, 1855, 1857, and condensed in one volume, Leipzig, 1870); Joseph Salvador, born in Montpellier, France, 1796, died in Paris, 1873, although a physician, devoted his attention to Jewish history. He published a "Histoire de la Domination Romaine en Judée" (two volumes, 1847), translated in German by Dr. Ludwig Eichler (Bremen, 1847). He is ingenious, looks on Judaism mainly as a protest against Christianity, and makes little use of Jewish sources. His "Histoire des Institutions de Moïse et du Peuple Hébreu" (three volumes, 1828), passed through several editions, and was translated into German by Dr. Essenna with a preface of Dr. Gabriel Riesser (Hamburg, 1836). The work protests against those who tried to find in the Bible a justification for the oppression of the people and against the Rationalists, who attacked the Bible as the stronghold of despotism and feudalism, by proving that the Kingdom of Jehovah is identical with the dominion of freedom, justice, reason and truth; in short, that liberty, equality, and fraternity are the elements of the Mosaic legislation. Salvador lays more stress on the political and social than on the religious moment of the institutions of Israel. Dr. Moses Kaiserling, Rabbi in Buda-Pesth (born at Hannover, June 17, 1829), devotes his historical researches to the Iberian peninsula. His works which deserve special mention are, "A Holiday in Madrid," 1859, "History of the Jews in Spain," "History of the Jews in Portugal," "History of the Jews in Navarra" (Berlin, 1861), "The Jewish Women in History, Literature and Art" (Leipzig, 1879). Quite a number of special histories of the Jews in different cities have been published, some of which may find a place here, B. H. Auerbach, "History of the Jewish Congregation in Halberstadt" (Prague, 1866). H. Barbeck, a Christian writer, published a "History of the Jews in Nuernberg and Fuerth" (Nuernberg, 1878).

C. Brisch, a Jewish teacher in Muehlheim, published "History of the Jews in Coeln and Vicinity" (first volume,[1] Muehlheim, 1879). An excellent "History of the Jews in Coeln" was published by Ernst Weyden, a Christian, in 1867; Dr. Bergel, a physician, published a "History of the Hungarian Jews" (Leipzig, 1880); Berndt, a "History of the Jews in Gross-Glogau;" S. J. Bloch, "The Jews in Spain" (1880); M. Gruenwald, "History of the Jews in Bohemia" (vol. 1, Pissek, 1886); Dr. Guedeman, contribution to the "History of the Jews in Middle Ages" (3 volumes, Vienna, 1888); L. Herzfeld, "History of the Commerce of the Jews in Antiquity" (Braunschweg, 1879), a work distinguished—as are all the writings of Herzfeld—by deep research; G. Haenle, "History of the Jews in Ansbach" (1867); A. Jaraczewsky, "History of the Jews in Erfurt" (Erfurt, 1868); J. F. Herman, "History of the Jews in Bohemia" (Vienna, 1819); H. Jolowicz, "History of the Jews in Koenigsberg" (1867); G. Kreigk, "History of the Jews in Frankfurt in Middle Ages" (Frankfurt-on-M., 1862); J. Benjacob and S. G. Stern, "Shem Haggedolim" [names of great men] and "Vaad Lachachamim," edited by Asulai, corrected (Leipzig, 1844); S. Bonhard, "Biography of R. Joseph ben Kohen" (Lemberg, 1859), in Hebrew; Solomon Buber, "Biography of Elia Levita" (Leipzig, 1856), in Hebrew; S. L. Friedenstein, "Ir Gibborim, History of the Jews in Grodno" (Wilna, 1880); Loewenstein, "History of the Jews on the Bodensee" (Konstanz, 1879); J. Perles, "History of the Jews in Posen" (1865); D. J. Podiebrad, "Antiquities of the Josefstadt Jewish Cemetery and Synagogues in Prague" (Prague, 1882); K. Schaab, "Diplomatic History of the Jews in Mainz" (Mainz, Victor v. Zabern, 1855).

The last-named book contains 480 pages, and was written by the Vice-President of the Circuit Court in Mainz in the ninety-fourth year of his life. It would be a blessing for American Judaism, if our Jews of to-day would comprehend as well as this Christian what we stand for. Much wild, foolish talk, which is so popular in our lodges, the nonsensical declamations about our race, would cease then. He says, in the preface, that the Jews are an extraordinary appearance in history, which can only be explained from the *religious* point of view. "It must be acknowledged that the Jews are a religious people, and that *the religion is their essential bond of union.* They possess one faith, one hope, one fate."

To this class belong Dr. A. Stein's "History of the Jews in Dan-

[1] I do not think that a second part appeared. The first part ends with the "Black Death" (1348).

zig" (Danzig, 1860), from the fourteenth century to this time; H. Stern-
berg's " History of the Jews in Poland ;" O. Stobbe's " The Jews of
Germany During the Middle Ages " (1860) ; S. Tausig's " History of
the Jews in Bavaria ;" Prof. G. Wolf's " History of the Israelitish
Congregation of Vienna from 1816 to 1861 " (Vienna, 1862) ; " Contribution to the History of the Jews in Worms " (Berlin, 1862) ;
" Ferdinand II. and the Jews " (Vienna, 1859) ; " Expulsion of the
Jews from Bohemia " (1861) ; M. Friedlander's " History of the Jews
in Moravia " (1876) ; L. Donath's " History of the Jews in Mecklen-
burg " (1874) ; E. Carmoly, " Biographies of Old and Modern Israelites "
(Metz, 1828) ; only one volume was published ; S. L. Rappaport,
" Kore Hadoroth," history of the Jews from the Hasmoneans to the
destruction of the Second Temple, one volume (Warschau, 1838) ;
Jos. Epstein, " History of Russia," with special regard to Jewish history (Wilna, 1872) ; E. Schreiber, " History of the Jewish Congregation in Bonn " [1] (Bonn, 1879), published in honor of the dedication
of the Synagogue ; Dr. Samuel Meyer, " The Jurisprudence of the
Israelites, Romans, and Athenians " (three volumes, 1876). The
first volume treats on " Public Right," the second on " Private
Right," the third on " The History of the Penal Laws of all Civilized
Nations from Moses, Solon, etc., to the Present Day " (Trier, Fr. Lintz,
703 pages). The first two volumes were published by Baumgaertner
in Leipzig. The author, who officiated as Rabbi in Hechingen, practiced at the same time law in that city. The mass of material stored
up in this scholarly work is something stupendous. It is a standard
work to this day. Dr. Julius Fuerst published a " History of Kara-
ism," in three volumes (Leipzig, 1862–69) ; Franz Delitzch, " Anecdota
to the History of Mediæval Scholastic " (1841) ; S. Pinsker, *Likkute
Kadmoniyoth*, contributions to the " History of the Karaites " (Wien,
1860, in Hebrew) ; A. Neubauer, " From the Petersburg Library
Documents to the History of the Karaites and their Literature "
(Leipzig, 1866).

Geiger, Firkowitch, Chwolson, Deinard, J. Kasas, M. Toetter-
mann, A. Harkavy, and Strack have done great work in this branch
of Jewish history. Dr. Berliner published " Inner Life of the German Jews in Middle Ages " (Berlin, 1871). Dr. S. Baeck's " The

---

[1] I was requested by the Congregation of Bonn, where I officiated as
Rabbi from 1878 to 1881, to write this history, which gives also a justification of my recommendation and introduction of Geiger's Prayerbook in
the Synagogue of Bonn, a step which is considered even to-day radical in
Germany.

History of the Jewish Nation and its Literature from the Babylonian
Exile to the Present" (Lizza, 1877) is a good school-book. We object,
however, to the term "Jewish Nation." In the same style are Des-
sauer's "History of the Israelites" (Breslau, 1870), Emanuel Hecht's
"Israel's History" (Leipzig, 1865 and 1885). The latter deserves
recommendation. M. Braunschweiger published a "History of the
Jews in the Roman States 700 to 1200 b. Chr." (Wien, 1865); Dr.
Dozy, "The Israelites at Mecca from the Time of David to the Fifth
Century"[1] (Leipzig, 1864); E. B. Feder, "Israel's Temple of Honor"
(3 volumes), 1840; Friedman, "Pictures of Jewish History" (Pest,
1860); S. Goldschmidt, "History of the Jews in England in the
XIth and XII Century" (Berlin, 1886); Finn, "Kirjah Neemanah,
History of the Jews in Wilna" (Wilna, 1860, 333 pages); Zimmerman,
"History of the Jews in Silesia" (Breslau, 1791); Kaiserling, "Li-
brary of Jewish Preachers" (two volumes, Berlin, 1870-72), contain-
about forty short sketches of the lives of prominent Jewish preachers and
samples of their sermons; M. Horowitz, "Rabbis of Frankfort" (in
four volumes, Frankfort on the Main, 1885); A. Jellinek, "History
of the Crusades" (1853); I. Gastfreund, "Biography of the Tannai
Rabbi Akiba ben Joseph" (Lemburg, 1871); G. M. S. Ghirondi,
"Onomasticon of Jewish Scholars" (Triest, 1853); Julius Fuerst,
"Biography of Dr. Marcus Herz" (Berlin, 1850); M. L. Belinson,
"Toldoth Jashar, Biography of Solomon del Medigo," from the Ger-
man of Dr. Abraham Geiger (Odessa, 1864); Malvezin, "Histoire
des Juifs a Bordeaux" (Bordeaux, 1875); Aretin, "History of the
Jews in Bavaria" Landau, 1803); H. Baerwald, "The Old Cemetery
of the Israel Congregation in Frankfort on the Main" (Frankfort,
1883); Brieglieb, "Expulsion of the Jews from Nurnberg" (1868);
A. Gierse, "History of the Jews in Westphalia" (Naumburg, 1879);
Heffner, "The Jews in Franken" (Nurnberg, 1855); J. M. Zunz,
"History of the Rabbinate in Krakau from the Sixteenth Century to
the Present" (Lemberg, 1874).

F. W. Weber, "The Jews and the Church of the Middle Ages"
(Noerdlinger, 1862); C. F. Walsher, "History of the Jews in Wuer-
temberg" (Tuebingen, 1852); L. Landshut, "Berlin Rabbis, Toldot
Anshe Hashem" (Berlin, 1883); J. Ritter, "The Jewish Free School
in Berlin" (Berlin, 1883); R. Hoeniger, "The Black Plague in Germany" (Berlin, 1882); Sheppler, "The Abolition of the Body-tax for
the Jew" (Hanau, 1805); K. Lieben, "Galed, Epitaphs at the Old

[1] Translated from the Dutch into German.

Cemetery of the Jews in Prague" (Prague, 1856); Dr. Marcus Jastrow, "Four Centuries of the History of the Jews from the Destruction of the First Temple to the Dedication of the Second Temple under the Maccabees" (Heidelberg, 1865).

M. Joel, "Relation of Albert Magnus to Maimonides ;" Prof. M. A. Levy, "Don Joseph Nassi Hagay of Naxos" (1859); L. Levysohn, "Sixty Epitaphs at the Cemetery in Worms, from the Year 905 to the Present," with biographies (Frankfort, 1855); Moccatta, "The Jews in Spain and Portugal," translated into German by Kaiserling (Hanover, 1878); J. Muenz, "Jewish Physicians in the Middle Ages" (Berlin, 1887); L. Oelsner, "Silesian Archives to the History of the Jews" (Vienna, 1864); Ph. Philippson, Biographical Sketches of Jos. Wolf, Moses Philipsohn, Gotthold Salomon and others, in three parts (Leipzig, 1866); Salfeld, "Biography of Dr. Sal. Herxheimer" (Frankfurt, 1885); Emanuel Schreiber, "Abraham Geiger as Reformer of Judaism" (Loebau, 1879, 158 pages); N. Samuely, "Pictures of Jewish Life in Galicia" (Lemberg, 1885); H. Schlesinger, "Chronological Hand-book of the History of the Jews" (1872); Moise Schwab, "Histoire des Israelites, depuis l'edification du Second Temple jusqu'à nos jours" (Paris, 1866); Leopold Loew (pseudonym Dr. Weil), "Aron Chorin" (Szegedin, 1863); E. Willstaetter, "General History of the Israelitish People" (Karlsruhe, 1836), for schools.

Of greatest importance to the historical literature of the Jews in this century are the numerous year books and magazines, of which I mention, Leopold Zunz's "Magazine for the Science of Judaism" (Berlin, 1823); Abraham Geiger's "Scientific Magazine for Jewish Theology" (1836–1843); most valuable and instrumental in creating the historical-critical school of Reform-Rabbinism.[1]

Jost's "Annals for History," etc. (1839–41); Zach. Frankel's "Magazine for the Religious Interests of Judaism" (1844–1846); "Monthly for the Science of Judaism," continued by Graetz (1851–1882); now again taken up by Dr. Brann. "Year-book for the History of the Jews and Judaism," four volumes (Leipzig, 1860, 1861, 1863, 1869, Oscar Leiner), under the auspices of the Jewish Publication Society in Germany, under the management of L. Philippson, Jost, Goldschmidt, Herzfeld and others.

Buechner's "Year-book for 1864;" Joseph v. Wertheim's "Year-book for Israelites" (1854–1868), with contributions from Jellinck,

---

[1] See my "Reformed Judaism and its Pioneers" (1892), pages 284–286.

August Frankel, Kompert and others; M. Bresslauer's "German Almanac for Israelites" (1850–51), has contributions from the pen of Zunz, Geiger, Honigman, Munk, Dr. F. Cohn, Jos. Wertheimer and others. The German-Israelitish Confederation of Congregations (Gemeindebund), published in 1889 a statistical year-book. Year-books were also published by Klein and Isidor Busch, the latter in Vienna (1840–1847).

But the palm must be given to the "Year-book for Jewish History and Literature," edited by Dr. Nehemias Bruell, the erudite successor of Geiger in the Rabbinate of Frankfort-on-the-Main. Mints of historical material are preserved in the volumes of these year-books (1874–1889), which give *multum in parvo*. We meet here in every respect with the scientific acumen and courage of opinion of a Zunz and Geiger. Fuerst's "Orient" (1841–1851); Loew's "Ben Chananya" (1858–1867); Stein's "Volkslehrer" (1851–69); "Revue des Etudes Juives" (Paris, 1880), still in existence, and Prof. Ludwig Geiger's "Magazine for the History of the Jews in Germany," which is published since 1887 under the auspices of the German Israelitish "Gemeindebund," offer treasures to the Jewish historiographer.

The history of modern Judaism, *i. e.*, of Judaism since Moses Mendelsohn is comparatively not well represented. The reason for this peculiar state of affairs can easily be discovered. The Jewish historiography of to-day is to a great extent in the hands of the Rabbis, who, while certainly able to treat the subject, are not blessed with the necessary courage of opinion and manliness to do justice to such a subject. The present generation of Rabbis in Germany is in this respect different from the leaders of German Judaism half a century ago, when men like Geiger, Holdheim, Einhorn, Samuel Hirsch, Wechsler, and Hess were not afraid to tackle the burning questions and live issues of the day. The Rabbis of to-day in Germany are shrewd business men, and therefore avoid to write on subjects and persons within the memory of men for fear they might make an enemy on the one or the other side of the camp. They therefore shrewdly live up to the maxim, "silence is gold," are happy and contented, live in peace and rest, without being disturbed or disturbing others. "If there be only peace in my days," *Rak sholom jihjeh b'yamai*. Aprés nous le déluge.

Dr. Sigismund Stern's "History of Judaism from Mendelsohn to the Present" (Frankfort-on-the-Main, 1857); Dr. Immanuel Ritter's

15

"History of the Jewish Reformation," 3 volumes;[1] Geiger's life in letters (Vol. V of his posthumous works, Berlin, 1875, Gerschel); my "Abraham Geiger as Reformer," and Zirndorf's "Jost and his Friends" (Cincinnati, 1886), are about all the German works of that period. Stern was the man, whose electrifying lectures on the "Mission of Judaism" (Berlin, 1845), and on the "Religion of Judaism" (1846), have aroused the indifferent Berlin Jews from lethargy and brought about the formation of the famous "Reformgenossenschaft," now "Reform-Gemeinde" in Berlin, which was presided over by Holdheim, and is to this day the only radical Reform-Congregation in Europe. But while Stern was a fiery German orator and appeared on the scene at the proper time, he was not endowed with sufficient theological scholarship as to enable him to do full justice to the subject. His "history" is interestingly written for the masses. Ritter's "history" is written from the point of view of the Berlin "Reform-Gemeinde," almost ignoring and belittling the work of others in this direction, and showing little understanding for the *causa movens* of the great struggle. Aside from this, Ritter was no theologian.

In this connection I mention Samuel Holdheim's "History of the Origin and Development of the Jewish Reform-Congregation in Berlin" (Berlin, 1857, Springer, 254 pages, which is very valuable); Ludwig Geiger's "Abraham Geiger's Life in Letters" (Berlin, 1875, Gerschel); and my criticism on Graetz's history, "Graetz's Geschichtsbauerei" (Berlin, 1881, Issleib).

We have seen that German scholarship has contributed the lion's share, so far as Jewish history is concerned.

We possess very few books on the subject in the English language. Following deserve special mention:

"An Apology for the Honorable Nation of the Jews and all the Sons of Israel," by Edward Nicholas (London, 1648, 15 pages), is a readable pamphlet in which the misfortunes of the British Isle are attributed to the expulsion of the Jews from England. Tovey, "Anglia Judaica, or the History of the Jews in England" (Oxford, 1738); Manasse ben Israel's "Humble Address and Declaration to the Commonwealth of England," and "Vindiciae Judaeorum, or a letter in answer to certain questions Impounded by a Noble and Learned Gentleman touching to reproaches cast on the nation of the Jews" (London, 1656). This work was translated into Hebrew and German,

---

[1] First part, Mendelsohn and Lessing; II, David Friedlander (1861); III, Holdheim (1865).

by Moses Mendelsohn, under the title, "Rettung der Juden" (*Teshuath Yisroel*, 1848).

Milman, "History of the Jews from the Time of Abraham to 1830;" Dean Stanley, "History of the Jewish Church" (3 volumes), both from a Christian point of view, the latter scholarly and in accord with modern science.[1] This work is the result of the lectures which Stanley delivered in Oxford (1862). Samuel M. Smucker, "History of the Modern Jews from the Destruction of Jerusalem to the Present Time" (Philadelphia, 1860, D. Rulison). While the author is well-meaning and unbiased, he has very little knowledge of the subject. He styles, for instance, as "modern Jews," all the Jews living after Jesus. The following is certainly far from correct: "Both parties, the radical and conservative, adhere to the great cardinal doctrine, that the promised Messiah is yet to come, and will establish a *temporal kingdom of superior power and splendor at Jerusalem*" (p. 329).

The fact is, that the Reformers have long given up this belief, and it is a question whether, in America, even the so-called "conservative" Jews subscribe to this doctrine.

Prof. Abraham De Sola, Rabbi at Montreal, published "Notes on the Jews in Persia," "Life of Sabbathai Zebi," "History of the Jews in France," and "History of the Jews in England," in Isaac Leeser's *Occident*. The first Jew who published in good English a "Post-Biblical History of the Jews, from the Close of the Old Testament to the Destruction of the Second Temple" (2 volumes, Philadelphia, 1856, Moss & Brothers), was the New York Rabbi, Morris J. Raphall, born Sept. 1798, in Stockholm, Sweden, died June 23, 1868, in New York. The work, written in good English, exhibits profound knowledge, a strict conformity to truth, and enthusiastic love and patriotism for the United States of America and its free institutions. It is not a learned work, as the author himself says, but it is instructive, interesting and fair. The author justly remarks, that rigid impartiality can not well be maintained, inasmuch as "he is not the abstraction of a Jew, but one living, acting, feeling warmly for men whose descendant he is, whose deeds and sufferings he is about to relate." The first volume contains 405, the second 486 pages. The same period of history is treated by Humphrey Prideaux in the English language.

Our venerable Dr. I. M. Wise is to my knowledge the first Rabbi who has undertaken the dangerous task to write, as early as 1854, his well-known "History of the Israelitish Nation" from its very begin-

---

[1] The American edition, New York, 1884, Charles Scribner.

nings. Not one of the Jewish historians possessed the courage to write a history of Israel from a radical point of view. Graetz published the first volume of his "History" one year before Wise commenced with the "Four Generations of the Tanaaim," thus starting with the *fourth* volume. Although it is claimed that Graetz did so because he wanted to find material for biblical history in Palestine, it is an open secret, that considerations of policy prompted him not to touch on ground, by which he could easily forfeit his position as teacher in a Seminary for the training of conservative Rabbis.

In his first volume, which treats the history from Abraham to the destruction of Jerusalem by Nebukadnezzar, we notice all the strong and weak points of rationalism. This name covers the attempt to save the letter at the expense of the spirit, reduces biblical miracles to commonplace, natural occurrences, and makes of the prophets jugglers, sleight-of-hand performers, and conscious frauds, who performed seeming miracles, or reported them as miracles, contrary to their better knowledge of the actual facts. Renan's "Life of Jesus," and in fact also his later writings on the "Origin of Christianity," and the first two volumes of Graetz's "history," although published in the seventies, still bear the stamp of this sham liberalism which makes of the Bible a book of fiction, the child of crafty priests and artful impostors, who merely wanted to delude the people. Barring this objection, the book is not only instructive, but written with a heart full of enthusiasm and fiery zeal for Judaism and its world-redeeming mission.

The second volume of this work, although an independent publication, is entitled: "History of the Hebrews' Second Commonwealth" (Cincinnati, 1880, Bloch & Co.), and contains 386 pages. A great progress is discernible to him who compares the two books. The author justly claims for the work to be "a history without miracles, history constructed on the law of causality, where every event appears as the natural consequence of its preceding ones." The learned author has carefully consulted ancient and modern sources, especially the Rabbinical Midrashic literature, and has thrown some new light on the most important period of our history. The treatment of "Herod and Hillel," "The Messianic Commotion," "John the Baptist," "The Religion of Jesus," "The Policy of Jesus," "Crucifixion," "Paul of Tarsus," "Great Synod," "Sanhedrin," "Apocrypha," is in many points original, brilliant, and ingenious. The practicable division and subdivision of the work in chapters and paragraphs, recommends it particularly to students of theological seminaries, Jewish and Christian. We can not agree with the author in many points, particularly in his own views on the "Pharisees and Sadducees," and hope that his investigations will ultimately lead him to fall in line with the vast and increasing galaxy of theological scholars who accepted Geiger's theory on the subject.

The first, which means the fourth volume, of Graetz's "history" was translated by Rev. James Gutheim (New York, 1873), under the auspices of the American Publication Society, now defunct.[1] "Eminent Israelites of the Nineteenth Century" is the title of a book published in Philadelphia (1880, Edward Stern), by Henry S. Morais. The book contains one hundred short sketches of Jewish men and women, and is in spite of errors quite instructive for Sunday-school pupils, and the great mass of people, who are ignorant of modern Jewish history. The author attempted to appear impartial and unbiased. My "Reform Judaism and its Pioneers," which was published last year, is what it claims to be, simply a contribution to the history of Reform Judaism, and as such it certainly fills a long-felt want considering the fact that very little was written on this subject, and this little in a spirit far from doing justice to the men whose biographies I have given. Some critics who were shocked at my strong criticism of their idol, Graetz, found fault with my work, because I did not treat Reform Judaism in America. They have no doubt overlooked the paragraph in the preface to my book, where I plainly stated: "The following chapters are an earnest attempt to set aright before the people the men who were partly slandered, partly ignored or belittled by Graetz."

Should God grant me health I shall publish a complete "History of the Jewish Reform-movement to the Present Day." Aside from this, to write a "History of Reform-Judaism in America" is too premature for the present, from the fact that some of the most active men and conspicuous figures in this still waging battle for Reform are still living and laboring in the good cause.

May they live long, and continue to make history!

---

[1] The present publication society published "Outlines of Jewish History," by Lady Magnus, and two volumes of Graetz's history in English translation. Both works are reprints from England.

ORTHODOX OR HISTORICAL JUDAISM.

BY REV. DR. H. PEREIRA MENDES.

Our history may be divided into three eras—the biblical; the era from the close of the Bible record to the present day; the future. The first is the era of the announcement of those ideals which are essential for mankind's happiness and progress. The Bible contains for us and for humanity all ideals worthy of human effort to attain. I make no exception. The attitude of historical Judaism is to hold up these ideals for mankind's inspiration and for all men to pattern life accordingly.

The first divine message to Abraham contains the ideal of righteous Altruism—"Be a source of blessing." And in the message announcing the Covenant is the ideal of righteous egotism. "Walk before Me and be perfect." "Recognize me, God, be a blessing to thy fellow-man, be perfect thyself." Could religion ever be more strikingly summed up?

The life of Abraham, as we have it recorded, is a logical response, despite any human feeling. Thus he refused booty he had captured. It was an ideal of warfare not yet realized—that to the victor the spoils did not necessarily belong. Childless and old, he believed God's promise that his descendants should be numerous as the stars. It was an ideal faith, that also and more, was his readiness to sacrifice Isaac— a sacrifice ordered to make more public his God's condemnation of Canaanite child-sacrifice. It revealed an ideal God who would not allow religion to cloak outrage upon holy sentiments of humanity.

IDEALS IMPARTED TO MOSES.

To Moses next were high ideals imparted for mankind to aim at. On the very threshold of his mission the ideal of "the Fatherhood of God" was announced—"Israel is my son, my first born," implying that other nations are also his children. Then at Sinai were given those ten ideals of human conduct, which, called the "ten commandments," receive the allegiance of the great nations of to-day. Magnificent ideals! Yes, but not so magnificent as the three ideals of God revealed to him—God is mercy, God is love, God is holiness.

"The Lord thy God loveth thee." The echoes of this are the commands to the Hebrews and to the world, "Thou shalt love the Lord thy God with all thy heart, with all thy soul and with all thy might." "Thou shalt love thy neighbor as thyself." "Thou shalt not hate thy brother in thy heart; ye shall love the stranger." God is holiness! "Be holy! for I am holy;" "it is God calling to man to participate in His divine nature."

To the essayist on Moses belongs the setting forth of other ideals associated with him. The historian may dwell upon his "proclaim freedom throughout the land to its inhabitants." It is written on Boston's Liberty Bell, which announced "Free America." The politician may ponder upon his land tenure system, his declaration that the poor have rights; his limitation of priestly wealth ; his separation of church and state. The preacher may dilate upon that Mosaic ideal, so bright with hope and faith—wings of the human soul as it flies forth to find God—that God is the God of the spirits of all flesh ; it is a flashlight of immortality upon the storm-tossed waters of human life. The physician may elaborate his dietary and health laws, designed to prolong life and render man more able to do his duty to society.

MOSAIC CODE OF ETHICS.

The moralist may point to the ideal of personal responsibility ; not even a Moses can offer himself to die to save sinners. The exponent of natural law in the spiritual world is anticipated by his "Not by bread alone does man live, but by obedience to divine law." The lecturer on ethics may enlarge upon moral impulses, their co-relation, free will, and such like ideas; it is Moses who teaches that the quickening cause of all is God's revelation, "Our wisdom and our understanding," and who sets before us "Life and death, blessing and blighting," to choose either, though he advises "choose the life." Tenderness to brute creation, equality of aliens, kindness to servants, justice to the employed ; what code of ethics has brighter gems of ideal than those which make glorious the law of Moses?

As for our other prophets, we can only glance at their ideals of purity in social life, in business life, in personal life, in political life, and in religious life. We need no Bryce to tell us how much or how little they obtain in our commonwealth to-day. So, also, if we only mention the ideal relation which they hold up for ruler and the people, and the former "should be the servants to the latter," it is only in view of the tremendous results in history.

For these very words license the English revolution. From that very chapter of the Bible, the cry, "To your tents, O Israel," was taken by the puritans, who fought with the Bible in one hand. Child of that English revolt, which soon consummated English liberty, America was born—herself the parent of the French revolution, which has made so many kings the servants of their peoples. English liberty, America's birth, French revolution! Three tremendous results truly! Let us, however, set these aside, great as they are, and mark those grand ideals which our prophets were the first to preach.

PEACE, BROTHERHOOD, HAPPINESS.

1. Universal peace, or settlement of national disputes by arbitration. When Micah and Isaiah announced this ideal of universal peace, it was the age of war, of despotism. They may have been regarded as lunatics. Now all true men desire it, all good men pray for it, and bright among the jewels of Chicago's coronet this year is her universal peace convention.

2. Universal brotherhood. If Israel is God's first born and other nations are therefore His children, Malachi's "Have we not all one Father?" does not surprise us. The ideal is recognized to-day. It is prayed for by the Catholics, by the Protestants, by Hebrews, by all men.

3. The universal happiness. This is the greatest. For the ideal of universal happiness includes both universal peace and universal brotherhood. It adds being at peace with God, for without that happiness is impossible. Hence the prophet's bright ideal that one day "All shall know the Lord from the greatest to the least." "Earth shall be full of the knowledge of the Lord as the waters cover the sea," and "All nations shall come and bow down before God and honor His name."

Add to those prophet ideals those of our Ketubim. The "seek wisdom" of Solomon, of which the "Know thyself" of Socrates is but a partial echo; Job's "Let not the finite creature attempt to fathom the infinite Creator;" David's reachings after God! And then let it be clearly understood that these and all ideals of the Bible era are but a prelude and overture. How grand then must be the music of the next era, which now claims our attention.

The era from Bible days to these is the era of the formation of religious and philosophic systems throughout the Orient and the classic world. What grand harmonies, but what crashing discords sound through these ages. Melting and swelling in mighty diapason they come to us to-day as the music which once swayed men's souls, now lifting them with holy emotion, now rocking, now soothing, now exciting. For those religions, those philosophies were mighty plectra in their day to wake the human heartstrings. Above them all rang the voice of historical Judaism, clear and lasting, while other sounds blend or were lost. Sometimes the voice was in harmony ; most often it was discordant as it clashed with the dominant note of the day. For it sometimes met sweet and elevating strains of morality, of beauty, but more often it met the debasing sounds of immorality and error.

JUDAISM AND ZOROASTRIANISM.

Thus Kuenen speaks of " the affinity of Judaism and Zoroastrianism in Persia to the affinity of a common atmosphere of lofty truth, of a simultaneous sympathy in their view of earthly and heavenly things." If Max Muller declares Zoroastrianism originally was monotheistic, so far historic Judaism could harmonize. But it would raise a voice of protest when Zoroastrianism became a dualism of Ormuzd, light or good, and Ahriman, dark or evil. Hence the anticipatory protest proclaimed by Isaiah in God's very message to Cyrus, King of Persia, " I am the Lord, and there is none else." " I formed the light and create darkness." " I make peace and create evil." " I am the Lord, and there is none else ;" that is, I do these things, not Ormuzd or Ahriman.

Interesting as would be a consideration of the mutual debt between Judaism and Zoroastrianism, with the borrowed angelology and demonology of the former compared with the " ahmiyat ahmi Mazdan anma" of the latter manifestly borrowed from the " I am that I am " of the former, we can not pause here for it.

Similarly, historical Judaism would harmonize with Confucius' instance of belief in a Supreme Being, filial duty, his famous " What you would not like when done to you, do you not unto others," and of the Buddhistic teachings of universal peace. But against what is contrary to Bible ideal it would protest, and from it, it would hold separate.

In 521, B. C., Zoroastrianism was revived. Confucius was then actually living. Gautama Buddha died in 543. Is the closeness of the dates mere chance? The Jews had long been in Babylon. As Gesenius and Movers observe, there was traffic of merchants between China and India, via Babylonia with Phœnicia, and not unworthy of mark is Ernest Renan's observation that Babylon had long been a focus of Buddhism and that Boudasy was a Chaldean sage. If future research should ever reveal an influence of Jewish thought on these three great oriental faiths, all originally holding beautiful thoughts, however later ages might have obscured them, would it not be partial fulfillment of the prophecy, as far as concerns the orient, "that Israel shall blossom into bud and fill the face of the earth with fruit?"

SEPARATENESS OF HISTORICAL JUDAISM.

In the West as in the East, historical Judaism was in harmony with any ideals of classic philosophy which echoed those of the Bible. It protested when they failed to do so, and because it failed most often historical Judaism remained separate.

Thus, as Dr. Drummond remarks, Socrates was "in a certain sense monotheistic, and in distinction from the other gods mentions Him who orders and holds together the entire Kosmos," "in whom are all things beautiful-and good," "who from the beginning makes men,"—as historical Judaism commends.

Again, Plato, his disciple, taught that God was good or that the planets rose from the reason and understanding of God. Historical Judaism is in accord with its ideal "God is good," so oft repeated and its thought hymned in the almost identical words, "Good are the luminaries which our God created : He formed them with knowledge, understanding and skill." But when Plato condemns studies except as mental training and desires no practical results, when he even rebukes Arytas for inventing machines on mathematical principles, declaring it was worthy only of carpenters and wheelwrights, and when his master, Socrates, says to Glaucon, "It amuses me to see how afraid you are lest the common herd accuse you of recommending useless studies"—the useless study in question being astronomy—historical Judaism is opposed and protests. For it holds that even Bezaleel and Oholiab is filled with the spirit of God. It bids us study astronomy to learn of God thereby. "Lift up your eyes on high and see who hath created these things, who bringeth out their host by number. He calleth them all by name, by the greatness of his might, for he is strong in power; not one faileth." Even as later sages practically teach the dignity of labor by themselves engaging in it. And when Macaulay remarks "from the testimony of friends as well as of foes, from the confessions of Epictetus and Seneca, as well as from the sneers of Lucian and the invectives of Juvenal, it is plain that these teachers of virtue had all the vices of their neighbors with the additional one of hypocrisy," it is easy to understand the relation of historical Judaism to these with its ideals. "Be perfect."

WORSHIP RATHER THAN DOUBT.

Similarly the sophist school declared "there is no truth, no virtue, no justice, no blasphemy, for there are no gods; right and wrong are conventional terms." The sceptic proclaimed, "we have no criterion of action or judgment; we can not know the truth of any thing; we assert nothing." Not even the Epicurean school taught pleasure's pursuit. But historical Judaism solemnly protested. What are those teachings of our Pirke Aboth, but protests, formally formulated by our religious heads? Said they: "The Torah is the criterion of conduct. Worship instead of doubting. Do philanthropic acts instead of seeking only pleasure. Society's safe-guards are Law, Worship, and Philanthropy." So preached Simon Hatzadik. "Love labor," preached Shemaia to the votary of Epicurean ease. "Procure thyself an instructor," was Gamaliel's advice to any one in doubt. "The practical application, not the theory, is the essential," was the cry of Simon to Platonist or Pyrrhic. "Deed first, then creed." "Yes," added Abtalion, "deed first, then creed; never greed." "Be not like servants who serve their master for price; be like servants who serve without thought of price—and let the fear of God be upon you." "Separation and protest" was thus the cry against these thought vagaries.

Brilliant instance of the policy of separation and protest was the glorious Maccabean effort to combat Hellenist philosophy.

If but for Charles Martel and Poictiers, Europe would long have been Mohammedan, then but for Judas Maccabeus and Bethoron or Emmaus, Judaism would have been strangled. But no Judaism, no Christianity. Take either faith out of the world and what would our civilization be? Christianity was born—originally and as designed and declared by its founder not to change or alter one tittle of the law of Moses. If the Nazarene teacher claimed tacitly or not the title "Son of God" in any sense save that which Moses meant when he said, "Ye are children of your God," can we wonder that there was a Hebrew protest?

JUDAISM JOINED NO HERESIES.

Historical Judaism soon found cause to be separate and to protest. For sect upon sect arose—Ebionites, Gentile Christians, Jewish Christians, Nazarenes, Gnostic Christians, Masboteans, Basilidians, Valentinians, Corpocratians, Marcionites, Balaamites, Nicolaites, Enkratites, Cainites, Ophites or Nahasites; evangels of these and others were multiplied, new prophets were named, such as Paschor, Barkor, Barkoph, Asmagil, Abraxos, etc. At last the Christianity of Paul rose supreme, but doctrines were found to be engrafted which not only caused the famous Christian heresies of Pelagius, Nestorius, Eutyches, etc., but obligated historical Judaism to maintain its attitude of separation and protest. For its Bible ideals were invaded. It could not join all the sects and all the heresies. So it joined none.

Presently the Crescent of Islam rose. From Bagdad to Granada Hebrews prepared protests which the Christians carried to ferment in their distant homes. For through the Arabs and the Jews the old classics were revived and experimental science was fostered. The misuse of the former made the methods of the Academicians the methods of the Scholastic Fathers; but it made Aristotelian philosophy dominant. Experiment widened men's views. The sentiment of protest was imbibed — sentiment against scholastic argument, against bidding research for practical ends, against the supposition "that syllogistic reasoning could ever conduct men to the discovery of any new principle," or that such discoveries could be made except by induction, as Aristotle held against the official denial of ascertained truth, as, for example, earth's rotundity. This protest sentiment in time produced the Reformation. Later it gave wonderful impulses to thought and effort, which has substituted modern civilization, with its glorious conquests, for medieval semi-darkness.

Here the era of the past is becoming the era of the present. Still historical Judaism maintained its attitude.

FRUITS, NOT FOLIAGE.

As the new philosophies were born, it said, with Bacon, "Let us have fruits, practical results, not foliage or mere words." But it opposed a Voltaire and a Paine when they made their ribald attacks. It could not praise the success of a Newton as he "crowned the long labors of the astronomers and physicists by co-ordinating the phenomena of solar motion throughout the visible universe into one vast system." So it could only cry "Amen" to a Kepler and a Galileo. For did they not all prove the unsuspected magnificence of the Hebrew's God, who made and who ruled the heavens and Heaven of heavens, and who presides over the circuit of the earth, as Isaiah tells us? So he cried "Amen" to a Dalton, to a Lineus; for the "atomic notation of the former was as serviceable to chemistry as the binominal nomenclature and the classificatory schematism of the latter were to zoology and botany." What else could historic Judaism cry when the first message to man was to subdue earth, capture its powers, harness them, work? True historical Judaism means progress.

A word more as to the attitude of historic Judaism to modern thought. If Hegel's last work was a course of lectures on the proofs of the existence of God; if in his lectures on religion he turned his weapon against the rationalistic schools which reduced religion to the medium compatible with an ordinary, worldly mind, and criticised the school of Schleiermacher, who elevated feeling to a place in religion above systematic theology, we agree with him. But when he gives successive phases of religion and concludes with Christianity, the highest, because reconciliation is there in open doctrine, we cry, Do justice also to the Hebrew. Is not the Hebrew ideal God a God of Mercy, a God of Reconciliation? It is said, "Not forever will He contend, neither doth He retain His anger forever." That is, He will be reconciled.

We agree with much of Compte, and with him elevate womanhood, but we do not, can not, exclude woman as he does, from public action; for, besides the teachings of reverence and honor for motherhood; beside the Bible tribute to wifehood "that a good wife is a gift of God;" besides the grand tribute to womanhood offered in the last chapter of Proverbs, we produce a Deborah or woman-president, a Huldah as worthy to give a Divine message.

If Darwin and the disciples of evolution proclaim their theory, the Hebrew points to Genesis ii, 3, where it speaks of what God has created "to make," infinitive mood, not "made" as erroneously translated. But historic Judaism protests when any source of life is indicated, save in the breath of God alone.

JUDAISM ALWAYS LOOKS TO GOD.

We march in the van of progress, but our hand is always raised, pointing to God. This is the attitude of historical Judaism. And now to sum up. For the future opens to us—

1. The "separatist" thought. Genesis tells us how Abraham obeyed it. Exodus illustrates it. We are "separated from all the people upon the face of the earth." Leviticus proclaims it, "I have separated you from the peoples." "I have severed you from the peoples." Numbers illustrates it, "Behold, the people shall dwell alone." And Deuteronomy declares it, "He hath avouched thee to be His special people."

The thought began as our nation; it grew as it grew. To test its wisdom, let us ask who have survived? The 7,000 separatists who did not bend to Baal or those who did? Those who thronged Babylonian schools at Pumbeditha or Nahardea, or those who succumbed to Magian influence? The Maccabees who fought to separate, or the Hellenists, who aped Greek or the Sectarians of their day? The Bne Yisrael remnant recently discovered in India, under the auspices of the Anglo-English Association, the discovery of Theaou-Kin-Keaou, or

" people-who-cut-out-the-sinew," in China, point in this direction of separation as a necessity for existence.

And who are the Hebrews of to-day here and in Europe, the descendants of those who preferred to keep separate, and therefore chose exile or death, or those who yielded and were baptized? The course for historic Judaism is clear. It is to keep separate.

2. The protest thought. We must continue to protest against social, religious, or political error with the eloquence of reason. Never by the force of violence. No error is too insignificant, none can be too stupendous for us to notice. The cruelty which shoots the innocent doves for sport—the crime of duelists who risk life which is not theirs to risk—for it belongs to country, wife, or mother, to child or to society; the militarianism of modern nations, the transformation of patriotism, politics, or service of one's country into a business for personal profit, until these and all wrongs be rectified, we Hebrews must keep separate, and we must protest,

CONTINUE SEPARATE AND PROTESTING.

And keep separate and protest we will, until all error shall be cast to the moles and bats. We are told that Europe's armies amount to 22,000,000 of men. Imagine it! Are we not right to protest that arbitration and not the rule of might should decide? Yet, let me not cite instances which render protest necessary. "Time would fail, and the tale would not be told," to quote a Rabbi.

How far separation and protest constitute our historical Jewish policy is evident from what I have said. Apart from this, socially, we unite whole-heartedly and without reservation with our non-Jewish fellow-citizens; we recognize no difference between Hebrew and non-Hebrew.

We declare that the attitude of Historical Judaism, and, for that matter, of the Reform School also, is to serve our country as good citizens, to be on the side of law and order, and fight anarchy. We are bound to forward every humanitarian movement; where want or pain calls there must we answer; and condemned by all true men be the Jew who refuses aid because he who needs it is not a Jew. In the intricacies of science, in the pursuit of all that widens human knowledge, in the path of all that benefits humanity, the Jew must walk abreast with non-Jew, except he pass him in generous rivalry. With the non-Jew we must press onward, but for all men and for ourselves we must ever point upward to the Common Father of all. Marching forward, as I have said, but pointing upward, this is the attitude of Historical Judaism.

Religiously the attitude of Historical Judaism is expressed in the Creeds formulated by Maimonides, as follows:

"We believe in God the Creator of all, a unity, a Spirit who never assumed corporeal form, Eternal, and He alone ought to be worshiped.

"We unite with Christians in the belief that Revelation is inspired. We unite with the founder of Christianity that not one jot or tittle of the Law should be changed. Hence we do not accept a First Day Sabbath, etc.

"We unite in believing that God is omniscient and just, good, loving, and merciful.

"We unite in the belief in a coming Messiah.

"We unite in our belief in immortality. In these, Judaism and Christianity agree."

DEVELOPMENT OF JUDAISM.

As for the development of Judaism, we believe in change of religious custom or idea only when effected in accordance with the spirit of God's law and the highest authority attainable. But no change without. Hence we can not, and may not, recognize the authority of any conference of Jewish Rabbis or ministers, unless those attending are formally empowered by their communities or congregations to represent them. Needless to add, they must be sufficiently versed in Hebrew law and lore; they must live lives consistent with Bible teachings and they must be advanced in age so as not to be immature in thought.

And we believe, heart, soul and might, in the restoration to Palestine, a Hebrew state, from the Nile to the Euphrates—even though, as Isaiah intimates in his very song of restoration, some Hebrews remain among the Gentiles.

We believe in the future establishment of a Court of Arbitration, above suspicion, for a settlement of nations' disputes, such as could well be in the shadow of that temple which we believe shall one day arise to be a "house of prayer for all peoples," united at last in the service of one Father. How far the restoration will solve present pressing Jewish problems, how far such spiritual organization will guarantee man against falling into error, we can not here discuss. What if doctrines, aims, and customs separate us now?

There is a legend that when Adam and Eve were turned out of Eden or earthly Paradise, an angel smashed the gates, and the frag-

ments flying all over the earth are the precious stones.   We can carry
the legend further.

FAITH SET IN THE GATES.

The precious stones were picked up by the various religions and
philosophers of the world.   Each claimed and claims that its own frag-
ment alone reflects the light of heaven, forgetting the settings and in-
crustations which time has added.   Patience, my brothers.   In God's
own time we shall, all of us, fit our fragments together and reconstruct
the Gates of Paradise.   There will be an era of reconciliation of all
living faiths and systems, the era of all being in at-one-ment, or atonement with God.   Through the gates shall all people pass to the foot of
God's throne.   The throne is called by us the mercy-seat.   Name of
happy augury, for God's Mercy shall wipe out all record of mankind's
errors and strayings, the sad story of our unbrotherly actions.   Then
shall we better know God's ways and behold His glory more clearly, as
it is written, "They shall all know me, from the least of them unto the
greatest of them, saith the Lord, for I will forgive their iniquity and
I will remember their sins no more" (Jer. xxxi, 34.)

What if the deathless Jew be present then among the earth's
peoples?   Would ye begrudge his presence?   His work in the world,
the Bible he gave it, shall plead for him.   And Israel, God's first-born,
who, as his prophets foretold, was for centuries despised and rejected
of men, knowing sorrows, acquainted with grief and esteemed stricken
by God for his own backslidings, wounded beside through others'
transgressions, bruised through others' injuries, shall be but fulfilling
his destiny to lead back his brothers to the Father.   For that we were
chosen; for that we are God's servants or ministers.   Yes, the attitude of Historical Judaism to the world will be in the future, as in
the past—helping mankind with His Bible—until the gates of earthly
Paradise shall be reconstructed by mankind's joint efforts, and all nations whom Thou, God, hast made shall go through and worship before Thee, O Lord, and shall glorify Thy name!

THE POSITION OF WOMAN AMONG THE JEWS.

By DR. MAX LANDSBERG.

The scope of the subject assigned to me is so wide, it extends over so long a period of time, and covers so large a territory that only a sketch can be attempted in a paper destined to be read at a gathering where but very limited time can be given to each of the many subjects engaging the interest.

The consideration of Woman's position among the Jews must naturally be divided into three parts coincident with the three great periods of Jewish history.

The first period embraces the biblical time down to the destruction of the Jewish nationality by the Romans.

The second period includes the long time of suffering from the fall of Jerusalem to the removal of political disabilities of the Jews which in France and the United States began at the end of the last century.

The third marks the growing intercourse of the Jews with non-Jews and their active participation in the social, political, and intellectual life of the nations in whose midst they live and of which they constitute an integral part. The beginning of this period varies among the different nationalities according to the time of the removal of political disabilities, from the last years of the last century to the second half of our own, and is continued to the present day. In Russia and the oriental countries the third period has not yet commenced.

It is generally supposed that the status of woman in the first period is most universally known, since the biblical writings are open to every body, and hosts of scholarly and popular books are available on the subject. Nothing however is further removed from the truth; and it can safely be asserted that little or nothing is known about the condition of woman among the ancient Hebrews before the eighth or seventh century, B. C., except what can be inferred from occasional notices in which historical reminiscences seem to be preserved with exceptional faithfulness.

Those, of course, who still measure the biblical writings by a

16

different standard from that applied to all other productions of the
human mind, and suppose that they were produced in some supernatural manner and revealed to those who were yet utterly unpre-
pared to understand and appreciate them, may still assert that from
the very beginning an ideal relation existed between man and woman
among the Hebrews, and will have a hard task to reconcile therewith
the traces widely scattered of a condition in direct conflict with this
advanced position.

The rude and barbarous manners found here and there in historic
accounts and especially recognizable in the ancient legislation are indeed evidences of the reality, while the beautiful legend of the creation of woman, setting forth a full understanding of her dignity and
of the sacredness of matrimony—generally represented as the exclusive growth of modern civilization—and the wonderful descriptions of the characters of women in the Bible, are the result of the
teachings of the prophets, which became religious and moral sentiment
incarnated in the Jewish people.

The ancient Hebrews had an origin and a beginning not by any
means different from the rest of humanity. At first they were savage
hordes like the ancestors of all other nations; they were cultivated
and refined by a long development and a slow growth, until they had
reached so high a state of advancement that they could be led to
suppose themselves to have commenced their career on the height of
refinement and civilization.

The biblical stories do not give evidence of the condition of the
people at the time which they attempt to describe, but reflect the
sentiments and the culture of their writers who represented the most
advanced religious and ethical views of their age. So it is true even
of the biblical period, what a distinguished scholar so well states as
a general truth in his latest work, "The Jewish religion has made
the Jew."[1]

The finest flower then of the prophetic religion we find in the
position assigned to woman in the history of her creation, where the
perfection of matrimony in the close union of one man and one wife
for life is expressed in such an exalted manner, that not only all
conceptions of antiquity are put in the shade, but that the highest
civilization, yet attained, can not conceive of a more sublime ideal.

"God said, It is not good for man to be alone, I will make him a
helpmate suitable for him," that is equal to him. The perfect equality

[1] C'est le Judaisme, qui a fait le juif. A. Leroy-Beaulieu, Israel chez
les nations, p. 18.

of man and wife is here taught, which is still further impressed by the idea that woman is made out of man and confirmed by man's exclamation, "This is bone of my bones and flesh of my flesh ; she shall be called *Isha*" (that is man with the feminine termination) ; man and wife supplement each other; man and wife are one. And not satisfied with the force of even this statement, the author adds : "Therefore shall a man leave his father and his mother, and shall cling to his wife ; and they shall become one flesh." [1]

It is characteristic for the condition of our present civilization to note how often this last wonderful sentence is misquoted by reversing therein the position of man and wife. To my knowledge, sufficient stress has never yet been laid upon the significant suggestion of the text, which does not say, woman, the physically weaker one, shall cling to her husband, but man, the physically stronger one, shall cling to his wife, who in a high condition of humanity is morally and ethically his superior. A wealth of sentiment, so universally ascribed exclusively to modern ideas, is contained in this ancient Hebrew phrase. It indicates the glory of the prophetic thought, it furnishes the keynote for the exalted position of woman among the Jews, so strangely exceptional, when compared to that of all the ancient and many of the modern nations.

It may be incidentally remarked that this high ideal was ascribed not to the supposed ancestors of the Israelites alone, but set up as the norm for all humanity, of whom Adam and Eve were represented as the common father and mother.

We can not be surprised to meet with a much lower standard in the legislative parts of the Pentateuch which represent the real condition of a much earlier time, and besides practical law never does readily conform with the ethical lessons of the most advanced teachers. But even here the ancient Jews need not blush when compared with other and especially with contemporaneous nations.

While the father had a right to sell his daughter for a slave, she was protected against being made the object of brutal lust. When she had born a child or when she was given to the son of the house, she became thereby a free woman and entered upon the rights of the legal wife. Even when divorced, care was taken that she should be amply provided for. [2]

The abomination of prostitution for religious purposes, in vogue among all oriental nations, was branded as the most heinous crime. [3]

[1] Genesis ii, 18. 21-24. [2] Exodus xxi. 7-11. [3] Lev. xix, 29.

The young married man was exempted from public duties for a whole year, that he might make his wife happy.[1]

The duties to father and mother were perfectly alike. The women were not excluded from the society of men. They were not confined to the innermost part of the house and kept there in utter ignorance of every thing except their household duties, but freely took part in all that concerned their husbands and fathers, and were benefited by the education and training gained by such free intercourse. Choruses of women were admitted to public celebrations. Evidence of this is not wanting. Miriam is reported to have celebrated the escape from Egypt at the head of a host of women with music and song;[2] David, after his victory, received the laurel wreath from the maidens of his people,[3] and religious processions were conducted by women.[4] On Sabbaths and New Moons they appeared at the places of worship " to seek God," and went to the schools of the prophets to listen to their religious instruction.[5]

Thus, far from being unconditionally subject to man, shut up in the harem and protected by isolation, they could move freely and unsuspected among men, participate in public affairs and were not excluded from the highest positions. They were judges and prophets. One of the oldest songs was by a woman,[6] and one of the finest prayers on record was placed in the mouth of the mother of Samuel.[7]

Upon the basis of the practical equality between man and wife grew up that chastity, continency and temperance which are never promoted by legislation, but by the moral self-government of man, brought about by the recognized dignity of woman.

It is significant that the laws against sexual excesses make no distinction between the two sexes. To how high a degree moral sentiment was educated is shown in the tradition preserved in Judges xix to xxi. The outrage committed is declared unheard of "since Israel left Egypt," it arouses the indignation of the whole people, and the refusal to surrender the guilty ones causes a war whose motives remind us of the expedition against Troy. But while Paris had violated the hospitality of a mighty chief and robbed him of his queen, the men of the city of Benjamin had offended a common and unknown wayfarer and his spouse whose honor was to be vindicated.

This high spirit of honor due to woman is evident in the old family legends where the wife is by no means the slave of man. Sarah,

[1] Deut. xxiv, 5.   [2] Ex. xv, 20.   [3] I Sam. xviii, 6, 7.
[4] Psalms lxviii, 26.   [5] II Kings iv. 23.   [6] Debora, Judges v.
[7] I Sam. ii.

Rebekkah, Michal,[1] Abigail,[2] the woman of Shunem,[3] were all the mistresses of the house as described in Proverbs which exhort man to remain true to the wife of his youth and find satisfaction in her love;[4] for a good wife is the crown of her husband,[5] a gift of God;[6] a virtuous woman more valuable than pearls.[7] A celebration of true and faithful love as we have it in the Song of Songs and the charming character represented in that beautiful idyl the Book of Ruth could be produced only where the highest ideals of woman's nobility were conceived and accepted.

This exceptional position of woman among the Israelites stands out in high relief if we compare it with her status amongst the most advanced nations of antiquity, the Greeks and Romans, where the abominable custom was tolerated of lending the wife to a friend, as it was done even by a Socrates, a Cato, a Cicero.

The only apparently just criticism of woman's position among the Jews is the absence of a law against polygamy. An analogous objection might be made against the permission of slavery. But in the one case as in the other legislation was powerless to abolish these abominable customs, but did all in its power to mitigate and to check them.[8]

Better even than the laws, the old family legends prove that monogamy was the rule and polygamy the rare exception, indulged in only by kings and powerful chiefs. Abraham, after having resigned every hope of posterity, takes Hagar only after the urgent request of his wife. Isaac had one wife, Jacob intended to marry Rachel alone, Joseph, Moses, Aaron, lived in monogamy. The word concubine is not even mentioned in the legislative code, it was a foreign word,[9] which never once occurs in the last four books of the Pentateuch. With what disfavor the relation is regarded, is evident from the very old law, quoted before,[10] defining the father's power over his daughter and the master's over his female slave.

Compare with these humane provisions, at least twenty-six centuries old, the following account given on the present condition of similar relations among a people so far advanced as the Japanese, upon the development of whose civilization, however, the Jewish religion never had the slightest influence:

----

[1] II Sam. vi, 29. [2] I Sam. xxv, 14, ff. [3] II Kings, iv, 8, ff.
[4] Prov. v. 18. [5] Prov. xii, 4. [6] Ib. xix, 14.
[7] Ib. xxxi, 10. See also xxxi, 11, ff. and Ecclesiasticus xxvi. 1-4.
[8] Cf. Deut. xxi, 15-17.
[9] פִּלֶגֶשׁ πάλλαξ.
[10] Page 243; Exod. xxi. 7-11.

"In Japanese households the concubine or *mekake* occupies a position similar to that of a servant, so far as her rights are concerned. The wife is always the mistress of the house, and looks upon her husband's *mekake* in the light of a maid. Should the concubine become a mother, she has no claim upon the child, who belongs to her master and mistress, and who is taught to regard them only as his natural parents. Indeed, most frequently the *mekake* is employed in a family for the sole purpose of securing an heir; and no sooner has the child been born and weaned than the concubine is discharged.

"The *mekake* has no prerogatives above the other servants of the house, and is subject to immediate dismissal whenever the master of the house desires it. . . . She is simply a convenience, and has been secured from some employment bureau, just as any other servant, and receives regular wages. . . . Not only is the present emperor himself the child of a *mekake*, but so also is the present heir-apparent to the throne."[1]

All the pictures of domestic felicity in the later poetry, as in Proverbs so often, and in Psalms cxxviii, 3, point evidently at one only wife ruling in the house as queen. The prophets could find no better illustration to bring home to the people the relation of God to them, than that of marriage with the wife of his youth.[2]

While therefore no general law existed abolishing polygamy, long before the origin of Christianity monogamy among the Jews was the universally established custom. There is no indication of such a provision in the New Testament nor in the early Church. And long after monogamy was proclaimed as a law under the name of Rab. Gershom ben Jehuda, at the Synod of Worms, in 1020, Christian dignitaries, and even Protestant reformers, continued to regard the polygamic connections of Christian princes with a most lenient eye.[3]

When considering the wonderful early development of the exalted position of woman among the early Jews, we appreciate the sentiment expressed by Heinrich Heine : "Judea has ever appeared to me like a piece of Occident lost in the midst of the Oriental countries."[4] The ingenious poet would have done better justice to Judea had he expressed his wonderment that the finest features of Occidental ethics

[1] From Moral Life of the Japanese, by Dr. W. Delano Eastlake, Popular Science Monthly, July, 1893, p. 344.

[2] Hosea ii. 16-22; Is. liv, 6-8; and the forceful adhortation to conjugal fidelity, Mal. ii, 13-16.

[3] For a collection of evidences see die Frau der Vergangenheit in A. Bebel, die Frau und der Socialismus.

[4] Geständnisse, Sämmtl. Werke, Vol. 14, p. 315.

and morality were the flower and fruit of that which Judaism has
taught humanity.

Being so often repeated it is generally regarded as an axiom that
the Christian religion has emancipated woman from her slavery and
delivered her from her subordinate position. Let me give as a speci-
men of this popular idea a quotation from Dr. John Lord:[1]

"Only Christianity," he says, "recognizes what is most truly attractive and ennobling among women." "The Jewish women seem to
have been more favored and honored than women were in Greece or
Rome, even in the highest periods of their civilization. But in Jewish
history woman was the coy maiden, or the vigilant housekeeper, or
the ambitious mother, or the intriguing wife, or the obedient daughter,
or the patriotic songstress, rather than the sympathetic friend. Though
we admire the beautiful Rachel, the heroic Deborah, or the virtuous
Abigail, or the fortunate Esther, or the brave Judith, or the generous
Shunamite, we do not find in the Rachels and Esthers the hallowed
ministrations of the Marys, the Marthas and the Phœbes, until
Christianity had developed the virtues of the heart and kindled the
loftier sentiments. Then woman became not merely the gentle nurse
and the prudent housewife and the disinterested lover, but a friend,
an angel of consolation, the equal of man in character, and his superior in the virtues of the heart and soul."

How unjust this assertion is, the author himself might have known,
had he but remembered that the Marys and the Marthas were Jewish
women, born from Jewish parents, grown up and educated solely under
Jewish influence, and made, what they were, by the instrumentality
of the Jewish religion. How much superior the conception of woman's
place was among the Jewish Prophets than it was understood by the
apostle Paul can be learned from I Corinthians vii, I Timothy ii,
11–14, and other passages. The depreciation of marriage became indeed the rule in the Christian Church.

Full justice to the Jews in this respect has been done from a Christian side lately by Nahida Remi, in her book, "The Jewish Woman,'
where, pages 18 to 32, she gives a full collection of the passages from
the New Testament and the early fathers of the Church, showing how
they regarded woman and matrimony. She is fair enough to say,
"The higher fancy is strained to exalt the mother of Jesus, the more
proud the Jews can be to see the gentle, quiet Mary originate from
their people."

Far from attempting to deny that among Christian nations the

[1] Beacon Lights of History, Vol. 5, Great Women, pp. 58, 64 and 65.

dignity of woman has been elevated and tardy justice is being done to her, we are entitled to assert that this is the result of that part of Christianity which is essentially Jewish.

In the long period which succeeded the blotting out forever of the Jewish nationality, the natural development of Jewish religion and ethics was rudely interrupted, its stream led into a new channel and exposed to a great variety of unfortunate conditions. Hated, persecuted, and tempest-tossed, the only preventive against total dissolution and loss of identity was found in the minute elaboration of the formal and ceremonial part of religion, with which the Jews surrounded themselves as with a protecting wall.

The Talmud, representing a development especially in Babylon under oriental influences, became the power ruling supreme. Rigid conservatism, a result of terrible oppression continued through centuries, furthered isolation and preserved existing conditions even in occidental countries. If, indeed, Judea had seemed like a piece of Occident in the midst of the oriental countries, now the Jews represented orientalism in the midst of the Occident. Every department of life was so influenced, and the position of woman was materially altered. Women were excluded from the participation in all those ceremonies which to the popular mind were the principal expression of religion.[1] Women were gradually placed on a level with children and slaves, their testimony was not admitted on the witness stand, not even to testify for the appearance of the moon.[2] From Deuteronomy xi, 19,[3] it was deduced, against the rules of the Hebrew language and the plain sense of the words, that daughters must not receive religious instruction, and, while Ben Asai taught that it is a duty to give such instruction to them,[4] the opinion of R. Elieser to the contrary became so popular as to be used as a proverb.[5] Finally a benediction was introduced in the daily ritual for men, thanking God, that he had not made them a woman.[6] This sentiment, however, sadly as it has influenced the position of woman for many centuries, was far from being universal in the early part of this period. The spirit of the Jewish

[1] כצות עשה שהזמן גרמה Menachot 13, b.

[2] Rosh Hashana 22a.

[3] ולמדתם אותם את בניכם ולא את בנותיכם

[4] Sota III. 4. חייב אדם ללמד את בתו תורה

[5] Ib. כל המלמד בתו תורה כאלו לומדה תפלות ישרפו דברי תורה ואל ימסרו לנשים

[6] Menachot 43, b; Tos. Berachot 7, 18; Jer. Berach. 13, b.

religion was too strong ever to be entirely suppressed by this narrow-mindedness, and the Jewish woman was far from being degraded thereby, as might be supposed.

Not all the prominent Rabbis indorsed the opinion of the above-mentioned R. Elieser, who silenced a scholarly woman that asked him about the explanation of a biblical passage with the impolite words, "A woman's scholarship should be confined to the spinning wheel." [1] Many were of the same view as Ben Asai. So it is reported, when a halachic question was discussed at one time, the son and daughter of Chanina ben Teradion answered it each in a different manner, and Jehuda ben Baba said, he approved of the answer of the daughter. [2] A conversation on religious topics is recorded of R. Jose ben Chalafta with a woman, [3] and there are many other indications of a similar nature. Women occupied high positions in the congregations. Prof. Emil Schürer furnishes evidence that women were made "Archisynagogos," [4] and that the title of "mater synagogae" not unfrequently occurs in the inscriptions. [5] The same author takes it for granted that at the time of Christ the sexes were strictly separated in the synagogue, although there is no mention of this in ancient records and even in the Talmud no separate place for women is spoken of anywhere. But this is by no means certain. The indications rather tend to prove that the strict separation of the sexes at the synagogues was caused by later oriental influence, while greater freedom seems to have been the rule in older times. The court of women at the temple was by no means reserved for women alone ; many functions connected with the service were performed there by men, [6] and the halls under the court of the Israelites opened into it.

St. Paul's injunction, "Let your women keep silence in the churches," [7] etc., shows that such rule had not been obligatory upon the Jewish women and a Baraitha [8] gives women the right to read from the Thora at the public services, and it is added that the custom was abolished only on account of the dignity of the congregation (which means of course as understood in oriental countries).

[1] אין הכמה של אשה אלא בפלכה Jer. Sota 19a; Babli Joma 66b.
[2] יפה אמרה בתו כבנו Tos. Kelim I, 4. 17.   [3] Tanchuma, Ber.
[4] Geschichte des jüdischen Volkes II, p. 367.   [5] Ib., p. 520.
[6] Middoth II, 15, there the Nazirs cooked their offerings and cut their hair, and priests who could not approach the altar examined the wood, to see whether it was worm eaten.
[7] I Corinth. xv, 34, 35.
[8] Meg. 23, a, quoted by Löw, Lebensalter. p. 201.

During the middle ages the higher or lower position of the Jewish women was determined by the condition of the nations in whose midst the Jews lived. It was better in Italy where women in general took an active part in the higher culture than in Germany and France. Still, even from those countries, a number of names of scholarly women has been preserved.[1]   -

The daughter of Rashi was his secretary when he fell sick ; Hannah, the sister of Rabbenu Tam, instructed the women of her town in their religious duties, and renowned Rabbis quote as religious authorities distinguished and learned women.[2]

Pellicanus, one of the best known theologians and hebraists in Germany at the beginning of the sixteenth century, tells in his autobiography that he was induced to take up the study of Hebrew because he had heard that a Doctor of Theology in a discussion with a Jew on the Christian religion was defeated by the arguments not only of the Jew, but also of a Jewess.[3]

In Italy the number of learned Jewish women was much greater. Among them, the Roman woman, Paula, a descendant of Nathan, the author of the Aruch, who made a beautiful copy of many commentaries of the Bible. Immanuel of Rome mentions a number of Jewish women who wrote creditable poetry.   .

But, although, after all, women of scholarly attainments were the rare exceptions, we must not forget that the same was the case everywhere, and that the few Jewish women so distinguished deserve the greater credit if the terrible conditions are considered under which the Jews were laboring. No degree of oppression, however, could rob the Jewish woman of the halo of chastity and unexceptional purity with which she was surrounded, and which shines with the most brilliant luster when compared with the moral rottenness which, according to the testimony of Christian moralists and preachers, was the rule in the sexual relations among the Christians of the same period.[4] All the Jewish girls were trained in their duties as wives and mothers; even the most ignorant ones among them were very prominent in domestic virtues and morality, and many sacrificed their lives as martyrs to save their womanly honor and to remain faithful to their religion. In accordance with this distinction was the treatment they received from their husbands and sons, and the high esteem in which they were

[1] See Zunz, Zur Gesch., p. 172.   Berliner, Aus dem innern Leben, p. 51.
[2] See Güdeman, Gesch. des Erziehungswesens, etc., Vol. I, pp. 231, 232.
[3] W. Bacher in Monatsschrift zur Gesch. u. Wissensch. des Judenth, June, 1893, p. 402.
[4] See Güdeman, Gesch., etc., Vol. I, p. 234; Vol. II, p. 217 ff.

held. R. Meir ben Baruch, of Rothenburg, in the second half of the thirteenth century, could proudly say: "It is utterly unheard of for a Jew to beat his wife, as it is customary among other people." [1]

While, thus, the recognition of woman's nobility and of her claim to refined treatment and high consideration remained through all times a characteristic feature of Jews of all classes and all countries, the peculiar position assigned to her with reference to religious practice low, though it was in theory, was far from exercising a degrading influence upon her spiritual life. On the contrary, it had evidently the opposite tendency.

Excluded as she was from most of the ceremonial part of religion, so excessively developed, and exempt from the practice of those manifold duties which lent to the Jews their peculiar oriental aspect, she was largely saved from the dangers of that formalism which so easily crushes under its weight all truly religious sentiment. She was led to concentrate her efforts upon the essential part of religion, upon that which is alike the true end and aim of all religions independent of creed or denomination. She remained the representative and preserver of idealism and of that genuine prophetic spirit which tends to promote the glorification of Judaism, and to further the realization of the brotherhood of humanity. This was constantly appreciated, and explains the singularly elevated and ideal position of the female sex among the Jews. As far removed from the unhealthy worship of feudal chivalry which made woman an object of a playful cult, as from the extreme views of those who, clamoring for woman's rights, wish to obliterate all the natural distinctions between the two sexes, the Jews always and every-where appreciated the high significance of woman's work for the noblest goods, the gain of true liberty, and the conservation of religious sentiment. The whole history of the Jews and their literature testify to this. Aggadists and preachers never got tired of dwelling thereon, showing their own views of woman by the use they make of scriptural texts. It was owing to the merit of the pious women, the preachers said, that Israel was delivered from Egypt.[2] On Sinai Moses was instructed to win over the women first to accept his teachings.[3] They taught their children love of God and love of their fellow-men, the practice of unlimited charity, and filled them with enthusiasm for noble works.[4]

---

[1] Responsa ed. Cremona No. 291. אין זה דרך בני עינו להכות
נשותיהם כמנהג א"ה

[2] Sota 11.   [3] Mechilta Jethro.

[4] Schir Rab. 28. ישהו מזרזות במצות.

Rabbi Joseph Jabez relates that the Jewish women in Spain encouraged their despondent husbands to remain true to their faith, and rather suffer the agonies of death on the pyres of the Inquisition than to deny the truth which it was their mission to teach.[1]

They found their noblest work in faithfully discharging their duties as wives and mothers; they were the priestesses at the sacred hearth of the home, gave the family a religious atmosphere, and infused it with that affection, sincerity, and holiness by which it is proverbially distinguished, they saved Judaism from becoming a church religion, and made it most emphatically a religion of life.

This wonderful religious power the Jewish woman acquired by being saved from spending her energy on much of that formal part of Judaism which had such an exuberant growth. So she could and did become the most important factor in cultivating that part of religion which has its root in the heart.

This explains also how it happened in the last epoch, since the shades of darkness gradually began to lift and the sun of liberty and justice to shine for the Jews, that wherever the Jews stripped their religion of the old oriental garments forced upon them through a thousand years, wherever they could emerge from their compulsory exclusiveness and were permitted to take part in the common labors of humanity, and especially where many of the ceremonies by which men alone were formerly distinguished have been recognized in their true value and to a great extent dropped, the Jewish woman was at once ready to take the most active and public part in every branch of religious work: that she even excelled man in enthusiasm and devotion.

As soon as the spirit of liberty began to purify the air, and the nations were delivered from the undisputed sway of intolerance, the Jews were aroused from their lethargy and their leading men began with energy to demand the emancipation of the Jewish wives and mothers and daughters from their religious minority and their legal restoration to the position which they had never totally ceased to hold in fact. How modest and insignificant these demands were at first can be learned from the literature of fifty years ago, when it was regarded as a great achievement to insist upon the abolishment of the obsolete chalitza and to reform laws, made for an entirely different state of civilization, which condemned Jewish wives to the bonds of a hopeless widowhood, and when scholars spent their learned efforts to prove

---

[1] Or ha Chayim, Ch. 5. הן הנה הנשים הספרדיות באו והביאו את
בעליהן על קדושת השי״ת, quoted by Jellinek.

that, according to Jewish law, married women are not obliged to cut off their hair and cover their heads.[1]

Great strides in advance have since been made among the Jews in all civilized countries. Nobody in Europe, outside of the semi-barbarous nations where mediaevalism yet reigns supreme, nobody in America would still think of subscribing to the preposterous idea that woman is inferior to man in a religious sense; that she has not the same rights and the same obligations. Nobody would think of denying that she is the most powerful factor in the promotion of religious life and religious sentiment. Religious instruction is therefore given with equal thoroughness to the boys and girls alike, and well is the fact appreciated, that the flourishing condition of our Jewish congregations in America, where the work done and the sacrifices made are entirely spontaneous, could not exist without the noble and active co-operation of our women. Their work in the department of active and especially organized charity is as zealous in the smallest as in the largest congregations. It grows in scope in accordance with the larger opportunities offered in the great centers of population. It is as distinguished and elaborate at Paris and London, at Berlin and St. Petersburg, as it is at New York and Chicago.[2]

In all our progressive Jewish congregations, women render the most valuable services as teachers at the schools of religious instruction, and it is well known that they furnish the largest contingent in the attendance at religious services.

Nevertheless, it can not be denied that work has been only begun,

[1] See Geiger, Wissensch. Zeitschrift, Vol. III, pp. 1 and 354.

[2] It is a source of great regret that complete statistics are not available of the charitable work of Jewish women everywhere. A successful attempt has been made in this direction in the book, " Woman's Mission," edited by the Baroness Burdett-Coutts, and published by the Royal British Commission of the Chicago Exhibition. An account as interesting as it is gratifying is there given of the Jewish women's philanthropic work in London, where they conduct every kind of preventive and rescue work. Among other charitable institutions they have a Jewish ladies' loan society, which has worked well for the last forty-six years, and has met with marked success. It assists the deserving poor with loans of money without interest in sums from ten shillings to ten pounds, which are repaid in weekly installments of one-twentieth until the debt is liquidated. During 1892, 359 loans were granted, the loans amounting to £2,032 10s., the repayment being £1,908. It is added that the good offices of the Jewish ladies are by no means confined to their co-religionists, but are very largely extended also to the Christians, and many of them gladly co-operate in efforts for the spread of education, wholesome recreation and temperance with Christian workers. Pp. 143, 144.

that much remains to be done, and that it will not be completed until perfect religious equality has been established between men and women.

There is no conceivable reason why our women should not have a voice in the management of our congregations, why they should not enjoy all the privileges of active membership, why they should not be elected to lend their aid, their wisdom and enthusiasm, as trustees and members of the school boards.[1]

Only if this last step has been taken, when our women will be enabled to contribute their full share to our religious activity, shall we have some prospect of removing that baneful indifferentism of which there is so much complaint everywhere.

They will again restore to Judaism, purified from the dross of former ages, its fire and inwardness which inspire all to make noble sacrifices, not only of their substance, but of their personal service.

From our magnificent temples they will again transplant genuine religious spirit into the bosom of the families, they will cause Judaism to be placed in its proper light before the world, they will be instrumental in bringing its influence to bear upon the people at large by educating a generation which, with the old fidelity and enthusiasm, will exclaim: "All that God has spoken we will do."

---

[1] For a number of years women have served as members of the school board of my congregation at Rochester.

STATE AND SOCIETY.

JUDAISM AND THE MODERN STATE.

By RABBI DAVID PHILIPSON, D.D.

The modern state may be said to date from the year 1789, when, on the one hand, the French revolution, violent outburst of an oppressed nation, become conscious of the wrongs inflicted upon it and of the rights whereof it had been deprived, opened a new era in the history of government, not alone in France, but in Europe at large, and on the other hand, the adoption of the Constitution in this United States demonstrated that the doctrine of the equality of men politically had at last been realized. New principles of statecraft came into vogue. The age of the absolutism of hereditary rule had passed. The period of the reign of the people had dawned. The shot of emancipation had been fired that had been heard around the world. The new evangel of human right and human liberty had been proclaimed, and whatever occasional relapses the cause of freedom may have suffered in the years that have since ensued, the course has been steadily onward and upward, the spirit awakened in 1789 has never quite disappeared from the rulings and doings of men. The primary principles whereon the modern state rests are the individual freedom of men and popular representation in the councils of state; these may be said to have been first effectually declared by the English Puritans. Their descendants, the American fathers, founders of this republican government, imbibed their thoughts and embodied them in the Declaration of Independence and the Constitution of the United States. Now, the Puritans were guided in their thoughts and lives almost altogether by the Old Testament writings, hence the doctrines that lay at the foundation of the modern state, notably as represented by government in this country, were through these political disciples of the Jews of old drawn from the pages of the Jewish bible that regulated the formation and government of the old Jewish state. The political philosophy of the mediæval state was laid on the lines marked out by Rome, the political philosophy of the modern state on the ideas first promulgated by the great Jewish law-giver of the olden days; therefore the first proposition in regard to the relation of Judaism to the modern state is the broad declaration that the principle of government of the modern state was

17

anticipated by Jewish legislation in the far past. And with the up-growing of the modern state, the living descendants of those who in that far past first outlined its principles, obtained the rights of which, under the vicious legislation of the mediæval state, they had been entirely deprived.

In the mediæval state, the Jews and Judaism were unknown factors. They had no position whatsoever. The state was Christian, the church and the state were closely connected, and in a Christian state there was no room for any but Christians; there were no rights for any but Christians. The Jew plainly then had no rights. In the eyes of the state, dominated by the church, the Jew was an existing evil, living under a curse; Judaism was a *superstitio et perfidia*, a perfidy and a superstition. True, in constitutions, edicts, bulls, there were frequently paragraphs devoted to the Jews, but these set forth not their rights, but their lack of rights.

The church legislation as embodied in the rubrics of church councils and synods was the inspiration for the regulations of the state. The Jew could hold no office, was not admitted into the army, was not eligible as a witness in the courts, had no free right of residence, but was compelled to dwell in such districts and quarters as might be set aside for him and his, could not travel from place to place without paying the Jew-toll, could not tarry in a town without paying a special tax, and even then often not longer than over night; in short, the Jew had no standing as a citizen or a man, all the laws and regulations dealing with him were restrictive; he was permitted to exist (and at times not even that), but to live a free life was not to him granted. The story of the relation of the Jew to the mediæval state presents a monotonous sameness in all lands, it is the tale of the man without a country, for however eagerly and anxiously the Jew may have desired to serve the land of his adoption he was repelled; he was only an alien tolerated until it might please the powers that were to drive him forth. In a word, he had no legal or civic standing; he was excluded from the enjoyment of every right; he was *in* the state, but not *of* it. It is not my purpose to dwell upon the dread persecutions and oppressions to which the Jews were continually subjected nor to call up the harrowing scenes of plunder, pillage, outrage, murder, that blacken the records of those days; man's inhumanity to man has never appeared in more lurid light than in this martyrdom of the Jewish people, illustrating marvelous constancy on the one hand and incredible cruelty on the other. Thus did it continue until the dawn of the new time when the first gray streaks of light appeared on the horizon and the oppressed classes every-where began to be the objects of the consideration of statesmen and law-making bodies. It is not necessary for me to state that there are no cataclysms in history; we name the year 1789 as the beginning of the new time, the modern state, but it is remarkable merely as the date when the ideas as to human rights that had been in the air for many years found active expression; thus too the anomalous position of the Jews struck the attention of thinkers, and in the year 1781 the statesman, Johann Konrad Wilhelm von Dohm, published his book on the improvement of the civil condition of the Jews, the first serious attempt at treating the question historically, philosophically, and humanly; he pleads for the removal of civil disabilities from the Jews and for placing them on an equal footing with other subjects.

The first effective step taken toward the emancipation of the Jews was the celebrated Edict of Toleration of the Emperor Joseph II of Austria in the year 1782. Although it was far from granting full freedom to the Jewish subjects of the empire in every respect, yet it was a sign of the times, the first real result in Europe of the working of the new spirit and the new ideas. It was the first recognition on the part of the state of the fact that the Jew was also entitled to consideration, the forerunner of the legislation of the modern state. The atmosphere was clearing during the closing years of the eighteenth century. Class rights, class distinctions, class exclusions, vicious class legislation, were to disappear in the light of the new time. The first clear note sounded from this side of the world: "Congress shall make no law respecting the establishment of religion, or prohibiting the free exercise thereof." Unmistakably the separation of church and state was here proclaimed; no special legislation regarding Chatholics, Protestants, Jews, infidels; no classes or sects mentioned; all equal as men. Not having past traditions to hamper them, the framers of the constitution took as their text the equality of all men as men and labored accordingly. There was no question as to the relation of any religious body to the state on these shores; this is the correct, the ideal attitude of the state, characteristic of the modern state in its true realization. So that it would seem that, as far as this land is concerned, the question of the relation of the Jews to the state is an idle one, but unfortunately it was not, as we shall have occasion to see later on.

France, true to the principles of the Revolution, granted full emancipation to its Jewish subjects by the act of the National Assembly of September 27, 1791, by which it declared that all Jews who took the oath of citizenship and assumed the duties of citizenship should be considered Frenchmen. But it was not without a struggle that this was accomplished, and it will be interesting to briefly recount the steps of the struggle, since it involves the consideration of Judaism's attitude to the state. In the year 1789 the question of the emancipation of the Jews was before the Assembly; the Abbe Gregoire, one of the deputies, who before this time had already espoused their cause, arose and exclaimed: "As a minister of a religion that regards all men as brethren, I invoke the intervention of the Assembly in favor of a proscribed and unhappy people." But his expression was unfortunate; this was the very thing that those who opposed the granting of full rights to the Jews insisted on, viz., that the Jews were a people, that they considered themselves a nation with national hopes and expectations of their own, that they were an *imperium in imperio*, and hence could not be truly patriotic. This has been the cry of the enemies of Judaism and the Jews ever since, and still to-day we hear it; and that, too, in spite of the fact that on every battlefield during this century Jewish blood has been spilled and Jewish lives have been sacrificed for their country, and that, too, in spite of the fact that on every possible occasion the Jewish pulpit and the Jewish press have uttered the most patriotic sentiments, and that, too, in spite of the fact that time and time again Jewish representative men have declared, and it has come to be an accepted tenet of modern Judaism that the Jews do not constitute a nation, but only a religious community; that they do not look for the coming of a personal Messiah who will lead them back to Palestine and reconstruct the Jewish state, that they have no political hopes or ideals other than those of the nation in whose midst they dwell and of which they form component parts. As long ago as 1806 the Emperor Napoleon called together an assembly of representative Jews of France and Italy. This assembly is known as the French Sanhedrin; before this body the Emperor laid twelve questions for discussion and answer; the responses to these questions were to stamp the attitude of Judaism in regard to matters that involved the commonweal, and particularly the relation of the professors of the faith to those standing outside of its ranks. Three of these questions bear directly upon the subject in hand, the fourth, fifth and sixth; they were as follows: "Are the French regarded by the Jews as strangers or as brothers? How are the Jews to deport themselves toward the French legally? Do the Jews born in France regard this as their fatherland, and do they consider themselves bound to defend it? do they owe obedience to the law of the land?" The responses were as follows: "The Jews look upon the French as brethren. Moses long ago commanded kindness toward strangers; how much more must the Jews regard those as brethren with whom they live in one land, under one law; yea, through whose humanity they are now enjoying the best imaginable condition of citizenship. The attitude of Jews toward non-Jews is exactly the same as toward Jews. Only in their religion do they differ. The French Jews regarded France as their fatherland, even in time of great oppression; how much more now, after being placed on an equal footing with all citizens. The Jews have often given testimony of their love of country in battle." In the year 1842 a number of Jews of Frankfort, in meeting assembled, declared, among other things (and this may be taken as a brief and clear expression of Judaism's attitude toward the modern state), "We neither expect nor desire a Messiah who will lead the Israelites back to Palestine; we know no fatherland but that to which by birth and civic relations we belong;" and in that remarkable document known as the Declaration of Principles, adopted by the Conference of Rabbis, assembled in Pittsburgh in November, 1885, and hailed with acclaim as one of the clearest and most comprehensive statements of the teachings of Judaism that had ever been formulated, we find this paragraph bearing upon the subject in hand, which, being the latest public deliverance, may be set down as the true expression of Jewish teaching: "We recognize in the modern era of universal culture of heart and intellect the approaching of the realization of Israel's great Messianic hope for the establishment of the kingdom of truth, justice and peace among all men. We consider ourselves no longer a nation, but a religious community, and therefore expect neither a return to Palestine nor a sacrificial worship under the sons of Aaron, nor the restoration of any of the laws concerning a Jewish state."

The position of Judaism then in regard to the state is very clear; its followers are Jews in religion only, children of their fatherland, whatever or wherever it may be, in all that pertains to the public weal. Judaism discountenances the connection of church and state. Each shall attend to its own. Judaism teaches its confessors that if any contingency should arise (an occurrence, however, of which I can not conceive) in which it, the religion, should be in conflict with the state, the religion must take the second place, for we recognize no power within a power; the two, religion and civil government, have distinct and individual provinces, neither shall, neither need encroach upon the other.

Thus run Judaism's teachings as affecting the state. Let us now briefly review the attitude of the modern state toward the Jew and Judaism, showing how gradually right was done and emancipation from mediaeval shackles and restrictions gained during the course of this century. We have seen how in France the National Assembly of 1791 declared the Jewish residents of the country French citizens with all the rights of citizenship; nor with all the many changes of

government was this act ever reversed; true, during the reigns of
Louis XVIII and Charles X, after the fall of Napoleon, the church
gained great ascendancy, but the rights of the Jews as citizens was
never revoked. After the July revolution, in 1830, the final step toward a complete recognition of the equal standing of Judaism with the
Christian faiths was taken when the ministers of the Jewish church
were placed on the civil list and paid their salaries by the government,
and the very last vestige of the regulations of the mediaeval state
anent the Jews disappeared when, in 1839, through the efforts of
Adolphe Cremieux, the oath *more Judaico*, the special form of oath prescribed for the Jews as distinct from the Christians, was abolished.
In France the attitude of the modern state has been fully upheld for
over a century. In civil matters there is no question of Jew or Judaism, of Catholic or Catholicism, of Protestant or Protestantism ; the
state deals with men, not with opinions or beliefs. But one other
state of Europe has a like record of justice to present. On the declaration of the Batavian Republic, the National Assembly of Holland, in
1796, invested its Jewish subjects with the full rights of citizenship.
Louis Napoleon, when king of the country, ratified the act, modified
the form of oath, and admitted the Jews to military service ; and after
1814, William I, proceeding in a like manner, regulated the legal and
civil position of his Jewish subjects in the most liberal spirit, and
swept away every distinction that marked them in the mediaeval legislation. These two countries present the bright side ; into the other
governments of Europe the principles of the modern state, as founded
upon the natural rights of man, gained slow entrance as far as the
Jews were concerned. True, the victories of the armies of the French
Republic and Empire carried the principles of the Revolution into
other lands, and in the early years of the century those countries that
came particularly under French influence, such as Westphalia, the
kingdom of Jerome Bonaparte, the Rhine provinces, and Italy extended to the Jews rights of citizenship. Most of the German kingdoms, in fact Prussia, Baden, Bavaria, began to take steps in a like
direction and to recognize the right of the Jews to be treated as men.
The new spirit was working every-where ; but after Waterloo came the
reaction. Mediaevalism in thought and practice became the fashion.
The Congress of Vienna, in 1815, passed a resolution seemingly favorable
to Jewish emancipation, but it meant nothing. The Jews in the German states were forced back into the old situation. This was the more
bitter to bear after the high hopes that had been aroused. Disgrace-
ful scenes of pillage and persecution were re-enacted in German towns.
In Wurzburg, Frankfurt, and others the hep-hep cry again resounded,

the night of mediaevalism again threatened to settle upon Jewry ; but this could not last. The Jews themselves, men trained in the modern spirit, took up the fight and bravely struggled for human rights, men who would not sell their birthright for a mess of pottage, who would not renounce their Judaism to gain the rights of citizenship. Chief among these, the leader in the struggle for Jewish emancipation, was Gabriel Riesser, who with word and pen advocated the cause, urged the formation of clubs for the furtherance of emancipation, addressed statesmen and legislators, called upon the Jews to demand full equality not as a *favor* but as a *right*, clearly demonstrated the principles of the modern state in the matter, and lived to see his cherished hopes realized, for the year 1848, year of storm and stress, finally brought to fruition the seeds sown in 1789. In that year, or shortly thereafter, the states of Western Europe expiated the wrongs of centuries and expunged from their statute books the special, discriminating, degrading regulations against their subjects of the Jewish faith. In that year, Baden and Sweden, in the following, Denmark, in 1850, Prussia did the act of justice. In 1860, Bavaria, in 1867, Austria, in 1874, Switzerland fell into line. As early as 1821, Portugal, that in 1506 had expelled the Jews, following the example of Spain in 1492, two-faced year, re-admitted them with full rights.

In Italy the cause had its ups and downs. Joined to the fortunes of France by the conquests of Napoleon, the Italian states, too, were included in the French legislation on the rights of the Jews, but with the fall of Napoleon and the return of the Pope in 1815, the same story of reaction that I have told as characterizing the German states can be rehearsed. The Jews of Rome were driven back into the Ghetto and the work of emancipation was slow. 1849 witnessed Sardinia proclaim equal rights to all without distinction of faith. Tuscany and Lombardy, followed in 1859 ; Umbria in 1860, Naples and Sicily in 1861, Venice in 1866, and finally Rome, with the establishment of the Italian kingdom in 1870.

England was in the fore front of all European governments in agitations for the emancipation of the Jews. As early as 1753 a bill was passed in Parliament granting the Jewish residents of the country the rights of citizenship, but, owing to the protests of the merchants of London and other towns, the bill was reconsidered and repealed. A long time elapsed ere the question of Jewish emancipation again became the subject of parliamentary discussion. In 1833, Robert Grant introduced a bill to that effect. Lord Macaulay supported it with his well known speech on the civil disabilities of the Jews. The bill was passed time and again ; ten times by the House of Commons, and the Lords rejected it as often. In 1847, Baron Lionel De Rothschild was elected a member of Parliament. He could not enter upon his office because he would not take the oath of allegiance "in the true faith of a Christian." Not till 1858 was he able to take his seat, when the House passed Sir John Russell's bill, which permitted Jews to omit these words. This was first made a special resolution, but, in 1866, the Parliamentary Oaths Act Amendment was passed removing the words in question from the oath altogether. In 1885, Lord Rothschild (Sir Nathaniel) took his seat in the House of Lords, the first Jewish English peer.

In this country, from the very inception of the government, there was as a matter of course no such thing possible as civil disability on account of religious faith ; all who possessed the qualifications and fulfilled the legal requirements of citizenship were equal before the law ; there was no religious test. This was true as far as the Federal government was concerned, yet could the separate states enact special legislation demanding religious tests.

This was, for example, the case in Maryland as far as the Jews were concerned. The thirty-fifth section of the constitution of 1778 reads as follows : "No other test or qualification ought to be required, on admission to any office of trust or profit, than such oath of support and fidelity to this state and such oath of office as shall be directed by this convention or the legislature of this state and a declaration of belief in the Christian religion." By this, of course, the Jews were excluded. In 1818, a bill was introduced into the legislature known as the "Jew Bill," whose object it was to remove the civil disabilities of the Jewish citizens of the state. For eight years the struggle lasted, and the bill was finally passed in 1826. In consequence of this, we find in the new constitution adopted in 1851 the following addition to the above quoted clause : "And if the party shall profess to be a Jew, the declaration shall be of his belief in a future state of rewards and punishments." In the constitution of 1864 (Declaration of Rights, Art. 37), we find still further progress of the spirit of liberty, the article being amended to read as follows : " No other test or qualification ought to be required, on admission to any office of trust or profit, than such oath of allegiance and fidelity to this state and the United States as may be prescribed by this constitution or the laws of the state and a declaration of belief in the Christian religion or in the existence of God, and in a future state of rewards and punishments;" and, finally, to trace this matter one step further, in the constitution of 1867 (Declaration of Rights, Art. 37), all distinction between religious sects is done away with by the following declaration : "No religious test ought ever to be required as a qualification for any office of trust or profit in this state other than a declaration of belief in the existence of God, nor shall the legislature prescribe any other oath of office than the oath prescribed by this constitution."

In North Carolina, too, the Jews, or rather the non-Christians, were discriminated against. The constitution of the state adopted in 1776 declared that " no person who shall deny the being of God or the truth of the Protestant religion or the divine authority either of the Old or New Testaments . . . shall be capable of holding any office or place of trust or profit in the civil department within this state." In the year 1835 the words "Christian religion" were substituted for "Protestant religion." This removed the civil disabilities of the Catholics but not of the Jews. No further step was taken in this measure until 1861 and 1862, during the rebellion, when Colonel Wm. Johnston proposed in the constitutional convention the removal of the Jewish disabilities, stating that he " saw Jewish blood and Christian blood spilt on the same battle-field, running of the same hue and commingling with each other." My informant, Rev. S. Mendelssohn, of Wilmington, North Carolina, to whom I am indebted for these facts, writes me that he does not know whether this amendment was adopted, but that all the enactments of this convention and all other conventions held in the state during the War of the Rebellion were nullified by the United States government. I find that it was only as late as 1868, under the Reconstruction regime, that the civil disabilities of the Jews were fully and finally removed, the oath to be taken on the assumption of office being as follows (Art. VI, sec. 4): " I, —— ——, do solemnly swear (or affirm) that I will support and maintain the constitution and laws of the United States and the constitution and laws of North Carolina not inconsistent therewith, and that I will faithfully discharge the duties of my office, so help me God;" and section five of this same article declares that only such shall be disqualified for office who "shall deny the existence of Almighty God."

Others of the thirteen original states in their constitutions adopted prior to the adoption of the constitution of the United States in 1789, had also religious tests for office, but these were for the most part changed shortly after the establishment of the federal government. Thus the constitution of the State of Delaware of 1776 (Art. 22) ordains that the following declaration be made on taking office: "I do profess faith in God the Father, and in Jesus Christ his only son, and in the Holy Ghost, one God, blessed for evermore, and I do acknowledge the holy scriptures of the Old and New Testament to be given by divine inspiration ;" but in the constitution of 1792 (Art. 1, sec. 2) we read that " no religious test shall be required as a qualification to any office or trust under this state." In the constitution of Massachusetts (Chap. vi, art. 1) the oath of office included the statement, " I do declare that I believe the Christian religion and have a firm persuasion of its truth." This was amended in 1822 to read, " I do solemnly swear that I will bear true faith and allegiance to the commonwealth of Massachusetts and will support the constitution thereof; so help me God."

The constitution of New Jersey of 1776 (Art. 19) declared that " no Protestant inhabitant of this colony shall be denied the enjoyment of any civil right merely on account of his religious principles, but that all persons professing a belief in the faith of any Protestant sect . . . shall be capable of being elected into any office of profit and trust . . . ." This stood until 1844, when the following declaration appears (Art. 4): " There shall be no establishment of one religious sect in preference to another; no religious test shall be required as a qualification for any office or public trust, and no person shall be denied the enjoyment of any civil right merely on account of his religious principles."

The constitution of Pennsylvania of 1776 (Sec. 10) discriminated against Jews by prescribing the following oath for members of the House of Representatives: " I do solemnly believe in one God, the Creator and Governor of the Universe, the Rewarder of the good and the Punisher of the wicked. And I do acknowledge the scriptures of the Old and New Testaments to be given by divine inspiration." But the constitution of 1790 (Art. 9, sec. 4) declares that " no person who acknowledges the being of a God and a future state of rewards and punishments shall on account of his religious sentiments be disqualified to hold any office or place of trust and profit under this commonwealth." The constitution of South Carolina of 1778 (Art. 38) declared " The Christian Religion is deemed and is hereby declared to be the established religion of the state," but the constitution of 1790 (Art. 8, sec. 1) states that " the free exercise and enjoyment of religious profession and worship without discrimination or preference, shall forever hereafter be allowed within this state to all mankind."

The members of the House of Representatives of the state of Vermont had to make the following declaration (Constitution of 1777, Chap. 2, sec. 8): " I do believe in one God, the Creator and Governor of the Universe, the Rewarder of the good and Punisher of the wicked ; I do acknowledge the scriptures of the Old and New Testament to be given by divine inspiration and own and profess the Protestant religion." This was repeated in the constitution of 1786, but omitted in that of 1793.

Rhode Island, Connecticut, Virginia, and Georgia, had no religious test in their original state constitutions. The newer states, admitted after the formation of the government, naturally declare expressly in their constitutions against a religious test.

The latest deliverance on our subject was given at the Congress of Berlin in 1878, when the representatives of the powers of Europe made the civil and political emancipation of the Jews a condition of the recognition of the independence of Roumania. Sad to say, this condition has been violated by that government and the lot of the Jews in that land is very sad.

With this statement I close the necessarily brief review of the progress and attainment of Jewish emancipation under the ægis of the modern state. In lands such as Russia and Morocco, in which the principles of the modern state have found no foothold, neither the Jew nor Judaism have any recognized rights; the horrors of Russian and Moroccan inhumanity against the Jewish subjects are still too fresh and vivid in the minds of all to require more than a mere mention here.

For the modern state, then, founded upon the principles of the equal rights of all men, mankind's divisions into churches and religious parties have no existence. As for Judaism's attitude to the state, I have already outlined it, and need only point to the patriotic acts of Judaism's confessors in every land in time of war and in time of peace to show how fully and positively the Jews have proven, by actions that indeed speak louder than words, that they are Jews in religion alone, citizens of their fatherland wherever it may be in every thing else, that their faith has no interests that are at variance with the common weal, that they are not a class standing apart, but their hearts and hopes are bound up with every thing that conduces to civic advancement and their country's honor and political triumphs; that they recognize in all men brethren and pray for the speedy coming of the day when all the world over religious differences will have no weight in political councils; when Jew, Christian, Mohammedan, agnostic as such will not figure in the deliberations of civil bodies anywhere, but only as men. This is the political philosophy of the modern state; this is the teaching of Judaism; the two are in perfect accord.

JUDAISM A RELIGION AND NOT A RACE.

By RABBI A. MOSES, of Louisvlile, Ky.

THE ARYAN RACE — THE SEMITIC RACE — THE PURITY OF THE JEWISH RACE.

Some time ago an officer in the Austrian army called a Jewish physician "an impudent Semite." The latter retorted and called the officer "an arrogant Aryan." A bloody duel was the outcome of the altercation. The two men slashed one another to vindicate the honor of their respective race. If there be evil powers that hover between heaven and earth, watching the doings of mortals, and rejoicing in their follies and crimes, they must have taken a fiendish delight in the sight of Jew and Gentile driven by the figment of an Aryan and Semitic race to spill each other's blood. There was precious little Aryan blood in the race-proud warrior, and the doctor, though a Jew, was not much of a Semite. There is no Aryan race anywhere in existence. And the Jews can certainly not lay claim to being pure Semites. This honor, if honor it be, belongs exclusively to the Bedouins of Arabia. During the first third or half of this century the imagination of certain famous linguists gave birth to the myth of a great and homogeneous Aryan race, which, with the exception of the Basques in Spain, the Magyras in Hungary, the Turks and the Finns, comprised all the nations of Europe, the inhabitants of Northern India, of Persia and of Armenia. Because all those nations were found to speak kindred languages, the philologians, with pardonable but unscientific rashness, jumped to the conclusion that they were all of one blood, of one race, that their common ancestors must have one day lived somewhere in Asia as a united people, governed by the same laws and institutions and worshiping the same gods. On the basis of this fiction the scholars went on building up a spurious science of a common primitive Aryan culture, of Aryan religion and mythology, of law and government, of their racial characteristics, their emotional and intellectual traits. Imaginative writers, such as Max Mueller, drew charming pictures of the idyllic life which his reputed Aryan ancestors, the forefathers of the Hindoos, the Iranians, the Luthuanians, the Teutons and the Selavs once upon a time led in their central-

Asian home, dwelling together almost under the same roof. Ernest Renan, with his all-knowing retrospective imagination, did most to elaborate into a consistent system the luckless legend of an Aryan race, perennially opposed in its innermost nature, in its habits of thought and modes of feeling, in its conception of nature and life, to a fictitious Semitic race, embracing the ancient Babylonians and Assyrians, the Arameans or Syrians, the Hebrews, with their kindred the Ammonites, the Moabites and Edomites, the Phoenicians and Carthaginians, all the inhabitants of Arabia, and largely also the tribes of Ethiopia. He describes the Aryans as the most valiant, the noblest and lordliest of races, endowed by nature with a rich and creative imagination, an intellect vigorous, profound, metaphysical, rather inclined to mysticism, and possessing constructive political powers of the highest order. He but voices, though he exaggerates, the views of the other Aryomaniacs. He exalts above all others the stock, of which he believes all the European nations to be the living representatives, he glorifies it as earth's natural born aristocracy, and magnifies it as the imperial race of the world, destined to bear sway over all the children of men by the grace of its high and indestructible native qualities. How did Renan and the whole school, of which he was the most eloquent exponent, come to know with such wonderful exactness and fullness of detail all the emotional and artistic, all the mental, moral and religious characteristics of the hypothetical Aryan race? By a simple process of selection and combination which requires no large discourse looking before and after. He selected the finest qualities of the noblest Grecian tribes, as displayed in the season of their richest flowering and fruit-bearing, and spoke of them as inborn qualities of the whole Aryan race. He took the grandest and ripest achievements of the Hellenic genius in the fields of poetry, art and science, and deduced from them instinctive tendencies of the imaginary Aryan race. The rare capacity of the Roman people for military and political organization, slowly developed under favorable conditions during centuries of fierce contest and growing experience, the sturdiness, the unyielding tenacity, the undaunted courage, the iron will and domineering spirit of the Roman nation, were turned by a mere slight of hand into innate attributes of whole Aryan families. Whatsoever things good, whatsoever things true, whatsoever things beautiful and great, the Italians and the Spaniards, the Dutch, the English, the French, the Germans and the Americans have accomplished in course of many ages in war and peace, in art, poetry, philosophy, science and commerce, were by a delusive fancy traced back to hereditary racial powers peculiar to the fancied Aryan stock. The hymns

of the Rigveda, composed by successive generations of swarthy poets
on the banks of the Indus, are spoken of with comical enthusiasm as
the hymns of *our ancestors*, as the oldest poems of our race. The
pantheistic speculations of the Indian thinkers, and the refined mysticism of Persian Sufism are claimed no less than the ideal philosophy
of Plato, the monumental system of Aristotle, the epoch-making
meditations of Descartes and Kant's revolutionary Critique of Pure
Reason as emanations of the Aryan spirit.

All the greatest men of the Occidental world, all the kings of
poetry from Homer to Shakespeare and down to Goethe, the Indian
poet Kalidasa, Firdusi, the famous poet of the Persian epic, Shah
Nameh, the immortal master of art from Phidias to Canova, the most
renowned statesmen from Alexander and Cæsar to Charlemagne and
Napoleon, the most celebrated scientists from Archimedes to Newton
and Darwin, were compelled to yield their best parts in order to make
up the psychology of the Aryan race. A composite photograph was
taken of the supreme men of India and Persia, of Hellas and Italy, of
Spain and Portugal, of Holland and England, of Germany and
America, of the glorious men who within the space of nearly three
thousand years appeared at long intervals in the sky of humanity.
This composite photograph looking so ideal, so beautiful, was declared
to be the true likeness of the Aryan race. It was indeed ideal, but
absolutely unreal, the fanciful picture of a fancied race. This imaginary superior and aristocratic race, poetic, artistic, polytheistic, philosophical, imperial in virtue of incredible instincts, finds its natural
contrast and historical antagonist in another fictitious race, the so-called
Semites, whom the omniscient Renan, with his usual promptness and
recklessness of judgment, brands as an inferior race. The method by
which the most famous linguists, with the adventurous Renan for
their spokesman, managed to draw a pen-picture of the emotional, intellectual, moral, and religious nature of the Semitic race corresponds
to that adopted in delineating the character of the Aryan race, and
forms one of the most discreditable chapters in the annals of modern
scholarship. The monotheism of Israel, a belief in one only God, the
maker of heaven and earth, which was the result of at least a thousand
years of moral and religious development, was changed by Renan with
audacious self-assurance into a general characteristic, into a necessary
mental state of the whole race, into a religious sentiment peculiar to
all Semites past and present. In the opinion of Renan and his numerous followers, all the nations regarded as members of the Semitic race,
because they are known to have spoken or to speak the Semitic languages, have been and are monotheists by an invincible necessity of

their mental constitution. They can not help believing in one God only. Just as spiders weave their web, as bees gather honey by instinct, so were Semites compelled by the form of their mind to believe in and to worship only one divinity. The Semitic mind, he says, is too narrow, too unimaginative, to believe in more than one God, to conceive of more than one divine power ruling all the phenomena of nature. The expansive imagination and creative intelligence of the Aryan race could not rest content in so narrow a faith, so beggarly an idea of the supreme power. They peopled the universe with a host of self-conscious, self-determined divinities. Every natural phenomenon was personified, and represented as a divine individual. Even after the Aryans of Europe had been converted by persuasion or force to a Semitic religion, the indestructible tendencies of their polytheistic soul speedily turned the barren Semitic idea of an absolute divine unity into the richer and profounder idea of a divine trinity. The belief in only one God is good enough and natural enough for the inferior Semites. But as to the Aryans, heaven forbid that they should be satisfied with one only God ruling in the heavens above and on the earth beneath. However hard History tried, she could not change the immutable nature either of the Aryan or of the Semite. The two races are like opposite poles. Some sort of polytheism is in the blood, the feelings and intellect of the Aryan, while monotheism, uncompromising, fanatical, poor in ideal contents, is bound up with the very nature of the Semite. The chain of reasoning by which he and other Aryomaniacs arrived at this startling generalization is as plain as it is delusive, as simple as it is false. Israel glories in the fact that it has given the religion of monotheism to the world. But did not the people of Israel belong to the inferior Semitic race? How should the spirit of originality in this one particular field, in the province of religion, have departed from the great creative race, the standard-bearer of civilization and progress, the chosen Aryan race, and come to manifest itself in so signal a manner in the midst of the Semitic Hebrews? Does it not seem like a perversion of the laws of nature and history? Starting from such false premises, only one answer could be given by thinkers who believe in blood, instinct, race, inherited tendencies, as the cause of causes, as an all-sufficient explanation of all things animate, of all things human. The Semite Israelites were believers in one God only, because they were Semites. All Semites are born monotheists, just as it is the nature of sheep to grow wool and bleat. The syllogism is perfect. The Hebrews were Semites; hence all Semites were monotheists. You ask for proofs? Proofs shall be forthcoming. Are not the Semitic Arabs monotheists? Is not the Semitic East monotheistic? On the other hand, the whole Aryan Occident, all Europe, is Christian, trinitarian. Is this not convincing evidence? What if history protests against such an unwarranted assumption, and is indignant at such a willful perversion of her facts, at such reckless falsification of her records! What if every page of history bears witness to the fact that the so-called Semitic nations, the Babylonians, the Assyrians, the Syrians, the Phœnicians, and the rest of the Cananites and the Arabs down to Mohammed's time, were steeped in idolatry the most abominable, believed in innumerable gods, male and female, in gods of heaven and gods of earth, gods of the seas and of the rivers, in mountain gods and forest gods, divinities of the sun, divinities of the moon, divinities of the stars, divine rulers of life and death and the underworld? What if proofs irrefragable go to show that the Israelites themselves had for ages been rank polytheists, that there had been as many gods in Israel as there were cities in the land, that it required a thousand years of prophetic teaching—nay, that the nation as such had to be destroyed—before the leaven of heathenism was overcome, and a small remnant was thoroughly and permanently converted to the belief of one God. If the facts contradict, down with the facts! Let them perish, in order that the theory of Aryan superiority and Semitic inferiority may live and prosper.

The Semites are all born monotheists, instinctive worshipers of one God. This is the first, though far from praiseworthy characteristic of the race! The despots of Babylonia and Assyria are known to have been fierce and cruel conquerors. There are to be seen on the ancient monuments harrowing scenes representing acts of cruelty done by the ruthless victors upon the vanquished. King David treated the conquered inhabitants of Rabbath Ammon in a manner which, to our refined humanity, must appear exceedingly inhuman. What inference is drawn from these facts? Why, they were generalized into a race quality of the Semites, and renowned writers did not hesitate to teach, with an air of scientific infallibility, that savage cruelty toward vanquished foes was a distinguishing feature in the character of the Semite race. And what a glaring contrast such Semitic bloodthirstiness is made to form to the gentleness and sweet uses of humanity usually displayed by Aryans against their enemies! Several days after he had slain Patroclus in battle, Achilles, the hero of the Aryan Greeks, tied the corpse of his great foe to his chariot and dragged it, driving furiously, 'round and 'round the camp, in order to appease his wrathful and vengeful heart. Yet no one ever asserted that the savage action of the ideal Greek was characteristic of the whole Aryan race. Alexander the Great destroyed the glorious city of Corinth, one of the centers of Hellenic civilization, and sold all its inhabitants into slavery. Yet no writer ever held that in so doing Alexander simply acted in obedience to the ferocious instincts of the Aryan race. Great Cæsar one day ordered a whole German people, some sixty thousand persons, to be massacred in cold blood, sparing neither age nor sex. That fearful butchery is declared by historians to have been dictated by motives of far-seeing policy. But the Aryan race is not dragged in to stand god-father to it. Was it by virtue of his brutal Aryan nature that Titus caused over a hundred thousand Jewish warriors to fight with wild beasts in the arena? Hadrian hunting the conquered Jews of Cyprus and other lands like wild beasts, is not declared by historians to have acted out the inhuman disposition of his whole race. Historians have diverse kinds of judgment for what they regard as the Aryan and for what they designate as the Semitic race. Urged and favored by their geographical position, the ancient Phœnicians were enterprising and shrewd merchants. Ages of remorseless exclusion and restriction have compelled the Jews after their dispersion to eke out a livelihood by trade. What follows? Why, the Semites of all lands and all times are born traders and money-getters. The Babylonians and Canaanites are known to have been lascivious in their religious practices and sensual in their private conduct. Forthwith the conclusion was reached, that the whole Semitic race was and is exceedingly sensual by nature. The peculiar characteristics of the Bedouin tribes of Arabia have been worked as a rich mine of adjectives, to be applied indiscriminately to all the people speaking Semitic tongues. The Bedouin is avaricious and rapacious, both a miser and a spendthrift according to his varying moods. So are all the Semites. He is unscrupulous in his dealings, lacking in truthfulness, unreliable; faithful to his guests as long as they are in his tent, treacherous as soon as they have left it. In all these respects, the modern Bedouin is declared to be the typical Semite. The Bedouin is in his usual demeanor calm and dignified, but when aroused, he is capable of the wildest outbursts of uncontrollable passion. He is revengeful and cruel. Lo and behold, they cry, the true son of Shem. He dislikes physical labor, and wishes to earn his bread with as little muscular exertion as possible. He is of migratory habits. He is superstitious, fanatical; his religion is mainly one of fear. In all these points he is held up as the true representative of the Semitic race. In this curious way there has been formed a complete, but most incongruous, picture of the Semites. What a strange animal the hypothetical

18

Semite is made to be. What an incredible creature he is, made up of irreconcilable contradictions. He is moved by the invisible wires of instinct, to utter forth with a prophet's tongue the deepest truths regarding God and the moral dignity of man, such as the wisest of the wise among the Aryans did not dream of, and at the same time he adores vile and vicious gods, and pays homage to them in ways unmentionably abominable. He preaches the gospel of love and mercy, of universal brotherhood and broadest humanity in Jerusalem, and in Babylon and Tyre he is a blood-thirsty despot.

In a word, he is all things to all men and all times. Yet he does not act out his part in the free play of spontaneous development in harmony with his changing surroundings, but he is compelled to be what he is, and to do whatever he does by the fatality of his immutable racial nature! Through all times and all lands he forms by the indestructible laws of his being an enduring contrast to the Aryan. They have met in thousands of places and times. They have exchanged innumerable services, they have adopted from one another the arts of civilization and learned one another's wisdom of life. But they have never blended. There is a natural gulf of separation between them. There is a deep-seated mutual sympathy between the Aryan and the Semitic race! Many scholars have sinned against the holy spirit of history and humanity by giving expressions to such perverted and mischievous views. But it was chiefly the witchcraft of Renan's marvelous powers as a writer that gave currency to those pernicious theories of race, and made them popular throughout Europe and America with the educated and half-educated, from whom they gradually percolated down to the masses. Without knowing it, without willing it, Renan was in a sense the intellectual father of modern anti-Semitism. He with others sowed the poisonous seed of the baleful theory regarding the Semitic race and its eternal antagonism to the Aryan race, from which in course of a few decades the upas tree of anti-Semitism has grown, to their own dismay and disgust. The very term anti-Semitism bears the birthmark of its origin in the lucubrations of philosophers. Linguists and historians gave birth to the idea of Semitism; knavish or insane agitators tacked on to it their malignant "anti." Strange fate and nemesis that Renan, the gentlest and sweetest tempered of men, as true a lover of his kind as ever lived, should have fathered a theory, the practical consequences of which became the shame and curse of our century. Like many wise men before him, he did not give heed to his words, and did not calculate the effect which his theory might have on natures in which the instinct and ideas of the savage lay dormant, and which only required

the right word to be awakened to full life. With savages blood
kinship is every thing. Right and wrong, love and hate are derived
exclusively from the bonds of race. For thousands of years the
prophets of Israel and their disciples tried to substitute the moral
dignity of man and the brotherhood of all men for the brutal conception of descent and race. Barely had these supreme ideas of humanity begun to make a deeper impression and to translate themselves
into a humanizing practice, when leading scholars came up with their
theories of an Aryan race, and a Semitic race, drawing hard and fast
lines of separation between these two races, and tracing all the grandest achievements of the human mind back to racial qualities, to
hereditary instincts and tendencies. The fanaticism of nationalism in
our days and the still fiercer fanaticism of race is largely due to the
influence of such teachings. Since the Jews are Semites and we are
Aryans, the anti-Semites say, and since Semites and Aryans are forever separated from one another by their physical and also by their
moral and emotional constitution, the Jews are and forever will remain
strangers in our midst, aliens that can not be assimilated with us.
And since the Semites are an inferior race, their presence in our midst
is a perpetual danger to our higher Aryan life and character.

Fortunately, a deeper and more conscientious research, a science
based on fact and not on fancies, has during the last ten or fifteen
years begun to deal staggering blows to the ill-starred fiction of an
Aryan and a Semitic race, and bids fair to soon drive it entirely from
the temple of knowledge and rob it of all power to affect the view of
men for evil. Certain eminent scholars, foremost among them the
distinguished French anthropologist Broca, were not dazzled by the
splendor of the Aryan theory, and asked themselves in sober earnestness, what evidence there was for assuming that nearly all the nations
of Europe and many people of Asia form one vast homogeneous race.
True, the nations in question do speak languages which are closely related to one another, and may in a sense be regarded as but widely
divergent dialects of one common speech. But does community of
language prove community of race?

There are eight million negroes in the United States and several
more millions in the West Indies who speak English, the language of
the New Englanders, the language of Gladstone and Tennyson. Will
any one contend that the blood of Washington and Cromwell rolls in
the veins of the South Carolina blacks? The Spaniards, the Portuguese and the French speak Latin tongues, yet there is scarcely a
trace of Roman blood in these nations. The Mexicans speak Spanish,
a Latin dialect. Still, of pure Spaniards there is but a dwindling

number in Mexico. The overwhelming mass of the natives are of Aztec blood. The present inhabitants of Greece are largely a Slavonic race, which in the eighth century occupied the lands and learned the speech of the Greeks. The Bulgarians speak a Slavonic language, but they belong to the Turkish race. The Arabic language is spoken to-day by all the Egyptians, the lineal descendants of the Hamitic pyramid builders, by the Berbers and Kabyls of Algiers, Tunis, Tripoli and Morocco, the descendants of the ancient Lybians and Mauritanians. By adopting the speech of the Bedouins they did not exchange their blood for that of the Arabs. The Arabic has killed off all the native languages of Asia Minor, of Mesopotamia, Syria and Palestine. But in their racial features the populations of those countries have continued substantially what they were before the Arab conqueror had set foot there. The speech of Tunis has been in turn Numidian, Phoenician, Latin, Vandal and Arabic. The inhabitants of Southern Germany speak German; but, taken as a whole, they belong to the Celtic stock. They exchanged their Celtic speech for German within historic times.

Instances too numerous to mention could be adduced from every part of the inhabited earth to prove that, under certain conditions, there is a tendency in language to spread from people to people. Spanish, Portuguese, French, German, Arabic, and above all, English, are steadily invading new territories, occupied by races physically and mentally the most varied. Such causes as conquest, slavery, the necessities of commercial intercourse and religious propaganda co-operate to give to certain languages dominion over vast areas and over multitudinous tribes of men wholly unrelated to the people whose speech they have come to adopt. What has taken place within historical times, what is happening before our very eyes, has, under the operation of the same causes, doubtless been going on in pre-historic ages. One such universal language, split up into numerous branches, is the Aryan speech, which is spoken by about six hundred millions of human beings through the length and breadth of Europe, in northern India and all Persian lands, in the south of Africa, and in the two Americas and Australia. Many, many thousand years ago, in the dim past of mankind, it originated somewhere in Europe, but not in Asia, in the midst of a people which scholars are agreed to call the Aryans. It must have been a masterful people, since, like the English, the Spaniards and Arabs of these latter centuries, they imparted their own speech, be it by conquest or by the powers and arts of a higher civilization, to the various distinct races which inhabited and still inhabit Europe.

Which of the modern European nations may be regarded as the

descendant of the original and true Aryans? Most probably none. The original Aryans very likely mingled and blended with the conquered alien stocks, and disappearing as a distinct race, left only their language behind them as the record of their power and far-reaching influence. There exists an Aryan language, but no Aryan race in Europe. The population of that continent and of other continents settled by European colonists, consists of four distinct and easily recognizable races. Any man with an observant eye can, in a large assemblage of Europeans or Americans, readily enough distinguish extremely divergent types, being the living representations of the several races which have occupied Europe from time immemorial. Here you see a man small in stature, of slender build, swarthy of complexion, with black eyes and black hair. His head is long, his forehead narrow and nearly perpendicular. He is either a Welshman from Dembigshire or an Irishman from Kerry, Donegal or Galway. Or you may discover that he or his ancestors came from the Basque provinces of Spain. But it is just as probable that he hails from the island of Corsica. He belongs to the Iberian race. The Berbers, of northern Africa, and the Guanches, of Teneriffe and the Canary Islands, are his close racial kinsmen. The bones of his remote ancestors are found in sepulchral caves in England, France, Corsica and other parts of Europe. Next to your Iberian you may see another small, dark-complexioned man with black hair and black eyes. He too has a straight forehead. And yet he belongs to quite a different race. His head is extremely short. If you inquire you are sure to learn that he or his forefathers came from central France, and more specifically where the Auvergnats dwell. Or he will tell you that he is a Savoyard or a Swiss. The skeletons of his savage ancestors are found in Belgian caves and in the round barrows of central France. Though they speak French or German, they are as to their race the brothers of the Laplanders. They and the Lapps have, of all existing races, the shortest heads. They resemble one another in their swarthy complexion, their black hair and eyes. The head of the Auvergnats and Lapps is alike abnormally narrow across the cheek bones and wide at the temples. They belong to the Ligurian race, which once inhabited large parts of Italy.

Besides those representatives of these Iberian and Ligurian races, you may notice, in any large gathering in American cities, a number of tall men with blue eyes and blonde hair and a white skin and somewhat projecting jaws. They have very long heads. You will, at a glance, recognize them as Swedes or Frisians or North Germans of the fair type. They belong to the Scandinavian race. The bones of their ancestors are found in numerous graves in the south-west of Germany, in Holland and Sweden, in Burgundy and many other parts of Europe. These primitive Teutons were the oldest inhabitants of Europe. They were muscular, athletic and of great stature. They were nomad hunters, who sheltered themselves in caves, but were without fixed abodes or even any sepulchers. These savages were the direct forefathers of the Germans and Englishmen who represent the pure Scandinavian type.

Besides those three races, the Iberian, the Ligurian, and the Scandinavian, there lives in Europe and in many other parts of the world a numerous race, the Celtic. The living representatives of this race are like their pre-historic forefathers, men of tall stature, with light eyes and yellowish red or brownish red hair. They have long and prominent jaws and florid faces. They are marked off from the Scandinavian race mainly by the fact that they are brachycephalic or short-headed. The great mass of the English, Scotch, and Irish are the descendants of the ancient Celtic Britons. The other element which has entered into the composition of the British people, are the dark-skinned Iberians and, to a certain extent also, the Teutonic Anglo-Saxons. The fiction of an Anglo-Saxon race is one of those delusions which the pride of the English and the American hugs to its heart. They speak with unbearable vanity of the noble, glorious, invincible, creative, liberty-loving Anglo-Saxon race on both sides of the Atlantic. In listening to the Fourth-of-July spread-eagle eloquence on the Anglo-Saxon race, one would imagine that every American and every Englishman had nothing but the purest blood of the purest-blooded Anglo-Saxon invaders in his veins. But in reality the present Americans are a mixture of all the European races. And even the English and their purest descendants in America have at best but a streak of Anglo-Saxon blood to boast of. Only a number of noble families in England may lay claim to being largely the offspring of the invading Anglo-Saxons. But the English as a mass are Celts and Iberians. For even the Danes, who settled in certain parts of England, are like the Danes of Denmark itself, no Teutons, no genuine Scandinavians, but teutonized Celts, as is evidenced by their racial characteristics, chiefest among which is their being short-headed, instead of long-headed, like the true Scandinavians. The same short-headed Celtic race inhabited as Gauls and Celts large provinces of France. The French people thus consist of a mixture of Iberians, Ligurians, and Celts, with a sprinkling of Teutons. The present Spanish people is composed of Iberians and Celts, and in a measure, also, of Phoenicians and Jews. The south of Germany as far north as the Teutoburger Wald, the Thuringen Wald, and the Riesengebirge is in the main Celtic in race, though German in speech. The Swiss people, whose ancestors erected pile dwellings around the Swiss lakes, belong, together with the people of Northern Italy, to the same Celtic race, with a large mixture of Etruscan and other blood. The southern Italians are of quite a different race. All the nations of Slavic speech, except the great Russians or the Russians proper, are members of the same far-spreading race. They have short heads, light hair, and light eyes. Yet let not the Celts of France and England believe and boast that they represent the genuine high-born Aryan race. For the despised tribes of Siberia, the barbarous Finno-Tartaric tribes, that speak Turkic languages, belong to the same aristocratic race. All of them are short-headed. Most of them have blue eyes and flaxen or red hair. The Turcomans are usually blonde. The heads of the Mongols are precisely like those of the ancestors of the short-headed English.

All of the foregoing details will suffice to convince the most skeptical mind that the belief in a close racial kinship between all the Aryan-speaking nations is a mere fiction refuted by incontrovertible facts. There exists an Aryan language, but no Aryan race. And as the fiction of an Aryan race has in the light of careful inquiry vanished like a mist, so has the myth of a Semitic race recently been condemned by the spirit of true knowledge and made to pass into the limbo of exploded delusions. Eight nations, the Babylonians, the Assyrians, the Hebrews, the southern Arabs or Sabaeans, the Phoenicians, the Armenians, the Abyssinians, and the Arabs proper, are known to have spoken or still to speak languages so closely related that they may be regarded as merely dialects of one language. In their vocabulary, in their grammatical structure, and above all in the law that every root must consist of three consonants, they form among themselves the most intimate unity and stand in striking contrast to all other languages. From this community of speech, the deduction has been made that all the above-mentioned nations belonged to the same race, the Semitic race. But the facts brought out by the most searching investigations of the foremost anthropologists of our time flatly contradict this assumption. Sixty thousand heads or skulls belonging to those various nations have been examined with circle and tape-measure, and the result has been "not unity of race, but a bewildering variety of racial characteristics." Only the Bedouins of Arabia form a surprising exception. They alone can be regarded as a physically homogeneous race, among whom the variations are reduced almost to a minimum. Just as their speech, though in a literary sense two thou-

sand years younger than Babylonia, has, with wonderful tenacity, preserved the oldest and fullest forms of the original Semitic languages,
so do they in their physical qualities represent the genuine Semitic race
in almost absolute purity. They have invariably long and narrow
heads. As such, as a people with long and narrowed heads, they appear depicted on numerous ancient monuments of Egypt. This goes
to prove that the Bedouins of to-day are the lineal and unmodified descendants of the primitive inhabitants of Arabia. These Arabs are
without exception of a dark complexion with black eyes and black
hair. But, what is most to be noted is the fact that the Arabs have
short and small noses which are hardly curved at all. They form in
every respect a striking contrast to what the vulgar regard as the
typical curved Jewish nose. The physical traits of these genuine and
unmixed Semites seem to connect them in some as yet unaccountable
way, with the long-headed and dark-skinned Iberian race, which, in
prehistoric-times, occupied England and many other parts of Europe.

Which of the so-called Semitic nations, living or departed, does
or did, in their racial characteristics, most closely resemble these pure
Arabs? Only the ancient Phoenicians can be looked upon as true
Semites, as the full brothers of the Arabs. Many Phoenician skulls
have been most carefully examined by eminent anthropologists, and
bear out the testimony of the Egyptian pyramids, on which Phoenicians are represented as pronounced long-heads, and otherwise showing
the distinguishing marks of the pure Semitic or unmixed Arabic
stock. Now, what has anthropology, after years of most conscientious
searching, after collating and comparing many thousands of facts, ascertained regarding the Hebrews and Syrians, both of ancient times
and of the present day? Are the Syrians, are the Jews pure Semites,
or even largely Semitic? There are numerous and life-like representations of Hebrews and Syrians on the monuments of ancient Egypt.
Those carefully-drawn pictures of the Egyptian artists of Hebrews
and Syrians tally to perfection with the observations made by modern
investigators on Syrians and Jews. And what do we learn from both
these reliable sources of information? Only five per cent of the Syrians and the Jews are found to be true long-heads, and to bear the
other distinctive features of the genuine Semites. Stranger still, fully
eleven per cent of the Jews and Syrians have blue eyes and blonde
hair, and display the other characteristics of the Scandinavian and the
fair North Germans. No less than fifty per cent are veritable short-
heads, and consequently do not belong to the Semitic race. Of these
a good many are the happy possessors of so-called typical Jewish
noses. How come there to be eleven per cent blue-eyed and blonde-

haired genuine Aryans among the Jews and the Syrians? Fortunately the ancient Egyptians have preserved for us on their imperishable monuments a clear and decisive answer to this important query. The Amorites, one of the seven nations that inhabited Palestine before and after the invasion of the Israelites, are depicted on those monuments as tall, white-skinned, blue-eyed and blonde-haired men. These Amorites are called in Egyptian Tamehu, the people of the North land. These Tamehu or Northmen are described by the Egyptian writers as white savages, who were dressed in skins and, in Indian fashion, adorned their heads with feathers. It is certainly no disgrace to the blue-eyed and blonde-haired among the English, the Americans and Germans, that their ancestors were living in Europe, in North Africa and Palestine, as savages long after the Babylonians and Egyptians had reared the grand edifice of their civilization, that their fore-fathers were dressed in skins and dwelt in caves at the time Moses had laid the foundation of the kingdom of righteousness and humanity. Nor are we Jews specially proud of the fact that a good deal of the blue blood of the blue-eyed Aryans is rolling in our veins, almost as much of it as is to be found in Southern Germany, in many parts of England and in most parts of America. We only wish to call attention to the fact that they who pride themselves on being Aryans did not receive a charter from nature, to be exclusive standard-bearers of civilization and the privileged creators of the arts and the wisdom of a higher life. At the same time we desire to point to the fact that we Jews are after all, by the ties of blood, second or third cousins to the very people who, as Aryans, regard us as Semitic aliens.

But whence do the fifty per cent short-heads among the Jews and Syrians come, who are evidently no Semites? Prof. Felix von Luschan, whose data I am freely using and whose lines of reasoning I am closely following in this lecture, has, in a paper recently read before the German Anthropological Society, given a satisfactory solution to this great problem. The fifty per cent of the Syrians and Jews that have short heads, dark eyes, and dark hair are the descendants of the once great, very numerous, and powerful Hittites, one of the seven nations found by the Semitic Israelites when they conquered Canaan. The Hittites belonged to the wide-spread race called by Luschan the Armenoid, by Hommel the Alarodian stock. The modern Armenians are the purest representatives of that race. The Armenians have short heads, dark eyes, dark hair, and the most pronounced typical Jewish noses. They resemble in every respect the ancient Hittites, as represented on numerous Hittite monuments. The same race forms the main stock of the population of Asia Minor. Most of the Greeks and Turks bear

the features of that race. The ancient Pelasgians, the aboriginal inhabitants of Greece, were a branch of the same race. The latter,
again, are very probably identical with the Ligurians, whose descendants form the bulk of the population of Southern Italy, and make up
a very large part of the French and Swiss.

The result of the foregoing discussion is: The so-called Aryans
consist of four distinct races, the Semites do by no means form a racial
unit, and lastly, we Jews are far from being a pure race. On the contrary, we are a very mixed race. Three elements have entered into
the composition of the Jewish people: The true Semitic race, the
blue-eyed, or, if you choose, the Aryan Ammorites, and the Hittites,
have mixed their blood to produce the Jewish or Israelitish people.
The Aryan Amorites and the Armenian Hittites were turned into Israelites, into worshipers of Yahve and followers of Moses, by a small
but masterful Semitic tribe, the Bene Israel. Many a Jew will
doubtless groan in spirit or be filled with indignation on being told
that he shall no longer vaingloriously boast of being a member of the
purest race on earth! "What are we then," many of these race-Jews
will cry, "if we are not unmixed and lineal descendants of one of the
tribes of Israel? Alack the day! We are told by a teacher of the
religion of Israel that we are not pure Israelites. All our glory will
depart from us, and the faith of the prophets will lose its hold on
the Jews, if they should come to think that we are after all a very
mixed race, if we can not all lay claim to being lineal descendants of
those that went forth from Egypt." To this lament of race-Jews, I
reply: Let the voice of your ignorance and irreligion be hushed.
There has never been a great people on earth that was of an unmixed
race. Only among savages do you find pure races. The English,
French, and German nations, on whose shoulders rests the civilization of Europe, have been composed out of four distinct races at
least. The valiant, free, rich, and progressive American people is the
most mixed of all peoples. There is hardly a race on earth that has
not contributed some of its blood toward the making of this youngest
nation. All the greatest nations known to history; the civilizers of
the world, the Hellenes; the conquerors of the world, the Romans;
the Egyptians, before whose stupendous works we stand in speechless
wonder; the Babylonians and the Assyrians, who gave to the world
the art of writing, of architecture and sculpture, the science of astronomy, and the elements of mathematics; all grew out of an amalgama-
tion of various races. And should the people of Israel, that has given
to the world something more precious than all the gifts bestowed by
all other nations, namely, the belief in the one only God, the Maker

of heaven and earth, and the Father of all men, the belief in Yahve, the righteous and merciful, that has given birth to the Bible, and enriched the families of the earth with the highest spiritual treasures, should that people alone have formed an exception to the universal rule and done its life-work as a pure race? Savages exist as a race just as animals form distinct species. All the civilized nations of the earth were welded together into a living unity by spiritual forces.

The Israelites were closely considered no people in the narrow and accepted sense. They were from the very beginning a religious community. It was the supreme genius of one man, of Moses, that delivered a few small Semitic tribes and a multitude of non-Semitic people from the bondage of Egypt. It was through him that the infinite mystery of all manifested itself for the first time as Yahve, the just God, who loves the stranger, pities the oppressed, and wreaks vengeance on the cruel oppressor. For the first time in history oppression exercised in the name of race and nationality, was resisted and overcome in the name of human rights, defended by a God that loves right and hates wrong. It was on Mount Sinai that the hero of justice promulgated the leading principles of social and individual morality as a revelation of the Deity. It was there that he made a covenant between Yahve and the freedmen, not as between a tribe and its divinity, but as between the redeemed ones and their Redeemer, between a God of righteousness and the people that was to walk in the ways of justice. With this step taken by Moses, the spirit of mankind broke through the bounds of race and made the attempt to establish a commonwealth on the foundations of human rights as laid down and made sacred and inviolable by the will of Yahve. The people of Israel, as fashioned and inspired by Moses, had in itself a spiritual power of attraction and assimilation. No race and no class could be excluded from a community which had for its animating and unifying principle the belief in Yahve, the protector of the weak and oppressed and the lover of right.

As the Israelites marched through the wilderness they attached to themselves a number of Midiantish tribes. Though by no means a numerous people, they conquered Canaan and made it the land of Israel and of Yahve, not so much by the prowess of their arms, but by the spiritual power inherent in their religion. The seven nations were not annihilated, as a late legend would make us believe, but were assimilated by the Israelitish spirit and incorporated into the people of Yahve. Translated to Babylonia, the Jews converted the population of whole provinces to Yahvism and incorporated them into the body of the Jewish people. Only about 50,000 Jews returned from the Babylonian captivity. But in spite of the vehement protests of the puritan nationalists against intermarriage nearly all the Pagan inhabitants of Palestine were transformed into Yahve-worshiping Israelites. In every province and city of the Roman empire numerous Gentiles embraced the faith of Israel and formed flourishing congregations. And the blood of these Gentiles still rolls in our veins. In a modified form as trinitarian Christianity, the religious spirit of Israel has conquered and assimilated the best part of mankind and made it Israelitish. But Yahvism, pure and simple, did not cease to gain accessions. The blood of the converted Turanian Chazars has mixed with the blood of the Russian Jews. Teutonic, Celtic, Slavic, and Latin were elements that have entered into our composition. The very vigor and vitality, physical and mental, of the Jews, is next to the perenially active influences of their moralizing religion, due to the fact that they are an extremely mixed race.

Some of those who hear and many more who will read this lecture will exclaim : " If we are not Jews by race, if we are not Jews by the sacred and indissoluble ties of blood, why should we continue to be Jews, why should we hold to Judaism ?" To such we answer : " If you are not Jews by faith, but by race, the sooner you will depart from us, the better it will be for you, the better it will be for the mission of Yahve, for the religion of Moses and the prophets, the religion of the psalmists and sages who worked and prayed, who lived and died not to glorify a race but to glorify the God of humanity. If I knew that there is not a drop of Semitic, not a drop of Jewish blood in my veins, I would yet cling with every fiber of my being, as long as there was breath in me, to the religious community of Israel, to the Church of Yahvism, to the monotheistic faith of pure humanity. Abraham is not our father, Isaac did not beget us, Jacob we know not, but Yahve, the Maker of heaven and earth, the Father of all men, the Father of justice and mercy. He is our Father and our God, He is the Redeemer and Guide of spiritual and universal Israel from generation to generation.

POPULAR ERRORS ABOUT THE JEWS.

By RABBI JOSEPH SILVERMAN, D. D., NEW YORK.

Human life has often seemed to be a "comedy of errors." Each generation is busy correcting the mistakes of the previous one, and, at the same time, making others for the next generation to correct. History is only, as it were, a record of the world's mistakes.

There would be no science if God had revealed the whole truth to mankind. We are constantly groping in the dark. Every doctrine which to-day was a fact, becomes merely a theory to-morrow; the next day a myth. All is mystery. There is scarcely any truth save the false, any right save the wrong. Knowledge is only opinion about facts, and most opinions are errors, or will be to-morrow.

One of the keenest and most injurious evils that can befall a man or a people is to be misunderstood; perhaps worse is to be misrepresented. The individual who has experienced both knows the vital sufferings that were his. To worship truth and be accused of falsehood; to be religiously virtuous and be charged with vice; to aspire to heaven and, by the world, be consigned to purgatory; to be robbed of one's identity and be clad in the garb of another, of an inferior being; to see one's principles distorted, every motive questioned, one's words misquoted, every act misunderstood, one's whole life misrepresented, and made a caricature in the eyes of all men, without the power of redress, is to suffer all the unmitigated pangs of inner mortification. You breathe the air, you see the world, you live; but the air is poison, the world a snare, and life a delusion. Those are not the greatest martyrs who died for any cause; but those who have lived and struggled in a world which not only did not believe or trust them, but filched from them every blessed endowment and acquired virtue.

If any one were to attempt to analyze the character of the Jew on the basis of what has been said about him in history (so called), in fiction, or other forms of literature, both prose and poetry, he would find himself confused and baffled, and would be compelled to give up his task in despair. The greatest paradoxes have been expressed about the Jew. The vilest of vices and crimes, as well as the greatest of virtues, have been attributed to him. Pictures of him have been

painted as dark as Barabbas and as light as Mordecai, while between
the two may be found lines of every shade of wickedness and goodness.

There can be no doubt but that many errors and misconceptions
about the Jew can be traced to this source. The opinions of the world
are, to a great extent, formed by what men read in history or fiction,
in any form of prose or poetry. In this way so great an injustice has
been done to the Jew that it will be impossible for mankind ever to
rectify it or atone therefor. To cite but one example out of an infinite number, I refer to Shakespeare's portrayal of the Jew in his character of Shylock. This picture is untrue in every heinous detail.
The Jew is not revengeful as Shylock. Our very religion is opposed
to the practice of revenge, the *"lex talionis"* having never been taken
literally, but interpreted to mean full compensation for injuries. The
Jew, in all history, is never known to have exacted a pound of human
flesh cut from the living body as forfeit for a bond. Such was an
ancient Roman practice. Shylock can be nothing more than a caricature of the Jew, and yet the world has applauded this abortion of
literature, this contortion of the truth, more than the ideal portrait
which Lessing drew of Israel in his "Nathan, the Wise."

If any one coming from another world were to inquire of the inhabitants of this world regarding the character of the Jew, their beliefs
and practices, he would obtain the most incongruous mixture of opinions. A dense ignorance exists about the Jews regarding their social
and domestic life, their history and literature, their achievements and
disappointments, their religion, ideals and hopes. And this ignorance
is not confined merely to ordinary men, but prevails also amongst
scholars. Ovid, Tacitus, Shakespeare, Voltaire, and Renan, most
heathen and Christian writers, have been guilty of entertaining and,
what is more culpable, of disseminating erroneous ideas about the descendants of ancient Israel.

"In regard to the Jews," said George Eliot, "it would be difficult to find a form of bad reasoning about them which had not been
heard in conversation or been admitted to the dignity of print, but the
neglect of resemblances is a common property of dullness which invites all the various points of view, the prejudiced, the puerile, the
spiteful, and the abysmally ignorant. Our critics have always overlooked our resemblances to them (the Jews) in virtue; have, in fact,
denounced in Jews the same practices which they admired in themselves."

There is no doubt but that prejudice against the Jews is as much
a cause of ignorance and false reasoning as a result therefrom.

When I sometimes hear or read a certain class of opinions concerning the Jews. I am reminded of an anecdote about Bishop Brooks. He attended a meeting in England, at which an Englishman declared, "All Americans are narrow-minded and illiberal. They are in spirit, just as in body, small, dwarfed and pigmy." The late Bishop Brooks then arose in all the majesty of his colossal stature, and called out in his stentorian voice, "And here is one of those American dwarfs."

For the sake of completeness I will speak of the error ordinarily committed, of referring to the Jew as a particular race. Hebrew is the name of an ancient race from which the Jew is descended, but there have been so many admixtures to the original race that scarcely a trace of it exists in the modern Jews. Intermarriage with Egyptians, the various Canaanitish nations, the Midianites, Syrians, etc., are frequently mentioned in the Bible. There have also been additions to the Jews by voluntary conversions, such as that in the eighth century, of Bulan, Prince of the Chasars, and his entire people. We can, therefore, not be said to be a distinct race to-day.

We form no separate nation and no faction of any nation. Nor is there any general desire to return to Palestine and resurrect the ancient nationality. We can only look with misgiving, rather with indifference, upon an organized effort undertaken by fanatic believers who are deeply concerned in the fulfillment of certain Biblical prophesies. They overlook the fact that those prophesies have either already been or need never be fulfilled.

We form merely an independent religious community and feel keenly the injustice that is done us when the religion of the Jew is singled out for aspersion, whenever such a citizen is guilty of a misdemeanor. Jew is not to be used parallel with German, Englishman, American, but with Christian, Catholic, Protestant, Buddhist, Mohammedan or Atheist.

Over fifty years ago the late Isaac D'Israeli wrote that "the Jewish people are not a nation, for they consist of many nations. They are Russian, English, French, or Italian, and, like the chameleon, reflect the color of the spot they rest on. They are like the waters running through the countries, tinged in their course with all the varieties of the soil where they deposit themselves."

An eminent Jewish divine, in a spirit of indignation at some harsh criticism cast upon the Hebrew nation, so-called, asked: "If we are a separate nation, where is our country; where our laws; where our armies; where our courts of justice; where our flag?" To this question the critic made no reply. But we, here in congress assembled, can unitedly answer: "The land of our nativity or of our adoption is our country, its laws we obey, in its armies we find our comrades, by the decision of its courts we abide, under its flag we seek protection, and for it we are ready to sacrifice our substance and our lives and to pledge our sacred honor.

We are furthermore often charged with exclusiveness and clannishness, with having only narrow, tribal aspirations, and with being averse to breaking down social barriers. Few outside of that inner close circle that is to be met in the Jewish home or social group know aught of the Jew's domestic happiness and social virtues. If there is any clannishness in the Jew, it is due not to any contempt for the outside world, but to an utter abandon to the charm of home and the fascination of confreres in thought and sentiment.

However, if there is a remnant of exclusiveness in the Jew of to-day, is he to blame for it? Did he create the social barrier? We must agree with Mr. Zangwill when he says: " People who have been living in a Ghetto for a couple of centuries are not able to step outside merely because the gates are thrown down, or to efface the brands on their souls by putting off the yellow badges. The isolation from without will have come to seem the law of their being." (Children of the Ghetto, 1. 6.)

None is more desirous of fraternity than the Jew, but he will not gain it at the loss of his manhood. He will not accept fraternity as a patronage, but would rather claim it as a simple matter of equality. That is a point which our critics and detractors do not understand. Again, if the Jew is exclusive, it is due to the fact that while he is willing to come to any truce for brotherhood, he declines to do so and be regarded as legitimate prey for religious conquest. And that is a point which the missionaries can not understand.

The fact that Jews are, as a rule, averse to intermarriage with non-Jews, has been quoted in evidence of Jewish exclusiveness. Two errors seem to underlie this false reasoning : The one, that Judaism directly interdicts intermarriage with Christians, and the other that the Jewish Church disciplines those who are guilty of such an act. The Mosaic law, at best, only forbade intermarriage with the seven Canaanitish nations and, though the only justifiable inference would be that this interdiction applies also to heathens, still, by rabbinical forms of interpretation it has been made to apply also to Christians. The historical fact is that the Roman Catholic Council held at Orleans, in 538 A. C. E., first prohibited Christians to intermarry with Jews. This decree was later enforced by meting out the penalty of death to both parties to such a union. Jewish Rabbis, then, as a matter of self-protection, interdicted the practice of intermarriage. And though to-day, men are free to act according to their tastes, there exists on the part of the Jew as much repugnance to intermarriage as on the part of the Christian. Such ties are, as a rule, not encouraged by the families of either side, and for very good cause. And even if there exists, on the part of the Jew, a greater aversion to intermarriage, this can not and should not be charged to a desire for clannishness or exclusiveness, but rather to those natural barriers that separate Jewish from Christian society.

It is not my purpose, at present, to lay the blame for the creation or continuance of such barriers, but only to submit that social ostracism, as that term is understood to-day, has never in any form been undertaken by Jews. A sense of just pride even constrains me from strongly protesting against the social ostracism that, at times, manifests itself against the Jew. I desire here merely to point out the error that seems to inspire it, namely, the grievous error that ostracism is supposed to purify the one side of all objectionable characters, and to stamp all ostracized as the outcast of the earth. We are familiar with that false logic that infers a broad generality from a few isolated particulars, which imputes the sins of an individual to the class of which he may be a member, which charges the misdemeanor of one upon a whole people, which condemns a religion because of the wickedness of a few hypocrites, which punishes the guilty with the innocent. And it is such fallacious reasoning that is time and again applied to Jews, with this exception, that the virtues of a Montefiore or a Baron de Hirsch are not generalized in the same manner. We are convinced that Jews who have outlived the terrors of the Inquisition will be able to live down all abuse, all false reasoning, and maintain the majesty of their manhood even outside the charming circle of self-appointed censors of social life. But we must protest against the error which mistakes ostracism for exclusiveness. In this case the latter is a virtue, the former a vice—a crime. Let the verdict of history say, who is guilty?

We have even been charged with exclusiveness in our religion— so little is our practice known. I have myself been lately asked by a lady who makes some pretense to education, whether she should not go to the synagogue in order to see the offering of animal sacrifices and the burning of incense. She had supposed that the Jewish religion was a secret, mysterious rite, to witness which was only the privilege of the initiated. Frequently we are asked whether non-Jews are permitted to enter a Jewish house of worship. Error and misrepresentation about Judaism are common. A Christian divine once remarked that the offering of the Paschal lamb in the Synagogue, at this very

19

day, contains a sublime picture of the transfiguration of Christ. And recently in New York (and perhaps in other cities also), a missionary was giving performances in Christian churches, showing how the Jews still offer the Paschal lamb. If such gross errors and misrepresentations are current and are taught in this country with the connivance of men who know better, it is not difficult to understand how benighted peasants in Europe can be made to believe that Jews use the blood of Christian children at the Passover services, and how such monstrous calumnies could rouse the prejudice and vengeance of the ignorant masses.

So little is Judaism understood by even educated men outside of our ranks, that it is commonly believed that all Jews hold the same form of faith and practice. Here the same error of reasoning is used to which reference has already been made, in speaking of the character of the Jew as an individual and as a class. Because some Jews still believe in the coming of a Personal Messiah, or in bodily resurrection or in the establishment of the Palestinian kingdom, the inference is at once drawn by many, that all Jews hold the same belief. Very little is known by the populace of the several schisms in modern Judaism denominated as Orthodox, Conservative, Reform, and Radical. It is not my province to speak exhaustively of these sects, and it must suffice to merely remark here that Orthodox Judaism believes in carrying out the letter of the ancient Mosaic code as expounded by the Talmudic Rabbis; that Reform Judaism seeks to retain the spirit only of the ancient law, discarding the absolute authority of both Bible and Talmud, making reason and modern demands paramount; that Conservatism is merely a moderate Reform, while Radicalism declares itself independent of established forms, clinging mainly to the ethical basis of Judaism.

Reform Judaism has been the specially favored subject of misunderstanding, of ignorance. Recently an eminent Christian divine of St. Louis objected to extending an invitation to a Reform Rabbi to lecture before the Minister's Association, on the plea that "all Reform Jews are Infidels." A still grosser piece of ignorance is the identification of Reform Judaism with Unitarianism. As scholarly and finished a writer as Frances Power Cobb, in a recent article on "Progressive Judaism," made bold to show her extreme interest in this Reform movement, believing it to evidence a breaking up of Judaism altogether and a turning toward Christianity. Far from breaking up Judaism, Reform has strengthened it in many ways and retained in the fold those who would have gone over, not to Christianity, but to Atheism. Judaism can never tend toward Christianity,

in any sense, notably to Unitarianism; the latter rather is gradually
breaking away from Christianity and tending toward Jewish belief.
For the present, however, Reform Judaism still stands opposed to even
the most liberal Unitarians and protests against hero-worship, against
a second revelation, and the necessity of a better code of ethics than
the one pronounced by Moses and the prophets.

To prevent the inference that Judaism is no positive quantity, and
that there are irreconcilable differences dividing the various sects, I
will say that all Jews agree on essentials and declare their belief in
the Unity and Spirituality of God, in the efficacy of religion for spiritual regeneration, and for ethical improvement in the universal law of
compensation, according to which there are reward and punishment,
either here or hereafter, in the final triumph of truth and fraternity of
all men. It may be briefly stated that the Decalogue forms the constitution of Judaism. According to Moses, the prophets and the historical interpretation of Judaism, whoever believes and practices the
" Ten Commandments " is a Jew.

Errors about the Jew pertain not only to questions of race and
nationality, not only to his individual, domestic and socal character,
not only to his religion, but also to his inherent power to resist the condemnation and opposition of an evil enemy, and his persistent existence in spite of the destructive forces of a hostile world. The very
fact that after so many fruitless efforts to destroy the Jew by persecution and inquisition, similar efforts are still put forth, only proves that
the invincibility of Israel has ever been, and is still, underestimated.
It is a fact that the cause of the Jew is strengthened in times of
persecution. When the hand of the oppressor is felt, the oppressed
band together, encourage one another, become more faithful to their
God, firmer in their conviction, and more zealous in behalf of their religion. It has been said that martyrdom is the seed of the Church.
This is no less true of Judaism. The very means adopted to destroy it
have only plowed up the fallow land and planted a stronger faith.
Persecution against any religion is a wanton error, a monstrous blasphemy.

The very traducers and persecutors of the Jews are the real enemies of Christianity. Russia has set Christianity one or two centuries
backward. Anti-Semitic agitation in Germany will have a similar result. The church is committing a monumental blunder in conniving
at this nineteenth century outrage, and must sooner or later be over-
taken by her Nemesis. The church should in her own interest, in the
name of her own principles and teachings, rise up in arms against unholy Russia and unrighteous Germany.

When persecution had done its work to no avail, when inquisition failed to make any impression on the Jew, in order to induce him to leave his brethren, detraction and ostracism were resorted to in order to weaken the hold of the Jew upon his co-religionists. We have already referred to some forms of this persecution, and wish to add that Jews were falsely charged with having poisoned wells, with having spread contagious diseases, and been the cause of the black death and every public calamity. Strenuous efforts have also been made to impair their commercial relation with the world. Jews have been condemned as a people of usurers, of avaricious money-lenders, as consumers in contradistinction to producers. " In the Midddle Ages," says Lady Magnus (Outlines of Jewish History), " 'Jew' meant to the popular mind nothing more than money-lender. Men spoke of having their 'Jews' as we speak of having our grocers and druggists. Each served a particular purpose and was primarily regarded in connection with that service. The real reason was never recognized by popular judgment, and the rude peasant of mediæval Europe firmly believed that the Jew amassed more money than those about him, not because he was more industrious or more frugal, but because he was meaner, trickier, more deceitful, and, if necessary, positively dishonest." Whatever may be the reprehensible practice of individuals, such an aspersion does not apply to the Jewish character, Jewish teaching, both in Scripture and Talmud, being opposed to usury and overreaching of whatever kind.

It is malicious slander to class the Jews as consumers, as distinguished from producers. The Jew is by birthright a tiller of the soil. Of this birthright he has been robbed by rapacious governments. Through centuries of persecution, when he was but a wandering sojourner on the earth, with no country he could call his own, no government to love, no flag to revere, he was like a tortoise that carries his house with him. The Jew was compelled to traffic in moneys and gems which he could take with him from place to place as necessity demanded. To-day, however, he is found in all trades and professions; to-day he is agriculturist, mechanic and artist, partakes of all the bounties of free citizenship, and must be counted among the producers of the world. And what shall we say of the Bible, the Talmud, music and poetry, art and science, which the Jews have contributed to the intellectual and material wealth of mankind! To still repeat the old thread-bare charge is worse than malicious slander; it is a criminal detraction, a subversion of all fact, a travesty upon truth.

There is sufficient reason to believe that all persecution and detraction of Jews rest on the further fundamental erroneous supposition that Jews can, in some way or other, be converted to Christianity. When men think they can destroy the Jew and his religion, they forget his indomitable patience, his untiring perseverance, his almost stolid obstinacy. When they endeavor to crush him, they overlook his hardened nature, steeled by trials and misfortune. When they expect to lure him from his associates, and wean him from his religion, they lose sight of his keen wit, his sense of the humorous and ridiculous. When they endeavor to punish him with ostracism, they fail to note his cheerful disposition, his happy home, and charming social instincts. When they endeavor to injure his influence by slander and detraction, they are blind to his utter disregard for public favors and to his ability to rise to any emergency. When they look forward to converting him by force or persuasion, by threat or bribe, they disclose their ignorance of his deep-seated conviction of the truth of his own religion.

The meager results achieved by missionaries and tracts have proved how futile are all efforts to convert the Jews. And even those few who have changed their faith have done so, there is ample reason to believe, only through mercenary motives, only because abject poverty forced them to accept the bribe that was temptingly held out toward them. I believe there are many sincere missionaries, and that, perhaps, amongst savages they accomplish some good as a civilizing leaven, but amongst the Jews their labors are uncalled for and misdirected.

This whole modern system of anti-Semitic agitation, and of attempts to convert the Jews by any means, reveals to us the erroneous impression entertained by many, it seems, that Jews have entered into a kind of secret competition with the rest of the world for the supremacy of Judaism and its followers. Nothing could be further removed from the truth. Jews do not aspire to supremacy (perhaps unfortunately) religiously, socially or politically. They desire no distinction as a particular sect apart from the rest of the world, in dress, habits, manners, social features, or politics. Jews have renounced the title of "Peculiar People," and regard such a sobriquet rather as a reproach than a compliment. They claim the name of Jew merely as a term denoting their particular faith and practice. In religion only are Jews different from others, and they claim the right as free men to worship their God in peace, according to the dictates of their own and not another's conscience.

The Jew is tolerant by nature, tolerant by virtue of his religious teaching. He believes in allowing every man, what he claims for himself, the right to work out his own salvation and make his own

peace with God. He has only one important request to make of
Christian teachers and preachers, namely, that they desist from teaching their school children and congregations the prevailing error that
the Jews have crucified Jesus of Nazareth. Because of this great
error the believing world looks upon the Jew through an imperfect
medium, one that enlarges faults and minimizes virtues. It is this
error which has caused so much prejudice, bitter hatred, and unjust
persecution. If it were once corrected, the way would be opened for
the correction of many other errors. Now is the great opportunity of
the age for rectifying it. Let the truth be told to the world by the
assembled Parliament of Religions, that not the Jews but the *"Romans
have crucified the great Nazarene teacher."*

And until the Jew has been set before the world in the right
light, let us exert our utmost toward correcting mistakes, false impressions, and malicious slander. The work of this congress is in that
direction. But it alone is not sufficient. Let us also use every agency
in our power, the pulpit, the press, and platform, the vehicles of general literature, for the purpose of disseminating the truth and destroying the false about Israel. In addition to this, our Union of Congregations, Rabbinical Conference, and Publication Society could and
should establish a competent Literary Bureau for the sole purpose of
pointing out errors about the Jews, defending our principles and institutions, of rebutting attacks, silencing slander, righting wrongs, and
demanding justice and equality from all the world. Such a Bureau
could do valuable service in reviewing press and magazine articles, as
well as books, and calling the attention of the world to fallacious reasoning, false statements, and unjust criticism. If it were known that
a competent literary bureau was on the constant watch to expose in-
nuendo and slander, fallacy, misrepresentation, and error, it would
induce many writers and speakers to be more circumspect in their
statements and arguments. With every agency thus working in behalf of the right, error and falsehood must in time succumb. They
are, even without any defense on our part, engaged in an unequal
contest with Israel, for God is with us, and, it may take long, but the
truth will prevail.

THE OUTLOOK OF JUDAISM.

BY MISS JOSEPHINE LAZARUS.

The nineteenth century has had its surprises; the position of the Jews to-day is one of these, both for the Jew himself and for the most enlightened Christians. There were certain facts we thought forever laid at rest, certain conditions and contingencies that could never confront us again, certain war-cries that could not be raised. In this last decade of our civilization, however, we have been rudely awakened from our false dream of security—it may be to a higher calling and destiny than we had yet foreseen. I do not wish to emphasize the painful facts by dwelling on them, or even pointing them out. We are all aware of them, and whenever Jews and Christians can come together on equal terms, ignoring differences and opposition and injury, it is well that they should do so. But, at the same time, we must not shut our eyes, nor, like the ostrich, bury our head in the sand. The situation, which is so grave a one, must be bravely and honestly faced, the crisis met, the problem frankly stated in all its bearings, so that the whole truth may be brought to light, if possible. We are a little apt to look on one side only of the shield, especially when our sense of justice and humanity is stung, and the cry of the oppressed and persecuted—our brothers—rings in our ears. As we all know, the effect of persecution is to strengthen solidarity. The Jew who never was a Jew before becomes one; when the vital spot is touched, "the Jew" is thrust upon him, whether he would or not, and made an insult and reproach. When we are attacked as Jews, we do not strike back angrily, but we coil up in our shell of Judaism and intrench ourselves more strongly than before. The Jews themselves, both from natural habit and force of circumstance, have been accustomed to dwell along their own lines of thought and life, absorbed in their own point of view, almost to the exclusion of outside opinion. Indeed, it is this power of concentration in their own pursuits that insures their success in most things they set out to do. They have been content for the most part to guard the truth they hold, rather than spread it.

Amid favorable surroundings and easy circumstances, many of us had ceased to take it very deeply or seriously that we were Jews.

We had grown to look upon it merely as an accident of birth for which we were not called upon to make any sacrifice, but rather to make ourselves as much as possible like our neighbors, neither better nor worse than the people around us. But with a painful shock, we are suddenly made aware of it as a detriment, and we shrink at once back into ourselves, hurt in our most sensitive point, our pride wounded to the quick, our most sacred feelings, as we believe, outraged and trampled upon. But our very attitude proves that something is wrong with us. Persecution does not touch us; we do not feel it when we have an idea large enough and close enough to our hearts to sustain and console us. The martyrs of old did not feel the fires of the stake, the arrows that pierced their flesh. The Jews of the olden time danced to their death with praise and song, and joyful shouts of hallelujah. They were willing to die for that which was their life and more than their life to them. But the martyrdom of the present day is a strange and novel one, that has no grace or glory about it, and of which we are not proud. We have not chosen and perhaps would not choose it. Many of us scarcely know the cause for which we suffer, and therefore we feel every pang, every cut of the lash. For our own sake then, and still more perhaps for those who come after us, and to whom we bequeath our Judaism, it behooves us to find out just what it means to us, and what it holds for us to live by. In other words, what is the content and significance of modern Judaism in the world to-day, not only for us personally as Jews, but for the world at large? What power has it as a spiritual influence? And as such, what is its share or part in the large life of humanity, in the broad current and movement of the times? What actuality has it, and what possible unfoldment in the future?

No sooner do we put these questions than we are at once confronted with every phase of sentiment, every shade and variety of opinion. We sweep the whole gamut of modern, restless thought, of shifting beliefs and unbelief, from the depths of superstition, as well as of skepticism and materialism, to the cold heights of agnosticism; from the most rigid and uncompromising formalism, or a sincere piety, to a humanitarianism so broad that it has almost eliminated God, or a Deism so vast and distant that it has almost eliminated humanity. Nothing is more curious than this range and diversity of conviction, from a center of unity, for the Jewish idea survives through every contradiction, as the race, the type, persists through every modification of climate and locality, and every varying nationality. Clear and distinct, we can trace it through history, and as the present can best be read by the light of the past, I should like briefly to review the ideas on which our existence is based and our identity sustained.

What an endless perspective! Age after age unrolls, nations appear and disappear, and still we follow and find them. Back to the very morning of time, before the primal mist had lifted from the world, while yet there were giants in the earth, and the sons of God mingled with the daughters of men, we come upon their dim and mythical beginnings. A tribe of wanderers in eastern lands, roaming beside the water-ways, feeding their flocks upon the hill-sides, leading their camels across the lonely desert wastes, and pitching their tents beneath the high, star-studded skies. From the first, a people much alone with their own souls and nature, brought to face the Infinite— self-centered, brooding, and conscious of a something, they knew not what—a power, and themselves, that led their steps and walked and talked with men. Already in those earliest days great types loom up among them, the patriarchal leaders, large, tribal, composite figures, rather than actual persons, and yet touched with human traits and personality, moving about in pastoral and domestic scenes; men, already, in their own crude way, preoccupied of God, and his dealings with themselves and with the world. Upon a background of myth, and yet, in a sense how bold, how clear, stands Moses, the man of God, who saw the world aflame with Deity—the burning bush, the flaming mountain top, the fiery cloud, leading his people from captivity, and who heard pronounced the divine and everlasting name, the unpronounceable, the Ineffable I Am. In Moses, above all, whether we look upon him as semi-historic or a purely symbolic figure, the genius of the Hebrew race is typified, the fundamental note of Judaism is struck, the word that rings forever after through the ages, which is the law spoken by God himself, with trumpet sound, midst thunderings and lightning from heaven. Whatever of true or false, of fact or legend hangs about it, we have in the Mosaic conception, the moral ideal of the Hebrews, a code, divinely sanctioned and ordained, the absolute imperative of duty, a transcendent law laid upon man which he must perforce obey, in order that he may live. "Thou shalt," "Thou shalt not," hedge him around on every side, now as moral obligation and again as ceremonial or legal ordinance, and becomes the bulwark of the faith, through centuries of greatness, centuries of darkness and humiliation.

Amid a cloud of wars, Jehovah's sacred wars, with shadowy hosts and chieftains, the scattered clans unite, the kingdom forms, and we have the dawn of history. Jerusalem is founded, at once a stronghold and a sanctuary, and the temple built. The national and re-

ligious life grow as one growth, knitting themselves together, and mutually strengthening and upholding one another. Then the splendors
of Solomon's reign, the palace with royal state, and above all the ever-
growing magnificence of the temple service, with more and more
sumptuous rites. The true greatness of Israel was never to consist in
outward greatness, nor in the materializing of any of its ideas, either
in the religious or the secular life, but wholly in the inner impulse and
activity, the spiritual impetus which was now shaping itself into
Prophetism. And here we strike the second chord, that other source
and spring of Israel's life, which still yields living waters. In Hebrew
prophecy we have no crumbling monument of perishable stone, the
silent witness of a past that is dead and gone, but the quickening
breath of the spirit itself, the words that live and burn, the something
that is still alive and life-giving because it holds the soul of a people,
the spirit that can not die. The prophets owned the clearer vision that
pierced below the surface and penetrated to the hidden meaning, the
moral and spiritual interpretation of the law in contrast with its outer
sense.

Throughout their history we find that the Jews as a nation have
been the "God-intoxicated" race, intent upon the problem of understanding him and his ways with them, his rulings of their destiny.
With this idea, whether in a high form or a law, in spiritual or material fashion, their whole existence has been identified.

In the Hebrew writings we trace not so much the development of
a people as of an Idea that constantly grows in strength and purity.
The petty, tribal god, cruel and partisan, like the gods around him,
becomes the universal and eternal God, who fills all time and space, all
heaven and earth, and beside whom no other power exists. Throughout nature, His will is law, His fiat goes forth, and the stars obey Him
in their course, the winds and waves: "Fire and hail, snow and vapors,
stormy wind, fulfilling His word."

"The lightnings do His bidding and say 'Here we are' when He
commands them."

But not alone in the physical realm, still more is He the moral
ruler of the Universe; and here we come upon the core of the Hebrew conception, its true grandeur and originality, upon which the
whole stress was laid, namely, that it is only in the moral sphere,
only as a moral being that man can enter into relation with his
Maker, and the Maker of the Universe, and come to any understanding of Him.

"Canst thou by searching find out God? Canst thou find out

the Almighty unto perfection? It is as high as heaven; what canst
thou do? deeper than hell; what canst thou know?"

Not through the finite, limited intellect, nor any outward sense-
perception, but only through the moral sense, do these earnest teachers bid us seek God, who reveals Himself in the law which is at once
human and divine, the voice of duty and of conscience, animating the
soul of man.   Like the stars, he too can obey, and then his righteousness will shine forth as the noon-day sun, his going forth will be like
the dawn.   It is this breadth of the divine that vitalizes the pages of
the Hebrew prophets and their moral precepts.   It is the blending of
the two ideals, the complete and absolute identification of the moral
and religious life, so that each can be interpreted in terms of the
other, the moral life saturated and fed, sustained and sanctified by the
divine, the religious life merely a divinely ordained morality, this it
is, that constitutes the essence of their teachings, the unity and grand
simplicity of their ideal.   The link was never broken between the human and the divine, between conduct and its motive, religion and
morality, nor obscured by any cloudy abstractions of theology or metaphysics.   Their God was a God whom the people could understand;
no mystic figure relegated to the skies, but a very present power,
working upon earth, a personality very clear and distinct, very human
one might almost say, who mingled in human affairs, whose word was
swift and sure, and whose path so plain to follow, "that wayfaring
men, though fools, should not err therein."   What He required was no
impossible ideal, but simply to do justice, to love mercy, and walk
humbly before Him.   What He promised was: "Seek ye me and ye
shall live."   How can one fail to be impressed by the heroic mold of
these austere, impassioned souls, and by the richness of the soil that
gave them birth at a time when spiritual thought had scarcely dawned
upon the world.   The prophets were the "high lights" of Judaism;
but the light failed, the voices ceased, and prophetism died out.   In
spite of its broad ethical and social basis, its seeming universality, it
never became the religion of the masses, because in reality it is the
religion of the few, the elect and chosen of God, who know and feel
the beauty of His holiness.

The people needed something more penetrating and persuasive, or
else something more congenial to their actual development at the time;
namely, some concrete and sensuous form in which Deity could be
brought into life.   Therefore the code was devised, or rather it evolved
and grew like a natural growth out of the conditions and constitution
of Judaism.   The "Torah" was literally the body of the law, in
which the spirit was incased as in a mummy shroud.   In order that

Israel should survive, should continue to exist at all in the midst of the ruins that were falling around it, and the darkness upon which it was entering, it was necessary that this close, internal organization, this mesh and network of law and practice, of regulated usage covering the most insignificant acts of life, knitting them together as with nerve and sinew, and invulnerable to any catastophe from without, should take the place of all external prop and form of unity. The whole outer framework of life fell away. The kingdom perished, the temple fell, the people scattered. They ceased to be a nation, they ceased to be a church, and yet, indissolubly bound by these invisible chains, as fine as silk, as strong as iron, they presented an impenetrable front to the outside world, they became more intensely national, more exclusive and sectarian, more concentrated in their individuality than they had ever been before. The Talmud came to reinforce the Pentateuch, and Rabbinism intensified Judaism, which thereby lost its power to expand, its claim to become a universal religion, and remained the prerogative of a peculiar people.

With fire and sword the Christian era dawned for Israel. Jerusalem was besieged, the temple fired, the Holy Mount in flames, and a million people perished, a fitting prelude to the long tragedy that has not ended yet, the martyrdom of eighteen centuries. Death in every form, by flood, by fire, and with every torture that could be conceived, left a track of blood through history, the crucified of the nations. Strangers and wanderers in every age, and every land, calling no man friend, and no spot home. Withal the ignominy of the Ghetto, a living death. Dark, pitiable, ignoble destiny! Magnificent, heroic, unconquerable destiny, luminous with self-sacrifice, unwritten heroism, devotion to an ideal, a cause believed in, and a name held sacred! But destiny still unsolved; martyrdom not yet swallowed up in victory.

In our modern rushing days, life changes with such swiftness that it is difficult even to follow its rapid movement. During the last hundred years, Judaism has undergone more modification than during the previous thousand years. The French Revolution sounded a note of freedom so loud, so clamorous that it pierced the Ghetto walls, and found its way to the imprisoned souls. The gates were thrown open, the light streamed in from the outside, and the Jew entered the modern world. As if by enchantment, the spell which had bound him hand and foot, body and soul, was broken, and his mind and spirit released from thrall, sprang into re-birth and vigor. Eager for life in every form and in every direction, with unused pent-up vitality, he pressed to the front, and crowded the avenues where life was most crowded, thought and action most stimulated. And in order to do this movement, naturally and of necessity, he began to disengage himself from the toils in which he was involved, to unwind himself, so to speak, from fold after fold of outworn and outlandish customs. Casting off the outer shell or skeleton, which, like the bony covering of the tortoise, serves as armor, at the same time that it impedes all movement and progress, as well as inner growth, Judaism thought to revert to its original type, the pure and simple monotheism of the early days, the simple creed that Right is Might, the simple law of justice among men. Divested of its spiritual mechanism, absolutely without myth or dogma of any kind, save the all-embracing unity of God, taxing so little the credulity of men, no religion seemed so fitted to withstand the storm and stress of modern thought, the doubt and skepticism of a critical and scientific age that has played such havoc with time-honored creeds. And having rid himself, as he proudly believed, of his own superstitions, naturally the Jew had no inclination to adopt what he looked upon as the superstitions of others. He was still as much as ever the Jew; as far as ever removed from the Christian standpoint and outlook, the Christian philosophy and solution of life.

Broad and tolerant as either side might consider itself, there was a fundamental disagreement and opposition, almost a different make-up, a different caliber and attitude of soul, fostered by centuries of mutual alienation and distrust. To be a Jew was still something special, something inherent, that did not depend upon any external conformity or non-conformity, any peculiar mode of life. The tremendous background of the past, of traditions and associations so entirely apart from those of the people among whom they dwelt, threw them into strong relief. They were a marked race always, upon whom an indelible stamp was set, a nation that cohered not as a political unit, but as a single family, through ties the most sacred, the most vital and intimate, of parent to child, of brother and sister, bound still more closely together through a common fate of suffering. And yet they were every-where living among Christians, making part of Christian communities and mixing freely among them for all the business of life, all material and temporal ends. Thus the spiritual and secular life which had been absolutely one with the Jew, grew apart in his own sphere, as well as in his intercourse with the Christians—the divorce was complete between religion and the daily life. The outer world allured him, and the false gods, whom the nations around him worshiped: Success, Power, and Pride of Life and of the Intellect. He threw himself full tilt into the arena where the clash was loudest, the press thickest, the struggle keenest to compete and outstrip one another, which we moderns call life. All his faculties were sharpened to it, and in his eagerness he forgot his proper birthright. He drifted away from his spiritual bearings, and lost sight of spiritual horizons. He, the man of the past, became essentially the man of to-day, with interest centered on the present, the actual, with intellect set free to grapple with the problems of the hour, and solve them by its own un-aided light. Liberal, progressive, humanitarian, he might become, but always along human lines; the link was gone with any larger, more satisfying and comprehensive life. Religion had detached itself from life, not only in its trivial, every-day concerns, but in its highest aims and aspirations.

The something that the Hebrew prophets had, that made their moral teaching vital and luminous, was lacking, the larger vision reaching out to the unseen, the abiding sense of an eternal will and purpose underlying human transient schemes, an eternal presence, transfusing all of life as with a hidden flame, so that love of country, love of right, love of man, were not alone human things, but also divine, because they were embraced and focused in a single living unity, that was the love of God. How different now the cold, ab-stract and passive unity, the only article of their faith now left to them, that had no hold whatever, no touch with life at any point, no kindling power! In what of positive and vital did their Judaism con-sist? Were they not rather Jews by negation, by opposition, non-Christians, first and foremost? And here was just the handle, just the grievance for their enemies to seize upon. Every charge would fit. Behold the Jew! Behold one not of ourselves who would be one of us? Our masters even, who would wrest our prizes from us, whose keen wits and clever fingers have somehow touched the inner springs that rule our world to-day, and set its wheels in motion. Every cry could shape itself against them, every class could take alarm, and every prejudice go loose. And hence the Proteus form of anti-Semitism. Wherever the social conditions are most unstable, the equilibrium most threatened and easily disturbed, in barbarous Russia, liberal France and philosophic Germany, the problem is most acute, but there is *no country now*, civilized or uncivilized, where some echo of it has not reached; even in our own free-breathing America, some wave has come to die upon our shores.

What answers have we for ourselves and for the world in this, the trial-hour of our faith, the crucial test of Judaism? We, each of us, must look into our own hearts, and see what Judaism stands for in that inner shrine, what it holds that satisfies our deepest needs, consoles and fortifies us, compensates for every sacrifice, every humiliation we may be called upon to endure, so that we count it a glory, not a shame to suffer. Will national or personal loyalty suffice for this, when our personality is not touched, our nationality is merged? Will pride of family or race take away the sting, the stigma? Lo! we have turned the shield and persecution becomes our opportunity! "Those that were in darkness, upon them the light hath shined." What is the meaning of this exodus from Russia, from Poland, these long black lines, crossing the frontiers or crushed within the pale—these "despised and rejected of men," emerging from their Ghettos, scarcely able to bear the light of day? Many of them will never see the Promised Land, and for those who do, cruel will be the suffering before they enter, long and difficult will be the task and process of assimilation and regeneration. But for us, who stand upon the shore, in the full blessed light of freedom and watch at last the ending of that weary pilgrimage through the centuries, how great the responsibility, how great the occasion, if only we can rise to it! Let us not think our duty ended, when we have taken in the wanderers, given them food and shelter, and initiated them into the sharp daily struggle to exist upon which we are all embarked; nor yet guarding their exclusiveness, when we leave them to their narrow rites and limiting observance, until, breaking free from these, they find themselves, like their emancipated brethren elsewhere, adrift on a blank sea of indifference and materialism. If Judaism would be any thing in the world to-day it must be a spiritual force. Only then can it be true to its special mission, the spirit, not the letter, of its truth.

Away then with all the Ghettos and with spiritual isolation in every form, and let the "spirit blow where it listeth." The Jew must change his attitude before the world, and come into spiritual fellowship with those around him. John, Paul, Jesus himself, we can claim them all for our own. We do not want "missions" to convert us. We can not become Presbyterians, Episcopalians, members of any dividing sect, "teaching for doctrines the opinions of men." Christians as well as Jews need the larger unity that shall embrace them all, the unity of spirit, not of doctrine.

Mankind at large may not be ready for a universal religion, but let the Jews, with their prophetic instinct, their deep, spiritual insight, set the example and give the ideal.

The world has not yet fathomed the secret of its redemption, and "salvation may yet again be of the Jews."

The times are full of signs. On every side there is a call, a challenge and awakening. Out of the heart of our materialistic civilization has come the cry of the spirit hungering for its food, "the bread without money and without price," the bread which money can not buy, and "thirsting for the living waters, which, if a man drink, he shall not thirst again." What the world needs to-day, not alone the Jews, who have borne the yoke, but the Christians, who bear Christ's name, and persecute, and who have built up a civilization so entirely at variance with the principles He taught—what we all need, Gentiles and Jews alike, is not so much "a new body of doctrine," as Mr. Claude Montefiore suggests, but a new spirit put into life which will re-fashion it upon a nobler plan, and consecrate it anew to higher purposes and ideals. Science has done its work, clearing away the dead wood of ignorance and superstition, enlarging the vision and opening out the path. It is for religion now to fill with spirit and with life the facts that knowledge gives us, to breathe a living soul into the universe. "Return unto me, and I will return unto you, saith the Lord of Hosts." "All we like sheep have gone astray," Christians and Jews alike have turned from the true path, worshiping upon the high places and under every green tree, falling down before idols of gold and silver, and making graven images of every earthly and every heavenly thing. Thus have we builded a kingdom, wholly of the earth, solid and stately to the eye of sense, but hollow and honeycombed with falsehood, and whose foundations are so insecure that they tremble at every earthly shock, every attempt at readjustment, and we half expect to see the brilliant pageant crumble before our sight and disappear like the unsubstantial fabric of a dream. Christians and Jews alike, "have we not all one Father, hath not one God created us?" Remember to what you are called, you who claim belief in a living God who is a Spirit, and who therefore must be worshiped "in spirit and in truth,"—not with vain forms and meaningless service, nor yet in the world's glittering shapes, the work of men's hands or brains,—but in the ever-growing, ever-deepening love and knowledge of His truth and its showing forth to men. Once more let the Holy Spirit descend and dwell among you, in your life to-day, as it did upon your holy men, your prophets of the olden times, lighting the world as it did for them with that radiance of the skies; and so make known the faith that is in you, "for by their fruits ye shall know them."

WHAT HAS JUDAISM DONE FOR WOMAN?

BY MISS HENRIETTA SZOLD.

The whole education conferred by Judaism lies in the principle that it did not assign to woman an exceptional position; yet, on the other hand, by taking cognizance of the exceptional position assigned to woman by brute force, and occupied by her on account of her physical constitution and natural duties, Judaism made that education effectual and uninterrupted in its effects.

In the tangled maze of history, let us single out the thread that marks the development of Jewish woman. In Jewish history, as in that of the rest of mankind, leaders are only mile-stones.

Our question calls for the spiritual data about the typical woman whom Judaism has prepared for nineteenth century work. To discover them, we must go back to twice nineteen hundred years ago, to the woman that presided over the tent of Abraham.

In that tent, whatever incipient Judaism did for man, that precisely it did for woman: it made man, created male and female, aware of his human dignity, and laid it upon him as a duty to maintain that dignity. With the defining of man's relations to his family, begins the refinement, the humanity of civilization.

Abraham stands out in a historic picture of mankind as the typical father. He it was of whom it was known that he would "command his children and his household after him, that they shall keep the way of the Lord, to do righteousness and justice."

What was Sarah's share in this paramount work of education? Ishmael was to be removed in order that Isaac, the disciple of righteousness and justice, might not, by bad example, be lured away from "the way of the Lord." In connection with this plan, wholly educational in its aims, it is enjoined upon Abraham: "In all that Sarah may say unto thee, hearken unto her voice."

The next generation again illustrates, not the sameness in function, but the equality in position, of man and woman. Isaac and Rebekkah differ in their conception of educational discipline and factors.

20

Yet whatever may have been the difference of opinion between them with regard to interference in their children's affairs, before their children, father and mother are completely at one, for when the first suspicion of displeasure comes to Esau, it reaches him in Isaac's name alone. We are told that "then saw Esau that the daughters of Canaan were evil in the eyes of Isaac, his father." Isaac, the executive, had completely adopted the tactics of Rebekkah, the advisory branch of the government.

In Rebekkah we are shown the first social innovator, the first being to act contrary to tradition, and the iron-bound customs of society. She refuses to yield to birth its rights, in a case in which were involved the higher considerations of the guardianship of truth. And this reformer was the traditionally conservative woman, Rebekkah.

Such are the ideals of equality between man and woman that have come down to us from the days of the Patriarchs. Such, furthermore, was the basis upon which the position of woman in Judaism was fixed, and such in turn, the ideal toward which the Jewish woman was to aspire.

Women continued to be held in high esteem. We hear of the mothers of the greatest men, of Jochebed, the mother of Moses, and of Hannah, the mother of Samuel, and the sole director of his career. We still hear of fathers and mothers acting in equal conjunction, as in the disastrous youth of Samson. The law ranges them together: "If a man have a stubborn and rebellious son, who hearkeneth not to the voice of his father, or to the voice of his mother, and they chastise him, and he will not hearken unto them, then shall his father and his mother lay hold on him." We have evidence of woman's dignity in the parallel drawn by the prophets between the relation of Israel to God and that of a wife to her husband, most beautifully in this passage which distinguished between the husband of a Jewish woman and the lord of a mediæval Griseldis: "And it shall happen at that day, saith the Lord, that thou shalt call me *Ishi* (my husband), and shalt not call me any more *Ba' ali* (my lord). And I will betroth thee unto me forever: yea, I will betroth thee unto me in righteousness and justice, and in loving kindness, and in mercy. And I will betroth thee unto me in faithfulness."

But Israel was a backsliding nation. Even its purity of family life was sullied, as for instance at Gibeah, and by David. Yet it remains true that through good and evil times the ideals were maintained, and in the end practice was influenced into conformity with them. Subtler signs than gross historic events show both truths— show that practice degenerated, and show that it was reconstructed on the basis of never-abandoned ideals. Emphatic assertions of the exalted position of women are dangerous. They involve the concession that man has the authority to establish or refuse, instead of leaving the economy of the moral world as God has ordained it. Any tendency to create an inequality, be it to the detriment or to the aggrandizement of woman, is fatal to her true dignity.

The prophet Malachi sets forth the whole misery of those later days, culminating in disregard of woman, and on the other hand, the Jewish principle and ideal of woman's co-equality with man, as well as the cause of her dethronement from his side. He says: "The Lord hath been witness between thee and the wife of thy youth against whom thou hast indeed dealt treacherously; yet is she thy *companion* and the wife of thy *covenant*."

The last of the prophets, the contemporary of the Scribes, ushers us into the halls of the Talmud. Here the prophet's utterances still reverberate: "He who forsakes the love of his youth, God's altar weeps for him;" "A man should be careful lest he afflict his wife, for God counts her tears." Less suggestive of disordered affairs is: "He who sees his wife die before him has, as it were, been present at the destruction of the sanctuary itself, around him the world grows dark." "Love your wife like yourself, honor her more than yourself," smacks of the equivocal distinction of mediæval times, and of a convulsive desire to hide the existing condition of affairs. "If thy wife is small, bend down to her to take counsel from her," indicates a return to natural, unstrained relations. "He who marries for money, his children shall be a curse to him," is a practical maxim applicable not only in ancient times, and finally, the early ideal is realized in "A man's home means his wife."

The question arises, how came it about that the early realities turned into fit subjects for poetry, aphorism, and chivalrous sayings, but were absent from every-day life sufficiently often to justify the prophet's wrath? It all lies in this: Israel's sons married the daughters not of a stranger, but of a strange god.

It was the Israelite's crown of distinction that his wife was his *companion*, whose equality was so acknowledged that he made with her a *covenant*. But this crown was dragged in the mire when he married the daughter of a strange god.

Direst misfortune taught Israel the folly of worshiping strange gods, but the blandishments of the daughters of a strange god produced the enactment of many a law by the rabbis of the Talmud. Here was the problem that confronted them: Israel's ideals of womanhood were high, but the nations around acted according to a brutal standard, and Israel was not likely to remain untainted. They solved it in a truly Jewish way—both in the Jewish spirit and on a Jewish basis. As always in Judaism, they dealt with a condition, and strove, by modifying it, to realize the ideals of their theory.

Judaism had taken cognizance of the fact that the practice of the nations about, with regard to women, varied widely from Jewish ideals. Clear of vision, the Lawgiver-Prophet could not fail to see that Israel, stiff-necked, unmindful of its mission, participating in the human fault of asserting brute strength over the physically weak, would soon adopt the lower standards unless restrained by iron-handed law. Thus Mosaic legislation recognizes the exceptional position occupied by woman, and profits by its knowledge thereof to lay down stringent regulations ordering the relation of the sexes. We have the rights of women guarded with respect to inheritance, to giving in marriage, to the marriage relation, and with regard to divorce. But woman's greatest safeguard lay in the fact that both marriage and divorce among the Jews were civil transactions, connected with a certain amount of formality.

An authority describes the Jewish view of marriage as standing between that of the common law, which, according to Blackstone, "considers marriage in no other light than as a civil contract," and that of the Roman Catholic Church, which "holds marriage to be a sacrament and as such indissoluble." He says: "Between these two extremes stands that of the Jewish law." The act of concluding marriage is there certainly also considered as a contract, which requires the consent of both parties and the performance of certain formalities similar to other contracts, and which under certain circumstances can be dissolved. But, inasmuch as marriage concerns a relation which is based on morality and implies the most sacred duties, it is more than a mere civil contract. In such a contract, the mutual duties and rights emanate from the optional agreement of the contracting parties, while those who enter upon the state of married life must submit to the reciprocal duties which have been imposed by religion and morality. Adultery is not merely infidelity toward the conjugal partner, but a violation of a divine order, a crime which can not be condoned by the offended party; it invalidates the very foundation of that marriage, so as to make its continuation absolutely impossible. Under Jewish jurisdiction, the husband was compelled to divorce his wife who had been found guilty of adultery.

The laws and regulations of divorce are full and detailed. A passage often quoted, in order to give an idea of the Jewish divorce law, is the following : "The school of Shammai"—inclining to Biblical ordinances—"says that a wife can be divorced only on account of infidelity. The school of Hillel says that the husband is not obliged to give a plausible motive for divorce—he may say that she spoiled his meal. R. Akiba expresses the same idea in another way : he may say that he has found a more beautiful woman." And those that wish to throw contempt upon the Jewish law add that the school of Hillel, the milder school, is followed in practical decisions. This is one of the cases in which not the whole truth is told. In the first place, a woman has the same right to apply for a divorce, without assigning any reason which motives of delicacy may prompt her to withhold. The idea underlying this seeming laxity is, that when a man or a woman is willing to apply for a divorce on so trivial a ground, then, regard and love having vanished, in the interest of morality a divorce had better be granted, after due efforts have been made to effect a reconciliation. In reality, however, divorce laws were far from being lax. The facts that a woman who applied for a divorce lost her dowry, and in almost all cases a man who applied for it had to pay it, would suffice to restrain the tendency. Rabbinowicz remarks about a certain law, that it shows that the rabbis sought to diminish divorce as much as possible. Moreover, and this is the clinching fact, divorces were very rare.

The important points characterizing the Jewish divorce law, and distinguishing it far beyond that of other races of antiquity, are these : A man, as a rule, could not divorce his wife without providing for her ; he could not summarily send her from him, as was and is the custom in eastern countries, but was obliged to give her a duly drawn up bill of divorcement ; and women as well as men could sue for a divorce.

Besides these important provisions regulating woman's estate, there are various intimations in the Talmud of delicate regard paid to the finer sensibilities of women.

These and such are the provisions which, originating in the hoary past, have intrenched the Jewess' position even unto this day. Whatever she may be, she is through them. But what is she ? You have heard of the Jewish custom which bids the Jewish mother, after her preparations for the Sabbath have been completed on Friday evening, kindle the Sabbath lamp. That is symbolic of the Jewish woman's influence on her own home, and through it upon larger circles. She is the inspirer of a pure, chaste family life, whose hallowing influences are incalculable ; she is the center of all spiritual endeavors, the confidante and fosterer of every undertaking. To her the Talmudic sentence applies: " It is woman alone through whom God's blessings are vouchsafed to a house. She teaches the children, speeds the husband to the place of worship and instruction, welcomes him when he returns, keeps the house godly and pure, and God's blessings rest upon all these things."

ORGANIZED FORCES.

A SABBATH-SCHOOL UNION.

By DR. S. HECHT.

In presenting the subject of "Sabbath-School Union," on this
memorable occasion, as one of the topics falling under the head of
"What can Organized Forces do for Judaism?" I do not presume
upon any startlingly new or original ideas, calculated to revolutionize
the status of Judaism in America.

Recognizing, moreover, the soberness of the question which on its
very face precludes alike flights of fancy, bursts of eloquence, and
depths of erudition, I will not attempt more than a plain, matter-of-
fact exposition of the subject.

I do hope, however, to be able to say something, born of a deep
love and earnest solicitude for our ancestral religion. The subject assigned to me touching the future of Judaism, concerning the coming
men and women in Israel, is so near my heart, its import and effect are
far-reaching, that I unhesitatingly declare as my innermost conviction:
"Within the broad limits of the modern rabbi's activity, there is no
aim worthier of his best and noblest efforts than that which affects the
moral and religious growth of the young." Here is the point in which
all the hopes, aims and aspirations of Judaism converge. All that is
good and commendable in the Jew, all that tends to make him and his
religion strong, respectable and respected, has its seat, its root, in the
young. And when we read that play of words in the ancient literature אַל תִּקְרָא בָּנַיִךְ אֶלָּא בּוֹנַיִךְ, it seems to strike the key-note
for this consideration.

To my mind בָּנַיִךְ and בּוֹנַיִךְ are to a great extent interchange-
able terms, and if Judaism be indeed, as we hear it so often and so
persistently claimed, a structure upon which generations to come shall
have to build, as generations past have builded, it clearly follows that
the builders of the future must be well, must, indeed, be better
equipped than were they who laid the foundation. The work of the
future requires a thorough knowledge of the basic conditions, in order
that the superstructure may become sound and safe and useful. But
it requires more. The builders to come must be in sympathy and har-

mony with the founders, to be sure, but they must possess likewise, the ability of happily blending strength with beauty, and soundness with grace.

Such equipment for the builders of the future can best, and perhaps solely, be supplied or furnished by the proper religious training of the young. And, therefore, I feel justified in repeating, that the noblest task of the rabbi of to-day consists in that training of the young which gives them at once the knowledge of right and truth and the means practically to apply that knowledge in the different walks and relations of life.

In making these emphatic statements concerning the necessity of religious education, I am not unmindful of the principles on this point held by our fathers of old and transmitted by them to their posterity, even to us. The sacred duty, sacredly performed by them, was ever לִלְמֹד וּלְלַמֵּד, to learn and to teach. The study of the word of God occupied the time and attention of our wisest and greatest teachers, and the care they bestowed upon the development of the religious life of the Jewish youth is unremitting.

But I am dealing with the present time, in this land and under modern conditions, and these, you will concede, widely differ from and strangely contrast with the times, country and conditions of our ancestors.

Here, where the line of demarkation between secular and sectarian education is so sharply drawn to-day, that the state recognizes its duty to the future citizen to afford him an opportunity for secular education only; under existing conditions, which absorb almost all the time, interest and attention of the *practical* man, and ignore the claims of the heart and the soul; the religious development of the children is certainly at a disadvantage and would be entirely lost were it not for the several religious institutions established and maintained by the religions.

But unable, for obvious reasons, to transplant to this country the seats of learning which flourished in Palestine and Babylon, or their methods, dependent on the time which the secular instruction did not claim, we learned from, and adopted the plan of our Christian brethren, and as they used the Sunday for their work among the young, we began to utilize the Sabbath, or the Sunday, or both, for the dissemination of religious knowledge among our children. And we have done well, for we have done the best that could be done under existing circumstances. False pride was not allowed to interfere with, and on the plea of "patterning after the Christians," to jeopardise the entire future of Judaism. We rather exemplified our approval of the defini-

tion of wisdom as given by the interlocutors of Alexander the Great,
viz: **איזהו חכם הלמד מכל אדם**, "Wise is he who adopts the
good wherever he may find it."

The pioneer work in the direction of religious education among
the young Israelites in America was done by that noble Jewess,
Rebecca Gratz, of blessed memory, who some fifty years ago or more
established the first school for religious instruction in the city of
Philadelphia, and thus laid the foundation to our Sunday-schools,
which we fondly and firmly hope may become a power for good in
the land. That modest beginning in the city of brotherly love, that
tiny seed, sown upon the fertile soil of a religious community, has
grown and brought forth a rich harvest, so that to-day there are but
few places, if any, inhabited by Jews in which the religious training
of the young does not receive some attention and care.

Fifty years of experimenting are behind us, half a century of
Sunday-school work has completed its circuit. What are the results
achieved? Which are the fruits enabling us to judge of the quality
of the tree upon which they have grown? Have we the right to feel
proud of the one, or to rejoice in the other? Are our schools fulfilling
their ideal purposes? Do they fit the young among us for the great
work devolving upon them as builders of the future?

Truth compels us to say that, with all the efforts and energies
which have been brought to bear upon the young, our Sunday-schools
still remain in the experimental stage. We know, of course, that
there is an interest taken in the religious training of our children,
that the education of their heart is not ignored, and while this is certainly an advantage, it is, I fear, in many of our communities, the
only one we may boast. For with the exception, perhaps, of the
schools connected with our larger and wealthier congregations in the
large cities of our country, and of those smaller communities, fortunate enough to possess some able and devoted persons, to conduct
the schools, there is a woeful lack of system, of method, and of aim.
And even in these schools there exist so many drawbacks, that the
real purpose and end of religious education is lost sight of.

Too much mechanism and rote work frequently tend to defeat
the aims of religion, the heart of the young remains cold, and their
life irresponsive to the call of duty. Children are drilled on historical
data, crammed with a lot of names, or taught to memorize abstract
and abstruse philosophical and metaphysical phrases, and then exhibited as prodigies of religious knowledge. The ethical beauties of
the Bible are treated superficially, and the influence upon the life and

deeds of the young does not find adequate consideration. So that children are able faultlessly to recite the Decalogue, without knowing that by refusing respect to their parents, love to their brothers and sisters, and kindness, truth and justice to every one, they are guilty of a wrong, or acting in violation of the "Ten Commandments." They may know the entire history of Abraham and Lot, of Joseph and his brothers, and not dream of the virtue of peace, of the duty of hospitality and kindness, or of the sin of jealousy, of selfishness, and indifference, which that history means to emphasize.

Many, alas! who have passed through the course of Sunday-school instruction, carry with them into life unpleasant recollections of those years, look back upon them as upon a time most unprofitably spent, nor wonder at the apathy and reluctance characterizing the attendance of their younger brothers and sisters, or of their children, reflecting, as they are in a large measure, their own sentiments and their own experience. And these unsatisfactory conditions are not ascribable to the school, they can not be laid at the door of the teachers or pupils, much less can religion be held responsible for them. It is a chain of circumstances which militates against success, and frustrates and brings to nought the best intentions, the highest aims, and loftiest purposes. To break that chain, that force of circumstances is the imperative requirement of the time upon us.

The gloomy and depressing atmosphere of many a school-room, the misunderstandings concerning the essence of religion, the inexperience of a large number of teachers, the insufficiency of existing text-books, the lack of plan, method, and means, which so largely exist, these, and many other drawbacks to successful and practical religious training, combine and form a solid and impenetrable phalanx against which all, even the best individual efforts, remain fruitless. The wonder to-day, therefore, is not that our schools are inadequate,— the wonder is that they exist at all.

What then is the remedy? The answer as briefly as possible is: *Concentration of forces.* Were an illustration, an object lesson needed, the great wonder of the world exhibited in this city, and attracting millions of people from every part of the earth, would furnish it. The triumph of the human mind here achieved, the grandeur of the work here accomplished, the creation of the magic "White City" here called into existence, eloquently sets forth the answer to the question here under consideration, "What can organized forces do?"

However great the men, however skillful the mechanic, however practical, inventive, and original the individuals may have been, who were active in the production of these marvelous results, they could not have been obtained without the concentration and organization of the many individual forces which entered as factors into this stupendous enterprise.

It is so in the domain of charity. Its noblest results do not depend upon the wealth of the one, nor upon the liberality of the other, nor upon the wisdom of the third, but upon the combination of these and similar elemental factors.

It is so in all material pursuits, in all spiritual aspirations. The individual, with his best efforts and purest aims, with all his means and with all his good will, can accomplish nothing. With these efforts, means, and aims of the individuals, united, and properly directed, there is nothing which could *not* be accomplished, which would be impossible.

A Sunday-school Union in word and deed is the great desideratum; the Judaism of the future needs it, and the re-establishment, the re-organization of such a Union is the burden of my plea to-day.

Far be it from me, however, to advocate a suppression of the individuality, or to favor a machine-made man. The idea of a Sunday-school Union, as it lives in my mind, does not mean the abolition of the independent thought of the thinker or the individual work of the worker: it means a pooling of issues, a contribution of ideas, that should be well digested and then made the common basis for our work. It means that we agree upon what we want; it means that we cease to grope in the dark; it means that all who are engaged in the work be thoroughly and clearly informed as to its scope. This done, we may safely leave the details of the work to the individual, to be adjusted in accordance with local requirements and available material. Such a Sabbath-school Union with a well defined aim would be like the Public Schools, or like the Christian Sunday-schools, either of which, having the masses with them, arouse public interest, stimulate the efforts and propagate the cause to which they are devoted. Such a Union, which would embrace all our schools, and marshal all our children of school age, would inevitably enforce the recognition, on the part of our people, of its importance, a recognition which is now denied our schools, and this advantage gained, alone would do away with most, if not all, of the drawbacks enumerated above, the school would, more generally, be assigned to cheerful and inviting quarters and surroundings, teachers and pupils would gain a spirit of emulation, text-books, appealing with irresistible force to instructor and instructed, would be produced, the work of the Sunday-school and its influence would not remain confined to the hour of instruction, but certain agencies, such as magazines and weekly papers, would be called into existence and keep alive the interest during the week, erroneous notions about religion would be rectified by making it a factor of every day life; the school would thus become a delight to those attending it, and the hours of instruction invested with an interest and attractiveness, which, eventually, would make them appear as the pleasantest and most profitable period of youth—in one word—such a union would make the component parts thereof, to answer fully and satisfactorily their great purpose of fitting the young to be successful builders of the future.

Let then this year, so fraught with valuable lessons, impress upon our minds the possible results of organized, concentrated forces. Let a systematic effort be made to secure the co-operation of all our individual schools. Let the large and influential congregations with their well appointed schools extend the hand of helping fellowship to those of their sisters less favored by circumstances, and let these not be misled by false pride, but come forward, grasp that extended hand, and help the common cause. Every school, even the smallest, will aid in increasing the number of our working forces, enlarge the scope of our labor and the field of our usefulness. Long enough have we, has our cause suffered under the baneful effects of self-sufficiency, of false pride and petty jealousy. It is time that we learn the better way. No matter how large the individual school, no matter how well equipped, no matter how competent the superintendent and the teachers, it will never, by itself, rise to that dignity, or win that success which our schools need.

Together, with forces united, let us advance together with one aim in view, let us remove the obstacles, until the more than two hundred schools, with the more than thirty thousand children, shall feel one common interest, shall be able to further it, and by their influence give shape and beauty, glory and honor to the structure of Judaism, to the name of Jew. Then, and not till then, will be verified the prophecy ורב שלם בניך וכל בניך למדי יהוה; then only and not till then, will peace and strength be our portion through our children, the builders of the future!

ON INSTRUCTION IN THE POST-BIBLICAL HISTORY OF THE JEWS IN OUR SABBATH SCHOOLS.

By. DR. B. FELSENTHAL.

Is it necessary, or is it even desirable, that our rising Jewish generation shall receive instruction in the post-biblical history of our people? I am of the opinion that now-a-days very few among us will raise such a question. I believe that a large majority of the superintendents of Jewish Sabbath Schools and of the teachers in such schools will agree with me when I say, post-biblical history of the Jews ought to be a branch of instruction in each and every Jewish Sabbath School, *provided* it is kept within proper limitations and is imparted in the proper spirit and in a proper method.

Such an instruction has thus far been too much neglected. And the consequence is, that we so often meet among our co-religionists with a great ignorance in Jewish matters, with an ignorance which certainly should not prevail. For it is one of the main sources of the wide-spread indifference toward Judaism. Furthermore, the Jew who lacks all knowledge of Jewish History is unfitted to clearly understand the present conditions of his people and of his religion, since these present conditions are rooting in the past and are the outcome of historical causes.

And aside from this, it is to be taken into consideration that even a limited knowledge in Jewish History is apt to inculcate a new love for Judaism and a stronger attachment for the same into the hearts of our sons and daughters, and may fill with more self-respect, aye, with a noble pride, the minds of our youth, so that again they might confess and exclaim in joy, in enthusiasm, and before all the world, "*Ibhri anokhi*, yes, I am a Hebrew; yes, I am a Jew; and I am proud of my people and of my religion!"

The question now arises, in how far and to what extent shall Jewish History be taught in our Sabbath Schools?

Considerations of various kinds will force the conclusion upon us that the teacher in a Sabbath School will have to restrict himself to the main points, and that he must be satisfied if the pupils in his classes become more or less familiar with the outlines of this branch of study. For the time which we can devote to our Sabbath School work is very limited, and this time is therefore to be husbanded economically and wisely. Besides this, the children have to study so many other branches, many of which may well claim precedence to Jewish History and greater importance, since they weigh heavier in the scale of the general culture of the age than Jewish History does. And a Jew of whom it might be said that he possesses the average culture required in the present times of a well educated person, must, in the opinion of many, be more at home in Universal History than in Jewish History.

Furthermore, it can not be the aim and object of the Sabbath Schools to educate profound scholars and thorough specialists in Jewish History. If good foundations are laid and a comparatively small number of the most important names and dates and events are stored in the memory of the pupils in becoming chronological order, and if the teacher succeeds in awakening sufficient interest in the minds of the pupils to widen their knowledge by their own private readings and in other ways open to them, then we may be well contented.

The next question is, What are the main points that deserve, foremost of all, to be selected and to be taught in the Sabbath School? I answer: First, those points which will help the young students to better understand the religious life and the religious institutions of the Israelites in the present times; secondly, those points by which the learners may be lifted up religiously and morally, and by which a deeper love for our religion may be called forth.

Let me illustrate this by going a little into details.

The child visiting the Sabbath School is also a visitor of the Synagogue. And it is to be expected that it shall remain a regular attendant of the divine services after having left the school and having reached the years of manhood or womanhood. Our synagogal service is of an historical growth. Many parts of it can only be understood properly and appreciated properly if we know how they originated and how they grew. It is therefore desirable that in our Sabbath Schools the children should learn what is meant by the terms *Sha'harith*, *Musaph*, *Minchah*, *Ma'aribh*; by the words *Siddur*, *Ma'hzor*, *Piyyutim*, *Selihoth*, *Kinoth*; by *Keriath ha-Torah* and *Haphtarah*, and so forth; and they should be instructed how that what is designated by these words came gradually into existence in the course of times, and accepted the present shapes and forms. The children will also not fail to notice that besides the biblical festivals, we Jews celebrate also a semi-festival of post-biblical origin, our *Hanukkah*, and that every four weeks *Rosh 'Hodesh* is announced, and that the same in some way is distinguished from other days by certain features in the ritual. Why 'Hanukkah is celebrated, and when the rules were laid down by which the Roshé 'Hodashim were to be calculated and the lunar years of the Jews were to be arranged—this the pupils ought to learn in the historical lessons given in our Sabbath Schools. And similarly it should be in regard to many other points in our ritual and in our ceremonial usages and customs.

By the Sabbath School lessons in Jewish History also, so much should certainly be taught that in later years the audiences listening to the discourses and sermons of the Rabbis could follow intelligently these discourses and sermons. The Rabbi quotes occasionally from the Talmud or the Midrash or other parts of the Jewish literature; he mentions occasionally the Halakhah or the Haggadah; he speaks occasionally of Pharisees and Sadducees, of Samaritans and Karaites, of Rashi and Maimonides. How discouraging must it now be to the Jewish preacher to know that his discourses, in so far as they allude to historical persons and facts and presuppose some substantial knowledge of our past, are not appreciated and not understood, because his listeners are so grossly ignorant! Shall now the Jewish preacher ever and anon restrict himself exclusively to appeals to the emotional side of our soul life? to exhortations and expostulations? or to the platitudes of empty harangues? A *Jewish* sermon must be instructive, and must have matter and substance, and a *Jewish* preacher must speak to the intellect and not merely to the heart. Therefore, Jewish audiences must be prepared to a certain degree, they must at least be familiar with the main points of Jewish history and Jewish literature. They must know what is to be understood by such words as Talmud, Targum, etc. They must have an idea who these eminent men were whose names they hear sometimes mentioned by the Rabbi, and of whom they read occasionally in their periodicals. And to learn that much, opportunities must be offered by our Sabbath Schools.

In the beginning of this essay it has also been remarked that by the instruction imparted in the Sabbath Schools a deeper love and warmer attachment to Judaism might be created. For this purpose such points must be selected which show that our ancestors in times past were indeed heroes in their sufferings, heroes who remained true and faithful to their God and their religion, even then when they had to sacrifice all their earthly possessions, even when they had to renounce their liberty, their country, their lives. Also such points must be laid stress upon which demonstrate that education, learning, poetry,

21

that, in short, many other ideal objects were constantly held in high esteem by our ancestors in former times, notwithstanding the dark days of persecution and the cloudy days of the Middle Ages, and notwithstanding the fact that they were surrounded on all sides by enmity and fanaticism. Thus great lessons will be impressed upon the minds of the Jewish children, the lessons that there are higher objects to be pursued than accumulating earthly possessions and enjoying fleety sensual pleasures: that gold and silver and even life itself must not be considered as the sole and best realities to be aimed after; that religion, moral conduct, fulfillment of our duties, the building up of a world resting upon truth, justice, and peace is of an immensely higher value than those things which by so many in our materialistic age are put into the foreground. And thus the Sabbath School will have an educational influence upon the children, and will not impart merely a dead and unproductive knowing of a number of facts, to be stored away in the chambers of our memory.

As to the text-books to be used in our Sabbath Schools, I am of the opinion that we need three such books—one for children from seven to ten years, one for pupils from ten to fourteen years, and one for post-graduates from our schools who desire to enlarge their knowledge of Judaism and of its history. These books must not treat exclusively of Jewish history; they might comprise whatsoever the young student ought to know of Jews and of Judaism. To require of the children that in each grade they should buy and respectively study one special catechism of the Jewish religion, one special manual of Biblical History, and another special manual of Post-biblical History would be unwise for many reasons.

The text-books for the lower classes in the Sabbath Schools should contain the substance of all Jewish learning which the young children visiting these classes should receive and could understand and digest. The most necessary points in Jewish dogmatics, in ethics, in biblical history, and in post-biblical history can well be compressed in one small volume, containing from 100 to 150 pages. What such young children could learn and digest of *Jewish Dogmatics* might be said upon two or three pages of the text-books. There is a God above us, one God. In the beginning God created the heavens and the earth. He is the Ruler of all the world, He is our kind and merciful Father. He is the Judge who calls us to account for our moral shortcomings. We can not comprehend the essence of God, nor His thoughts and ways. He is beyond our understanding. Man in his moral conduct is a free agent; he possesses an immortal soul, endowed with reason and with a conscience, and he is responsible for whatever he is doing. All mankind is one great family, of whom God is the Father. This, I think, is more than sufficient for younger children—and, perhaps, for grown people too—to learn of Jewish-Dogmatics. To enter with them into more dogmatical details, to speculate, as the gnostics of old did and the gnostics of modern times do, upon metaphysical and really unknowable matter, as for instance, upon the positive attributes of the Absolute Being, of the nature of the Life Hereafter, etc., would be more than unwise, it would be misleading and harmful. A few short sentences, clothed in plain words, must suffice for the children. To *Ethics* some more space is to be devoted in the text-book and some more time in the school. Duties incumbent upon the children in their relations to their parents, teachers, friends, and to other people in general, charity toward the poor and needy, truth, justice, honesty, etc., etc.—these are matters of ethical instruction, and the paragraphs in the text-book regarding them should be well memorized, after the teacher has thoroughly explained them and appropriately illustrated them by facts from history, from fiction, and from every-day-life. In support of the ethical instructions, about fifty or sixty well selected passages from the Bible, and also some ethical sayings from the Talmud and from our post-talmudical literature, should be accepted into this text-book, and the children should commit them to memory. Such ancient authoritative sentences are often great moral aids in hours of temptation, and in times when we may be in doubt in what direction we should go, they might prove to be guides showing us the paths of duty. By far the largest part of the text-book should be devoted to *Biblical and Post-biblical History*, or let us rather say, to a selection of such stories from the Bible and from post-biblical times which can be understood by young children, and by which they can be led upward in their religious and moral life. As it is at present the case in many Sabbath Schools, much is taught there which ought to be omitted altogether, or which at least should be left for a maturer age ; as for instance, the biblical cosmogony, the details of the ancient temple service, the political history of Israel in the times of the Judges and of the Kings, etc. Let our text-book for the lower classes contain about one hundred short stories, of which seventy or seventy-five may be biblical stories and twenty-five or thirty post-biblical stories. Each of these stories might in the average fill one page. The language should be plain and easy, without being childish. The story number One might have as its superscription, "Abraham's migration into Canaan and his separation from Lot," and the story number One Hundred (the last in the book), "Moses Montefiore, the great philanthropist and the devoted friend of Israel."[1]

The text-book for the next higher grade, for the pupils from ten to fourteen years, might be somewhat larger; it might be a book containing from two hundred to three hundred pages. And these pages also should contain the entire substance of what the more advanced ones ought to learn in our Sabbath schools. To the *dogmatical part* from ten to twelve pages might here be devoted—not to teach essentially more of such metaphysical matters, for in reality none of us knows more of these things than we teach to the smaller children : but it may probably be well to make here a commencement in teaching the children in this grade how to look at Jewish dogmatics from a historical and from a comparative standpoint. A few elementary paragraphs showing in general outlines how Jewish dogmas grew and developed in the course of time, and in how far they differ from the corresponding dogmas of other religious systems, this it is what should be contained in these pages. As to *ethical instructions*, we should now certainly widen the limits and enlarge the field. Although children of twelve or fourteen years are not ripe enough to understand systematic ethics and their last philosophical foundations, yet they can be impressed with the sacredness of the duties which we have to fulfill as citizens of the state in which we live, as members of the human family to which we belong, as component parts of society in which we move, and to the amelioration of whose conditions we should contribute, etc. Also beginnings might be made now in defining such moral conceptions as virtue and vice, good and evil, truth and untruth, selfishness and unselfishness, etc. *Biblical History* should be supplemented now by chapters which in the lower grade had necessarily to be omitted, and which to explain the time may now have come. The book need also not longer to consist of isolated and disconnected stories, but Biblical History ought to be treated now as an organic History, and it ought to show how Israel became a nation and how Israel's religion developed in the course of centuries. Immediately following the Biblical History, and in close connection with it, the most important parts of *Post-Biblical History* are to be given. We have already indicated what, in our view, these more important parts are, and we can therefore be brief here. Let the substance be presented in chronological order. Omit whatsoever is of interest only to

---

[1] I may be permitted to refer the reader to the *Hebrew Review, Vol. 1, p. 89, seq.,* and to the *Menorah, Vol. VII, p. 330, seq.,* where I have expressed myself more in detail on the true method of teaching Biblical History in our Sabbath Schools.

the specialist and do not burden the memory of your pupils with heavy and unimportant details.   If these views are correct, then, to give an example, the text-book for the second grade of our Sabbath Schools might comprise upon ten to fifteen pages whatever the pupils in this grade need to learn of Jewish history in the times between the return from the Babylonian captivity and the destruction of the second temple.   Without any particular disadvantage to the pupils in this grade the names of the High Priests during this period and their historical sequence, and the intricate history of the Asmonean dynasty and of the Herodian princes can be omitted entirely.   Sufficient it is if brief mention is made of the fact that at first the Jews were subjects to the Persian kings, then to Alexander the Macedonian, and then to the Syrians, that subsequently they became more or less independent (or some time under the rule of the Asmoneans and of the Herodians, until finally Palestine became a conquered province of the Roman empire and remained it till the second Jewish commonwealth ceased to exist in the year 70 A. C.   More important than these outer facts of the political history of the Jews in this period are for our children the story how 'Hanukkah originated during this time; the fact that the first translation of the Sacred Scriptures, the Septuagint, was made in this period; that two great parties took now their rise among the Jews, viz., the party of the Pharisees and the party of the Sadducees; that the books comprised in the Bible were then collected and put into the same order in which we still possess them; that the authors of the so-called Apocrypha, that furthermore Philo, Josephus, and some others, enriched the Jewish literature by writings in the Greek language; that in this period the Jerusalem temple ceased to remain the sole house of Jewish worship, and that gradually synagogues arose in the various cities and villages where Jews were living; that our oldest prayers, which are still retained in our rituals, the institution of publicly reading from the Torah in the synagogues, the translation of the lessons read into the Aramaic (the Targumim) originated in these days, etc.   It is also important to tell the children in a discreet and well considered manner how it came that Christianity germinated, and that finally the Christian Church separated from the Jewish Synagogue. In proceeding to the next period of our Post-Biblical History, to the history of the talmudic age, the pupils must learn how gradually the Jews became dispersed over many parts of the known world; but of still more importance is it for them to learn who Johanan ben Zakkai, Rabbi Akibha, R. Jehudah ha-Nasi were, and for what reasons we look upon them as great men in our history.   The pupils in this grade should also receive an idea what is meant by Mishnah, Jerusalem

Talmud, Babylonian Talmud, Halakhah, Haggadah, Midrash, Massorah, etc. In coming down to still later periods, the children should receive some instructions regarding Geonim, Karaites, Kabbalists, regarding the most eminent scholars in biblical, in talmudical, in general lore, the great philosophers and poets who arose among despised Israel, and so on. All these pages might, however, well be compressed into a space of forty or fifty pages at the utmost. For permit me to repeat once more: Do not attempt to teach too much. תפסת מועט תפסת תפסת מרובה לא תפסת. If you attempt to reach too much, you will not succeed in your attempts: if you attempt less, you may succeed. From the entire realm of post-talmudical Jewish history certainly not more than at highest fifty names and dates should be garnered into the memory and treasured in the minds of the children.

One other manual is a desideratum—a book for classes of postgraduates. It might consist of a number of essays on topics from Jewish history and religion, each one complete in itself, and yet connected in some systematic and logical way of arranging them. By these essays the young student may be led somewhat deeper into the spirit which fills our history and our religion. Here selections from our prayers, some of the Piyyutim and some other poetical productions, in classical translations, of course, might also be embodied; likewise translations of single chapters from our ethical literature, aye, even from our halakhic literature, also some pages from our philosophers, etc. These specimens from our Jewish literature should be read attentively, and should be commented upon in introductory chapters by the author and in verbal explanations by the teachers, and thereby the young students should learn how to properly esteem and appreciate our literature and to judge it from a literary and from an historical standpoint. For without leading our rising youth, or at least the maturer ones among them, to the sources, they might be filled with pretensions and deceptive idea and might be induced to indulge in the baseless self-glorification that they really master the history of the Jews and of their religion and literature, while in reality they would not know more than names, nothing but names. And can this be called mastery of the science of history?

And here let me close. Let me close in the hope that some of my thoughts may be found worthy of further consideration, and eventually of practical application.

THE JEWISH PUBLICATION SOCIETY OF AMERICA.

By MISS HENRIETTA SZOLD.

Five years ago, through the efforts of the union of several local committees in Philadelphia, eighty-eight persons became interested in the plan to effect, for the third time in the history of American Jews, an organization for the purpose of publishing and circulating works bearing upon Jewish life and literature. At the instance of this small band there assembled at Philadelphia, in June, 1888, an unusually large as well as representative convention of men and women, who realized the importance of the work to be undertaken. Besides, the gathering was thoroughly national in character. The delegates, for the most part self-constituted—delegates by virtue of their unflagging interest in Jewish communal affairs—came from all sections of the country. The laity and the clergy were represented, the professors and the world of business, the city congregations and the country districts. It was thus not unfounded assumption of representative character that prompted the quickly formed organization to call itself "The Jewish Publication Society of America."

The preamble to its constitution declares the object of the society to be the publishing of "works designed to foster a knowledge of Judaism, its religion, its literature and its history among the Jews of the United States." More explicitly the constitution defines its proposed task as two-fold: (1) "To publish works on the religion, literature and history of the Jews, and (2) to foster original work by American scholars on these subjects."

The government of the society was intrusted to a president and an executive committee of twenty-one members. The literary policy is determined by a publication committee, selected by the executive from among the members of the society. The officers elected at the first convention have since, with but few minor changes, continued to preside over the society. In the composition of the executive some new names may be noted, and the publication committee has had one new member added to its original number. But the character of the changes has not been such as to affect materially the policy under which the society began to act. The work of the society is, therefore, a unit, and may be reviewed as such.

A society whose purpose it is to foster a knowledge of Judaism by publishing works on the religion, literature and history of the Jews, acts as an educator and propagandist. Stress is laid upon the latter function in the constitution, by which "the Executive Committee is authorized to distribute copies of the society's publications among such institutions as may be deemed proper, and wherever such distribution may be deemed productive of good for the cause of Israel." All those interested in Jewish educational work in this country can bear witness to the fact that the enthusiasm of the student and the ability of the teacher are as naught before the obstacle interposed by the lack of works on Judaism in the English language. Jewish doctrines have, in our country, hitherto depended for their promulgation and exposition almost entirely upon the spoken word, reaching only a limited number, and quickly fading from memory, or upon the timely but chiefly ephemeral and often polemic productions, to which a place can be given in the Jewish press. The library now bearing the seal of the Jewish Publication Society holds out the promise of better facilities in the future. Indeed, the first work published, Lady Magnus' "Outlines of Jewish History," by its wide sale, testified to the fact that the organizers of the society had rightly conceived of its province. It has been adopted by our educators as a charmingly written text-book on post-Biblical Jewish history, for our religious schools and the satisfaction it gives shows that, in the language of the trade, it supplies "a long-felt want." Furthermore, the welcome accorded the "Outlines" may not unfairly be interpreted as stamping with legitimacy the propaganda aims of the society, in so far as they tend to effect the better understanding of Judaism among its own adherents. Although the society added much new matter to Lady Magnus' book, which enhances its value as a literary work, it is a fact that her book, so far as its qualifications as a text-book go, might have been used some years before the society republished it from the English edition. But it is another fact that it was not so used. The work of the society, in this instance, then, was to render a good book accessible to wide circles, and that it has notably done.

The "Outlines" were followed by "Think and Thank," "Rabbi and Priest," "The Persecution of the Jews in Russia," "Voegele's Marriage and Other Tales," "Children of the Ghetto," "Some Jewish Women," and two volumes of "Graetz's History of the Jews."

The most important work published hitherto is doubtless Graetz's "History of the Jews." When completed the work will consist of

five volumes. averaging five hundred pages. Up to the present Vol
umes I. and II. have been issued, and the third will soon appear. The
English book is an adaptation of Graetz's eleven-volume history, together with some new matter, partly taken from the author's *Volks-
thuemliche Geschichte*, in three volumes, the work of adaptation having
been done under the superintendence of the lamented author. It differs from the famous eleven-volume work in the omission of the scholarly notes appended to the latter. It thus loses in cumbersomeness
without losing in value as a product of Jewish literature.

The publishing of Graetz's History was earnestly objected to by
serious-minded men of good judgment. The fact that objections were
raised is here adverted to only because an examination of some of the
arguments may serve to define the literary policy followed by the society. It was said "that the work is not of a nature to appeal to the
popular taste," and it was suggested "that what is needed are especially
prepared works for the society, each complete in itself. and treating of
the great epochs in Jewish history and literature." The suggestion as to
the course to be pursued by the society in selecting works for publication naturally grew out of the objection. It is implied that our American Jewish public can not respond to the enthusiasm and vigor of a
great work on Jewish history—the greatest ever produced ; that before
it can be made responsive to what is strong and good, it needs to be
toned up by works especially compounded to suit its case ; and that
thus dosed, it may gradually be led on to the appreciation of what
truly deserves the name literature. A course of this kind is destructive of its own aims. The mind grows by what it feeds upon. As
men are prepared for liberty by the enjoyment of liberty, so for good
literature by the reading of good literature. Perhaps we may need
easy reading, but surely not *adulterated* reading. Books produced for a
set purpose make good campaign literature for effecting some practical
object. But gross means will certainly not compass the intangible results which a Jewish Publication Society should hope to realize. The
books that we need are those that will hold in *English* solution the fine
fervor, the subtle spirit that has ever pervaded Jewish literature, no
matter what the language in which it was couched. We do, indeed,
need books of instruction on our history, our religion, our literature,
but they, in turn, must be works which posterity may be willing to
rank as *literature*, each in its own department. We that have at last
ceased to be wanderers, and may honestly call ourselves citizens of a
country, in whose classic literature we take the joy and the pride that
come only through identifying one's self with that spirit that produced
it—we surely, if only a tithe of the enthusiasm for country be left for

race and religion, are not willing to put up with Jewish literature, so far below the classic, artistic standard that it openly avows its *tendenz* origin. The work of the Society, in other words, is, indeed, educational, but it is not school work, as its propagandism is not proselytizing.

Another book published by the Society that aroused general discussion and criticism, in this case *after* its publication, is Mr. Zangwill's "Children of the Ghetto." This book, which many believe is destined in the future to be looked upon as a classic of *English* literature, owes its origin directly to the Jewish Publication Society. It would certainly not have been written at this precise juncture if the Society had not urged its author on to the task. Mr. Zangwill did, indeed, write that a novel on the English ghetto was in him, and would come out at some time or other, but it remains true that this substantial contribution to literature was made through the encouragement which the Jewish Publication Society was able to offer its author. Its special value to the Jewish reading public lies in the fact that it is a virile and artistic reproduction of a phase of life among the Jews rapidly sinking out of view of the present generation into the shadows of the past. Mr. Zangwill has for English readers rescued from oblivion dear and quaint customs. It is the first time that the peculiar charm which makes Kompert's ghetto novels works of art has found congenial expression in the English language. Before "Children of the Ghetto" was written, most of us that had laughed and cried over pictures of old Jewish life, such as Kompert, Herzberg-Fraenkel, Kohn, Kulke, and Bernstein have drawn for us, would have declared it impossible for Jewish portraits to preserve their flesh tints after being transferred to an Anglo-Saxon canvas and frame. And who will deny that a book like Mr. Zangwill's has an educational—nay, to the historian of culture, a scientific—value?

It is noteworthy that each one of the three works discussed in detail—the "Outlines," Graetz's History, and "Children of the Ghetto"—invited criticism, for one reason or another, of the methods of the Publication Committee, yet they are the publications that have met with greatest success. Mere success would indicate nothing more than that the committee had properly gauged the desires and needs of the public. But that works of admittedly high literary character have been well received proves that the purpose of the society—to foster a knowledge of Judaism by publishing works on its religion, literature, and history can be effected best by *bona fide* literature—not by books written with the purpose in view of enlightening a certain class of people, but by books of intrinsic merit.

The fact that the society is educational in its character and aims
naturally forces upon its Publication Committee the exercise of careful
choice in the selection of books to be published. That is to say, not
every work of merit on a subject of Jewish interest which may be submitted can be given to its subscribers. Every book published should
be a book of merit, but not every book of merit can be published by
it. There was a time—some of us remember it, some of us have
heard our fathers tell of it—in which almost every Jew had a library
of Jewish works. Often the possessor could not read them because
they were in Hebrew, or, if he knew the words of their language, he
could not understand them because they were abstruse in subject and
conception. The possession of such a library certainly did not indicate, on the part of its owner, the desire to make an idle boast of intellectual attainments. He acquired it because he conceived it to be his
duty to help on book production, since he himself could not increase
the spiritual treasures of the world by producing books. Now, although the members of the Publication Society are banded together
primarily for educational purposes, we can not belie our intellectual
instincts. The society recognizes the legitimacy of the old Jewish
feeling, that every worthy spiritual enterprise, whether or not we are
to be directly and materially benefited by its success, should be supported and encouraged. Therefore, its second object is "to foster
original work by American scholars on these subjects," namely, history,
religion, and literature of the Jews. At the last biennial convention,
in June, 1892, the committee on the part of the report relating to
publication said: "In the nature of things, there are two classes of
works which the society is excluded from publishing:

"(1) Works of a costly character, for obvious reasons.

"(2) Works of a distinctly scientific character or such other works
as are beyond the present scope of the society.

"But we are of the opinion that the Society can very properly aid
in the publication of works falling under these two classes. Such aid
in the case of scholarly works is particularly needed and desirable:
and if it be urged that the members as such would receive no advantage from such aid given to the publications of this character, on the
other hand, the society would thus increase its usefulness, and would
also offer a return to the minority of its members for whom such
works are of importance whose publication would thus be rendered
possible. We accordingly recommend to the Publication Committee
that it set aside a sum for subventioning such scholarly publications as
they see fit, preference to be given to the production of American
scholars. In making this recommendation we are but urging the con-

sideration of the second clause of article 2 of the constitution, which places among the objects of the society the fostering of original work by American scholars on the religion, history, and literature of the Jews." This consideration is essentially Jewish—essentially in consonance with the history and principles of a' minority. And this consideration it is that will encourage our brave scholars, who have hitherto sacrificed not only time, labor and energy, but also their own not too abundant means, to produce works of mature learning and original research, works by virtue of which American Jews will fall into line with Jews of every land and age, and in the words of an appeal addressed in behalf of the society to the Jews of the United States, "works whose publication will pay a debt to our country, and increase the consideration in which our neighbors hold us."

That, however, is work for the years to come, and leads us to speak of the plans of the society. In the near future it will give to its members a book of sermons selected from those left to American Judaism as a legacy by one of its greatest spirits—Liebman Adler. The third volume of Graetz will follow, and a translation of essays by the eminent litterateur, Gustave Karpeles, now editor of the *Allgemeine Zeitung des Judenthums*, has already been prepared.   .

But the most important work proposed is first mentioned in the report above quoted in these words: "We look forward to the time when the society will furnish a new and popular English rendition of the book which the Jews have given to the world, the Bible, that shall be the work of American-Jewish scholars." It is this work which is now being approached by the Publication Committee with due care and tact. From among its members, a sub-committee was chosen and intrusted with the task of inviting consulting scholars, with their aid to formulate the *modus operandi* to be adopted in grappling with this truly monumental work. This sub-committee has, as you will remember seeing in the columns of the Jewish press, completed the task laid upon it, and now awaits the action of the Publication Committee. The work thus begun is stupendous, important, holy. Years may pass before it is wholly accomplished. But it is legitimate work for the Society, and once completed will form its charter of incorporation in perpetuity.

One other plan of interest and magnitude is under discussion. It is hoped that the ideas afloat among the members of the Publication Committee may soon crystallize, and that to American Judaism may be given a scientific Quarterly devoted to Jewish science, research and scholarship, as well as to all other spiritual aims of Judaism.

A word remains to be said of the work of the two chief commit-

tees of the Society. The results of the labors of the Publication
Committee are before the public, awaiting its verdict. Of the work
devolving upon the committee, it may be said that those not directly
concerned can have no idea of the amount of time given to the affairs
of the Society by individual active members of this committee. Their
work by no means ceases with the acceptance or rejection of a book,
or the discussions in the course of the frequent committee meetings.
It extends to all the minutiæ of the book-maker's art, and it has been
undertaken and executed, with rare fidelity, by men of wide experience, of tested devotion to Judaism, and of acknowledged attainments
in the field of Jewish literature and general culture.

To the Executive Committee, finally, all credit is due for the success of the Society. By means of its faithful administration of the
finances results great in comparison with the income have been produced. As in the case of the other committee, the work of its members has not been confined to that presented at its quarterly meetings.
Individual members have formed, at their own homes, as at Baltimore,
San Francisco and New York, auxiliary branches which have been
actively at work spreading abroad information about the achievements
of the Society, and have thus won numerous members. They proved
by their success in this direction that theirs is the only way to push
the work of the Society. The membership is now nearly three thousand, a number not before equaled in the annals of literary societies
among the Jews of America, and yet ridiculously small when, on the
one hand, the prosperity, the intelligence and the size of the American
Jewish community are taken into consideration, and, on the other
hand, the broad, all-embracing aims of the Society.

In the words of its President's first appeal, the Jewish Publication
Society of America again appeals to the public: "The cause is good,
the harvest is ripe, the workers are many, and success means a great
step forward for Judaism and for humanity."

TRAINING SCHOOLS.

By PROFESSOR G. BAMBERGER.

It is necessary to resort to radical measures, if we wish to help the poor. Confronted by the great misery of the so-called perishing classes, there is hardly a person of generous nature who does not attempt, at one time or another, to bring succor to the needy through the ordinary instrumentalities of charity. Such efforts have their value and ought on no account to be discouraged; but those who are most earnestly engaged in the cause of charity feel most keenly a lack of real satisfaction in their work. It seems so hopeless a task, so much like pouring water on a hot stone. The evil weed of poverty, when lopped off at the surface, continues to grow with unconquerable malignity from the roots. It were well if one could penetrate to the root itself and extirpate that—if one could help the poor to help themselves. Education is the only means of doing this, and, therefore, all those who have given the subject of human misery careful thought unite in the opinion that education—the best and most thorough education for the people—is what we pre-eminently need. And so one hears on all sides the cry, "Education!" Education is the one radical remedy which will solve these terrible problems. But while every one is ready to cry, "Education!" what is being actually done? we must ask. What steps are being taken to give the poor the right education? People are generally satisfied with having acknowledged the necessity of education, and nothing further is done. Nothing, did I say? Yes, something was done. There are here, in this city of Chicago, a number of such generous men and women who were not satisfied with the proclamation only, but who endeavored to, and succeeded in, establishing a school, the Jewish Training School of Chicago, a school in which such an education is to be given to the children of the poor, fitted and necessary to successfully check the growth of poverty in these quarters. It may seem presumptuous on my part to declare that in this institution mentioned, the looked-for remedy has been found. For the purpose of verifying, or rather illustrating, this statement, I have the pleasure of addressing you.

It must be evident to every thinking mind that the sort of education which the children of the people receive is not satisfactory. I do not wish to enter into any controversy to prove this, as the time allotted is limited. I shall content myself with referring to the opinions of distinguished educators and American writers whose views carry weight. Charles Francis Adams, Jr., W. T. Harris, Francis W. Parker, Felix Adler, Stanley Hall and many others have repeatedly expressed their dissatisfaction with the methods and results of our Common School Education.

A Training School Education differs widely from the Common School Education, and must, if properly carried out, be satisfactory in its results. This was the reason why the founders and supporters of this Training School were not in favor of sending the little children of the poor Refugees to Public School. I must also refrain from showing and proving in what respect the Training School Education is superior to the Public School Education. I shall only show you some of the great advantages such an institution gives to the children, and especially to the children of the Refugees.

In the first place, our Training School is an *educational* institution. We not only instruct, we educate our pupils. We are not satisfied with merely being with them during school hours; we follow them into their homes, we study their home surroundings, become acquainted with our co-educators, the parents; teach and interest them, and not only check by that method the evil influences that may be exercised, but change them into useful helpers for our task. We assemble the parents regularly every month, at which meetings teachers and parents are present, and in which the common sacred cause, the education of their children, is discussed.

Second. Because we take such a deep and sincere interest in them, they will send their children to school, and it is my conviction that fifty per cent of our pupils would not go to school at all if it were not the Training School.

Third. While we had in the first year—1890 to 1891—150 boys who went to the Cheder three to four hours a day, and six hours on Saturdays and Sundays, there were only twenty-four this year, and the time in Cheder was limited to one hour daily.

Fourth. We make it our special task to begin with the care for the physical condition of our pupils. " Cleanliness" is our watchword! We have ample facilities for this department and make the best use of them. Children come to school dirty, filthy and carelessly dressed. We wash them and correct every thing so long until they do it at home. It soon becomes the vital necessity for the child to be clean— a habit—and much is then gained. Parents, especially mothers, frequently complain that their children wash themselves too much, and too often at home, want shoe-blacking for every day's use, a hair-brush and the luxury of a tooth brush, etc. In these children we have then our strongest supporters and in many cases the little ones have favorably changed the conditions at home.

Fifth. Though we do not teach Religion, our school exercises a deep and true religious influence upon children and parents; they are, unbeknown to themselves, constantly imbibing ethical principles and acquiring moral habits from the discipline of the school and the nature of the subjects taught.

Sixth. The workshops especially have their good influence upon the pupils. In these shops they not only learn to better understand and digest the lessons taught in the class-room, but are also prepared for practical life, more especially learn to handle and to love mechanical work, and are thereby drawn away from the usual path of peddling and petit commerce, for which so many of them have a special preference. Our graduates will not become peddlers or junk dealers or paupers. Dr. Stolz, in his report as Secretary of the School, says: " In short, the Jewish Training School goes to the root of Jewish poverty; it kills the germs that produce it, instead of hiding its nakedness for a short time with a gift of money. Relief Societies may make paupers, Training Schools never can. Relief Societies may encourage improvidence, Training Schools teach providence; and we have every reason to believe that the lessons taught the children in our school will react upon the parents, and that in the course of time these children will not only be able to bring them substantial, material assistance, but will also bring cleanliness, order, beauty, and even culture, into the homes that are now uninviting and forbidding."

Seventh. The Training School is so arranged and conducted that not only the brightest and strongest, but also the dullest is made to feel that there is a station in life which he can occupy with credit and profit, and the weakest is made to feel that he need not despair of his weakness.

Our school is now three years old and we have good cause to be satisfied with the visible results in our graduates.

Of the thirty-one graduates of '91, eight returned to take another year of schooling, while of the twenty-three left, four girls became kindergartners, and one boy, Bennie Platchinsky, became the assistant to the teacher in the workshop in our school. Rebecca Aroner, one of the kindergartners, is still with us, assists in the kindergarten in the morning and studies in the Chicago Kindergarten Association with Mrs. Putnam in the afternoon. Bennie Platchinsky has been assistant during the last year in the sloyd department; has continued his literary studies successfully, and is to-day able to teach " wood sloyd " in the primary grades. Of the eighteen left, three are type-setters in the printing offices, two have become farmers, ten are engaged in business houses of this city and the remaining three we have not seen of late, so can not tell what they are doing.

Of the twenty-six of last year—1892—seven returned to take another year's course. The other nineteen are employed as follows : One Louis Platchinsky, is a pupil of the Art Institute, of this city. He is a member of the life class, and Mr. French, director of the Institute, has repeatedly praised Louis' progress and ingenuity. Another boy, Bennie Ellison, was a pupil of the Art School for six months. He is especially efficient in designing and mechanical drawing. He is continuing his studies in the night class since January of this year and is in business during the year. He gives satisfaction in both places. Three of the boys are type-setters, one boy and one girl are learning telegraphy, nine are in business—four of these nine are with Hart, Schaffner & Marx, and the firm seems to be pleased and satisfied with the progress and conduct of the boys. One girl is housekeeping at home and assists her mother ; being a perfect seamstress, she is a great help in the way of sewing the clothes for the children. She is also able to make her own and her mother's garments. We do not know what has become of the remaining two.

Of the twenty-five graduates of this year—1893—all except *four* found positions, the details of which are not yet known to me.

With the Training School is also connected a night school, for both men and women, who felt the need of mental culture and are desirous of acquiring the language of the country, and fitting themselves still further for the task in life. The night school is not an annex, but a necessary complement of the day school.

All show great eagerness to learn, which characterizes men such as one would suppose, on account of their age, to have outgrown the period of instruction. There is no question that those who attend the night sessions carry away with them knowledge which will be immediately available for them in their efforts to maintain themselves and their families.

The night school consists of two departments, male and female. Each department again consists of four classes. The male department receives instruction in the English branches only. The highest class is also taught book-keeping and commercial correspondence. All receive some instruction in the United States history and geography,

22

and are made familiar with the Constitution of the Commonwealth. Two hundred and sixty men were enrolled during the last year; the average attendance was 120; forty were above fifty years of age, sixty-two between thirty and fifty, eighty-four between twenty and thirty, and seventy-four between fourteen and eighteen years of age. All classes assemble four times a week in the evening, from 7:30 to 9:30; respite, 7:45 to 9:45.

The female department has 200 enrolled, with an average attendance of 105; there were only twenty-two above thirty years of age. The rest were girls from fourteen to twenty-two. The pupils of this department, too, are taught in four classes. Each one is compelled to study the elements of the English language. One-third of them took, in addition to English, a course in sewing and dress making, which department is optional. At the end of December thirty-two girls were dismissed from the dress making department who were able to finish a plain dress, waist and all, without any assistance, and all of them found positions in business houses as dress makers, or work in private families as seamstresses.

Ladies and Gentlemen—Allow me to conclude with the question: Has the Common School curriculum provided for all these needs indicated and met in our Training School?

PERSONAL SERVICE.

By Dr. A. Guttman.

I desire to press the stamp of approval upon that which has been said here to-night in behalf of the Jewish poor, and more especially of the Jewish immigrants. Now, it is true, Organized Charity, Jewish Training Schools, Popular Lecture Societies, Social Settlements, all these are comparatively new, they are yet in a state of incipiency; but on America's free soil, and bathed in the sunshine of love and enlightenment, they give fair promise to grow, to thrive, and to ripen into perfection. History is making fast in our time. Every year, we might almost say each day, brings new and wonderful accessions of knowledge. Science, with its marvelous reaches of discovery, its sublime generalizations and daring conjectures, outstrips anticipation and staggers prophecy. Not a province of thought, of knowledge, of action, that does not feel the push and the thrill that is imparted by the awakened spirit of our time. Man is subduing the earth, is slowly eliminating its barbarism and its savagery, and is to make the desert bloom and all the wilderness to blossom as the rose. He is subduing himself; slowly lifting himself to heights of intelligence, of a life illumined and swayed by thought and reason. The spirit of humanity is awakening, and *all* the strata of society, the lowest, the poorest, the most neglected in the past, are to be raised, warmed, enfranchised by its ray.

But how can this be done? How can we Jews, for instance, transform the immigrants coming to us from barbarous Russia, neglected, impoverished, discouraged, into resolute, self-helpful, alert men and women? How can we raise them to the plane of intellectual and moral worth of a true citizenship, and a fellowship of humanity? Can these new needs be met with an antiquated machinery? Can the existing evils be abolished by spasmodic and haphazard methods? No. As in every department of our complex civilization, we are bringing the power of system, of invention, and of organization to our aid, so we must do the same in the field of charity. New conditions require new methods. It is not sufficient that we give bread and coal and money to the poor, but we must give our hand, our heart and soul. It is not enough that we give our share by proxy, but we must give our own self; for it will ever remain true, that the greatest of all gifts that you can make to the poor is the gift of yourself. What is needed to-day, oh, so imperatively needed, is Personal Service. Personal service is the fairy wand which alone can change the shriek of despair into a song of triumph; transform our dependent immigrants into independent citizens, and develop their children into a higher type of manhood and womanhood. You remember what Elisha did with the son of the Shunamite woman. He said to his servant: "Run, take this staff of mine, and put it upon the dead child." And the servant ran and took the staff and put it upon the body of the dead child, but it did not do a bit of good. This expresses the result of charity by proxy.

Then Elisha went and stretched himself upon the boy, with his mouth to his mouth, his eyes to his eyes, and he was brought back to warmth and cheer and love of earthly life.

This expresses the power of Personal Service. If we would awaken the boys and girls of our immigrants to a better and purer life, if we would render them useful to themselves, useful to their parents, and useful to the whole community, we must get nearer to them; we must come in closer touch with them, and serve them with head, heart, and mind.

Time does not permit me to outline to you the sphere of Personal Service Societies, but let me say, that the Sisterhoods, with their "Circles of Ten," which have been recently organized in many of our congregations in the East, West, South, and North, are based upon the principles of Personal Service. These Sisterhoods blossom and bear fruit; they are alive and powerful in many of our larger congregations; and what has been possible in large congregations is also possible in small congregations, for all that is needed is a few women, imbued with the spirit of fidelity, love, and sympathy, and I venture to say such are to be found in every congregation, the smallest not excepted. To woman's loyalty and woman's self-sacrifice the world owes some of its greatest achievements. She has rocked its cradles and soothed its sorrows; she has taught its teachers and trained its heroes; she has wept over its miseries, and been the sunshine of its life, and she will continue to be the angel of mercy, the angel of love, in the midst of human society.

And now, before I conclude, I desire to make one or two practical suggestions.

1. Let the Sisterhoods in our large congregations send forth some

of their able members for the purpose of organizing similar Personal Service Societies in smaller congregations.

2. To the "Sisterhood" of Personal Service should also be added a "Brotherhood" of Personal Service. Not only women, but men too, are called upon to bring their sacrifices of kindness, sympathy, energy, and practical wisdom upon the altar of humanity.

> "If you have any task to do,
> Let me whisper, friend, to you,
> Do it.
>
> If you have any thing to love,
> As a blessing from above,
> Love it.
>
> If you have any thing to give,
> That another's joy may live,
> Give it.
>
> If you know what torch to light,
> Guiding others through the night,
> Light it.
>
> Whether life be bright or drear,
> There's a message sweet and clear,
> Whispered down to every ear,
> Hear it."

With these words ringing in our ears, let us go home, and as years roll by, may we more perfectly learn the lesson of loving, of giving, of serving, of serving the poor, the ignorant, and the suffering; and in serving them, we serve ourselves, we serve the country, we serve the world, and above all, we serve God.

POPULAR LECTURES.

By DR. A. M. RADIN, New York.

"What shall we do for the Russian immigrants?" This is a problem, the solution of which urgently demands our fullest attention. Whether they are desirable or undesirable as immigrants—we must take into consideration that they do not come to our hospitable shores by their own volition, prompted merely by an irresistible desire to emigrate to foreign countries; they come to the land of the free and the noble by compulsion. Expelled from their native country for no fault of their own, but simply on account of their fealty and adherence toward their ancestral faith, do they look for a place of refuge, which they can not possibly obtain in the European countries.

They are now in large numbers among us, and it is our duty to do all in our power for the amelioration of their material, moral, and mental conditions. Not only noble and philanthropic sentiments impose upon us the difficult task to take care of them until they become self-supporting, but practical wisdom, our own honor and social standing in the community at large continually admonish us to make efforts for their moral and mental elevation. We may be disinclined to identify ourselves with them, we may denounce them, we may join the un-American cry, "America only for Americans!" It will be of no avail. We can not deny our close connections to them by indissoluble ties of race and faith. The civilized world, and especially our American fellow-citizens, will make us responsible for their faults and shortcomings. If we, contrary to the historical traditions of our glorious past, should deny our solidarity with them, our brethren in faith, our friends and enemies among the other nations will constantly and emphatically remind us of the same. The saying of our sages, "All Israelites are accountable for each other," is and always will remain an undeniable truth, lasting as long as we should have a Jewish history.

But we have no reason whatever to be ashamed of the Russian immigrants and consequently no cause to denounce them. They became, in spite of the narrow-minded attacks made upon them by Senator Chandler and Dr. Senner, in a comparatively short time, good and useful citizens. They are neither paupers, nor a class of ignorant people; neither do they come hither with the intention of making America only their temporary home, as the Chinese and many of the Italians are doing. They are, as a general rule, peaceable and law-abiding people, loyal toward the public school and the American institutions—by far more than any other foreign element in the Union.

We assist the poor and needy among them in the first years after their landing to our shores, by granting them material help. But charitable institutions and individuals often fail to accomplish the de-sired end. Habitual beggars and undeserving people are sometimes benefited by the mode and method applied by us in dispensing of charity, while thousands of worthy and work-loving immigrants earn their livelihood without appealing to the generosity of their brethren.

Therefore, more useful and more desirable for them than material help and assistance is their moral and intellectual elevation. We should leave the education of their children entirely to the public school. They easily become Americanized with all the faults and virtues of Americans, with all their good peculiarities and bad habits; and children not seldom exercise even a beneficial influence upon their parents.

We must always keep before our eyes the grown-up immigrants. Some of them are naturally bright and gifted and are more or less familiar with the knowledge of Hebrew lore, though they did not enjoy the advantages of a scientific method and training. Nearly all of them are desirous of learning. The main trouble with the majority of the educated among the Russian Jewish immigrants is that they harbor in their minds false notions and conceptions of liberty. They often confound it with licentiousness. In Russia every intelligent man, including even some of the high officials, is a socialist, communist, nihilist, or anarchist. Religion, in the synagogue and in the church as well, consists there in obsolete ceremonies and observances; and men that are endowed with a sound judgment and commence to think for themselves, inevitably must be imbued with aversion and disgust at all religious doctrines and become atheists and agnostics. Alexander v. Humboldt, in his masterwork, "Cosmos," designates the volcanoes as the safety-valves of the earth. Without them, he says, we would be more frequently exposed to earthquakes. And so may we call liberty of the press and freedom of speech the safety-valves of every country. In Russia these safety-valves are tightly closed, and the immediate consequence of this despotic system of government is the disturbing and rebellious spirit that characterizes even in this country a considerable number of the intelligent Russian immigrants and those that are susceptible to liberal views.

This intellectual disease—*sit venia verbo*—can and must be cured by applying the proper remedies, the best of which are popular lectures, not on dry, scientific subjects; for those that wish to study them thoroughly will surely seek and find the proper sources and places, where they can acquire a profound knowledge of chemistry, mathematics, medicine, physics, astronomy, and the like. Select rather practical topics of everyday life. Try to explain to them, in plain language, intelligible to and understood by them, the difference between despotic Russia, the shame and disgrace of modern civilization, and free America, the pride and glory of our enlightened age; that, while in Russia nihilism or anarchism can easily be explained and to a certain extent even justified, it is criminal in this beloved country of ours; that every attempt to defy the law, or to overthrow it by brutal force of an ill-advised and misguided mob, or even the teaching of such a pernicious doctrine, is a danger to our free and noble constitution and must be thoroughly eradicated.

Popular lectures on history, spiced with anecdotes and bon mots, are strongly to be recommended. For the Russian Jews love historical studies and understand them quite well. Draw parallels from the events and occurrences of the past to their present conditions.

Many of the Russian immigrants have brought along with them the false notion that America is a country of swindlers and humbugs, and that immigrants can get rich here only by fraudulent manipulations and transactions. The endeavors of the lecturer should, therefore, be directed toward that end, to prove to them irrefutably that honesty is the best policy in this country, as elsewhere. Tell them the history of the struggles and labors and hardships of the first settlers on this continent, that they might possibly derive the conclusion that only through honest and hard labor, through patience, energy, and perseverance, could they possibly succeed to make a comfortable living and even to accumulate wealth.

Be careful not to hurt their feelings by denouncing them, as a whole, as unclean. Uncleanliness is never the cause of poverty, but the consequence thereof. In crowded quarters, used in daytime as sweating shops and during the night as sleeping-places for boarders, the unfortunate can not possibly observe the rules of cleanliness, as do our moneyed brethren in their palatial residences in the aristocratic quarters of the large cities. My experience in New York City and in other densely populated places of the Union has taught me that the immigrants give up their voluntarily selected ghettos as soon as they can afford to do so and keep themselves clean. But, indirectly, the lecturer may allude to the filthy quarters of the Chinese, Italians, and other nationalities, and they will take a lesson from such examples that cleanliness is next to godliness; that cleanliness of the body is closely connected with purity of the soul. Imbue them with the conviction that the frequent washings of our hands and bodies, prescribed by the rabbinical teachings, were intended to keep us pure and clean in body and soul.

The lecturer should by no means appear before them as if he were standing upon the exalted heights of culture and civilization, and has now descended to them in order to teach the semi-barbarians—as many of the so-called philanthropists choose to call the poor immigrants—morals and refinement. He would never accomplish the purpose he sincerely looks for. They would ridicule his wise instructions by saying: " It is easy for him to speak of all the good qualities which he possesses and in which we are wanting, because he was born and brought up under favorable conditions and surroundings. If he were born in Russia and suffered as much as we did, under the unbearable yoke of poverty and distress, of oppression and humiliation, he would have been much worse than we are."

Speaking of their faults and repulsive manners, the lecturer should not address them with the term " you," but he should rather use the word " we." By identifying himself with them, he would do no harm to himself ; he most decidedly would not fail to find entrance for his admonitions and good advice into their hearts and win their confidence.

The lecturer should make use of the vernacular when he speaks to those immigrants that are already familiar with the knowledge of the English tongue. To address the immigrants in English before they have acquired the knowledge of the same, would be useless, a loss of time and labor. It is true, they shall, and must, and will learn English. But you must first explain to them the necessity of learning the vernacular in a language which is understood by them. A plain and intelligible German, handled with skill, free from all poetical phrases and bombastic terms, is understood by almost all the Russian immigrants.

The popular lectures should contain Biblical and Talmudical quotations, also interpretations of allegorical sayings of our sages which are fully understood and appreciated by the immigrants ; these quotations should be of such a nature that they properly could be applied to their duties and prospects in this country.

The Hebrew-German dialect, the so-called Jüdisch-Deutsch, is un-

justly called jargon; for, as a language spoken by more than six
million Jews, it has the same right to exist as the Bohemian, Slavonic,
Servian, Roumanian, and Bulgarian languages. Nevertheless, should
this dialect under no circumstances be used by the lecturer that addresses the immigrants. The Jüdisch-Deutsch was the badge and
mark of disgrace of our German co-religionists till the beginning of
this century. The immigrants can sooner adapt themselves to modern
culture when we arouse in their minds the ambition of speaking a pure
language and to be benefited by the rich treasures of its literature.

Speaking on religious topics, the lecturer should not appear as the
representative and mouth-piece of orthodox or reform Judaism. He
must try to represent the neutral standpoint of our religion, as based
upon an enlightened faith and pure morality. If he makes himself
the defender of orthodox absurdities, he at once will be denounced by the
free-thinking immigrants. If he allows himself to appear as a reform
advocate, the obscure fanatics will seize the first opportunity to decry
him as an atheist and agnostic, as a hired tool of Christian missionary societies. Leave all ceremonies and observances out of question.
Speak only on the essence of Judaism, for therein prevails no difference of opinion among Jews. Admonish them to observe decency
and decorum in their synagogues in every form of worship and ritual
they find advisable to choose for themselves.

The lecturer should be, if possible, a countryman of theirs, who
was born and brought up under the same conditions and surroundings
with them, but was fortunate enough to receive his education either in
a civilized country of Europe or in America. He should at least be
a man who knows the Russian immigrants thoroughly with all their
good and bad qualities. He has not to speak, but he must understand
their jargon if you choose to so call their language. He must be
familiar with all the conditions, circumstances, and surroundings that
have produced the good and bad qualities, the favorable and unfavor-
able peculiarities of the Russian Jews. A physician can hardly cure
successfully the patient without knowing the cause and nature of the
sickness, without even understanding the language of the patient intrusted to his treatment. He would try to cure his headache while he
suffers from consumption. It is, therefore, a difficult task for a physician to give his medical treatment to infants that are yet unable to
speak. He is mostly compelled to guess the cause and place of his
patient's ailings, and he is not always successful.

The lecturer must, before all, feel himself attached to his immi-
grant brethren with fraternal love and sympathy. Without this at-

tachment he neither will exhaust all his power and energy in their behalf, nor will they submit to his treatment.

Unfortunately, those who stand at the head of our charitable organizations—not even the chief managers of the Baron de Hirsch fund excepted—do not know the true character and nature of the Russian Jew. They often assist the unworthy and refuse their support to those that are deserving. Though they are noble and generous enough not to hate the Russian Jew immigrants, they do not love them either. For that reason our charities do not accomplish that amount of good that could be expected from them, and sometimes are they an utter failure.

UNION OF YOUNG ISRAEL.

By S. ELDRIDGE.

WHAT THE YOUNG PEOPLE CAN AND SHOULD DO FOR JUDAISM.

Young Israel is awakening to its responsibilities.

This age of Congresses and organization is auspicious for the movement. We have our Y. M. H. A., our prospective Jewish Chautauqua, and the Jewish Publication Society, and other organized associations, striving to aid and uphold Judaism. Then why can not the young people organize a Young People's Religious Hebrew Endeavor Society, for the practice of charity and the advancement of Judaism, through their individual efforts and by their own methods.

About two years ago, through the columns of the Sabbath Visitor, the idea of a young people's religious society for American Judaism was advanced by one of the contributors to that paper. And through his efforts the idea was enlarged and promulgated.

The week of August, 1893, was arranged to perfect the national organization of that order, the results of which are now known to all. The objects of the Association are set forth and explained in this preamble: Whereas, the cultivation of morality, the advancement of the Jewish tenets of religion, and the practice of charity stand prominently among the duties of all Jews; and whereas, the most beneficial effects results from the efforts and acts of the young men and women of Israel; whereas, the establishment of an order based upon the Jewish teachings and for the cause of charity and the promulgating the tenets of Judaism to the world through young Israel is highly commended and believed to be productive of much good to Judaism and a vast benefit to all humanity; and whereas a higher standard in the code of morals, and the practice of charity and the disseminating the Jewish doctrine are greatly to be desired, therefore an Association to be known as the Young People's Hebrew Endeavor Association is hereby established, constituted, and ordained, and we, the founders thereof, do publish and declare for its government this constitution.

The National Association is in a sense supreme, being composed of auxiliary societies or branches. Each branch will be a separate, independent, self-governing society, conformable to the laws of the National Association. The National Society has its rules and regulations, and no changes can be made unless by a vote of a majority of the Branches. The purposes of the National Association is to meet and confer concerning different modes and methods that will benefit the religion at large and the Branches. For instance, a paper devoted to the order can and will be sustained by them.

It is even possible that the Union Sunday-school work might be successfully taken up by the National Order, so Jewish literature can be placed in the hands of all Jewish children at a nominal sum. And many other works will be in the scope of this part of the order, of which I will not now enter into details.

The Branches, which are the strength and hope of the order, is where the main work for our religion is to be done, and where the young people will be permitted to do active religious work.

The Branches should be composed of only earnest and serious workers for the advancement of Judaism, irrespective of age.

In seeking members you should look to the fact that they will be congenial, and if not congenial, make it so for them. It would not be a bad idea to make each one sign a pledge that he or she will attend meetings regularly and take part in the exercises and perform his or her duty.

Each Branch adopts its own program for their respective meetings, and also by-laws, so as not to conflict with the constitution and by-laws of the National Order. In order to make my plan clearer I will suggest an ideal program, as follows: After you have elected your officers, do not permit your offices to be badges of distinction, but only means by which you can better serve our cause. Let the President appoint some one to conduct the exercises for the following meeting, and also appoint an assistant in case of the leader's absence.

Exercises: Open with a song; Scripture reading by leader; song. Have a religious question or character for discussion and let each one express a thought on the subject. After all have spoken, have a song. Do not have the exercises over an hour. The program, of course, can be varied to suit the wishes of the members of the different Branches. When this short religious service is over, bring up the business before the society, which will be the report of different committees, sickness, death, and relief committee, which will report all the needy and indigent that have come under the observation of the committee, and relief be granted; membership committee, those on the lookout for new members; extension committee, those conferring with other Branches, with a view of extending the

order; Sunday-school and decoration committees, one to assist the
Superintendent of the Sunday-school and get new members, and the
other to assist in decorating the Synagogue on needed occasions;
entertainment committee, to get up an entertainment for each meeting, and also entertainments for raising funds for charity, and such
other committees as the wants of the Branches will demand.

After the business session is over resolve the meeting into a committee of the whole, and spend the time in meeting each other, and by
kind words and gentle expression make the young and old, rich and
poor, feel that they are amongst friends, and then spend a few moments pleasantly together. But do not let the "social feature" be
the controlling element. Let the downfall of other organizations on
this account prove a warning to us. That an organization of this nature is practical and necessary for American Judaism, has been fully
verified by the progress that our organization has made.

Hampered on all sides, receiving no encouragement from where
encouragement should come, our ministry, we have succeeded in arranging a National Meeting at Chicago, and have organized Branches
of the order in the following cities: Chicago, Ill.; St. Louis, Mo.;
Cincinnati, O.; Springfield, Ill.; Baltimore, Md.; Altoona, Penn.;
Jefferson, Tex.; and Sherman, Tex. All the Branches are making
good progress.

A society of this nature is needed in America especially for the
advancement of Judaism, for the practice of charity by the young
folks. And it will bring systematic religious work and exercises in
communities where otherwise religious spirit would be dormant.

To accomplish any thing to-day, it can only be done by organized
systematic work. Every vocation of life and all religious works are
now so conducted. There has always been a deficiency in our mode
of conducting our religious works in excluding the efforts of the children in behalf of religion. It is true we have our Sabbath Schools,
but that in a sense is peculiar to itself.

It has been suggested that the cause of this deficiency was because
heretofore no auxiliary aid was needed, and all religious work emanated from the synagogue or temple independently.

But since then many changes have taken place, and there is now
a very urgent demand for such work for Judaism. A society of young
people is especially needed in America for the advancement of Judaism by the young folks.

Give me a community of young workers, and religious torpidness
and indifference will not thrive. The organization should have unity

of action and purpose, and in its ranks it should know no orthodox, no conservative, no reform, but only members of the association with the sole purpose of doing good and helping our fellow-man.

With an organization of this nature as a means, much good can be done directly for Judaism. For here the young people can exercise originality and independence in religious matters. They can study the teachings of our religion, and instill within their own breasts that grand thought "that God is the fountain and first cause of all existence, and that we must love Him with all our heart, soul, and might," and in loving God there lies the secret of all our duties.

A study of the history of our nation can be pursued with great advantage, and the Bible can be properly and advantageously studied.

It is a noticeable fact that the young Jews of to-day seem to think their religious duties are at an end after leaving the Sabbath School, and that at a very tender age. This organization would be of great aid to the Sabbath School, and they could furnish scholars and teachers from their ranks, and aid the Superintendent in many ways.

The young people could practice active charity by visiting the sick and afflicted. Wholesome Jewish literature could be placed in the hands of those poor unfortunates who are denied that great pleasure. A national children's day could be instituted by them, by which means they could bring the sweetest of all offerings, a child's devotion. They could assist in decorating the synagogue on many of our beautiful fasts and feasts.

By beginning early in their religious work, a renewed love and admiration will be instilled in the hearts of the younger generation, and a grander impetus will be given to our religion.

With the children of to-day representing the learning and advancement of thousands of years back, serving Judaism with its eternal and ennobling principles, great will be the future in store for Judaism. And by the proper adherence to its principles, we will give to the world men of thought and of action and women of gentleness and of sweet influence.

We hope to place in every city, every town, and every hamlet one of these societies. Then no more will you hear the cry, no religious instruction, no Rabbi, no temples except on special occasions. This is the first combined effort of Jewish boys and girls to organize themselves into a religious body for the advancement of our blessed religion. Its growth and work is not to be confined to this continent, but we want it eventually to be welcomed and hailed with delight wherever any of our co-religionists reside.

The success and future of the organization depends on the encourment that we will receive from our ministers.

To the Jewish ministry, I consign it to your careful keeping and attention, hoping it will grow under your management.

Will you accept the charge?

WHAT ORGANIZED FORCES CAN DO FOR JUDAISM.

By RABBI HENRY BERKOWITZ, PHILADELPHIA.

The first three sessions of the Congress have been devoted properly to an exposition of doctrine. The Mother of Religions lifts up her voice in the hearing of her children, she rejoices with a mother's joy in their gathering together. She recalls the basic teachings of all religions—"There is a God." She emphasizes anew the distinctive injunction of Israel—"God is One." She sets herself at once to the task of reconciliation. Old misunderstandings, born of the ill-will of ages, are to be effaced; the wrongs of centuries, over which with bleeding heart and aching soul she has brooded so long in anguish, are at last to be righted. The first effort has naturally and spontaneously been directed to setting forth the religious and moral doctrines of our faith that our brethren of the church, of the mosque or shrine —all children of God—may know that we are for them not against them; that they are with us in the one-overshadowing and all-impelling motive of building up the righteous life.

Now, after the theoretical let us begin to consider the practical.

Our religious organizations—our moral forces—have become the property of the religious world. Church, Cathedral and Mosque trace their lineage to the Synagogue; use its incomparable text-book, the Bible; have adopted its ceremonialism, imbibed its spirit. Therefore, we pass on at once to consider educational forces, placing the primary emphasis on these in accordance with the Jewish maxim "תַּלְמוּד תּוֹרָה כְּנֶגֶד כֻּלָּם," "Education precedes all else."

In the so-called "Histories of Education" but scant notice is taken of the contribution of the Jews. And this notice is limited as a rule to the products of "the Biblical era." Nevertheless, it is true that a continuous record of great importance and undoubted worth has been inscribed in the annals of mankind by Jewish educators. The so-called "New Education," in very many of its principles and methods, is the Old Education of Judaism. Some of the greatest names in the history of educational development and progress are the

23

quaint and unknown names of the Rabbis who were by title and in life pre-eminently the *Teachers of Men.*

Two duties confront us to-day: To make known to our modern schoolmen the contribution of the Jewish Schools to education, and to bring the systems and disciplines of the modern schoolmen into fuller appreciation and practice within the organized forces of Jewish education.

The first of these duties is still all to be done. The latter we have been and are seeking to fulfill with increasing zest and success in the elementary work of our Religious Schools for children, and in the higher seminary education of our Rabbinical Colleges.

It is in the field of the systematic popular education that we are as yet derelict. After the religious school we have virtually nothing educational excepting for the specialist, the Rabbinical student. The normal school for teachers is a sadly missing desideratum, and the needs are not yet met of the general reader who is eager, or who should be made eager, to know of the history, the language, the literature which is the vehicle and product of Jewish thought, hope and life.

To bring Jewish knowledge to the people, to cast the light of information into the prevailing darkness is our most urgent duty. This is the cause I have come to champion.

I speak for the cause of popular education. There is no method provided, for either Jew or non-Jew, by which he may acquaint himself with Jewish history and literature. As yet this knowledge is the property of the few, It should become the knowledge of the multitudes. Objection has been made to such cheapening of knowledge. It is the glory of America, in contrast with Russia, that knowledge is cheap here, it belongs to all the people. Who shall dare to say that knowledge is to be confined to a certain class! Nay, let those who thirst come and drink of the waters of learning, and those who are hungry come and partake of the bread of life.

We need a system of popular education on Jewish subjects. True, we have our Young Men Hebrew Associations and Auxiliary Literary Societies of all names and all kinds. I should be the last to depreciate, by one iota, the worth of these organizations. My purpose is, if possible, to lend them a helping hand and aid them. It is well known to you who have had experience in these societies, that whenever they flourish, it is, as a rule, by the self-sacrifice of some one individual, some one who is willing to be the scapegoat, do the work, lay out the plans, and see that they are carried out. There is too little system, no bond of union, no conscious motive to unfailingly impel. Therefore these societies usually run off into social gatherings. To supply these needs and infuse into these organizations plan, motive, and method, has been the study of many. For a number of years, I have been casting about in my mind what could be done, have been looking over the methods of other denominations to learn how they succeeded, as they do unquestionably succeed, in winning the interest and holding the enthusiastic devotion of their young people to the cause of religion.

The best I know of is an institution most thoroughly American, most effective in its methods, well known under the title: "*The Chautauqua Literary and Scientific Circle.*" I have placed in your hands copies of a circular in which is set forth the object and purpose of this society. I want to induce you to try the method recommended by the Chautauqua Literary and Scientific Circle. Our purpose is not to segregate from our fellow-men, but truly to unite with all others, irrespective of their creeds, in the great work of education. Chautauqua claims to stand on this broad foundation. It has welcomed us with great generosity and broadmindedness, and it is a source of great joy to many that there is to be created a " Department of Jewish Studies " in the Chautauqua System of Education. There may be some here who are not familiar with this Chautauqua movement. I will briefly state its object for the benefit of such. It originated in a gathering of Sunday-school teachers at Lake Chautauqua, N. Y. It was organized to supply the crying need of teachers in religious schools. Out of a small beginning grew an institution of learning which seeks to supply the needs of all classes, ages, and talents, beginning with the youngest boys and girls and directing their minds into ever widening channels of knowledge, and supplying the needs of the old as well as the young. Aid is given especially to busy people, and the suggestion is that from three-fourths to one hour's reading, alone or in home circles or local gatherings, will enable a person to successfully carry through a course of four years' study. In the Summer time, the Assembly meets at Chautauqua Lake. This is an institution to gladden the heart of any lover of learning. I am able to speak from personal observation of the work done there. Among their teachers are professors from universities such as John Hopkins University, Yale, Harvard, Ann Arbor. The school has sixty classes— among these I noted three in Hebrew and one in Arabic; besides, there are specialties in all kinds of art work, scientific work, combining delightful outdoor pursuits with most delightful educational advantages. During two months every summer this work at Chautauqua is carried on. Men of note and ability bring there the result of their learning, experience, and travel, and detail it to all there in the most charming manner. During the winter months, the readings enable persons who have not had the advantage of an education to study at home, at the same time to make the family life mean something, by gathering the parents and children together in common educational interests. A Monthly Magazine is furnished, which fully advises people and supplies all needed information on the readings to those who have not access to public libraries or time to consult books of reference. In this way every thing that can be conceived of to enable people to educate themselves is done. The great result has been that thousands of people have been led to educate themselves. Among the number— fifty thousand graduates—there are not only young men and women of eighteen, but those of all ages up to seventy and eighty. All these have passed through the Golden Gate during August of each year, as a token of their having finished the course of reading and taken the certificates and seals of honor.

Now, we desire to attempt something of this kind. It is true, Chautauqua is Protestant, but the Catholics, with all their magnificent conservatism, have not hesitated to go there to study its plans and adopt them for their constituents. Shall we not be as ready to learn and as eager to apply instruction?

This is the plea I make. Let us adopt the Chautauqua plan. Its officials have volunteered to expunge all Christian readings for Jewish readers; the one book on Christianity is to be displaced by a book for Jewish readers, selected from the great store-house of Jewish learning. In addition to this, special courses shall be arranged for those who wish to pursue the study of Jewish history and literature. This department will be under some qualified instructor, a Jew, who shall outline the readings. Most important, a course of study for Sabbath School teachers shall be arranged. Also, a course in Hebrew and other branches, as the work may grow.

It is suggested to me that the Jewish people should not be committed to any one system. I respond, in championing Chautauqua: Nothing better is yet known to me. When something better appears, we shall be found, I trust, to have kept ourselves open-minded and open-hearted enough to eagerly seize upon it. In the meantime, I have taken upon myself, in the City of Philadelphia, to organize a circle. A formal contract has been entered into for the establishment of such a Department of Jewish Studies in the Chautauqua System of Education.

There are those who are eager for something of this kind in every community. I desire these circulars to be freely distributed, that we may place the subject before the Jewish people at large. Let us go forth from this Congress feeling that we have come here not merely to cry out against the evils Israel has suffered through all the ages, and declare again and again to those about us "We are your brethren," but to prove it by our own liberality. Let us not theorize simply on the agreements of religious people, but join hands in reality for the organization and maintenance of educational forces. As other religions are every-where made accessible to the student and the general reader—let us make Judaism accessible to all—remove the reproach of a false exclusiveness which is upon us. Drawing nearer together, we will accomplish the assured result that as Jews and Judaism become really known, popular errors and misapprehensions will fall away, prejudice will receive its quietus, and Jew and Gentile learn in truth that all men are brothers. Let us say practically to our friends, "Jews we are, Christians you are, yet brothers all of us and united in this grand work of Education."

THE SOCIAL SETTLEMENT.

By PROF. CHARLES ZEUBLIN, University of Chicago.

- -

Past environment, however disagreeable and repulsive, often confers on its subject a willingness to remain in like environment. The inheritance of centuries of persecution has led the Jew to adopt voluntarily as his home the Ghetto, into which he was so cruelly forced by stronger hands in ages past. Yet the adoption is not wholly voluntary. Segregation has become a law of life. The protection which association once held out to him against some of his religious persecutors he needs now against the industrial tyrants even in this land of refuge. Yet in his ignorance he is compelled to associate with the weak, and the spirit which might be helpful becomes a menace.

The problems of the age are intensified in the Chicago Ghetto. There we find the great race question: rapid multiplication of human beings of like temperament, habits, religion, language, in the midst, and yet not part of, another nation of different characteristics. There is the religious question: old forms preserved whose functions have ceased, and whose maintenance hinders progress. There is also the political puzzle of the Republic: a people familiar with other institutions exercising the right of suffrage without knowledge, or abstaining from any share in the government through suspicions formed under despotism. There, too, is the labor problem: what share shall the worker have in his product?—the chief question of the age, the solution of which shall solve all other problems. The Jew of the Ghetto is not only unskilled, he is not only physically weak, *he is the scapegoat of commercialism.* The sweater claims his stunted growth, his technical ignorance, his untiring perseverance. The capitalist puts his dirty work on the Jewish middleman. The latter enslaves his fellows. It is not enough that this age should perpetuate the indignities of past ages—Jew oppresses Jew. Many into whose lukewarm hearts a drop of humanitarianism has filtered from the liberal pulpits, refrain from oppressing, but despise. A little handful of the faithful show brotherly interest; of this limited number, the majority manifest sympathy by proxy.

What is to be done to make the Jew of the slums more of a man, less of an oriental? Four things: give employment to the industrious, decent homes to the deserving, intellectual opportunity to the ambitious, a social ideal to every one.

First—*Employ the industrious.* If one might judge by tradition, this would mean that every Jew in the community should have employment. There are doubtless examples in the Ghetto of those unwilling to work for society or self. It might even be asked concerning these unfortunates, whether intermittent employment and the speculative character of modern industries had not been the cause of negligence and indifference. But the vast majority of the indigent Jews have been forced to the wall by the irresistible power of *laissez faire.* The disgrace is society's, and the first element of reform is a provision of the means to earn a livelihood.

Second—*Give decent homes to the deserving.* One of the greatest curses of the Ghetto is the lack of good sanitation and the ignorance of hygienic laws. If the Mosaic code, designed for nomad life, could be expanded for use in a municipality, the religious nature of the people would make them seek healthful surroundings. It is a commonly quoted fact that the poor of the slums pay as much or more per cubic foot for their contracted, squalid surroundings as the rich of the avenues. This condition appears more horrible when one learns that many of these wretched homes are owned by the well-to-do and "respectable." The most persistent efforts of philanthropists can not teach people to observe hygienic laws when living in hovels. A safe and helpful investment would be the erection of blocks of model houses. Wealthy Jews could find here a means of helping their fellows, which might perhaps entail more personal effort than giving to the charity collector, but which would repay themselves economically and the inhabitants of the houses hygienically and socially. Blocks of " model" tenements would not meet the wants of the community. The deserving do not usually find homes there, and the large population which gathers in such buildings is generally in a worse condition than in their former shanties. The district needs homes.

Third—*Give intellectual opportunity to the ambitious.* No class of immigrants has as high intellectual qualifications as the Russian Jew. No class uses so faithfully the opportunities at hand. From the Talmud devotee to the scientific socialist, the development of the mind is a common ambition. The gatherings in the synagogues, the attendance at the evening classes of the Jewish Training School, the membership in the various clubs of Hull House, the groups in the Kosher restaurants, the agitation meetings of the socialists, all testify to this desire for knowledge. A larger proportion of useful citizens will be found among the young Russian Jews than any other nationality, if they are offered the needed opportunities.   Herein is one of the greatest demands for intelligent, sympathetic helpers from among the educated.

Fourth—*Give a social ideal to every one.*   Already many inhabitants of the Ghetto are more fortunate than their better situated fellow Jews, for they have not yet accommodated themselves to the false economic divisions of our "civilization." Unfortunately, the native American Jew often accepts the evil with the good in the existing system.   He even multiplies distinctions by adding to the breach between capital and labor, between Sephardim and Ashkenazim, another between the German and Russian Jew.   Such a difference can be neither Jewish nor American, it is Philistine.   Among a nation of priests there can be no class lines.   What the resident of the Ghetto has to forget is the difference between Jew and Gentile.   No social ideal can be realized without this.   Business integrity is impossible while the "brother" and the "stranger" receive different treatment. No true municipal or national life can be known while the Jew remains an oriental among occidentals.   More significant still, no social regeneration is possible while Jewish capitalist and Jewish laborer are opposed.   A social ideal can only be realized by affording every member of the Ghetto a chance to work, to have a home, to enjoy intellectual development, to feel himself a member of the social organism, with its privileges and duties.   No existing institution or effort can furnish these opportunities.   If they are possible at all, it will be through the co-operation of all existing and available forces.

Dr. Stolz's suggestion of the need of a Jewish Hull House, a social settlement, indicates the first step to be taken.   An attractive house located in the midst of the needy district, occupied by educated, devoted, broad-minded young men or women, or both, can prove the nucleus of these good works.   It can become the center of social life for the neighborhood.   Its residents can make themselves the friends of the community.   The need of each household can then be investigated by friends instead of strangers, the sanitary evils can be seen by sympathizers instead of perfunctory officials, clubs can be organized among the young and old, which shall promote the physical and intellectual life of all.   A Socialist Society will not be feared when composed of friends instead of unknown or unfavorably known agitators.   The real workers for the welfare of the district will be recognized when a neighborly feeling has removed distrust.   An employment bureau, a co-operative tailor shop, an emigration committee, even such common enterprises as a day-nursery or a reading-room, will be found possessing new possibilities when conducted by friends.

Those who are willing to make investments for the good of the neighborhood will find the way made easy by their own friends in the district.

Is the idea of a Jewish social settlement utopian? Not at all. Two young men have already signified their willingness to live in the Ghetto, and a determined group of friends is rallying to this newest and surest way to help one of the most needy yet hopeful factors in our municipality.

RELIEF SOCIETIES.

By MR. HENRY L. FRANK.

———

I hardly think I shall realize the high expectations set upon my ability to enlighten you on the very important subject of relief work. I shall not, in my remarks, dwell so much upon relief work in general as upon its relation to societies of other communities. In this connection there is one vital question which pushes itself to the foreground, namely, the Transportation Question. By this I mean the journeyings of the shiftless and their transference from one place to another by the aid of local relief societies.

The United Hebrew Charities of this city sent out invitations to a number of Jewish communities, principally of the larger cities, to discuss this important subject with us, and see what means can be devised to allay the evil. Some answered, some did not even deign to answer. Last evening there was a good deal said about religious indifference. Some of the reverend gentlemen complained about this, and justly so. But not only in the sphere of religion and political and social matters does this indifference manifest itself, in the domain of charity also it exerts its baneful influence. Allowance might be made for the disturbed condition of business, but our invitations were sent out before the panic had convulsed the business world, and thus we can ascribe the non-participation in a charity congress to nothing but general apathy.

I have jotted down just a few things bearing upon the subject of organization which, it seems to me, it would be well to bear in mind. Without co-operation on the part of the larger communities the task of checking pauperism is well-nigh hopeless. In order to trace the latter, to learn something of its antecedents, we must have the help of other relief societies. As between these and ourselves it means reciprocity pure and simple. Why should one community unload its undesirable dependents upon another? And why should thousands of dollars be expended for railroad fares in the useless endeavor to get rid of paupers? Ordinary safeguards would be the ascertainment of places of residence of applicant, the assistance rendered him by any local society, and length of sojourn. Also whether the applicant can show that any relative or friend at a distant place have promised to aid him before transportation is granted him. In fact, these supposed friends should be corresponded with before any steps are taken to change his domicile. I claim that through these precautions the useless expense of transportation can be minimized. I have gathered some data in order to bring more forcibly to your notice what this item costs. I have gone back to the year 1889 :

From 1889 to 1890 the United Hebrew Charities of this city
laid out for transportation (inclusive of some resident
poor to foreign countries)...................................... $1,034 95
From 1890 to 1891 .... 1,013 40
From 1891 to 1892 (108 transient cases)................ .... 1,593 75
    (36 transients received in cash, $113.50.)

Our collections in the first two years cited were about $14,000 each year ; in the last year they were about $20,000. We are thus nearing the ten per cent mark of total contributions. The figures given are from the printed reports issued annually. I could have wished a little more clearness in these (out of the material at hand I had to make the best). By resident poor, I should add, we mean such as have been living here six months or over. What the outlay for transients will be for 1892 to 1893 I can not state. Suffice it to say, that from obtainable data we can safely assume that it will not fall short of that of the previous year.

Inasmuch as the paupers prey upon every community they get into, it is highly necessary that a national organization be formed. Through it we can limit indiscriminate alms-giving. Not before people are made to understand that their money is thrown away will these indiscriminate bestowals cease. Every ten or twenty cents given to the undeserving means that much taken from the deserving. Whilst we ought not help swell the dividends of the railroad companies, we are, in justice to Chicago, compelled to engage in the shipment and re-shipment of the transients.

I have, in the foregoing, merely outlined the essential features and benefits of organization. May I ask the Rabbis assembled here to agitate the subject in their congregations ? I feel the responsibility resting upon me, a layman, in attempting to exhort Rabbis. But these are strange times, and I hope I shall be forgiven.

GENERAL.

THE VOICE OF THE MOTHER OF RELIGIONS ON THE SOCIAL QUESTION.*

By RABBI H. BERKOWITZ, D.D., OF PHILADELPHIA.

In this assembly of so many of her spiritual children, in the midst of the religions which have received from her nurture and loving care, Judaism, the fond mother may well lift up her voice and be heard with reverent and affectionate attention. It has been asked: "What has Judaism to say on the social question?"

From earliest days she has set the seal of sanctity on all that that question involves. From the very first she proclaimed the dignity, nay, the duty of labor by postulating God, the Creator, at work and setting forth the divine example unto all men for imitation, in the command: "Six days shalt thou labor and do all thy work." Industry is thus hallowed by religion, and religion in turn is made to receive the homage of industry in the fulfillment of the ordinance of Sabbath rest. Judaism thus came into the world to live in the world, to make the world more heavenly. Though aspiring unto the heavens she has always trod firmly upon the earth, abiding with men in their habitations, ennobling their toils, dignifying their pleasures. Through all the centuries of her sorrowful life, she has steadfastly striven with her every energy to solve, according to the eternal law of the eternally righteous, every new phase of the ever-recurring problems in the social relationships of men.

When the son of Adam, hiding in the dismal covert of some primeval forest, heard the accusing voice of conscience in bitter tones upbraiding him, he defiantly made reply: "Am I my brother's keeper?" then the social conflict began. To the question then asked, Judaism made stern reply in branding with the guilt mark of Cain every transgression of human right. From then until now, unceasingly through all the long and trying centuries, she has never wearied in lifting up her voice to denounce wrong and plead for right, to brand the oppressor and uplift the oppressed. Pages upon pages of her Scriptures, folio upon folio of her massive literature, are devoted to the social question in its whole broad range and full of maxims, precepts, injunctions, ordinances and laws aiming to secure the right adjustment of the affairs of men in the practical concerns of every day.

---

* Should have been placed in section, "State and Society."

In the family, in the community, in the state, in all the forms of social organization, inequalities between man and man have arisen which have evoked the contentions of the strong and the weak, the rich and the poor, the high and the low. Against the iniquity of self-seeking, Judaism has ever protested most loudly, and none the less so against the errors and evils of an unjust self-sacrifice. "Love thyself," she says, "this is natural, this is axiomatic, but remember it is never of itself a moral injunction. Egoism as an exclusive motive is entirely false, but altruism is not therefore exclusively and always right. It likewise may defeat itself, may work injury and lead to crime. The worthy should never be sacrificed for the unworthy. It is a sin for you to give your hard earned money to a vagabond and thus propagate vice, as much as it is sinful to withhold your aid from the struggling genius whose opportunity may yield to the world undreamed-of benefits."

In this reciprocal relation between the responsibility of the individual for society, and of society for the individual, lies one of Judaism's prime characteristics. She has pointed the ideal in the conflict of social principles by her golden precept, "Thou shalt love thy neighbor as thyself—I am God" (Leviticus xix, 18). According to this precept she has so arranged the inner affairs of the family that the purity, the sweetness and tenderness of the homes of her children have become proverbial.

"Honor thy father and thy mother" (Ex. xx, 12).

"The widow and the orphan thou shalt not oppress" (Ex. xxii, 22).

"Before the hoary head shalt thou rise and shalt revere the Lord thy God" (Lev. xix, 32).

"And thou shalt teach them diligently unto thy children" (Deut. vi, 7).

These, and hundreds of like injunctions, have created the institutions of loving and tender care which secure the training and nurture, the education and rearing of the child, which sustain the man and the woman in rectitude in the path of life, and with the staff of a devout faith guide their downward steps in old age to the resting-place "over which the star of immortality sheds its radiant light."

Judaism sets education before all things else and knows but one word for charity—Zedakah, i. e., Justice. She has made the home the basis of the social structure, and has sought to supply the want of a home as a just due to every creature, guarding each with this motive, from the cradle to the grave. With her sublime maxim, "Love thy neighbor as thyself—I am God," Judaism set up the highest ideal of society as a human brotherhood under the care of a divine Fatherhood. According to this ideal Judaism has sought, passing beyond the environments of the family, to regulate the affairs of human society at large. "This is the book of the generations of men"—was the caption of Genesis, indicating as the Rabbis taught, that all men, without distinction of race, caste or other social difference, are entitled to equal rights as being equally the children of one Creator. The social ideal was accordingly the sanctification of men unto the noblest in the injunction to the "priest-people:" "Holy shall ye be, for I, the Lord your God, am holy" (Ex. xix, 22).

The freedom of the individual was the prime necessary consequence of this precept. Grandly and majestically the Mosaic legislation swept aside all the fallacies which had given the basis to the heartless degradation of man by his fellowman. Slavery stood forever condemned when Israel went forth from the bondage of Egypt. Labor then for the first time asserted its freedom, and assumed the dignity which at last the present era is vindicating with such fervor and power. Judaism established the freedom to select one's own calling in life irrespective of birth or other conditions. For each one a task according to his capacities was the rule of life. The laborer was never so honored as in the Hebrew Commonwealth. The wage system was inaugurated to secure to each one the fruits of his toil. It was over the work of the laboring man that the master had control, not over the man. Indeed the evils of the wage system were scrupulously guarded against in that the employer was charged by the law as by conscience to have regard for the physical, moral and spiritual well-being of his employees and their families.

To the solution of all the problems, which under the varying conditions of the different lands and different ages, always have arisen and always will arise the Jewish legislation in its inception and development affords an extraordinary contribution. It has studiously avoided the fallacies of the extremists of both the communistic and individualistic economic doctrines. Thus it was taught: He that saith, "What is mine is thine, and what is thine is mine" (communism), he is void of a moral concept. He that saith, "What is mine is mine and what is thine is thine," he has the wisdom of prudence. But some of the sages declare that this teaching too rigidly held oft leads to barbarous cruelties. He that saith, "What is mine is thine and what is thine shall remain thine," he has the wisdom of the righteous. He that says that, "What is mine is mine and what is thine is also mine," he is utterly Godless. (Pirke Aboth, v, 13.)

24

Judaism has calmly met the wild outbursts of extremists of the anti-poverty nihilistic types with the simple confession of the fact which is a resultant of the imperfections of human nature: "The needy will not be wanting in the land" (Deut. xv, 11). The brotherly care of the needy is the common solicitude of the Jewish legislatures and people in every age. Their neglect or abuse evokes the wrath of prophet, sage and councilor with such a fury that even to-day none but the morally dead can withstand their eloquence. The effort of all legislation and instruction was directed to a harmonization of these two extremes.

The freedom of the individual was recognized as involving the development of unlike capacities. From this freedom all progress springs. But all progress must be made, not for the selfish advantage of the individual alone, but for the common welfare. "That thy brother with thee may live" (Lev. xxv, 36). Therefore, private property in land or other possessions was regarded as only a trust, because every thing is God's, the Father's, to be acquired by industry and perseverance by the individual, but to be held by him only to the advantage of all.

To this end were established all the laws and institutions of trade, of industry, and of the system of inheritance, the code of rentals, the jubilee year that every fiftieth year brought back the land which had been sold into the original patrimony, the seventh or Sabbatical year, in which the lands were fallow, all produce free to the consumer, the tithings of field and flock, the loans to the brother in need without usury, and the magnificent system of obligatory charities, which still hold the germ of the wisdom of all modern scientific charity. "Let the poor glean in the fields" (Lev. xix, 10), and gather through his own efforts what he needs, *i. e.*, give to each one not support, but the opportunity to secure his own support.

A careful study of these Mosaic-Talmudic institutions and laws is bound more and more to be recognized as of untold worth to the present in the solution of the social question. True, these codes were adapted to the needs of a peculiar people, homogeneous in character, living under certain conditions and environments which probably do not now exist in exactly the same order anywhere. We can not use the statutes, but their aim and spirit, their motive and method we must adopt in the solution of the social problem even to-day. Consider that the cry of woe which is ringing in our ears now was never heard in Judea. Note that in all the annals of Jewish history there are no records of the revolts of slaves such as those which afflicted the world's greatest empire, and under Spartacus threatened the national safety, nor any uprisings like those of the Plebeians of Rome, the Demoi of Athens, or the Helots of Sparta; no wild scenes like those of the Paris Commune; no procession of hungry men, women and children crying for bread, like those of London, Chicago and Denver. Pauperism, that specter of our country, never haunted the ancient land of Judea. Tramps were not known there.

Because the worst evils which afflict the social body to-day were unknown under the Jewish legislation, we may claim that we have here the pattern of what was the most successful social system that the world has ever known. Therefore does Judaism lift up her voice and call back her spiritual children, that in her bosom they may find comfort and rest. "Come back to the cradle of the world, where wisdom first spake," she cries, "and learn again the message of truth that for all times and unto all generations was proclaimed through Israel's precept, 'Love thy neighbor as thyself, for I am God'" (Lev. xix, 18).

The hotly contested social questions of our civilization are to be settled neither according to the ideas of the capitalist nor those of the laborer; neither according to those of the socialist, the communist, the anarchist or the nihilist; but simply and only according to the eternal laws of morality, of which Sinai is the loftiest symbol. The guiding principles of all true social economy are embodied in the simple lessons of Judaism. As the world has been redeemed from idolatry and its moral corruption by the vital force of Jewish ideas so can it likewise be redeemed from social debasement and chaos.

Character is the basic precept of Judaism. It claims as the modern philosopher declares (Herbert Spencer) that there is no political alchemy by which you can get golden conduct out of leaden instincts. Whatever the social system it will fail, unless the conscience of men and women are quick to heed the imperative orders of duty and to the obligations and responsibilities of power and ownership. The old truth of righteousness so emphatically and rigorously insisted on from the first by Judaism must be the new truth in every changing phase of economic and industrial life. Only thus can the social questions be solved. In her insistence on this doctrine Judaism retains her place in the van of the religions of humanity.

Let the voice of the mother of religions be heard in the parliament of all religions. May the voice of the mother not plead in vain. May the hearts of the nations be touched, and all the unjust and cruel restrictions of ages be removed from Israel in all lands, so that the emancipated may go in increasing colonies back to the native pursuits of agriculture and the industries so long denied them. May the colo-

nies of the United States of America, Argentine and Palestine be an
earnest to the world of the purity of Israel's motives; may the agri-
cultural and industrial schools maintained by the Alliance Israelite
Universelle, the Baron de Hirsch Trust and the various Jewish organizations of the civilized world from Palestine to California, prove Israel's
ardor for the honors of industry; may the wisdom of her schools, the
counsel of her sages, the inspiration of her lawgivers, the eloquence
of her prophets, the rapture of her psalmists, the earnestness of all
her advocates, increasingly win the reverent attention of humanity to,
and fix them unswervingly upon, the everlasting laws of righteousness
which she has set as the only basis for the social structure.

THE GENIUS OF THE TALMUD.

By REV. DR. ALEXANDER KOHUT.

The Talmud is the step-child of Literature. Used, misused, and abused, defamed and reviled, tortured into glittering falsehoods and tempered with deductive rays of perverted admiration, undisguised even by hatred, it has outlived the tragic auto-das-fé of malice and tyranny, and looms up with all the glamour and brilliance of its pristine splendor to-day, in every hamlet and metropolis of the universe—that huge ampitheater, upon whose stage the nineteenth century consumes the slowly flickering footlights of bigotry burning around the unhallowed bier of anti-Semitism.

No word reverberates more sonorously in the halls of science and research, no echo peals forth more harmoniously the tell-tale message of humanity's treasured truths, no thunder hurls the lightning alarms of conscience and righteousness, of equity and brotherhood, of morality and sanctity with more blasting force, or startles into godlier life the dormant faculties of self, than the silver voice of sage council and paternal monition, which rings out in clear signal tones of conviction and command from the watch-tower of the Talmud. The searchlight of lofty truth beaming in benignant glare from the stately peaks of Rabbinic lore illumines the shadows of the chosen race with glowing hues of immortality.

But *habent sua fata libelli!* The Talmud never fared well among strangers. No one *without* the pale of Judaism ever undertook to fathom this interminable abyss of wisdom, immeasurably more complex in its untarnished ethical simplicity than all the concentrated genius of antiquity. When men like Pfefferkorn, Wagenseil, Rohling, Justus, and other scandal-mongers, dipped their venom-dripping pens in the ire of fanatical vagaries, impulsed by vulgar arrogance and bestial delight to wreak vengeance upon imaginary foes, they took care to select and misinterpret the diverse ambiloquies, metaphors, and obscure allusions to heathenism as deliberate examples of Hebrew wisdom, disdaining to specify or designate them as mere hyperbolical illustrations of a hidden thought, as soulful and edifying, perhaps, as the latent suggestions of the fabulist deftly clad in flowers of allegory.

They did not perceive the embellishment of myth and riddle, the subtle magic of genuine delight, such as Longfellow's harp tunes to graceful melody :

> " It is but a legend, I know,—
> A fable, a phantom, a show
>   Of the ancient Rabbinical lore :
> Yet the old medieval tradition,
> The beautiful, strange superstition,
>   But haunts me and holds me the more.
>
> When I look from my window at night,
> And the welkin above is all white,
>   All throbbing and panting with stars,
> Among them majestic is standing
> Sandalphon, the angel, expanding
>   His pinions in nebulous bars.
>
> And the legend I feel is a part
> Of the hunger and thirst of the heart,
>   The frenzy and fire of the brain,
> That grasps at the fruitage forbidden
> The golden pomegranates of Eden
>   To quiet its fever and pain."

Despite the poetic portraiture of the noted Gentile bard, no plausible conception of this gigantic panorama of human ingenuity, so varied and gorgeous in its component hues, can be formed by the eager invader of this Andalusia of wonders. To unbiased minds the above would seem enticing indeed, if shorn of all graphic license, and modestly arrayed in colors of cold reality ; to lynx-eyed prejudice, ever on the alert to fasten a peccadillo of bribed conceit upon the fair name of righteous men, the rythmic vindication of brave America's well trained lyrist, sounds like overheated enthusiasm set to music out of tune—too gaudy for the naked gaze to view.

Perhaps a characterization, which we have in mind, free from the superlatives of exaggeration and unstrained by dry as dust details, elsewhere found, would not fail to convince the niggardly hesitator, or attract the indifferent, and if we be not too buoyant of hope—succeed in engaging the attention of even those who are already initiated in the intricacies of Rabbinic dialectics.

Well, then, what is the Talmud?

This query which has been raised by profound scholarship as

well as by dilettante superficiality; by philo-Semite, as well as by anti-Semite; by an eager thirst for knowledge, as well as by transient curiosity, has not yet been answered, at least in so far as it concerns the heart of the problem—the *contents* of this manifold encyclopædia of consummate utility, the production of which spans the period of a thousand years. If mild desire to know what this mammoth catalogue of human knowledge comprises, is thus irresistibly whetted by the curious—by whatever impulse instigated—we can not, in justice to the seekers after truth, forego the attempt to calmly elucidate the harassing enigma. " What does the Talmud not contain?" is our negative rejoinder.

It is a world in miniature; a spiritual universe, which because of its universality can not be defined in narrow limits. Its inexhaustible treasure-stores can barely be inventoried by means of words. We are here confronted with a state of things contrary to that which Goethe had in mind in his aphorism : " Where ideas are wanting, words come readily to relieve the want." To give a conception of the Talmud, of its wealth of thought and ideas, words are but helpless aids and useless means. Metaphor might more readily be utilized, though even here the poet's words apply :

> " Vergleiche nichts!
> Willst du dem Künstler seinen Werth dir rauben
> Dem Werk den Glanz, den Sternen ihren Schein—
> Vergleiche sie! dann hast du's leicht vollendet!
> Vergleiche Gott—du hast ihn abgesetzt."

Not only because every comparison limps, as the Latin proverb has it, should we abstain from attempting to describe the Talmud by means of metaphor, nor aside from the fact that the literature of the world presents nothing which in any degree or manner can be used for the purpose, but because every simile must needs be a depreciation of the Talmud, as it would fail to give any just conception of the work in its totality. And yet there has ever been a predilection for speaking parabolically of the Talmud as the sea; very ancient authors designating it as the "sea of the Talmud." For its breadth and depth, for the numerous objects of uncommon formation to be discovered in its recesses, and also for the dangers it abounds in, to those who venture to explore it without an accurate compass, it has truly been styled the Talmudic Ocean. It is true the term only gives but one phase of the object defined; but at least that phase is made conceivable, and through this medium some idea may be formed of the whole. The

sages secured this phrase from the scriptural verse: "Every thing
finite has a visible end, but Thy commandment reaches to infinity."

To him who never beheld the sea, the idea of it is limited to the
conception of an inexhaustible mass of water. The more thoroughly
versed, however, knows much more than this. He finds that the sea
has a topography of its own; its various currents; and that in the
endless flow and ebb of the water there are huge mountains, grand
natural formations, and images of the animal, vegetable and mineral
worlds. So, too, with the Talmud. Its wonderful treasures can only
be discovered by means of the most industrious and conscientious
special research. Externally and superficially we may say that the
Talmud is a complex work, whose typographical composition requires
2,957⅔ folio leaves, and that its twelve volumes contain the productions of 2,208 authors. This rather shallow estimate is hardly more
explanatory than the mention of the fact, that a great mass of water is
of certain dimensions in length and depth. Concerning the Talmud
as a whole, however, it is difficult to go further than this for the enlightenment of the amateur student, without doing injustice by one-
sidedness or weak inefficiency.

The contents of every other book, even of the Book of Books—
Holy Scriptures—can be readily summarized. Not so the Talmud.
A summary of its contents would require a detailed reference to each
page, frequently to each line, would seldom be continuous in its relationship between page and page, and would certainly not result in a
systematic view of the contents of the work. Nor would any other
result be expected if we consider the internal organism of the Talmud.
Other works of so great a scope, and certainly encyclopædic works,
have one or a number of editors, whose occupation it is to classify the
matter with which the work is to be concerned, to subdivide into
generic groups, and arrange the individual articles, so that the whole
will form a systematic mass whose single parts can be easily referred
to. But this was not the method used in constructing the enormous
intellectual edifice, whose completion involved ten centuries of earnest
thought and study—the result of the philosophizing, dissertating, teaching, preaching, explaining of the thinkers and poets and scholars of
various grades of culture, of different habits of thought and methods
of life, and all inspired with the purpose to keep this ebb and flow of
thought and speech alive with constant animation, and not to petrify
it by letter worship.

The Talmud is a museum with thousands upon thousands of rare,
choice and precious objects, whose values are not to be estimated by the
antiquarian standard, though they belong to such a remote past, but

may be permitted to influence us directly, as they have the thought and feeling of all Israel throughout its modern history.

They who traverse the sea of the Talmud (to refer for a while to our earlier image) are in so far like the travelers of the sea that the company is composed of characters with various habits of thought, of different stations in life, and of diverse grades of culture. But they vary from these in one important particular, in that insufferable dullness, dreary, stupid conversation and frivolous speech are banished from the Talmud. It is true, we are occasionally regaled with witty anecdotes, interesting stories and satirical sayings, but these and like humorous episodes, which are participated in by some even grave and earnest authors for the purpose of enlivening the otherwise monotonous Halachic discourses, contain none the less an ethical motive and a moral background, seeking either to impress more deeply a truth expounded, or to practically illustrate some abstract idea.

Moreover, such digressions and diversions occur only in the Haggadic portion of the Talmud. Those who are familiar with the work know that the Talmud may be subdivided into two principal parts, the Halachic and the Haggadic, which, like two powerful streams, now flow in parallel courses, then pursue their way together, and again separate, each passing its own path through the vast stretches of biblical exegesis and ideal thought.

Halacha signifies conduct, conduct of life: Haggada, expression of opinion. Both together constitute Midrash: research, study. The same meaning attaches to the word *Talmud*, or the Chaldaic form *Gemara*, which is an amplification of, and commentary upon, the Mishna, the latter again bearing the same relation to the Law. The titles and names bestowed upon the various schools of Mishnic preceptors, as *Tanaim;* the Talmudic authors, *Amoraim*, and the later *Saburaim*, are convincing evidences that the aim and object of the intellectual activity was learning, teaching, study, research. The title, *Halacha*, is a strong indication of this. The deliberations and discussions, ranging over every phase of the subject considered, as soon as they culminated in the establishment of a principle, with the force of law, should lead to the embodiment of the principles in operative rules for the conduct of life which are to be deduced from the Haggada. In this sphere the widest freedom of thought was exercised; here unrestrained speech held sway.

The Halacha begins with anxious questioning of the heroes of tradition, and with certain established and well defined rules of interpretation seeks to examine the religio-legal questions present for its consideration by means of research, now subdividing, analyzing, again

combining and comparing, by utilizing every logical apparatus to place
the subject in a clear and transparent light. The Halacha, freed from
the heavy bonds of method and rule of interpretation, is as lightly
feathered as thought, and as free and various in its phases as thought is.
Ranging upward through the intellectual realm, from the lowly plains
of a narrow-minded provincialism, it towers to the heights of lofty
conception. Beginning from the lower stage of fancy, mainly borrowed from Parsism concerning Dæmonology, or the Chaldaic Astrology, it ascends to the most profound philosophical distinctions. Starting with fables and weird tales, and sloping upward to the farthest-
reaching cliffs of intellectual conceptions concerning God and the universe, we behold the thousand artists of the Haggada observing every
thing and interested in all, sometimes stepping down to the level of
the people, and again lifting them up to their own moral plane, but
always appealing to their conscience, elevating, consoling, inspiring
them with hopes for a better future.

The Halacha offers inexhaustible nourishment for the coldly critical understanding. It is the domain of logic and of judgment. The
Haggada nurtures the heart, the spirit, the fancy. The Halacha occupies itself with working the gold bullion of the Jewish law to deco-
rate the soul. The Haggada brings into circulation the small coin for
the needs of the spirit. The mine is rich and inexhaustible, and the
miners are indefatigable.

God's omnipotence, omnipresence, omniscience; His all-benefi-
cence; the revelation of Himself in nature and in history, particularly
that of Israel; His relation to humankind, and the relations of man
to God; the manner and method of utilizing His manifold and various
powers, faculties, possibilities, and material things; the conduct of
man in joy and sorrow; the nature of a wise and pious course of life;
the need of following the good and avoiding the bad example; the reward for the former and the punishment for the latter; the sanctity of
the family; the sacredness of life; the many and various degrees of
acts of virtue; and the praiseworthiness of his occupation with the
study of the law. These and countless other details of knowledge
and subjects of reflection were drawn from the vast mine, and were
worked together with such profundity of thought, such fullness of
sympathy, and in such beautiful form, such power of convincing, that
even if we viewed it from the cold, antiquarian stand-point, we would
be compelled to offer our tribute of admiration and reverence to the
men whom we know as the sages of the Talmud and Midrash.

And yet not all is sparkling diamond, glittering gold, or shining
pearl. That pebbles and dross have attached themselves to the precious

stones and metal of thought, is so natural that it needs no long drawn
explanation. But because of the dross to ignore the gold; because of
the alien element to disdain the priceless gem, even to cast it aside—
that would be injustice and stupidity, and as we ourselves would be
the greatest losers, a most pitiful spite against ourselves!

Moreover, these insignificant utterances are of but a formal nature, and hardly deserve even that, if we cease to look upon them in
the light of our modern culture, and measure them by the standard of
mental habits of speech and thought and feeling. If we take this
point of view, we will gladly forgive the limited culture for the sake
of the childlike primitive naiveté; forget the hyperbole and bombast
in the vivid, unrestrained imagination; overlook the stilted flowery
language for the undeniable poetry; ignore the strange, because of the
fascinating novelty; overcome the difficulties of expression to attain
the keenness of thought; pass over the ambiguities for the spiritual
insight. We will then guard ourselves against labeling that which
seems unintelligible to us as meaningless, branding it with the stigma
of abomination, and declaring it to be dangerous to society. We
must rather strive to circulate the current beauties of legendary and
expository sentiment, which vie in exquisiteness of diction with the
comical pathos of Heine's inimitable strains, wafting the fragrant per-
fume of the Talmud—flowers from his enchanted garden—the con-
servatory of " Romancero :"

> " Beautiful old stories,
> Tales of angels, fairy fables,
> Stilly histories of martyrs,
> Festal songs and words of wisdom;
> Hyperboles, most quaint it may be,
> Yet replete with strength and fire,
> And faith how they gleam,
> And glow and glitter!   . . ."

We should endeavor to popularize the strange subtleties of Rabbinic allegory, narrated so quaintly in their chronicles of saga and
gnomic wisdom, to infuse its edifying councils and incomparable ethical
gleanings in the hearts of reticent humanity, that the latent spirit
which dwells therein may be released from the shell of false obscurity
and challenge the criticism of the most obstinate and impassioned
analysis.

But it is not now my purpose to idealize the Haggadic portion of
the Talmud, which, I would repeat, never arrogated to itself operative
force as legislation. I admit even that, as the sea-shore gathers, be-

sides the pearl shells, foam formations and a complexity of stones that are worthless, so there are many Haggadic utterances valueless for our times. Of this nature are some aphorisms, fables, and hyperbolical sayings, which perhaps, even in the time when they were fresh of utterance were considered eccentric, but for us have no more even the value of humor. We can only regret that the professional wisdom of the anti-Jewish guild of the caliber of Eisenmenger, Rohling, and others of that ilk, should choose just these incomprehensible passages, whose obscurity they confound still worse with their crass ignorance, and send them forth as specimens of Talmudical judgment. *Honney soit qui mal y pense!*

But there is one portion of the Haggada which these *soi disant* scholars cut out by preference and serve up in distasteful ragout as solid, healthy food, for those who, at every meal, would devour a Jew. This section comprises the vital passage which should demonstrate the intolerance of the Talmud toward non-Jews, and concerning which they who deal in human hate know so well how to juggle with. The truth of the matter is that the Talmud is a mirror which reflects the image of him who looks therein. The ugly, wicked face beholds in the shining surface of unbribed fidelity, his own hideous deformities and homely visage faithfully portrayed. The mirror of the Talmud reflects also, among other things, the heathen world, the follies of the heathen who scorn God, morals and righteousness; the now formed outgrowths of their fantasy, above all their nature-worship, their beastial idolatry. These served for many reproofs, and deserved the scourging administered by the sages of a people who were to be dominated by pure ethical and monotheistical ideas.

The *Haggada-Midrashic* denunciations of heathenism, aiming to secure respect for God and man, and therefore bitter and merciless in its expressions of disapprobation, may, for our part, be termed intolerant. But it must, at the same time, be called to mind that such invectives may be found on every hand in the New Testament and in the writings of the Church Fathers. And skepticism, that modified outgrowth of pampered heathenism, so much in vogue among liberalists of the nineteenth century, was not then universal. No Thomas Paine, the model of independent, aggressive freedom, and no Ingersoll, of infidel eloquence, were heard shooting their inflated torpedoes of rhetorical extravagance heavenward in a confusing medley of *semibarbaric* unbelief. The heathens of *antiquity* bowed in homage before the shrine of molded gods, and *our* petted pagans of advanced culture, worship the idols and deities of power. Had they been born under the summer skies of Oriental strictures, they would have shouted forth their folly to mute and impassable listeners under the ban of ex-communication.

The Haggada denounces the barbarity of the heathen; while the Patristic writers direct their fulminations against the mother religion—Israel.

The reproof, however, of heathen practices, rebuke based on judgment of the quality and character of conduct can not rightfully be termed intolerance. But to insinuate that these Talmudical utterances are leveled against Christianity is, let us emphasize, the topmost summit of bigotry and moral profligacy which modern professional sagacity has yet attained in the persons of those humane drivelers in science and theology, who seek to cover their intellectual nakedness with the moldy fig-leaves of Eisenmenger. What gross ignorance it requires to interpret עכו״ם familiarly known as an abbreviation of עובדי כוכבים ומזלות as a polemical reproach to the elder daughter of the Mosaic faith, and with obstinate effrontery to persist in such interpretation after its fallacy has been exposed.

This is all the more aggravating because it has long been the custom in the re-publications of the Talmud to expressly disavow any such intentions, either in the preface or on the backs of the title page. This zealous desire to fasten a false interpretation upon Jewish thought, is an anomaly, a historical anachronism, because, in the schools of Babylon, hardly any knowledge was had of young Christianity, which was then but sprouting. This is explicitly intimated of Nehardea, the central part of Talmudical learning, בנהרדעא דליכא מינין (Pesachim 56a).

In Palestine, however, where Christianity was known, it was very far from being ridiculed. The *worthy* founders of the new religion were treated with a large-minded tolerance, which the daughter has never shown to the mother. Let us gather some sentences from the writings edited in the Holy Land, in order to demonstrate more conclusively, that as concerns sufferance and high-minded humanity a brilliant light streams forth for guidance—luminous even to-day—from those despised sources of Hebraic morality.

Thus the Tosifta says: "The righteous among the people have a share in the future life," and this has been codified by Maimûni. Hillel, a generation before Jesus, taught, that the essence of all the six hundred and thirteen laws is contained in the sentence of Holy Writ: Love thy neighbor as thyself; that is original text, all else only commentary thereon. "There is, however," says ben Azai, "a Scriptural passage which teaches an even greater moral truth, and it is Genesis v, 1: "This is the history of the creation of man. In the day that

God created man, He created him in the likeness of God." The expression, "Love thy neighbor," may, by a strict interpretation, be construed as restricted in sense to those near to us by ties of blood and friendship. This is not possible, however, with the term אדם which unquestionably refers to all men, and places upon us the obligation to love all those who are "created in the likeness of God." Thus ben Azai finds in the verse a higher grade of humanitarianism. And Rabbi Meir dwells upon the word "man" in the Scriptural sense: "Which commands, when they are observed by man, insures him eternal life;" as showing clearly that not simply the Hebrew or the Levite, but every man can secure eternal bliss by the exercise of practical virtues.

A Palestinian authority teaches: "It is a far greater crime to rob a non-Jew than an Israelite, because it is a greater sacrilege committed against God's name." And the muchly scorned and little understood Talmud teaches explicitly: "It is forbidden to take advantage of a non-Jew, even in thought." In another instance it is remarked, that "in thirty-six, or according to another calculation, forty-eight, prohibitions is the deception of non-Jews in deed or word, condemned."

"To further the peaceful intercourse between Jews and non-Jews," says the humane Talmud, "a provision should be made for the alien poor, the same as for the Jewish poor, and their dead should be buried." The Tosifta adds: "Memorial services should be held in honor of deserving non-Jews." It is proper and praiseworthy to lend every moral support to non-Jews on appropriate occasions. From the use of איש in Leviticus xxii, 18, the Talmud concludes that it is permitted to receive sacrifice for the Temple at Jerusalem from every one, hence also from non-Jews.

"It is written," says the Midrash: "Thou shalt not hate thy brother in thine heart, as the all-holy forgives the sins of man without reservation and without any motive of evil or purpose of revenge, so do thou!" "Do not even in your heart store evil thoughts against any one." "Furthermore, even as God deems every pious man His friend and confidant, so you must construe the expression 'thy brother' as meaning the pious of the world, therefore also those of the non-Jewish world, who sincerely carry out God's will." Another Midrash adds: "We must gratefully acknowledge the results of scientific research, even of non-Jews." "Strangers, who reside not in Palestine, must not be considered as heathens, and therefore their religious belief and worship must be respected."

It is not within the limit of the space allotted to us to point out the rigid condemnation of all dishonest transactions, such as usury, illegal sale or barter, inadequate measures, and many other minor particulars to which the Rabbis of sterling honor devoted so much time to define, with an exactitude which rivals the specialties outlined in any modern criminal code. Nor is it practicable on this occasion, though we confess no more auspicious opportunity will again recur, wherein the demonstration of Talmudic legislation, in all its overtowering supremacy, would be received with more enthusiasm, to enter into the minutiæ of Hebrew jurisprudence, elsewhere elaborated; we will content ourselves for the present with citing the tribute rendered by the ablest jurist of our times, Professor Ed. Gans, who was not at sea in the overwhelming flood of Talmudic idiom, and needed no compass for guidance. "No *corpus juris* known to him," said he, "gives evidence of so much critical labor and so much penetration as the Talmudical law on inheritance and succession. The procedure in criminal cases prescribed in the Talmud is marked with the stamp of humanity in the slightest instance, and deserves the distinguished homage of all enlightened courts of justice."

We must likewise bridge over other branches of versatile stream, without even a glance at the picturesque cataract below. Natural science, geology, mineralogy, botany, zoology, biology, physiology, psychology, physiognomy, agriculture, horticulture, embryology, medicine, surgery, dentistry, bacteriology, all manner of trade, the most advanced grades of modern science, such as astronomy, electricity, caligraphy, and stenography, of art, literature, and education, music, philosophy, and etiquette, mathematics, numismatics, and philology, and countless other boastful accomplishments of our proud epoch, are all incorporated in this indispensable compendium of universal knowledge.

We will forego the satisfaction of collating the numerous terse aphorisms contained in the Talmud, to which parallels could be cited from Goethe, Schiller, Milton, Shakespeare, and other champions of *original* thought, and refrain from excepting the beautiful ethical sayings—three thousand of which we have prepared for publication—moral maxims for conduct which eclipse in lofty idealism the most select passages from Socrates, Seneca, Marc. Aurelius, Epictetus—eulogistic references to the dignity of woman, in contradistinction to the low estimate other nationalities held of her station; kindly, nay, complimentary allusions to aliens, whom they always counseled to regard with fraternal amity, will have to be omitted in our brief resumé. Quotations which should illustrate that the Rabbis of yore, contrary to anti-Semitic taunts, frsquently hurled in our face, were doughty foes of superstition, and chronicled mystic symbols and magic formulae as curious reminiscences from their relations with Chaldea and Parsism, as I have time and again argued, we can not now adduce. Suffice it to say, that those who would arrogate to themselves the authority of claiming to have discovered purely Cabbalistic elements in the Talmudic treasury of immaculate theory, only practice their own Abracadabras of fancy and folly. Here our necessarily brief survey must end. We are conscious of the fact that our bird's-eye view is essentially faulty and incomplete, compressed within the limit of a half-hour's lecture. Yet we can not help but acknowledge that much has been gleaned which is useful and edifying, in proportion to what has been unwittingly omitted from the entertaining forget-me-nots of Haggadic fancy and folklore, that odoriferous garden of stalwart lilies which blooms in a fertile soil impregnated with the sedate learning and earnest research of historic Israel. Perchance, this hasty side glance at the culture and attainments of our world-wise sages—all imbued with the fear of God and the love of man—will help toward allaying the thirst of the few for enlightenment, and dissipating the cancerous prejudice gnawing at the better impulses of that vaster herd called humanity.

If we have succeeded in overcoming the innate scruples of the wavering bigots, who, possessed by the erroneous idea (culled chiefly from calumnies of Jew haters) that the Talmud is a store-house of fetid superstition, where "corruption is virtue and every aim is vice," and proving that magic there *is* in the Talmud in so far as its attractive and cohesive power is concerned—that the magnetic needle which gravitates with the elasticity of buoyant inspiration and the diviner hope to spur our people on, is the only charmer's rod wielded by the Rabbis in every age and every clime, where scions of a once multitudinous but now sporadically scattered race abide, then we can triumphantly exclaim, with Darwin's royal judgment, "The fittest survive."

It is owing to the hoary Talmud, that ponderous volume of ancient *lore*, and ever modern *lore*, to the inexhaustible resources of that old curiosity shop, always open, even on the Sabbath, that Israel has no Ghetto—no spiritual fetters to weigh the soul immortal down—as Schleiden once tersely maintained.

To the Talmud, the associate-shepherd of our holier Writ, the *people of the Book* were at all times faithful, so as to the God commissioned agent to adjust Israel's weal or woe in this universe of

strife. And, although *habent sua fata libelli* runs the legend of its
life, it has a brighter, cheerier destiny in the domicile of Israel's devotion, by the fireside of Judea's glowing hearth, and in the gratitude of a scholar-nation's breast who lived eternally *sans peur et sans
reproache.*

25

ELEMENTS OF UNIVERSAL RELIGION.

By DR. EMIL G. HIRSCH, of Chicago.

The dominion of religion is co-extensive with the confines of humanity. Religion is one of the natural functions of the human soul; it is one of the natural conditions of human, as distinct from mere animal life. Man alone in the wide sweep of creation builds altars. And wherever man may tent, there also will curve upward the burning incense of his sacrifice or the sweeter savor of his aspirations after the better, the diviner light. A man without religion is not normal. There may be those in whom this function approaches atrophy. But they are undeveloped or crippled specimens of the completer type. A society without religion has nowhere yet been discovered. Religion may then in very truth be said to be the universal distinction of man.

Still, the universal religion has not as yet been evolved in the procession of the suns. It is one of the blessings yet to come. There are now even known to men and revered by them great religious systems which pretend to universality. And who would deny that Buddhism, Christianity, and the faith of Islâm present many of the characteristic elements of the universal faith? In its ideas and ideals, the religion of the prophets, notably as enlarged by those of the Babylonian exile, also deserves to be numbered among the proclamations of a wider outlook and a higher uplook. These systems are no longer ethnic. They have advanced far on the road leading to the ideal goal; and modern man in his quest for the elements of the still broader universal faith will never again retrace his steps to go back to the mile-posts these have left behind on their climb up the heights. The three great religions have emancipated themselves from the bondage of racial tests and national divisions. Race and nationality can not circumscribe the fellowship of the larger communion of the faithful, a communion destined to embrace in one covenant all the children of man.

The day of national religions is past. The God of the universe speaks to all mankind. He is not the God of Israel alone, not that of Moab, of Egypt, Greece, or America. He is not domiciled in Palestine. The Jordan and the Ganges, the Tiber and the Euphrates

hold water wherewith the devout may be baptized unto his service
and redemption. "Whither shall I go from thy spirit? Whither flee
from thy presence?" exclaims the old Hebrew bard.

The church universal must have the pentecostal gift of the many
flaming tongues in it, as the rabbis say was the case at Sinai. God's
revelation must be sounded in every language to every land. But,
and this is essential as marking a new advance, the universal religion
for all the children of Adam will not palisade its courts by the
pointed and forbidding stakes of a creed. Creeds in time to come
will be recognized to be, indeed, cruel, barbed-wire fences wounding
those that would stray to broader pastures and hurting others who
would come in. Will it for this be a godless church? Ah, no; it
will have much more of God than the churches and synagogues with
their dogmatic definitions now possess. Coming man will not be ready
to resign the crown of his glory which is his by virtue of his feeling
himself to be the son of God. He will not exchange the church's
creed for that still more presumptuous and deadening one of materialism which would ask his acceptance of the hopeless perversion that
the world, which sweeps by us in such sublime harmony and order, is
not cosmos, but chaos—is the fortuitous outcome of the chance play of
atoms producing consciousness by the interaction of their own un-
consciousness. Man will not extinguish the light of his own higher
life by shutting his eyes to the telling indications of purpose in history, a purpose which, when revealed to him in the outcome of his
own career, he may well find reflected also in the interrelated life of
nature. But for all this man will learn a new modesty now woefully
lacking to so many who honestly deem themselves religious. His God
will not be a figment, cold and distant, of metaphysics, nor a distorted caricature of embittered theology. "Can man by searching
find out God?" asks the old Hebrew poet. And the ages so flooded
with religious strife are vocal with the stinging rebuke to all creed-
builders that man can not. Man grows unto the knowledge of God,
but not to him is vouchsafed that fullness of knowledge which
would warrant his arrogance to hold that his blurred vision is the
full light.

Says Maimonides, greatest thinker of the many Jewish philosophers of the middle ages: "Of God we may merely assert that he
is; what he is in himself, we can not know. 'My thoughts are not
your thoughts, and my ways are not your ways.'" This prophetic
caution will resound in clear notes in the ears of all who will worship
in the days to come at the universal shrine. They will cease their
futile efforts to give a definition of him who can not be defined in

human symbols. The religion universal will not presume to regulate God's government of this world by circumscribing the sphere of his possible salvation, and declaring, as though he had taken us into his counsel, whom he must save and whom he may not save. The universal religion will once more make the God idea a vital principle of human life. It will teach men to find him in their own heart and to have him with them in whatever they may do. No mortal has seen God's face, but he who opens his heart to the message will, like Moses on the lonely rock, behold him pass and hear the solemn proclamation.

It is not in the storm of fanaticism nor in the fire of prejudice, but in the still, small voice of conscience that God speaks and is to be found. He believes in God who lives a Godlike, i. e., a goodly life. Not he that mumbles his credo, but he who lives it, is accepted. Were those marked for glory by the great teacher of Nazareth who wore the largest phylacteries? Is the sermon on the mount a creed? Was the decalogue a creed? Character and conduct, not creed, will be the key-note of the Gospel in the Church of Humanity Universal.

But what then about sin? Sin as a theological imputation will, perhaps, drop out of the vocabulary of this larger communion of the righteous. But as a weakness to be overcome, an imperfection to be laid aside, man will be as potently reminded of his natural shortcomings as he is now of that of his first progenitor over whose conduct he certainly had no control and for whose misdeed he should not be held accountable. Religion will then as now lift man above his weaknesses by reminding him of his responsibilities. The goal before us is Paradise.

This religion will, indeed, be for man to lead him to God. Its sacramental word will be duty. Labor is not the curse, but the blessing of human life. For as man was made in the image of the Creator, it is his to create. Earth was given him for his habitation. He changed it from chaos into his home. A theology and a monotheism, which will not leave room in this world for man's free activity and dooms him to passive inactivity, will not harmonize with the truer recognition that man and God are the co-relates of a working plan of life. Sympathy and resignation are, indeed, beautiful flowers grown in the garden of many a tender and noble human heart. But it is active love and energy which alone can push on the chariot of human progress, and progress is the gradual realization of the divine spirit which is incarnate in every human being. This principle will assign to religion once more the place of honor among the redeeming agencies of society from the bodage of selfishness. On this basis every man is every other man's brother, not merely in misery, but in active work.

"As you have done to the least of these, you have done unto me," will be the guiding principle of human conduct in all the relations into which human life enters. No longer shall we hear Cain's enormous excuse, a scathing accusation of himself, "Am I my brother's keeper?" no longer will be tolerated or condoned the double standard of morality, one for Sunday and the church and another diametrically opposed for week-days and the counting-room. Not as now will be heard the cynic insistence that "business is business," and has as business no connection with the decalogue or the sermon on the mount. Religion will, as it did in Jesus, penetrate into all the relations of human society. Not then will men be rated as so many hands to be bought at the lowest possible price, in accordance with a defined law of supply and demand, which can not stop to consider such sentimentalities as the fact that these hands stand for soul and hearts.

An invidious distinction obtains now between secular and sacred. It will be wiped away. Every thought and every deed of man must be holy or it is unworthy of men. Did Jesus merely regard the temple as holy? Did Buddha merely have religion on one or two hours of the Sabbath? Did not an earlier prophet deride and condemn all ritual religion? "Wash ye, make ye clean." Was this not the burden of Isaiah's religion? The religion universal will be true to these, its forerunners.

But what about death and hereafter? This religion will not dim the hope which has been man's since the first day of his stay on earth. But it will be most emphatic in winning men to the conviction that a life worthily spent here on earth is the best, is the only preparation for heaven. Said the old rabbis: "One hour spent here in truly good works and in the true intimacy with God is more precious than all life to be." The egotism which now mars so often the aspirations of our souls, the scramble for glory which comes while we forget duty, will be replaced by a serene trust in the eternal justice of him "in whom we live and move and have our being." To have done religiously will be a reward sweeter than which none can be offered. Yea, the religion of the future will be impatient of men who claim that they have the right to be saved, while they are perfectly content that others shall not be saved, and while not stirring a foot or lifting a hand to redeem brother men from hunger and wretchedness, in the cool assurance that this life is destined or doomed to be a free race of hag-

gling, snarling competitors, in which, by some mysterious will of providence, the devil takes the hindmost.

Will there be prayer in the universal religion? Man will worship,
but in the beauty of holiness his prayer will be the prelude to his
prayerful action. Silence is more reverential and worshipful than a
wild torrent of words breathing forth not adoration, but greedy re-
quests for favors to self. Can an unforgiving heart pray " forgive as
we forgive?" Can one ask for daily bread when he refuses to break
his bread with the hungry? Did not the prayer of the great Master
of Nazareth thus teach all men and all ages that prayer must be the
stirring to love?

Had not that little waif caught the inspiration of our universal
prayer who, when first taught its sublime phrases, persisted in changing the opening words to " Your father which is in heaven?" Re-
buked time and again by the teacher, he finally broke out: " Well, if
it is our father, why, I am your brother." Yea, the gates of prayer
in the church to rise will lead to the recognition of the universal
brotherhood of men.

Will this new faith have its bible? It will. It retains the old
bibles of mankind, but gives them a new luster by remembering that
"the letter killeth, but the spirit giveth life." Religion is not a question of literature, but of life. God's revelation is continuous, not
contained in tablets of stone or sacred parchment. He speaks to-day
yet to those that would hear him. A book is inspired when it inspires.
Religion made the Bible, not the book religion.

And what will be the name of this church? It will be known
not by its founders, but by its fruits. God replies to him who insists
upon knowing his name: "I am he who I am." So it will be with
the church. If any name it will have, it will be " the Church of
God," because it will be the church of man.

When Jacob, so runs an old rabbinical legend, weary and foot-
sore the first night of his sojourn away from home, would lay him
down to sleep under the canopy of the star-set skies, all the stones of
the field exclaimed: "Take me for thy pillow." And because all
were ready to serve him, all were miraculously turned into one stone.
This became Beth El, the gate of heaven. So will all religions, because eager to become the pillow of man, dreaming of God and beholding the ladder joining earth to heaven, be transformed into one
great rock which the ages can not move, a foundation-stone for the
all-embracing temple of humanity, united to do God's will with one
accord.

JEWISH CONTRIBUTIONS TO CIVILIZATION.

By PROF. D. G. LYON.

In this glad Columbian year, when all the world is rejoicing with us, and in this hall, consecrated to the greatest idea of the century, I could perform no task more welcome than that to which I have been assigned, the task of paying a tribute based on history. I shall use the word "Jew" not in the religious but in the ethnic sense. In so doing the antithesis to Jew is not Christian, but non-Jew or Gentile. The position of the Jews in the world is peculiar. They may be Englishmen, German, American, and, as such, loyal to the land of their birth. They may or may not continue to adhere to a certain phase of religion. But they can not avoid being known as the scattered fragments of a nation. Most of them are as distinctly marked by mental traits and by physiognomy as is a typical Englishman, German, or Chinaman.

The Jew, as thus described, is in our midst an American, and has all reasons to be glad as one belonging to the community at large, but his unique position to-day and his importance in history justify the inquiry, whether he may not have special reasons for rejoicing in this auspicious year.

I. Such ground for rejoicing is seen in the fact that the discovery and settlement of America was the work of faith. Columbus believed in the existence and attainableness of that which neither he nor his fellows had ever seen. Apart from his own character and his aims in the voyage of discovery, it was this belief that saved him from discouragement and held his bark true to its western course. What though he found something greater than he sought, it was his belief in the smaller that made the greater discovery possible.

What is true of the discovery is true of the settlement of America. This too was an act of faith. The colonists of Chesapeake and Massachusetts Bays left the comforts of the Old World, braved the dangers of sea, and cold and savage populations, because they believed in something which could be felt, though not seen, the guidance of a hand which directs the destiny of individuals and of empires.

Now the Jews, as a people, stand in a pre-eminent degree for faith.

They must be judged not by those of their number who in our day
give themselves over to a life of materialism, but by their best representatives and by the general current of their history.   At the fountain
of their being they place a man whose name is the synonym of faith.
Abraham, the first Jew, nurtured in the comforts and refinements of
a civilization whose grandeur is just beginning to find due appreciation, hears an inward, compelling voice, bidding him forsake the
land of his fathers and go forth, he knows not whither, to lay in the
distant West the foundations of the empire of faith.   The hopes
of the entire subsequent world encamped in the tent of the wanderer from Ur of Chaldæa.   The migration was a splendid ad-
venture, prophetic of the great development of it which was the beginning.

What was it but the audacity of faith which in later times enabled
an Isaiah to defy the most powerful army in the world, and Jeremiah
to be firm to his convictions in the midst of a city full of enemies?
What but faith could have held together the exiles in Babylon and
could have inspired them once more to exchange this home of ease
and luxury for the hardships and uncertainties of their devastated
Palestinian hills?   It was faith that nerved the arm of the Maccabees
for their heroic struggle, and the sublimity of faith when the daunt-
less daughter of Zion defied the power of Rome.   The brute force of
Rome won the day, but the Jews, dispersed throughout the world,
have still been true to the foundation principle of their history.   They
believe that God has spoken to the fathers and that He has not for-
saken the children, and through that belief they endure.

II. A second ground for Jewish rejoicing to-day is that America
in its development is realizing Jewish dreams.

A bolder dreamer than the Hebrew prophet the world has not
known.   He reveled in glowing pictures of home and prosperity and
brotherhood in the good times which were yet to be.   The strength of
his wing as poet is seen in his ability to take these flights at times
when all outward appearances were a denial of his hopes.   It was not
the prosperous state whose continuance he foresaw, but the decaying
state, destined to be shattered, then buried, then rebuilt, to continue
forever.   It was not external power, but external power in alliance
with inward goodness, whose description called forth his highest genius.
His dream, it is true, had its temporal and its local coloring.   His coming state, built on righteousness, was to be a kingdom, because this
was the form of government with which he was familiar.   The seat of
this empire was to be Jerusalem, and his patriot heart could have
made no other choice.   We are now learning to distinguish the essen-

tial ideas of a writer from the phraseology in which they find expression. A Jewish empire does not exist, and Jerusalem is not the mistress of the world. And yet the dream of the prophet is true. A home for the oppressed has been found, a home where prosperity and brotherhood dwell together. Substitute America for Jerusalem and a republic for a kingdom, and the correctness of the prophet's dream is realized. Let us examine the details of the picture.

1. The prophet foresees a home. In this he is true to one of the marked traits of his people. Who has sung more sweetly than the Hebrew poet of home, where every man shall "sit under his vine and under his fig-tree, and none shall make them afraid;" where the father of a large family is like the fortunate hunter whose quiver is full of arrows; where the children are likened to olive plants around the father's table, and where a cardinal virtue of childhood is honor to father and mother? And where shall one look to-day for finer types of domestic felicity than may be found in Jewish homes? Or, taking the word home in its larger sense, where shall one surpass the splendid patriotism of the Hebrew poet exile :

> " If I forget thee, O Jerusalem,
> Let my right hand forget her cunning.
> Let my tongue cleave to the roof of my mouth.
> If I remember thee not ;
> If I prefer not Jerusalem,
> Above my chief joy."

Yet notwithstanding this love of a local habitation the Jew has been for many cruel centuries a wanderer on the face of the earth. The nations have raged, the kings of the earth have set themselves and the rulers have taken counsel together, and the standing miracle of history is that the Jew has not been ground to powder as between the upper and the nether millstone.

But these hardships are now, let us hope, near their end. This young republic has welcomed the Jew who has fled the oppression of the Old World. Its constitution declares the equality of men, and experience demonstrates our power to assimilate all comers who desire to be one with us. Here thought and its expression are free. Here is the restful haven which realizes the prophet's dream. Not the Jew only, but all the oppressed of earth may here find welcome and home. The inspiring example of Columbia's portals, always open to the world, is destined to alleviate the ills and check the crimes of man against man throughout all lands. And what though here and there a hard and unphilanthropic soul would bolt Columbia's doors and recall her invitation or check her free intercourse with nations? This is but the eddy in her course, and to heed these harsh advices she must be as false to her own past as to her splendid ideal. Geary exclusion acts and some of the current doctrines of protective tariff are as un-American as they are inhuman.

2. But the Jewish dream was no less of prosperity than of home. America realizes this feature of the dream to an extent never seen before. Where should one seek for a parallel to her inexhaustible resources and her phenomenal material development? And no element of the community has understood better than the Jewish to reap the harvests which are ever tempting the sickles of industry. Jewish names are numerous and potent in the exchanges and in all great commercial enterprises. The spirit that schooled itself by hard contact with Judæan hills, that has been held in check by adversity for twenty-five centuries, shows in this free land the elasticity of the uncaged eagle. Not only trade, but all other avenues of advance, are here open to men of endowments, of whatsoever race and clime. In journalism, in education, in philanthropy, the Jews will average as well as the Gentiles, perhaps better, while many individual Jews have risen to an enviable eminence.

3. A third feature in the Jewish dream, an era of brotherhood and good feeling, is attaining here a beautiful realization.

Nowhere have we finer illustrations of this than in the attitude toward the Jews of the great seats of learning. The oldest and largest American university employs its instructors without applying any tests of race or religion. In its faculty Jews are always found. To its liberal feast of learning there is a constant and increasing resort of ambitious Jewish youth. Harvard, is, of course, not peculiar in this regard. There are other seats of learning where wisdom invites as warmly to her banquet halls, and notably the great Chicago University. The spectacle at Harvard is, however, specially gratifying, because there seems to be prophetically embodied in her seal, "*Christo et Ecclesiæ*," an anknowledgment of her obligations to the Jew, and a dedication of her powers to a Jewish carpenter and to a Jewish institution.

4. The era of brotherhood is also seen in the coöperation of Jew and Gentile to further good causes. To refer again, by permission, to Harvard University, one of its unique and most significant collections is a Semitic Museum, fostered by many friends, but chiefly by a Jew. And it is a pleasure to add here that one of the great departments of the library of Chicago University has been adopted by the Jews. Although taxed to the utmost to care for their destitute brethren who

seek our shores to escape Old World persecutions, the Jews are still ever ready to join others in good works for the relief of human need. If Baron Hirsch's colossal benefactions distributed in America are restricted to Jews, it is because this philanthropist sees in these unfortunate refugees the most needy subjects of benefaction.

5. But most significent of all is the fact that we are beginning to understand one another in a religious sense. When Jewish rabbis are invited to deliver religious lectures at great universities, and when Jewish congregations welcome Columbian addresses from Christian ministers, we seem to have made a long step toward acquaintance with one another. The discussion now going on among Jews regarding the adoption of Sunday as the day of public worship, and the Jewish recognition of the greatness of Jesus, which finds expression in synagogue addresses—such things are prophecies whose significance the thoughtful hearer will not fail to perceive.

Now what is the result of this close union, of which I have instanced a few examples, in learning, in philanthropy, and in affairs religious? Is it not the removal of mutual misunderstandings? So long as Judaism and American Christianity stand aloof, each will continue to ascribe to the other the vices of its most unworthy representatives. But when they meet and learn to know one another, they find a great common standing-ground. Judging each by its best, each can have for the other only respect and good will.

The one great exception to the tenor of these remarks is in matters social. There does not exist that free intercourse between Jews and non-Jews which one might reasonably expect. One of the causes is religious prejudice on both sides, but the chief cause is the evil already mentioned, of estimating Jews and non-Jews by the least worthy members of the two classes. The Jew who is forced to surrender all his goods and flee from Russian oppression, or who purchases the right to remain in the Czar's empire by a sacrifice of his faith, can hardly be blamed if he sees only the bad in those who call themselves Christians. If one of these refugees prospers in America and carries himself in a lordly manner, and makes himself distasteful even to the cultivated among his co-religionists, can it be wondered at that others transfer his bad manners to other Jews? But let Jew and non-Jew come to understand one another, and the refinement in the one will receive its full recognition from the refinement in the other. Acquaintance and a good heart are the checks against the unthinking condemnation by classes.

III. A third and main reason why the Jew should rejoice in this

Columbian year is that American society is, in an important sense, produced and held together by Jewish thought.

The justification of this assertion forces on us the question, What has the Jew done for civilization?

First of all, he has given us the Bible, the Scriptures, old and new. It matters not for this discussion that the Jews, as a religious sect, have never given to the books of the New Testament the dignity of canonicity. It suffices that those books, with one, or possibly two, exceptions, were written by men of Jewish birth.

1. And where shall one go, if not to the Bible, to find the noblest literature of the soul? Where shall one find so well expressed as in the Psalms the longing for God and the deep satisfaction of his presence? Where burning indignation against wrong-doing more strongly portrayed than in the prophets? Where such a picture as the Gospels give of love that consumes itself in sacrifice. The highest hopes and moods of the soul reached such attainment among the Jews two thousand years ago, that the intervening ages have not yet shown one step in advance.

2. Viewed as a hand-book of ethics, the Bible has a power second only to its exalted position as a classic of the soul. The "Ten Words," though negatively expressed, are in their second half an admirable statement of the fundamental relations of man to man. Paul's eulogy of love is an unmatched masterpiece of the foundation principle of right living. The adoption of the Golden Rule by all men would banish crime and convert earth into a paradise.

3. The characters depicted in the Bible are in their way no less effective than the teachings regarding ethics and religion. Indeed, that which is so admirable in these characters is the rare combination of ethics and religion which finds in them expression. In Abraham we see hospitality and faith attaining to adequate expression. Grant, if you will, the claim that part of the picture is unhistorical. Aye, let one have it who will, that such a person as Abraham never existed at all. The character, as a creation, does as much honor to the Jew who conceived it as the man, if real, does to the race to which he belonged. Moses is the pattern of the unselfish, state-building patriot, who despised hardships because " he endured as seeing Him who is invisible." Jeremiah will forever be inspiration to reformers whose lot is cast in degenerate days. Paul is the synonym of self-denying zeal, which can be content with nothing less than a gigantic effort to carry good news to the entire world.

And Jesus was a Jew. How often is this fact forgotten, so completely is he identified with the history of the world at large. We say to ourselves that such a commanding personality is too universal for national limitations. We overlook, perchance, the Judæan birth and the Galilean training. Far be it from me to attempt an estimate of the significance of the character and work of Jesus for human progress. Nothing short of omniscience could perform such a task. My purpose is attained by reminding myself and others anew of the nationality of him whom an important part of the world has agreed to consider the greatest and best of human kind.

I do not forget that the Jews have not yet, in large numbers, admitted the greatness of Jesus, but this failure may be largely explained as the effect of certain theological teachings concerning his person, and of the sufferings which Jews have endured at the hands of those who bear his name. But in that name, and that personality rightly conceived, there is such potency to bless and to elevate, that I can see no reason why Jesus should not become to the Jews the greatest and most beloved of all their illustrious teachers.

Viewing the Bible as a whole, as a library of ethics, of religion, of ethical-religious character, its influence on language, on devotion, on growth in a hundred directions, exceeds all human computation.

Along with the Sacred Writings have come to the race, through the Jews, certain great doctrines.

Foremost of these is the belief in one God. Greek philosophy, it is true, was also able to formulate a doctrine of monotheism, but the monotheism which has perpetuated itself is that announced by Hebrew seer, and not by Greek philosopher. Something was wanting to make the doctrine more than a cold formula, and that something the Jew supplied. It is the phase of monotheism which he attained that has commended itself to the peoples of Europe and America, to the teeming millions of Islam, and whose adoption by the remaining nations of earth is more than a pious hope.

This God, who is one, is not a blind force, working on lines but half defined, coming to consciousness only as he attains to expression in his universe, but he is a wise architect whose devisings all things are. The heavens declare his glory, and the firmament showeth his handiwork.

His government is well ordered and right. Chance and fate have here no place. No sparrow falls without him. The very hairs on your head are numbered. Righteousness is the habitation of his throne. Shall not the Judge of all the earth do right?

This one God, maker and governor of all things, is more, he is our Father. Man is created in his image, man's nostrils set vibrating with the divine breath. The prayer of all prayers begins: "Our

Father." What infinite dignity and value does this doctrine place upon the human soul! From God we come and his perpetual care we are. How this conviction lifts men above all pettiness and discouragement! Am I his co-worker with him on lines which he has preordained? Then mine the joyful task to work with zeal in the good cause whose sure success is seen by him though not by me.

If God be our Father, then are we brothers? The convenient distinctions among men, the division of men into classes, are all superficial, all based on externals. In essence men are one. If we be all brothers, then brotherly duties rest upon us all. Due recognition of our brotherhood would stay the act or thought of wrong, and open in every heart a fountain of love. Brothers! then will I seek the Father's features in every face and try to arouse in every soul the consciousness of its lofty kinship.

The immortality of the soul, though not distinctively a Jewish belief, is implied in much of the Old Testament, is clearly announced in Daniel, is well defined in the centuries preceding our era, and in the New Testament is often stated and every-where esteemed. This doctrine was rescued by the monotheism of the Jew from the grotesque features and ceremonies which characterized it among the Babylonians, the Egyptians, and the Greeks. The spiritual genius of the Jew, while asserting unequivocally the fact, and emphasizing the moral significance, has wisely abstained from an expression of opinion regarding a thousand details.

By the side of these great doctrines concerning God, his fatherhood, man's brotherhood, the soul, its dignity and immortality, we must place yet another, the Jewish conception of the golden age. This age to him is not past but future. He had, it is true, his picture of Eden, that garden of God where the first man held free converse with his Maker. But this picture is not of Jewish origin. It came from Babylon, and never succeeded in making a strong impression on the national thought. The Old Testament scarcely refers to it outside of the narrative in Genesis. In view of the emphasis given to the story by later theologies, the reserve in the New Testament is likewise most significant. The reason is clear. The age of gold is yet to be. Prophet and apostle and apocalyptic seer vie with one another in describing the glory of renewed humanity in the coming kingdom of God. The Jew can not fasten his thought on a shattered fortune. The brilliant castle which he is yet to build is too entrancing to his vision. There is here no place for tears over the remote past, but only a fond looking forward and working toward the dawn of the day of righteousness and of peace.

IV. I have spoken of our indebtedness to the Jew for the Bible and its great doctrines. We are under no less obligations for certain great institutions.

1. Whence comes our day of rest, one in seven, this beneficent provision for recreation of man and beast, this day consecrated by the experience of centuries to good deeds and holy thoughts? We meet with indications of a seven-day division of time in an Assyrian calendar tablet, but we are able to assert definitely by a study of the Assyrian and Babylonian commercial records that these people had nothing which corresponded to the Jewish Sabbath, the very name of which means rest. The origin of the Sabbath may well have to do with the moon's phases. But the Jew viewed the day with such sacredness that he makes its institution coeval with the work of creation. From him it has become the possession of the western world, and its significance for our well-being, physical, moral and spiritual, is vaster than can be computed.

2. I have spoken already of Jesus as a Jew. Then is the religion which bears his name a Jewish institution? It has elements which are not Jewish; it has passed into the keeping of those who are not Jews. But its earliest advocates and disciples, no less than its founder, were Jews. Not only so, but these all considered Jesus, His teaching and the teaching concerning Him, as the culmination of the Hebrew development, the fulfillment of the Hebrew prophets' hope.[1] Many causes have wrought together to insure the victory which Christianity has won in this world. But those who are filled with its true spirit and who are thoughtful can never forget its Judæan origin.

3. To the same source we must likewise trace institutional Christianity, the church. The first church was at Jerusalem. The first churches were among devout Jews dispersed in the great Gentile centers of population. The ordinances of the church have an intimate connection with Jewish religious usages. In the course of a long development other elements have crept in. But in her main features the church bears ever the stamp of her origin. The service is Jewish. We still read from the Jewish Psalter, we still sing the themes of Psalmist and apostle, the aim of the sermon is still to rouse the listener to the adoption of Jewish ideas; we pray in phraseology taken from Jewish Scriptures. Our Sunday schools have for their prime object acquaintance with Jewish writings. Our missions are designed to

---

[1] The greatest expounder of Christianity writes to the Romans that they have been grafted into the olive stock of which the Jews were branches by nature.

tell men of God's love as revealed to them through a Jew. Our church and Christian charities are but the embodiment of the Golden Rule as uttered by a Jew.

4. It may furthermore be fairly said that the Jew, through these writings, doctrines and institutions, has bequeathed to the world the highest ideals of life. On the binding and the title page of its books the Jewish Publication Society of America has pictured the lamb and the lion lying down together and the child playing with the asp, while underneath the picture is written the words, "Israel's mission is peace." The picture tells what Israel's prophet saw more than twenty-five centuries ago. The subscription tells less than the truth. Israel's mission is peace, morality and religion; or better still, Israel's mission is peace through morality and religion. This the nation's lesson to the world. This the spirit of the greatest characters in Israel's history. To live in the same spirit, in a word, to become like the foremost of all Israelites—this is the highest that any man has yet ventured to hope.

I have catalogued with some detail, though by no means with fullness, Jewish elements in our civilization. In most cases I have passed no judgment on these elements. If one were disposed to inquire into their value, he might answer his question by trying to conceive what we should be without the Bible, its characters, doctrines, ethics, institutions, hopes and ideals. To think these elements absent from our civilization is impossible, because they have largely made us what we are. Not more closely interlocked are the warp and woof of a fabric than are these elements with all that is best and highest in our life and thought. If the culture of our day is a fairer product than that of any preceding age, we can not fail to see how far we are indebted for this to the Jew.

My purpose has not been to inquire by what means the little nation of Palestine attained to its unique eminence. Some will say it was by a revelation made to them alone, others that they were fortunate discoverers, and yet others would explain it all by the spell, "development." Be one or all these answers true, the Deity can reveal Himself only to the choice souls who have understanding for the higher thought; discovery is made only by those who recognize a new truth when it floats into the field of vision; development is only growth and differentiation from germs already existing. Why should Israel develop unlike any other people, why discover truth hidden from others, why become receptacles for revelation higher than any attained elsewhere? This is one of the mysteries of history, but the mystery can in no wise obscure the fact.

However, explained or unexplained, the Jewish rôle in history belongs to the most splendid achievements of the human race. Alas, that these achievements are so often forgotten! Forgotten by the Jew himself, when he devotes his powers to the problems of to-day with such intensity as to be indifferent to his nation's past. Forgotten by those among whom he lives when they view him as an alien, and when in the enjoyment they fail to recognize the source of some of their greatest blessings. It is not alone the land which was discovered by Columbus, but the entire world owes to the Jew a debt of gratitude which never can be paid.

A practical closing question forces itself on our attention. The great rôle in history was played by this people while it had a national or semi-national existence. At present the Jews are separated from the rest of the community mainly by certain religious observances. Is the Jew of to-day worthy of the glorious past of his people, and is he entitled to any of the consideration which impartial history must accord to his ancestors? An affirmative answer, if it can be given, ought to do something to remove prejudices which yet linger among us, and to alleviate the fortunes of the Jew in lands less liberal than our own.

The ancient Jew was a man of persistence and of moral and spiritual genius. His modern brother is not lacking in either genius or persistence. His persistence and power to recuperate have saved him from annihilation. His genius shows itself chiefly in matters of finance, in the ability to turn the most adverse conditions into power. In literature, art, music, pholosophy, he is of the community at large, averaging high, no doubt, but with nothing distinctive. In the world's markets, in commerce and trade, he distances competition.

The extent to which he educates his children, and helps his poor to become self-supporting, and the very small percentage which he furnishes to the annals of crime, give to him a high character for morality. The Montefiores, Hirschs, Emma Lazaruses, Jacob Schiffs, and Felix Adlers show what power and spirit of benevolence and reform still belong to the Jew. It would perhaps be too much to demand further great religious contributions from this people. But it can hardly be that a people of such glory in the past and of such present power shall fail to attain again to that eminence in the highest things for which they seem to be marked out by their unique history.

26

INTRODUCTION TO A BIBLIOGRAPHY OF THE JEWISH PERIODICAL PRESS.

By DR. ISAAC M. WISE.

The fifth great power in this nineteenth century is JOURNALISM.

It is generally presumed that there are four great powers which govern society, viz., the sword, the pen, money, and woman. It might be supposed by further generalization toward the ultimate abstraction one could reduce the parallelogram of efficient causes to the mere parallel of money and woman. It must be admitted that money is mightier than the sword and the pen ; it directs and controls both. Capital is king every-where, in the capitols of nations, the parlors of society, the banks, the shops, and according to the *vox populi*, also in the laboratory of the pen. Not all is money, says the monometalist ; but money is all, woman excepted, anyhow the monomania of the century.

It is generally admitted that woman is mightier than sword and pen ; she controls and directs both. Where a king sits upon the throne, the queen or a queen governs the land. Woman wields the pen quite energetically. All your beautiful poetry is inspired by woman. It is no longer the pen, it is the typewriter, that does the mighty work, and woman is the queen at the typewriter. Long ago the pen was superseded by the types and type-setters, pressmen, and printer's devil. The steel pen dethroned your quill, and woman supersedes them all. The word pen is an antiquated symbolic term, and the sword is deposed abroad by the canon, and with us by the sovereignty of the people.

So you see in the ultimate abstraction of social powers, there is left money and woman. These, however, are stern realities and no abstractions. To be metaphysically correct, we can not reduce the parallelogram to a mere parallel. We can only change the antiquated terms of sword and pen in the concrete (like money and woman), emperors or kings, and the Press. Being myself a democratic man and this being the World's Fair, it would ill become me to dwell on emperors and kings. Having been connected with the Press these forty-five years, and this being a Press Congress, I might with propriety say something about the Press, with a capital P, as one of the great powers.

When we speak of the Press as one of the great powers, we do not mean that piece of mechanism called the power press, or any other of the same kind. We speak of that intellectual food which it multiplies so many thousandfold for the nutrition of human intellect. In this sense the Press is by no means a unit. It manufactures sense and nonsense, morality and its direct opposite, enlightenment and benightenment,[1] religion and superstition, bigotry and frivolity, faith and skepticism, truth and falsehood, justice and oppression, freedom and slavery, facts and fictions. It serves all masters, is every thing to every body; it can not be considered a unit. We must necessarily subdivide it. We might accomplish this on the following principle:

The substantial Press can not be divided by the criteria of its inner causes, for they are innumerable, as infinite as the products of reason and the sentiments of conscience. As none can count the follies of man to classify them, much less could he count or measure the infinite variety of the moral and intellectual waves which rise from the wide and deep sea of human ingenuity; and yet all of them are feeders of the Press, its inner cause and motive power. We must divide the Press and its products according to outward forms. Here we have since the advent of Guttenburg and Dr. Faust the Book Press, and in this nineteenth century the Periodical Press. If we may call the former Bookism, the latter is properly called Journalism. Here, then, is your fifth great power, its name is Journalism, the youngest offspring of old Dame Press, rapidly outgrowing the mother's fame, power, and usefulness. The journal is the people's book. What the book was to the select few, the journal is now to the multitude of mankind. What the book is to the student, the journal is to all classes of busy men. The magazine is the connecting link between the two, a kind of substitute for either, but the essay is no treatise; skimming the milk produces no butter, still it furnishes cream. It is something akin to university extension and Chautauqua classes. It is something which amounts to nothing in re.

The division of labor produced also the division in Journalism. We have all kinds of them in almost every country. The political and the impolitic, the scientific and the unscientific, with their ramifications in astronomical, medical, mathematical, ethical, esthetical law, etc., journals, and last, though not least, the religious press, with its kindred branches. All of them gather the news, each in its own de-

---

[1] This word is taken from the free coinage dictionary.

partment, with occasional excursions into the neighbor's field. The reviewer collects the literary news, as the society editor collects the gossip. The political organ gathers the current news of the day and deals or dabbles occasionally also in literature, science and religion. The religious organ does about the same. None remains within its sphere.

The religious journal as a specialty came into existence simultaneously with the American and French revolutions, because this was the practical start of separating Church from State. Prior to this separation the political was necessarily also the religious journal. When the State emancipated itself from the Church, and the Church was thrown upon its own resources, the political journal became semi-religious and the religious journal became semi-political, and there they abide yet, much to the disadvantage of both.

If the religious journal is the transportable pulpit, it can not afford to deal in politics. If the political journal is the mouth-piece and tutor of the people in all secular affairs, it must avoid interference in matters of religion, where Church and State are separated. They can assist one another only by keeping each strictly within its own sphere of journalism. The same is the case with all specialties in the periodical press.

The matter was different with the Hebrews. They could have no political journals; they were politically disfranchised the world over, when the periodical press began its work, and remained in this status till the constitution of the United States of America restored the inalienable rights of man to the maltreated portion of humanity, and the French revolution proclaimed Liberty, Equality and Fraternity. The Jewish journal not evolving from the political journal, could be but non-political at its inception. If here or there exceptionally, a Jewish journal seeks to make political capital, it is mostly for the sake of capital, and least for politics, where the Israelite has no particular interest in politics separate and apart from all his other fellow-citizens.

But Jewish journalism was involved in two difficulties. These were, and partly are yet, the defense of Judaism and the defense of the Jew. Both of them in the history of modern civilization were constantly kept on the defensive, as is invariably the fate of the minority opposite an overwhelming majority, where the sense of justice and truth not yet outbalances the consciousness and haughtiness of power and self-willed might. Where is this land, where this Eden, where? Echo responds, nowhere, and it was far, very far from there at the inception of Jewish journalism. It was obliged to contend at once with inimical systems of science, philosophy, theology and government from without, and an overgrown rabbinical legalism and cabbalistic mysticism—falsely called orthodoxy—from within. This made the Jewish press polemical in two directions, as it had made the Hebraic book press of prior centuries, and diminished its usefulness in its own legitimate field.

In the course of progress in this nineteenth century, the Jew and Judaism were but partially relieved from that defensive position. In the lands of absolutism the case underwent no change for the better. In the countries of transition from absolutism to the reign of justice the evil is but partially remedied ; the Jew suffers yet under political disabilities, and the cause for political polemics is not extinguished. In the lands of relative freedom the Jew is socially ostracised, and this ostracism peeps frequently and indecently through the crevices of social etiquette, and Judaism is quite recklessly and frequently attacked by pietistic pulpits, journals and hired missionaries to expedite Judaism out of existence. Discouraging and irritating factors of this kind exercise a humiliating influence upon the bulk of Hebrews, and their journalists are morally bound to take up the gauntlet thrown so petulantly at their feet. With all this, the contention with inimical systems of science, philosophy and theology from without, and against the overgrown rabbinical legalism and cabbalistic mysticism from within has not ceased, it is only moderated in the most civilized countries. No wonder then, that Jewish journalism has become polemic and frequently political in tone and tendency ; and as not all men are sweet-tempered and long-suffering, not all hold that language was invented to hide man's thoughts and feelings, it would be wonderful if, at some time or other, volleys of abuse and invective did not come down from that defensive position upon the heads of foes and friends.

These are the faults and shortcomings of Jewish journalism from its very inception, which impaired considerably its usefulness.

The merits and usefulness of the Jewish press consist of its universality, its liberality in dogmas, and its unceasing propaganda for science and art, civilization and culture.

When the distinguished philosopher, contemporary with Lessing, Herder and Kant, Moses Mendelsohn, of Dessau, made the first attempt to publish a Jewish journal in Berlin, he failed ; it was too soon. His disciples, however, during his lifetime, succeeded in establishing the *Measseph*, a periodical in the Hebrew language. This periodical product became to journalism and the new Hebrew language what Addison's "Spectator" was to the English. The *Measseph* was no less poetical, critical, reformatory in rhetorical forms, no less elegant and esthetic, and no more scientific and theological than the "Spectator."

The belletristic tone predominated in both. Both of these periodicals are landmarks pointing out the transition from crudeness to refinement, from the careless to the polished style.

The *Measseph* was Hebrew, because the bulk of the Hebrews in Germany, Austria, Hungary, the Danubian principalities down to the Black Sea, Germany, Poland and Russia—and these are the largest number of Israelites also in our days—as far as the German or Slavonic languages reached, the Hebrews, excepting some professional scholars, could read Hebrew only and no other language. The German and Slavonic languages had so long and so fiercely poured upon those neglected and persecuted Hebrews, insult and injustice in all forms of barbarisms, that the offended and insulted people considered it sinful to learn either of those hostile languages. They would read only Hebrew and the Aramaic which occurs in the Hebrew literature, which was to them so much more the holy language as the German and Slavonic bounded in profanities, insults and barbarisms.

The *Measseph* or "Compiler," was followed in course of time by *Bickure Ittim*, "First Fruits of the Times," *Kerem Chemed*, "Choice Vineyard," and two hundred and more other Hebrew journals, up to two daily papers appearing for some time in St. Petersburg and Warsaw. This style of journalism started in Germany, spread over Austria, especially Galicia, in Poland and Russia, into Turkey to the city of Jerusalem, became the main source of information to the Israelites in the Orient, turned them again westward and pitched its tent in almost every metropolis of the western world; in Vienna, Berlin, Amsterdam, Paris, London and New York, and became thus a universal organ to Hebrews and Hebrew scholars the world over, as was the Latin to Roman Catholics.

The amount of information spread by means of this kind among European Israelites, especially those who could not be reached by any other organs, was to them of great importance and benefit. All this was of more importance, however, to the Jews of Asia, who were thus brought in contact with European civilization and culture, and became in their turn the missionaries of civilization among their neighbors; and they are so yet this day. The sciences, especially the medical, were thus carried back into Asia; so was poetry, grammar, and a large amount of belletristic German, French and English literatures were circulated among them in Hebrew translations. Lessing, Schiller, Shakespeare, Milton, Byron and Dickens, recast in Hebrew, were carried into Russia and Asia and made the Jew acquainted with the world's literature and the progressive spirit of the century.

Hebrew journalism has accomplished another wonderful task. It has laid the foundation to the Science of Judaism, *i. e.*, the history and theology of Judaism, together with its vast literature reviewed and reconstructed in the light of modern methods and researches, which German and French writers completed to a modern science accessible to the students of all denominations and incorporated in the world's literature. And still another which is, perhaps, the most wonderful. Those journalists rejuvenated the Hebrew to a language of modern culture, with an abundant terminology for all sciences, industry and commerce, so that the ancient language of the Bible is now expanded to a complete vehicle of modern society.

Most important in Jewish journalism was the German press. The Israelites of Germany, Austria included, from and after the days of Moses Mendelsohn, established the modern scholarship, which produced the "Science of Judaism," accessible to the students of all denominations, and introduced it into the world's literature. The disciples of the German schools carried the new era of Jewish learning into France, England, Holland and America. The German Jewish journal was the mediator between the men of learning and the people in general. It carried upon its wings the higher conceptions of Judaism—its history and literature, its theology and ethics throughout western Europe and America, and to the eastern confines of civilization. What is called modern Judaism was begotten in Germany and German Austria, and carried by the press to all ends of civilization. This press became French in France, Dutch in Holland, English in England, America and Australia, Italian in Italy, Roumanian in Roumania, or also Magyar in Hungary ; still it is every-where the offspring of the Jewish Germanic mind and scholarship, and in most cases carried to all those countries by the sons of Germany and Austria. The first editors of Jewish journals in France, England and America were Germans by birth. The German language was carried by them into Russia and Poland, in the form of that German Jewish dialect spoken by that people, and reached also Paris, London and New York ; and the pure German was carried to Roumania, Hungary, Galicia, and to this country, where this day three German Jewish journals appear every week. In all these languages, however, it is chiefly the Germanic mind and scholarship which characterizes the editorial productions.

It is difficult to ascertain—there exist no statistics upon which to base—what influence this particular journalism exercised upon the progress of civilization and enlightenment beyond the limits of Judaism. We can but surmise on general principle that no department of literature, especially if it is as bulky as the Jewish press, fails to impress the world outside of its home circle. What we can maintain with certainty is that this Germanic Jewish press liberalized the masses politically and socially to a very wide extent. In Germany and Austria the Jew was disfranchised and even ostracised up to the year 1848, or even up to 1865 in Austria and 1870 in Prussia, and are even now to some extent under the ban of medieval ethics. But there was just enough freedom of the press left to complain loudly and publicly, and to argue logically from the principle of right and justice. Those Jewish editors stood up for the rights of their oppressed neighbors quite vigorously. They argued against injustice, oppression, absolutism, and despotism for all kinds of wronged people. The influence which Jewish journalism viewed from this standpoint, exercised on the hapless and helpless of all kinds and descriptions, is not fully ascertained, but it is loudly maintained and even exaggerated by extreme conservatives and re-actionists, so that they call all liberal and advanced organs Jewish, and claim that the whole press of Europe is in the hands of Jews.

The amount of prejudices, superstitions, errors, falsehoods, and injustice expedited out of existence or banished into the dark spots of illiterate and neglected humanity by Jewish journalism is prodigious in the eyes of those that love best the tin plates of their grandmothers, and would not have them replaced by silver vessels. With all its labors the Jewish press did not fully succeed in silencing or converting this class of people, either within or without the circle of Judaism; still it diminished their number and enfeebled their arguments. There is hope for the future.

A third division of Jewish journalism is the Spanish-Arabic, to which belongs also the new Greek published in Corfu, and the Hindoo published in Bombay. Some of them are in the Spanish-Jewish dialect, others in Hebrew. Those published in India are in the Menatic language. These prints have not reached the centers of literature like the Hebraic and German productions, hence their influence could have been local only. Still they are parts of the whole, and deserve the attention of the bibliographic student.

The mutual relations of the Jewish to the other religious press was very kindly in the countries where progressive ideas are cherished and a spirit of tolerance prevails. Jewish writers profited very much by reading what other religious denominations advanced. Whether this is the case also on the other side, it is hard to tell for one who was never engaged in that field. The political press exercises an influence on the religious press by its interpretation of the spirit of the age, which, after all, moderates and shapes ecclesiastical doctrine and practice with or without the consent of its presiding geniuses. On the other hand, the religious press, with its conservative nature, endeavors to correct public opinion and to expose the errors in the spirit of the age. So these two great powers may work into each other's hands without rivalry or animosity for the benefit of both and the progress of mankind toward higher conditions. The Jewish press in all lands of culture did take this position opposite the political press, and so the influence was mutual, friendly, and efficient. Therefore, the most influential political prints in America, England, France, Italy, and Germany are favorable to Jews and Judaism; only less important organs and those of despotic countries are hostile to the descendants of Abraham and the followers of Moses.

This may suffice as an introduction to the bibliography of Jewish journalism, which we attempt to contribute to the World's Congress in memory of the great event, The Religious Congress of all Nations and Denominations, an event without precedent in history.

THE ARCHBISHOP OF ZANTE ON THE BLOOD ACCUSATION.

[Rabbi Hirsch, in the absence of Dr. Barrows, presided at the evening session. He first introduced the Archbishop of Zante, who, after a gracious salutation to the platform occupants and the audience, said :]

"MOST HONORABLE LADIES AND GENTLEMEN:—I am not a Jew. I am a Christian, a profound believer of the truth of the Gospel. [Applause.] I am always bound to defend the truth, and for this reason I present a paper here to-night."

[Professor Snell then stepped forward at the Archbishop's request and said that his grace, the Archbishop, had asked him to read for him a statement regarding the belief current in the Orient and in many parts of Europe to the effect that Jews are in the habit of catching Christian children and sacrificing them upon the altar. This was the statement read :]

"In the East the belief is current among the ignorant masses of the population that the Jews use, for purposes of religious rites, the blood of Christian children, and, in order to procure such blood, do not shrink from committing murder. In consequence of this belief, outbreaks against the Jews are frequent, and the innocent victims are subjected to many indignities and exposed to great danger. In view of the fact that such erroneous ideas are also current among the ignorant of other countries, and during the last decade, both Germany and Austria were the scenes of trials of innocent Jews, under the accusation of having committed such ritual murder, I, as a Christian minister, ask this Congress to record our conviction, that Judaism forbids murder of any kind, and that none of its sacred authorities and books command or permit murder, or the use of human blood for ritual practices or religious ceremonies. The circulation of such slander against the adherents of a monotheistic faith is unchristian. The origin of the calumny must be traced to the Roman conceit, that early Christians used human blood in their religious observances. It is not consonant with Christian duty to allow this horrible charge to go unrebuked, and it is in the interest of Christianity's good repute that I ask this parliament to declare that Judaism and the Jews are innocent of the imputed crime, as were the Christians of the first century."

REMARKS ON ANTI-SEMITISM.

By ARCHBISHOP JOHN IRELAND.

LADIES OF THE CONGRESS :—It is with deep emotion of soul that I cross the threshold of this hall. I come among the representatives of an ancient people whom my own religion recognizes as having been during long ages the chosen people of God, whose history, replete with noble deeds and glorious names, goes back to remote ages, thousands of years before modern nations of Europe and America were heard of, whose literature is the first and best the world owns, worthy to have been the united product of earth and heaven.

When all humanity outside the frontiers of Judea was darkened by the fatal errors of polytheism and idolatry, one people, and one only, preserved pure and unsullied the religion of the spiritual world, and the worship of the one Infinite God. Moses and the prophets were the polar stars set in the firmament of intelligence, whence light and truth and hope came to men. The sweet songs of Israel have not been surpassed in sublimity of thought and exaltation of sentiment, and they are to-day the highest expressions of the human soul communing with God.

The Hebrew people were chosen by Jehovah to be the keeper of His revelation, the forerunner of all future civilization. All nations which worship one great God, and practice His pure religion, must avow themselves heirs of Israel, and repeat the words of the psalm : "If·I forget thee, O Jerusalem, let my right hand be forgotten. Let my tongue cleave to my jaws, if I do not remember thee, if I do not make Jerusalem the beginning of my joy."

The preservation of the Hebrew people through centuries, despite their sufferings and their dispersion among all the nations of the earth, is one of history's greatest miracles. Whatever the explanation which may be given of it, we must wonder and admire.

Christians and Hebrews have parted roads. But Christians look back to the Hebrews as having been for ages the people of God, and proclaim their own religion to be the result and complement of the Hebrew dispensation. The Founder of their religion is for Christians the Son of David and of Abraham, and his mother, Mary, is the Lily of Israel, the daughter of Nazareth.

I shall be pardoned for these remarks, which the sight of this Congress of Jewish Women elicits from me, and which, at the same time, are not altogether remote from the main question to which I am asked to speak.

You are holding a peace congress, offering peace to all, and asking peace from all. You desire that persecution and ostracism of the Jewish race cease through the world. I join with you most cordially in your hopes and wishes, and, while neither a prophet nor the son of a prophet, I know I can say that the reign of peace and security which you strive to establish is near at hand.

The duty of conscience to adhere to what is recognized as truth, to adhere most tenaciously with mind and heart to principles, is most firmly upheld by me, and most persistently proclaimed. Peace with men who differ from me does not mean the abandonment of my convictions. But I hold to the great rule of charity and common brotherhood to treat with amity, and as I would wish to be treated by them, all my fellow-men, in civil and political matters, however much they may differ from me in belief of religion, in race, in language, in color. There is no need that we refer this evening to historic conditions which are gone by under which Hebrews suffered; we live in the present, and we should busy ourselves most with the present which is with us and the future which is coming to us. I shall only make this remark, that while in past centuries Hebrews were not seldom exposed to dire persecutions in different nations of Europe, in the seven-hilled city of Rome, over which the chief of the Catholic Church held temporal sway, they were always secure at least in property and in life, and often thronged to Rome from other countries in search of peace and protection.

The present age is one of concord and peace, which builds itself up on the broad lines of humanity and common brotherhood. The United States of America gives the example in this matter to the world, and, hence, it is the most important that Americans carry out to the letter the principles of their constitution. There are some defects in their practice; ostracism of one kind or another on the mere basis of race is not totally unknown. Our first work is at home.

In other countries the ostracism is more marked; civil persecution even happens. In the name of humanity, we should work to alter such conditions. It does not matter which the particular people, or which the particular race, that is persecuted; all peoples and all races are concerned, for if one is persecuted to-day, another may be persecuted to-morrow. One class or one people is safe when all are safe. A government is bound to cause the observance of laws of social order and of justice; men violating these must be punished. But, when not violating them, men should not be disturbed. Let there be no distinction in citizenship, no discrimination of classes of citizens, no presumptive judgments against any portion of a people.

Public opinion is now-a-days the great arm of defense and conquest. The strongest governments go down before it. You have entered upon the road to success when you undertake to redress wrongs inflicted on the Hebrew race by awakening the world's public opinion. You will conquer, and the day is nigh when in America and in Europe, on the Mississippi, and on the Danube, and throughout the vast empire of Russia, all men shall be brothers, and treated by one another as brothers.

May God hasten the day!

INDEX.

Anti-Semitism. Renan the intellectual father of modern a.-S. 274. Anti-Semitic charges refuted, 285 ff. The effects of a.-S. on the Jew, 295 f. Remarks on the subject by Archbishop John Ireland, 411 ff.
Archbishop of Zante on the blood-accusation, 410.

Bamberger, Prof. G., paper on Training Schools, 334–338.
Berkowitz, Rabbi Henry, D.D., paper on what organized forces can do for Judaism, 353–357; on the voice of the mother of religions on the social question, 367–372.
Bible. Its authority among Jews and Christians, 58. Its influence on mankind, 42 ff, 397 ff. Religion made the B. 390. The B. of the Church Universal, ib. The B. (Old and New Testaments) written by Jews, 396. The B. as a classic of the soul, a hand-book of ethics, ib.
Biblical Criticism. The attitude of Reformed Judaism to B. C. 29 f. The share of Jewish scholars, 184 ff. 195.
Blood-accusation, the Archbishop of Zante on the, 410.

Character the key-note of the Gospel in the Church Universal, 388.
Christianity. Its attitude toward the Bible, 58. Messianic elements, 87. Relation of C. to Judaism, 114 ff. Rise of C. 176 ff. Jewish converts to C. 191 f. The attitude of the modern Jew toward the founders of C. 303. The debt of C. to Judaism, 395 f. 411 f.
Church. Its relation to the Synagogue, 114 f. The Early Church, 121 f. Mission of Church compared with that of the Synagogue, 122 f.
Church Universal, 126, 386 ff.
Civilization, Jewish contributions to, 391–401.

Deutsch, Gotthard, Ph.D., paper on the share of the Jewish people in the culture of the various ages, 175–192.
Dogmas in general, 1; in Judaism, 2, 24 f. 58.

Eldridge, S. L., paper on the union of Young Israel, 348 352.
Essenes, 115 ff.
Ethics of Judaism, 99–106; of the Talmud, 107 113; the ethical teachings of Synagogue and Church, 114–126; universal ethics of Prof. Steinthal, 127–146.

Felsenthal, Dr. B., paper on the Sabbath in Judaism, 36–41; on the instruction of post-Biblical history in the Sabbath Schools, 319–326.
Frank, Henry L., paper on Relief Societies, 362 f.

415